△▽△▽△▽△▽△▽△▽△▽△▽△▽△▽△▽△

Acknowledgments

The writer wishes to express his appreciation to the members of the reading department of Science Research Associates and to Miss Anne Coomer for assistance in the preparation of this book.

P. W.

How to improve your reading

by Paul Witty

Professor of Education and Director of the
Psycho-Educational Clinic, Northwestern University

 Science Research Associates, Inc., 259 East Erie Street, Chicago, Illinois 60611
A Subsidiary of IBM

05892

Note to the reader

How to Improve Your Reading is designed to help you develop a skill that will bring you immeasurable benefits. As you become a better reader, your horizons will be extended and your satisfactions will be intensified and deepened.

This book contains the key to successful reading and provides the steps by which you can acquire reading skill and check your progress. The rewards of your efforts to improve your reading will indeed be great.

contents

lesson 1. How Well Do You Read? 1

General Directions for the Practice
Reading and Reading Selection 10

article 1. Elephants—Giants on the Land 12

lesson 2. Why You Should Learn to Read Better 18

article 2. A Secret for Two 24
by Quentin Reynolds

lesson 3. What Is Reading? 29

article 3. A, B, and C—The Human Element in Mathematics.... 38
by Stephen Leacock

lesson 4. How You Can Remember What You Read 43

article 4. Jungle Zoo Without a Cage 51
by John Barkham

lesson 5. How You Can Get Main Ideas 56

article 5. The Lonesome Bear 61
by Harrison Kinney

lesson 6. How to Read for Details 67

article 6. Terror in the Woods 75
by Earl Doucette

lesson 7. How to Read to Follow Directions 80

article 7. Whales—The World's Largest Animals 92

lesson 8. How to Think About What You Read 97

article 8. Elastic Metal 109
by Elizabeth Rider Montgomery

lesson 9. How to Read at the Right Speed 114

article 9. Midshipman Aboard the "Half Moon" 129
by Lowry W. Harding

lesson 10. How to Read Illustrations 135

article 10. Clipper Ship Boy 150
by Louis Smith

lesson 11. How You Can Best Read Aloud 156

article 11. For the Benefit of All 178
by Ivan Ray Tannehill

lesson 12.   **How You Can Read Unfamiliar Words** 183

article 12.   **How We Kept Mother's Day** 196
by Stephen Leacock

lesson 13.   **How You Can Build a Better Vocabulary** 201

article 13.   **Ships and Masters** 210
by Robert Carse

lesson 14.   **How You Can Read Better for School Assignments** . . 215

article 14.   **Houdini—The Handcuff King** 227
by Beryl Williams and Samuel Epstein

lesson 15.   **How You Can Continue to Improve Your Reading** 233

article 15.   **How Long Is Life?** 240
by Paull M. Giddings

article 16.   **Mama Finds a Way** 246
by Kathryn Forbes

article 17.   **Motivations of the Space Program** 252
by A. R. Hibbs

article 18.   **Great-grandma** 257
by Ray Bradbury

Bibliography 262

Answer Key 266

How well do you read?

You can improve your reading ability. Studies show that we use only a small part of our capacity for efficient reading. In this we are like the modern automobile. The car today is a fine piece of machinery. But it is not very efficient. The best gasoline engine made today is only about 20 percent efficient.

What does this mean? It means that you get out of a gasoline engine only 20 percent of the energy you put into it. A diesel engine—the kind you see on big trucks and railroad trains—is about 40 percent efficient. The turbine—the kind of engine used to make electricity in a powerhouse—is about 50 percent efficient.

Right now the big automobile companies are beginning to put turbine engines in cars. By the time you get your driver's license, you may be able to drive a car with a turbine engine. A turbine engine is cheaper and easier to run than an ordinary gasoline engine and it makes far better use of fuel.

How about your reading efficiency?

Do you find that reading is hard work? Do you have to force yourself to pick up a book? Do you tire easily when you try to concentrate? Do you take as much time to read a story as to read a history lesson?

Even though your answer is no to all these questions, you are probably no more efficient in your reading than a gasoline engine is in driving a modern car. Most people do not read as well as they might. No matter how well *you* may read today, you can improve your reading. You can learn to read better.

This is an important fact to know. For the next few years your success in your main job—going to school—will depend on how well you read. And after you leave school, your reading skills will be even more important to your future success and happiness.

The lessons in *How to Improve Your Reading* are arranged to help you develop your reading skills. In this first lesson you will begin by finding out something about your present reading ability. In later lessons you will put this information to use in improving that ability. And you will keep a record of your progress as you go along.

How can you find out what your reading abilities are?

As you go through this book, you will learn that reading involves a great many separate skills. By taking the short tests in each lesson, you will find out how well you have developed these skills.

In this lesson you will get a good general idea of how you read by doing three sample exercises. You will also study your own particular reading needs. You will find out some of the skills in which you need special practice.

The exercises that follow will present three different kinds of reading material. Read each story at your usual rate—a rate that seems neither too slow nor too fast. After you finish each story, answer the questions in the test that follows it.

Exercise 1

Here is a short story that has been a favorite of young people for many years. It takes place in a frontier town a good many years ago. There is a young man who is tired of his job and is looking for excitement. He meets . . .

Gold-Mounted Guns[1]

by F. R. Buckley

Evening had fallen on Longhorn City, and already, to the south, an eager star was twinkling in the velvet sky. A spare, hard-faced man slouched down the main street and selected a pony from the dozen hitched beside Tim Geogehan's general store. The town, which in the daytime suffered from an excess of eye-searing light in its open spaces, confined its efforts at artificial lighting to the one store, the one saloon, and its neighbor, the Temple of Chance; so it was from a dusky void that the hard-faced man heard himself called by name.

"Tommy!" a subdued voice accosted him.

The hard-faced man made, it seemed, a very slight movement—a mere flick of the hand at his low-slung belt; but it was a movement perfectly appraised by the man in the shadows.

"Wait a minute!" the voice pleaded.

A moment later, his hands upraised, his pony's bridle reins caught in the crook of one arm, a young man moved into the zone of light that shone bravely out through Tim Geogehan's back window.

"Don't shoot," he said, trying to control his nervousness before the weapon unwaveringly trained upon him. "I'm—a friend."

For perhaps fifteen seconds the newcomer and the hard-faced man examined each other with the unblinking scrutiny of those who take chances of life or death. The younger, with that lightning draw fresh in his mind, noted the sinister droop of a gray mustache over a hidden mouth, and shivered a little as his gaze met that of a pair of steel-blue eyes. The man with the gun saw before him a rather handsome face, marred, even in this moment of submission, by a certain desperation.

"What do you want?" he asked tersely.

"Can I put my hands down?" countered the other.

The lean man considered.

"All things bein' equal," he said, "I think I'd rather you'd first tell me how you got round to callin' me Tommy. Been askin' people in the street?"

"No," said the boy. "I only got into town this afternoon, an' I ain't a fool any-way. I seen you ride in this afternoon, and the way folks backed away from you made me wonder who you was. Then I seen them gold-mounted guns of yourn, an' of course I knew. Nobody ever had guns like them but Pecos Tommy. I could have shot you while you was gettin' your horse, if I'd been that way inclined."

The lean man bit his mustache.

"Put 'em down. What do you want?"

"I want to join you."

"You want to *what?*"

"Yeah, I know it sounds foolish to you, mebbe," said the young man. "But, listen—your sidekick's in jail in Rosewell. I figured I could take his place—anyway, till he got out. I know I ain't got any record, but I can ride, an' I can shoot the pips out of a ten-spot at ten paces, an'—I got a little job to bring into the firm to start with."

The lean man's gaze narrowed.

"Have, eh?" he asked, softly.

"It ain't anythin' like you go in for as a rule," said the boy, apologetically, "but it's a roll of cash an'—I guess it'll show you I'm straight. I only got on to it this afternoon. Kind of providential I should meet you right now."

The lean man chewed his mustache. His eyes did not shift.

"Yeah," he said, slowly. "What you quittin' punchin' for?"

"Sick of it."

"Figurin' robbin' trains is easier money?"

"No," said the young man, "I ain't. But I like a little spice in life. They ain't none in punchin'."

"Got a girl?" asked the lean man.

The boy shook his head. The hard-faced man nodded reflectively.

"Well, what's the job?" he asked.

The light from Geogehan's window was cut off by the body of a man who, cupping his hands about his eyes, stared out into the night, as if to locate the buzz of voices at the back of the store.

"If you're goin' to take me on," said the young man, "I can tell you while we're ridin' toward it. If you ain't—why, there's no need to go no further."

The elder slipped back into its holster the gold-mounted gun he had drawn, glanced once at the obscured window and again, piercingly, at the boy whose face now showed white in the light of the rising moon. Then he turned to his pony and mounted.

"Come on," he commanded.

Five minutes later the two had passed the limits of the town, heading for the low range of hills which encircled it to the south—and Will Arblaster had given the details of his job to the unemotional man at his side.

"How do you know the old guy's got the money?" came a level question.

"I saw him come out of the bank this afternoon, grinnin' all over his face an' stuffin' it into his pants pocket," said the boy. "An' when he was gone, I kind of inquired who he was. His name's Sanderson, an' he lives in this yer cabin right ahead a mile. Looked kind of a soft old geezer—kind that'd give up without any trouble. Must ha' been quite some cash there, judgin' by the size of the roll. But I guess when *you* ask him for it, he won't mind lettin' it go."

"I ain't goin' to ask him," said the lean man. "This is your job."

The boy hesitated.

"Well, if I do it right," he asked, with a trace of tremor in his voice, "will you take me along with you sure?"

"Yeah—I'll take you along."

The two ponies rounded a shoulder of the hill: before the riders there loomed in the moonlight the dark shape of a cabin, its windows unlighted. The lean man chuckled.

"He's out."

Will Arblaster swung off his horse.

"Maybe," he said, "but likely the money ain't. He started off home, an' if he's had to go out again, likely he's hid the money someplace. Folks know *you're* about. I'm goin' to see."

Stealthily he crept toward the house. The moon went behind a cloud bank, and the darkness swallowed him. The lean man, sitting his horse, motionless, heard the rap of knuckles on the door—then a pause, and the rattle of the latch. A moment later came the heavy thud of a shoulder against wood—a cracking sound, and a crash as the door went down. The lean man's lips tight-ened. From within the cabin came the noise of someone stumbling over furniture, then the fitful fire of a match illumined the windows. In the quiet, out there in the night, the man on the horse, twenty yards away, could hear the clumping of the other's boots on the rough board floor, and every rustle of the papers that he fumbled in his search. Another match scratched and sput-tered, and then, with a hoarse cry of tri-umph, was flung down. Running feet padded across the short grass and Will Arblaster drew up, panting.

"Got it!" he gasped. "The old fool! Put it in a tea canister right on the mantel-shelf. Enough to choke a horse! Feel it!"

The lean man, unemotional as ever, reached down and took the roll of money.

"Got another match?" he asked.

Willie struck one and, panting, watched while his companion, moistening a thumb, ruffled through the bills.

"Fifty tens," said the lean man. "Five hundred dollars. Guess I'll carry it."

His cold blue eyes turned downward, and focused again with piercing attention on the younger man's upturned face. The bills were stowed in a pocket of the belt right next to one of those gold-mounted guns which, earlier in the evening, had covered Willie Arblaster's heart. For a moment, the lean man's hand seemed to hesitate over its butt; then, as Willie smiled and nodded, it moved away. The match burned out.

"Let's get out of here," the younger urged; whereupon the hand which had hovered over the gun butt grasped Will Arblaster's shoulder.

"No, not yet," he said quietly. "Not just yet. Get on your hawss, an' set still awhile."

The young man mounted. "What's the idea?"

"Why," said the level voice at his right, "this is a kind of novelty to me. Robbin' trains, you ain't got any chance to see results, like: this here's different. Figure this old guy'll be back pretty soon. I'd like to see what he does when he finds his wad's gone. Ought to be amusin'!"

Arblaster chuckled uncertainly.

"Ain't he liable to—"

"He can't see us," said the lean man with a certain new cheerfulness in his tone.

3

"An' besides, he'll think we'd naturally be miles away; an' besides that, we're mounted all ready."

"What's that?" whispered the young man, laying a hand on his companion's arm.

The other listened.

"Probably him," he said. "Now stay still."

There were two riders—by their voices, a man and a girl: they were laughing as they approached the rear of the house, where, roughly made of old boards, stood Pa Sanderson's substitute for a stable. They put up the horses; then their words came clearer to the ears of the listeners as they turned the corner of the building, walking toward the front door.

"I feel mean about it, anyhow," said the girl's voice. "You going on living here, Daddy, while—"

"Tut-tut-tut!" said the old man. "What's five hundred to me? I ain't never had that much in a lump, an' shouldn't know what to do with it if I had. 'Sides, your Aunt Elviry didn't give it to you for nothin'. 'If she wants to go to college,' says she, 'let her prove it by workin'. I'll pay half, but she's got to pay t'other half.' Well, you worked, an'—Where on earth did I put that key?"

There was a silence, broken by the grunts of the old man as he contorted himself in the search of his pockets; and then the girl spoke. The tone of her voice was the more terrible for the restraint she was putting on it.

"Daddy—the—the—did you leave the money in the house?"

"Yes. What is it?" cried the old man.

"Daddy—the door's broken down, and —"

There was a hoarse cry: boot heels stumbled across the boards, and again a match flared. Its pale light showed a girl standing in the doorway of the cabin, her hands clasped on her bosom—while beyond the wreckage of the door a bent figure with silver hair tottered away from the mantel-shelf. In one hand Pa Sanderson held the flickering match, in the other a tin box.

"Gone!" he cried in his cracked voice. "Gone!"

Willie Arblaster drew a breath through his teeth and moved uneasily in his saddle. Instantly a lean, strong hand, with a grip like steel, fell on his wrist and grasped it. The man behind the hand chuckled.

"Listen!" he said.

"Daddy—Daddy—don't take on so— please don't," came the girl's voice, itself trembling with repressed tears. There was a scrape of chair legs on the floor as she forced the old man into his seat by the fireplace. He hunched there, his face in his hands, while she struck a match and laid the flame to the wick of the lamp on the table. As it burned up she went back to her father, knelt by him, and threw her arms about his neck.

"Now, now, now!" she pleaded. "Now, Daddy, it's all right. Don't take on so. It's all right."

But he would not be comforted.

"I can't replace it!" cried Pa Sanderson, dropping trembling hands from his face. "It's gone! Two years you've been away from me; two years you've slaved in a store; and now I've—"

"Hush, hush!" the girl begged. "Now, Daddy— it's all right. I can go on working, and—"

With a convulsive effort, the old man got to his feet. "Two years more slavery, while some skunk drinks your money, gambles it—throws it away!" he cried. "Curse him! Whoever it is, curse him! Where's God's justice? What's a man goin' to believe when years of scrapin' like your aunt done, an' years of slavin' like yours in Laredo there, an' all our happiness today can be wiped out by a thief in a minute?"

The girl put her little hand over her father's mouth.

"Don't, Daddy," she choked. "It only makes it worse. Come and lie down on your bed, and I'll make you some coffee. Don't cry, Daddy darling. Please."

Gently, like a mother with a little child, she led the heartbroken old man out of the watchers' line of vision, out of the circle of lamplight. More faintly, but still with heartrending distinctness, the listeners could hear the sounds of weeping.

The lean man sniffed, chuckled, and pulled his bridle.

"Some circus!" he said appreciatively. "C'mon, boy."

His horse moved a few paces, but Will Arblaster's did not. The lean man turned in his saddle.

"Ain't you comin'?" he asked.

For ten seconds, perhaps, the boy made no answer. Then, silently, he urged his pony forward until it stood side by side with his companion's.

"No," he said. "An'—an' I ain't goin' to take that money, neither."

"Huh?"

The voice was slow and meditative.

"Don't know as ever I figured what this game meant," he said. "Always seemed to me that all the hardships was on the stickup man's side—gettin' shot at an' chased an' so on. Kind of fun, at that. Never thought 'bout—old men cryin'."

"That ain't my fault," said the man.

"No," said Will Arblaster, still very slowly. "But I'm goin' to take that money back. You didn't have no trouble gettin' it, so you don't lose nothin'."

"Suppose I say I won't let go of it?" suggested the lean man with a sneer.

"Then," snarled Arblaster, "I'll blow your head off an' take it! Don't you move, you! I've got you covered. I'll take the money out myself."

His revolver muzzle under his companion's nose, he snapped open the pocket of the belt and extracted the roll of bills. Then, regardless of a possible shot in the back, he swung off his horse and shambled with the mincing gait of the born horseman, into the lighted doorway of the cabin. The lean man, unemotional as ever, sat perfectly still, looking alternately at the cloud-dappled sky and at the cabin, from which now came a murmur of voices harmonizing, with a strange effect of joy, to the half-heard bass of the night wind.

It was a full ten minutes before Will Arblaster reappeared in the doorway alone and made, while silhouetted against the light, a quick movement of his hand across his eyes, then stumbled forward through the darkness, toward his horse. Still the lean man did not move.

"I'm—sorry," said the boy as he mounted. "But—"

"I ain't," said the lean man quietly. "What do you think I made you stay an' watch for, you young fool?"

The boy made no reply. Suddenly the hair prickled on the back of his neck.

"Say," he demanded hoarsely at last. "Ain't you Pecos Tommy?"

The lean man's answer was a short laugh.

"But you got his guns, an' the people in Longhorn all kind of fell back!" the boy cried. "If you ain't him, who are you?"

The moon had drifted from behind a cloud and flung a ray of light across the face of the lean man as he turned, narrow-eyed, toward Arblaster. The pallid light picked out with terrible distinctness the grim lines of that face—emphasized the cluster of sun wrinkles about the corners of the piercing eyes and marked as if with underscoring black lines the long sweep of the fighting jaw.

"Why," said the lean man dryly, "I'm the sheriff that killed him yesterday. Let's be ridin' back."

A comprehension test

For each of the ten questions below, several possible answers are given. Choose the answer that you believe is correct. Write the numerals 1 to 10 on a sheet of paper. Print your answer to each item.

1. The hard-faced man was
   A. Pa Sanderson
   B. the sheriff
   C. Will Arblaster
   D. Tim Geogehan
   E. Pecos Tommy

2. Sanderson's daughter had been
   A. away at college
   B. working in Laredo
   C. visiting her aunt
   D. seeing Pecos Tommy
   E. working in the bank

3. The young man knew that Pa Sanderson had money because
   A. he lived in a big house
   B. people in town had told him
   C. he saw Sanderson coming out of the bank with the money
   D. Sanderson always had money in his house
   E. Pecos Tommy told him so

4. The sheriff had Pecos Tommy's guns because
   A. he had found them somewhere
   B. he had killed Pecos Tommy
   C. Pecos Tommy had given them to him
   D. he had bought them
   E. he had stolen them

5. At the end of the story, the young man was
   A. ashamed of what he had done
   B. glad he had stolen the money
   C. afraid of the hard-faced man
   D. hopeful that he could join the hard-faced man
   E. afraid that he would be arrested

A vocabulary test

6. The town in the daytime suffered from an *excess* of eye-searing light. *Excess* means
   A. too little
   B. too much
   C. a flood
   D. lightning
   E. a bad storm

7. The hard-faced man's slight movement—a mere flick of the hand at his gun belt—was perfectly *appraised* by the young man. *Appraised* means
   A. understood
   B. surprising
   C. expected
   D. just what he wanted
   E. praised

8. The young man saw the *sinister* droop of a gray mustache over the lean man's mouth. *Sinister* means
   A. sudden
   B. unhappy
   C. suggesting danger
   D. stylish
   E. heavy

9. The newcomer and the hard-faced man examined each other with the unblinking *scrutiny* of those who take chances of life or death. *Scrutiny* means
   A. smile
   B. scowl
   C. doubt
   D. study
   E. fear

10. "I can shoot the *pips* out of a ten-spot at ten paces." *Pips* means
   A. lights
   B. buttons
   C. dollar signs on a ten-dollar bill
   D. eyes
   E. the spots on a playing card

The correct answers to Exercise 1 are shown in the answer key at the back of the book. Your score is important, but do not lose sight of the fact that you usually read for profit or enjoyment. If you enjoyed the story and if it helped you understand other people better, it was worth reading no matter what your score is.

Narrative is only one kind of writing. In the second tryout exercise, you will read in the field of science. You will find that scientific writing is also interesting, although the interest is different from that in narrative writing.

Exercise 2

If you enjoy reading about animals, go to the library and ask for *The Animal Kingdom*. This is a three-volume set of books filled with highly interesting articles written by experts. One of the articles is reprinted with some changes below.

Read this selection, too, at your regular rate. When you have finished, answer the questions in the test that follows.

The Shrew—A Small but Mighty "Mouse" [2]

Shrews are tiny mouselike animals. In fact, they are the smallest mammals in the world. In the United States and Canada, the common cinereous (gray) shrew when full grown weighs no more than three and a half grams—about the weight of a teaspoonful of water.

The typical shrew has a long pointed snout, beadlike eyes, and short rounded ears. Its body is covered with soft fur, usually brown, gray, or black.

The shrew is always hungry and is always eating. Every three hours it can eat as much as it weighs. That is like a hundred-pound boy eating his weight in food between six and nine o'clock in one evening. Because the shrew has such a ravenous appetite, it hunts for food all the time. The animal is on the move day and night.

---

[2] Reprinted by permission of Hawthorn Books, Inc., from *The Animal Kingdom* (Frederick Drimmer, editor in chief), Volume I: *Mammals*, by George C. Goodwin. Copyright 1954 by the Greystone Press.

For its food, the shrew catches beetles, crickets, grasshoppers, earthworms, and the larvae of flies and moths. Before eating, it may play with a beetle as a cat plays with a mouse. The shrew finds its fresh meat in grass, under fallen and rotting leaves, and under the ground.

Although most shrews prefer insects, some kinds feed on mice. When the American short-tailed shrew bites a mouse, its teeth inject poison from two glands near its jaws just as do the teeth of a cobra. Because the shrew's poison paralyzes the mouse's nerves, the mouse has fits or may even die. The shrew's poison, however, is not strong enough to harm a man.

The shrew is a fierce little animal. If two shrews are placed in a small cage, one will kill and eat the other within a few hours time.

Shrews have many natural enemies. These include hawks, owls, snakes, weasels, cats, foxes, and fish. A hawk, for example, will kill a shrew on sight—but will not eat it. That is because the shrew, like the skunk, has a pair of musk glands. These glands give off a strong odor that drives most animals away.

Shrews breed two or three times a year. Sometimes they multiply so fast that they swarm over the land. The female shrew has her first young early in the spring. She builds a leaf or grass nest in a hollow under a stump or in a hole in the ground. This nursery may be a ball-shaped bundle of grass about eight inches in diameter. The ball has a small hole for a door and a three-inch room in its center.

The mother shrew usually has six babies. At birth they are without hair and have wrinkled pink skin. Each of them is about the size of a honeybee. To feed herself and her babies, the mother is always active.

When one week old, the baby shrew begins to get fur. At the age of two weeks it has a fur coat. After the third week it has cut its first teeth and its eyes have opened. At one month the young shrew is weaned. Then it leaves the nest and looks for food on its own.

Because shrews are so small and because they live mostly under old leaves and grass and in runways just under the surface of the ground, you are not likely to see even one of these animals on a farm, in a field, or in the woods. But if you come across a shrew, you should let it alone. These animals kill and eat so many insects and mice that they are among the farmer's best friends.

A comprehension test

In this test there are ten statements about shrews. Some of the statements are true; some are not. You can tell which statements are true if you have read the selection carefully. Write the numerals 1 to 10 on your paper. Write **T** if you believe the statement is true. Write **F** if you believe the statement is false.

1. The shrew is the smallest mammal in the world.

2. The shrew looks like a tiny mouse.

3. In three hours a shrew eats more food than a hundred-pound boy eats for dinner.

4. Some shrews eat insects; others feed on mice.

5. Hawks kill shrews for food.

6. A shrew can paralyze a man with its poison glands.

7. Shrews multiply rapidly, as do mice and rabbits.

8. The mother shrew raises her babies in a nest that is usually high up in a tree.

9. When about three months of age, the young shrew first leaves the nest and hunts for food on its own.

10. Shrews are friends of farmers.

Correct answers to Exercise 2 are shown in the answer key at the back of the book.

Your score on this test may be different from your score on the first tryout exercise. In the first exercise you read a story. In the second exercise you read a different kind of material. Your second score shows how well you can read a scientific article at this time.

In the third exercise you will test your ability to read a newspaper story. It is a humorous story, the kind that newspaper editors call a human-interest story.

Exercise 3

Read this story mainly for enjoyment. But get the facts straight or you will miss some of the fun.

Everyone dreams of doing something he would like to do—something that just doesn't seem possible. Some people go ahead and make their dreams come true. There was a young man in Albany, New York, who wanted to ride in a balloon. He couldn't find a big balloon, so he . . .

Hitches Dream to Balloons and Away He Goes[3]

ALBANY, N.Y. (UP)—A jaunty young man in a beret floated high over Albany while roped to 70 red balloons.

Garrett Cashman, 27, built his flying machine from army balloons, a bosun's chair, a boat anchor, and a bicycle wheel.

His wife kissed him goodbye and gave him a meat loaf sandwich before Cashman —a hypnotist and dance teacher—began his 30-mile trip above the state capital.

Cashman said the flight was an experiment but that he "was a little nervous" as he soared into the sky.

Police Give Chase

On the ground, meanwhile, hundreds of persons rubbed their eyes and called the police. They reported "a man hanging onto a balloon," "a man in a red parachute," and a "whatever-it-is."

Harried state troopers chased after Cashman on both sides of the Hudson River, and a Trans-Canada Airline pilot reported a "parachute or balloon" in the sky—7000 feet over Albany and going east.

The balloons were filled with $43 worth of explosive gas and were tied to the bosun's chair. Cashman sat in the chair and ate his meat loaf sandwich.

"It was very good," he said later—the sandwich, that is. "I could see all of Albany and the river. But I got a bit scared when we went above the clouds.

"The sun got so hot some of the balloons began popping. I had a parachute

3 From the *Chicago Sun-Times*, September 10, 1954. Copyright by the United Press Association (UP). Reprinted with permission of the copyright holder.

rigged up, so I wasn't really worried, but I dropped some of the sand I carried for ballast."

Sinks to Earth

"I didn't have any idea where I was going. Part of the time I was in the clouds."

When he had had enough, Cashman cut some of the balloons adrift, sank slowly to earth, and rolled out of his chair.

He came to rest in an apple orchard and was greeted by a half-dozen state troopers. They took him before Justice of the Peace George Bigsbee in nearby Guilderland, where he was charged with flying without a license. Trial was set for September 17.

Cashman said that since he was eight years old "I have wanted to go ballooning and today I did."

Haven't you sometimes wished you could float in the clouds and look down at your school, your home, and your town? What would it be like up there? How would people and things on the ground look as you sailed over them?

Perhaps you envied the young man of the story. Perhaps you admired him for actually doing what he had always wanted to do. But you almost surely chuckled to yourself when you pictured the funny scenes in the story—the young man fixing up his balloons and chair, the young man calmly and happily eating his meat loaf sandwich 7000 feet up, the people below wondering what-is-it, and the young man landing in an apple orchard. You may have thought about the fun the reporter must have had covering and writing the story.

If you liked this story, you should practice reading it aloud—say, to your parents or to your younger brother or sister. Read the words of the story as accurately and as smoothly as possible. Put some expression into your reading—try to make the story and its different word pictures come to life for your listeners.

In reading this story, you may have come across words that were new to you or words whose meanings you were not quite sure of. The vocabulary test that follows contains words from the story. If you were reading carefully, you got the meaning of these words from the words near them.

A vocabulary test

Write the numerals 1 to 6 on your paper. Record your answer to each of the items below.

1. ". . . while *roped* to the red balloons."
   A. tied
   B. starting
   C. blowing
   D. letting go
   E. clinging
2. ". . . as he *soared* into the sky."
   A. sank
   B. prepared to fly
   C. looked
   D. exploded
   E. rose
3. "I had a parachute *rigged* up . . ."
   A. started
   B. right
   C. fixed
   D. helped
   E. thought
4. A *jaunty* person usually
   A. has a gay and carefree manner
   B. likes to take a walk
   C. tries to hide away from people
   D. is thoughtful and quiet
   E. plays ill
5. A balloonist drops part of his ballast when he wants to
   A. land
   B. fly at a lower altitude
   C. go higher
   D. change direction
   E. take measurements
6. If you are *harried*, you feel that someone is
   A. honoring you greatly
   B. tormenting you
   C. chasing you
   D. calling you names
   E. helping you out

Check your reading needs

Your scores may have varied on the three tryout reading exercises. You may have done well, or you may not be satisfied with your record. There are more exercises to come and more reading skills to study.

Before going on, try the checklist that follows. It will make you think about your reading and lead you to think about how to improve it.

Write the numerals 1 to 20 on your paper. For each question below, write "yes" or "no."

1. Do you read as well as you would like to?
2. Do you need to read better to do better schoolwork?
3. Do you read books often?
4. Do you use the public library?
5. Are you in the habit of reading newspapers and magazines regularly?
6. Do you remember well what you read?
7. Do you think about what you are reading?
8. Do you get the main ideas from stories when you read them rapidly?
9. Do you get the important details when you are reading in fields such as science?
10. Do you understand and follow directions quickly and accurately?
11. Do you understand pictures, maps, and graphs?
12. Can you read aloud with accuracy, clearness, and ease?
13. Can you figure out the meanings of new words when you meet them in your reading?
14. Do you know how to use a variety of books when you are studying?
15. Do you know the best sources of information?
16. Do you appreciate good writing?
17. Do you enjoy reading so much that you sometimes read just for fun?
18. Do you ever read to understand and improve yourself?
19. Do you read to become a good citizen?
20. Have you tried to improve your reading?

Now look at your answers to these questions. Read again the questions that you answered "no"; they point out some of your reading needs. Make a list of at least three things that you can do to meet these needs—that is, to improve your reading. The list of things to do is the first part of your reading improvement plan. But it is not all of it. You will find other things to do as you read this book.

Get acquainted with this book

Before you go further, you should learn something about the arrangement of this book.

1. Look at the title page. It gives the title of the book, the name and position of the author, and the name and address of the publisher.

2. Look at the next page. This is called the copyright page. It tells when the book was published.

3. Read the table of contents. This gives the titles of all the lessons and parts of the book.

4. Skim through the book. Turn the pages quickly. Look at the headings. They are useful guides to what the lessons contain. See if you can find out how the material is arranged in each lesson. Glance at some of the illustrations.

5. Note that each lesson contains two parts.

6. Turn to the answer section and look quickly over the charts.

In this book you will learn by doing. You will first read what you are to do, and then you will do it. Finally you will check on how well you did by taking a test.

General directions

Step 1. Do a practice reading.[4] Read in a book, magazine, or newspaper that you like.

Step 2. Record your practice reading in Chart 3 on page 8 of the progress folder.

Step 3. Record your starting time. Before you begin reading a selection, write down your starting time in the time record on page 4 or page 7 of the progress folder.

Step 4. Read the article as fast as you can, but make sure you understand what you are reading.

Step 5. Record your finishing time. After you finish the article, write down your finishing time in the time record.

Step 6. Take the reading test. Immediately after you read a selection, take the reading test that follows it. The test is made up of twenty items.

Step 7. Record your answers to the test in the answer record on page 4 or page 7 of the progress folder. As you choose your answer for each test item, mark the letter of this answer in the answer record.

Step 8. Correct your answers. Use the answer key in the progress folder or the one at the back of this book.

Step 9. Score your answers. Count the number of answers that you marked correctly. Write this score at the bottom of the answer record.

Step 10. Record your test score. Enter your score in Chart 2 on page 3 of the progress folder.

Step 11. Figure out your reading time for the selection. Use the time record on page 4 or page 7 of the progress folder (see Example 1).

Step 12. Change your reading time into your reading rate.

Step 13. Record your reading rate. Enter your reading rate in the time record and in Chart 1 on page 2 of the progress folder.

Step 14. Follow up. Read again each test item that you answered incorrectly.

In the article, find quickly and read carefully the sentence or paragraph that gives the correct answer.

Try to determine why you chose the wrong answer for the item, and why the answer given in the key is the right answer.

These follow-up steps will definitely help you improve your comprehension and your vocabulary.

---

4 You may do your practice reading with a device such as the Reading Accelerator® available from Science Research Associates. If your school or library has one of these devices, you can use it to increase your reading rate and comprehension.

Example 1

Directions for the time record

Keep the time record as shown in the example below.

1. If your starting time for Article 1 is exactly 12 minutes after the hour, write 12:00 to the right of "Starting time."

2. If your finishing time is 19 minutes 18 seconds after the hour, write 19:18 to the right of "Finishing time."

3. From your finishing time, 19:18, subtract your starting time, 12:00. The difference is 7:18—7 minutes 18 seconds. Write this difference to the right of "Reading time."

	Article 1
Finishing time	19:18
Starting time	12:00
Reading time	7:18

Practice Reading 1

In a book, magazine, or newspaper that you like, practice reading for speed and comprehension. Make a record of the reading in Chart 3 on page 8 of the progress folder.

Read the following selection to determine your present reading rate, comprehension, and vocabulary.

Record your starting time in the time record on page 4 of the progress folder. Then read the selection. Read as fast as you can, but make sure you understand what you are reading.

1
article

Elephants — giants on the land[5]

Elephants are the biggest and strongest of all land animals. For this reason, other wild animals seldom attack them. For this reason also, men have tamed elephants to work in the woods or to perform in circuses.

Wild elephants live naturally in only two places in the world—in Africa and in Asia. There they inhabit the tropical forests and plains. They are hot-weather animals. When the temperature is cool, an elephant catches cold and has muscle cramps. This is surprising, because its hide is leathery, tough, and one inch thick.

How large is an elephant?

The largest of all elephants is the African bush elephant. The bull weighs as much as 12,000 pounds. Its average shoulder height is eleven feet. That of the cow elephant is about seven feet.

The elephant of Asia is somewhat smaller than its African cousin. The Indian bull elephant reaches a shoulder height of about nine feet. Its average weight is 7000 pounds.

Although an elephant looks awkward, it can move through woodland and bush-covered country as silently as almost any other animal.

What does an elephant eat?

The elephant is a vegetarian. It likes grass, roots, bark, fruit, and leaves. Its favorite food is the tender twigs and branches that grow at the tops of trees. Often, if the elephant cannot reach a tree-top with its trunk, it simply pushes the tree down.

Because the elephant is so large, it needs to eat a lot of food. Every day an adult elephant must consume about five hundred pounds of fresh greens or about one hundred and fifty pounds of dry hay. Also, it must drink fifty gallons of water every day.

How important is the elephant's trunk?

The elephant has a truly wonderful trunk. It uses this trunk in feeding, in drinking, in smelling, and in lifting and carrying.

The elephant's trunk measures as long as eight feet from head to tip. Also, it bends and curls quite easily in almost any direction. This is extremely important, because the elephant's neck is short and hard to move or turn.

Scientists call the elephant's trunk a *proboscis*. This proboscis is a stretched-out nose, upper lip, and cheek. Outside it is covered with heavy skin. Inside it has many muscles.

At the end of its trunk the elephant has lobes that it uses as fingers. With these lobes the elephant picks leaves and grass and places them in its mouth.

Most people know that an elephant breathes through its trunk. Many believe that it also drinks through its trunk. But that is not true. The elephant sucks water

5 Reprinted by permission of Hawthorn Books, Inc., from *The Animal Kingdom* (Frederick Drimmer, editor in chief), Volume I: *Mammals*, by George C. Goodwin. Copyright 1954 by the Greystone Press.

into the lower end of its trunk. It then pours or blows the water into its mouth. With its trunk the elephant sometimes gives itself a shower bath or perhaps a dust bath.

The elephant uses its great trunk for lifting, carrying, and throwing things. With its trunk the elephant can raise and move a weight of nearly 2000 pounds. Or it can throw a man as far as forty yards.

Because the elephant's trunk has nerves that pick up odors, the animal is always moving its trunk around in every direction. In this way the animal gets the first faint scent of another elephant, or a lion, or a tiger, or a man.

What about family and herd life?

Elephants like their own company. That is why they live in a herd. The leader of a herd is usually a big bull, but sometimes a wise old cow. As among all herd animals, the older males fight one another to determine which is the strongest and the best. The winner of these battles becomes the leader of the herd.

About twenty-one months after mating, the cow elephant gives birth to a single calf. The newborn calf is covered with heavy black hair. It stands about three feet high at the shoulder and weighs about two hundred pounds. The calf usually stays under its mother's care until it is four or five years old.

The young elephant becomes an adult at age fourteen. Its total life span is fifty to sixty years.

How do elephants rest and move about?

The young elephant sleeps stretched out on its side. It easily lies down and gets up. The adult elephant, however, has difficulty in doing either of these things. That is why, from the age of about fourteen years until the time of death, an African bush elephant seldom, if ever, lies down. It even sleeps standing up. It can rest this way probably because its legs are built like four strong pillars.

An elephant walks at a rate of six to eight miles an hour—twice as fast as a man walks. When an elephant is angry or fright-

ened, it can run for fifty yards at a speed of twenty-five miles an hour.

When a herd of elephants is walking along in single file and comes to a riverbank the elephants sometimes make a slide for themselves. The first elephant may stretch its front legs forward and its hind legs backward. Then it slides down the slope on its belly, just for the fun of it. One by one the other elephants do the same.

When elephants are not disturbed, they make a strange rumbling sound that can be heard a quarter of a mile away. This sound seems to come from the working of their digestive systems. If the elephants smell danger, they at once stop making this sound. Then they are so quiet that they cannot be heard by an elephant hunter or by another enemy.

How well can elephants learn?

The elephant has a brain that is tiny compared to its head or body. Yet it is a very bright animal, next to the apes and monkeys in intelligence. An elephant can be taught to obey some twenty-five different commands.

Although the people of India can tame a wild elephant at any age, they usually catch such an elephant when it is eighteen or nineteen. At this age the animal can start doing light work. The Indians, however, would rather raise a tame elephant and then train it.

The tame young elephant "goes to school" for about ten years. By the time it is fourteen years old, it has a caretaker about its own age—an elephant boy. He and the elephant live together and work together year after year.

In India the man who feeds, waters, trains, and drives an elephant is called a mahout. The mahout knows his companion as well as he knows his best human friend. And he gives his companion the best of care.

When the adult elephant is twenty-five or older, it does heavy work. Often such an elephant has a hard life. It works all day and then has to find its own food during the evening and at night.

If an adult elephant is well cared for, it works three days in a row and rests two days. This goes on for about nine months. Then the elephant has a vacation—three months of complete rest.

How have men used elephants?

For centuries men have trained elephants not only to do peacetime work but to make war against an enemy. During battles before the birth of Christ, soldiers drove elephants like heavy tanks into the ranks of the enemy. Usually the enemy foot soldiers ran away or surrendered.

In 1882 the most famous elephant of all time was bought by P. T. Barnum and brought to the United States. This elephant was named Jumbo. It weighed 12,000 pounds and stood almost eleven feet at the shoulder. Before long its name came to mean something big. For example, a big candy bar or a large box of soap is the *jumbo* size.

Circus elephants are nearly always females. They are easier to train and to handle than bulls. These female elephants are so gentle that children can ride on their backs. They learn to parade, to play ball, to lie down, to stand on their hind legs, and even to stand on their heads—all tricks that many people enjoy seeing.

Elephants are not only giants on the land. They are also among the most interesting and unusual animals that have ever lived.

Record your finishing time in the time record for Article 1. Then take the reading test.

Read each test item and choose the answer you believe is correct. Write your answers in the answer record on page 4 of the progress folder.

Reading Test 1

Getting main ideas

1. The main purpose of the author is to

A. give facts about elephants
B. explain the birth of elephants
C. tell stories about elephants
D. compare elephants with other large animals
E. explain how elephants are trained

Understanding important details

2. One of the following facts about an elephant's trunk is *not* true: An elephant

A. breathes through its trunk
B. drinks through its trunk
C. lifts large and small objects with its trunk
D. showers itself with its trunk
E. throws things with its trunk

---

3. One of the following facts about elephants is *not* true: An elephant

A. can be trained to obey twenty-five commands
B. has no vacation at all
C. has a caretaker called a mahout
D. is trained for ten years
E. does heavy work when it is twenty-five years old

Remembering key facts

4. The cow elephant gives birth to

   A. a litter of four calves
   B. a litter of twelve calves
   C. twin calves
   D. a large litter
   E. a single calf

5. Wild elephants live naturally in only two places:

   A. Africa and Asia
   B. the United States and the Union of South Africa
   C. Africa and Europe
   D. China and Australia
   E. Texas and Vermont

6. Circus elephants are nearly always

   A. males
   B. old
   C. young
   D. females
   E. large

7. Elephants live

   A. alone
   B. in pairs
   C. in families of four
   D. in a herd
   E. in streams

8. Elephants move in the jungle

   A. in streams
   B. noisily
   C. as silently as other animals
   D. on roads
   E. on three legs

9. A newborn elephant calf is covered with

   A. large scales
   B. a blanket
   C. heavy black hair
   D. bark
   E. leaves

Choosing the best reason

10. Few wild animals attack elephants because elephants

   A. are the biggest and strongest of animals
   B. have too thick a skin
   C. move too fast
   D. hide in the water
   E. are too friendly

11. Elephants are always moving their trunks around because in this way

A. they can walk faster
B. they exercise their trunk muscles
C. they scratch their backs
D. they see enemies
E. they get the first scent of another animal or of man

12. Elephants catch cold easily. This is because they

A. have thick skin
B. live outside
C. are big
D. bathe a lot
E. are hot-weather animals

13. The adult elephant sleeps standing up

A. because it is in constant danger
B. because it has difficulty lying down
C. when it is on guard
D. because it is warmer that way
E. in the summertime

Understanding descriptive expressions

14. Elephants make a *rumbling sound*. This sounds most like

A. a screech
B. a song
C. a yell
D. a growl
E. a scream

15. If a candy bar is the *jumbo size*, it is

A. narrow
B. small
C. long
D. short
E. large

Knowing word meanings

16. The elephant is a *vegetarian*. It

A. eats meat
B. eats plants
C. eats fish
D. swims
E. runs fast

17. The elephant has *lobes* at the end of its trunk. The *lobes* are like

A. fingers
B. toes
C. hairs
D. tongues
E. tails

18. A stretched-out nose, upper lip, and cheek of an elephant form

A. a chunk
B. a tweak
C. a track
D. a trunk
E. a truck

16

Noting word relationships

19. *Automobile* is to driver as *elephant* is to

    A. bull
    B. pilot
    C. mahout
    D. leader
    E. calf

Recognizing the right word

20. The elephant's legs are built like

    A. pillows
    B. pens
    C. pillars
    D. pennies
    E. pelts

Follow the directions (Steps 8–13) on page 1 of the progress folder.

Why you should learn to read better

On a hot day last summer, thirty-six men with their books under their arms walked into a classroom on Northwestern University's downtown campus. They were enrolled in a class to improve their reading skills.

These men were in their thirties and forties. They were successful businessmen. (Most of them were college graduates.) They held important jobs in their companies. All of them could read well enough to get through the evening newspaper. And they could read well enough to understand the letters in their daily mail. They read a book occasionally, too. Yet they were back at school on a hot summer day.

They were learning to read more efficiently. The companies they worked for were paying the cost of their reading course and their living expenses for a month in Chicago. They were there because they had to learn to read better in order to do their jobs more efficiently.

It is hard for the average person to believe how much reading a top business executive has to do today. He must keep up with the daily news. He must read important articles in the business magazines and trade journals. He must read committee reports, accounts from research laboratories, and memoranda from the many other departments of his business.

There is so much for a businessman to read today that he must be able to read fast and accurately. He must know when to read sentence by sentence or phrase by phrase. He must know when he can skim. He must be able to pick out important facts and ideas.

That's why many business houses are willing to spend money to have their key men trained to read better.

"But," you may say, "I am not going to be a top business executive. I am going to be a housewife (or a mechanic or a forest ranger). Why is it important for me to become a better reader?"

So you are going to be a housewife? And you don't think you have to know how to read very well? Have you considered what kind of housewife you intend to be?

Do you expect to cook the same meals, using the same recipes, as your mother? Or do you want to use new foods and modern cooking methods? At least once a year the newspapers show pictures of the "dream kitchen of tomorrow," with wonderful machines for cleaning dishes, for cooking, for freezing foods. These machines cannot run themselves. *You* have to run them, and you can run them only if you can *read* directions accurately and don't have to wait to be told how to use each new gadget. Mistakes in reading directions can also be costly.

But why not turn on the television set and get all the new facts and ideas you need without bothering to read? Some of the television programs today are excellent, and many are well worth your time and attention. But once the show is off the air, it is beyond your reach. After a single hour has passed, you will probably not be able to recall more than two-thirds of what you saw and heard. And after a week, most people can remember less than half of what the program was about.

The only way to check your memory or to refresh your memory is to read and reread the facts in print. Events take shape so fast today and life changes so rapidly that you must be able to read efficiently to keep up with what is going on. Reading offers you a chance to study, review, and master facts in order to become well informed and knowledgeable. But you must be an *efficient* reader to get the most benefit from what you read.

What do you think?

How is reading going to affect your life? What reasons are there for you to improve your reading? Take a few minutes *right now* to make a list of reasons.

Your list will be your own. You will have some interests and needs that your classmates do not have. But your classmates and you will probably share many of the same reasons for becoming better readers.

Give some hard thought to your list of reasons. Write them out carefully. Then compare your list with the lists made by other students. Discuss the lists in class. The teacher may use the chalkboard to make a master list for the whole group.

Reasons for better reading

Better reading will help you—

- To become a more interesting person.
- To do better schoolwork and do it more easily.
- To get ready for more training and education in high school and after.
- To get and hold a more interesting and better-paying job.
- To prepare for military service.
- To become a better-informed citizen.
- To lead a fuller and happier life.

Frequent practice is a necessary means to reach these goals. When you have increased your reading efficiency, you will then enjoy reading for its own sake. It will give you pleasure that you can get in no other way.

Read better to become a more interesting person

Who is the most interesting person you know? Whoever it is, he is not likely to be the sort who has nothing to say. An interesting person is one with ideas, with information. *He* knows about the weight-to-power ratio in the latest sports cars. *She* knows about new styles in clothes or new ways of doing her hair.

An interesting person has something to say. He does not have to depend on what other people say for his conversation. He does not depend on gossip to interest his friends. He does not bore them by retelling the plot of the movie he saw last night, although he can discuss it intelligently. He is a good listener. He does not talk continuously but gains respect by the accuracy of his statements.

Where does he get his facts and ideas?

During World War II many young people had to leave school to go into the armed forces. Many boys entered the service before they finished high school. Both boys and girls left school to take factory jobs at high pay.

Indeed, so many young people dropped out of school that our federal, state, and local governments started a stay-in-school movement. They were aided by newspapers, magazines, radio stations, and motion picture companies.

One of the contributions to this movement was the popular movie *Going My Way*, starring Bing Crosby. In this picture Crosby sang "Swinging on a Star," a song that still has an important message for all young people.

The song is reprinted here. Read it carefully to make sure you understand what it says. See whether you can apply the ideas in the song to your own life.

Swinging on a Star[1]

Words by Johnny Burke
Music by Jimmy Van Heusen

Would you like to swing on a star,
  Carry moonbeams home in a jar,
And be better off than you are,
  Or would you rather be a mule?
A mule is an animal with long funny ears,
  He kicks up at anything he hears,
His back is brawny and his brain is weak,
  He's just plain stupid with a stubborn
    streak,
And by the way if you hate to go to school,
  You may grow up to be a mule.

---

1 "Swinging on a Star," by Johnny Burke and Jimmy Van Heusen. Copyright 1944 by Burke & Van Heusen, Inc.

Or would you like to swing on a star,
　　Carry moonbeams home in a jar,
And be better off than you are,
　　Or would you rather be a pig?

A pig is an animal with dirt on his face,
　　His shoes are a terrible disgrace,
He's got no manners when he eats his food,
　　He's fat and lazy and extremely rude,
But if you don't care a feather or a fig,
　　You may grow up to be a pig.
Or would you like to swing on a star,
　　Carry moonbeams home in a jar,
And be better off than you are,
　　Or would you rather be a fish?

A fish won't do anything but swim in a
　　brook,
He can't write his name or read a
　　book,
To fool the people is his only thought,
　　And though he's slippery, he still
　　gets caught,
But then if that sort of life is what you wish,
　　You may grow up to be a fish.
And all the monkeys aren't in the zoo,
　　Every day you meet quite a few,
So you see it's all up to you.
　　You can be better than you are,
You could be SWINGING ON A STAR.

Did you get the meaning of the phrase "swinging on a star"? To swing on a star, you would have to reach up. You would have to give up many of the unimportant little things that now waste your time. You might well have to be "better than you are."

Exercise 4

In List I are the names of the animals mentioned in the song. In List II are some habits and qualities of people. From what the song says about the animals, you should be able to match them with the items in List II.

Write the numerals 1 to 8 on your paper. Write the name of the animal that fits each of the descriptions of people.

List I—Animals

Mule
Pig
Fish
Monkey

List II—People

1. He fools around all the time; he never gets anything done.
2. He tries to get others to think that he is pretty good, but they find him out.
3. He thinks only of himself; he never considers the rights or feelings of other people.
4. He has a strong back and a weak mind.
5. He cannot read or write.
6. He has dirt on his face and clothes. His hair is always mussed.
7. He never listens to reason; he never gives an inch.
8. He does the same thing all the time.

The correct answers to Exercise 4 are shown in the answer key at the back of the book.

Read better to do better schoolwork

Do you know that the best students spend less time on their textbooks than many students who get poorer grades? Some students, of course, do not care whether they learn or not. But most students really care enough about the job of going to school to *want* to do good work.

If you want to do good work, you can do it more quickly and easily by learning how to read better. Your marks may improve a great deal. At the very least, you will show some improvement and at the same time reduce your study time.

The best students may spend less time on an assignment than others because they know how to read efficiently. They know where to look for the author's big ideas. They know how to fit examples and facts to these ideas in order to remember them more easily. They can tell the difference between a big idea and a statement that merely illustrates it.

To the untrained reader, one word on a page is about as important as another. He may read through an assignment slowly and carefully, but at the end all he has in his head is a mass of unrelated facts and ideas.

If you improve your reading as you go through this book, you will understand your other textbooks better. You will read them more rapidly and efficiently, and you will have time to read supplementary materials to get interesting sidelights on your studies.

Read better for more training and education

The farther you go in school, the better reader you have to be if you are to make the most of your opportunities. Your textbooks will have more information, more ideas, and more facts per page. You will need expertness and skill to deal with these more difficult facts and ideas.

As you move from one grade to the next, you will have more reading to do outside your textbooks. You will have to read magazines, newspapers, and reference books. You will want to read mature novels and biographies. With more reading and harder reading ahead, you will be more successful if you sharpen your reading skills this year.

Twenty-five years ago many educators thought that every student could learn all he would ever need to learn in reading by the end of the sixth grade. Educators no longer believe this to be true. Neither do the successful businessmen who take valuable time off from their work to learn how to cultivate better reading habits.

Very few people read as well as they might. Nearly everyone can improve his reading by thought and practice.

Some students in your school may be planning to drop out as soon as they are of legal age. Others plan to go no farther than high school. Do these students need to work now at improving their reading? Would they be wasting their time?

In Detroit, students who leave high school before graduating can come back to school after working hours. One of the most popular courses with those who come back is a course in reading and writing.

One of the most interesting facts about Americans is their thirst for knowledge and their desire to improve themselves. It is estimated that every year there are more than thirty million American adults taking part in some kind of adult education. For this work, whether it is accounting, drafting, or ancient history, these adults need to know how to read efficiently. The better they read, the more pleasure and satisfaction they will get from their courses.

A good many of the students in your school now will be taking adult education courses in a few years. Will you be one of them? Will your reading skill be good enough to get the most out of this work?

Read well to get and hold an interesting job

During the next year or two you will be planning for the job career you want to follow. You will need to read about the skills and training requirements. You will be interested in the rewards and opportunities that different jobs have to offer.

You are going to discover that most of the interesting jobs require a certain amount of reading. You will have to be able to read instructions fast and accurately. You will have to read directions for operating the wonderful new machines that industry is installing. Ten years ago there were just a few small companies that made a business of writing manuals for workers. Now there are hundreds of them, turning out printed materials that men in factory jobs have to read.

Every year the number of jobs open to skilled workers is increasing. Every year the number of men and women competing for unskilled jobs is greater, because the number of these jobs is not increasing. There are fewer opportunities every year for people to make a living in jobs that do not require good reading skills.

One of these days you will be reading the help-wanted advertisements in your daily newspapers. Will you be willing to settle for "Man Wanted" in large type? Or will you be able to read and understand the details about the more interesting jobs?

If you go into one of the professions—law, medicine, or teaching, for example—you will have to read a great deal to keep up with your work. But even in office jobs or service jobs you will have to read and understand letters, instructions, and other printed materials.

No matter what kind of work you finally go into, you will want to advance to a more responsible position with better pay.

To get advancement you may have to read training materials. If you are a good reader, these materials will seem easier to you.

Read better to get ready for military service

If you are a young man, you may go into one of the armed forces after you leave high school or college. In any of the military services, you will find that reading is an essential tool. In the army, for example, you will have to read and remember the *Soldier's Handbook* and training manuals in many fields. And you must be able to understand written orders that are given to you.

After basic training in any of the services, you may apply to an officer candidate school. Before you are accepted, you will have to take some tests. One of these will probably be a test of your reading ability. If you are admitted, you will have to do a great deal of reading. And your success will depend in large measure on your reading efficiency.

Read better to become a better-informed citizen

If you are brought into court on a charge of violating an ordinance or regulation, you cannot be excused because you did not know about the ordinance. "Ignorance of the law is no defense." As a citizen you are expected to know what the law is.

Keeping informed about the law is an important part of citizenship. But there are other things to do that are equally important and much more complicated. A responsible citizen takes an active interest in the problems facing his community and his country. He is frequently asked to vote and to express his opinion on important matters that affect the lives of many people.

Should taxes be reduced? Should a new school be built? How shall we pay for better roads and better public health? You cannot decide wisely on such questions without the facts. To get the facts you have to read widely and carefully.

Every year representatives in your national and local governments vote on matters about which people disagree. What kind of opinions will you have on such matters? If your opinions are to be sound, you will have to read extensively in order to evaluate the judgments of public leaders.

You cannot make up your mind about public problems without reading widely to get the facts. If you are not a good reader, wide reading will be hard work.

Read better to lead a happier and fuller life

So far we have been talking about reading as a tool that will help you to be effective as an individual and as a citizen. Now we will turn to the kind of reading you will enjoy in your leisure hours.

If you seldom read outside school, you are only partly living. You are missing out on a world that is filled with great adventure. Through books you can go exploring under the sea or far down inside the earth's caves. You can take part in the great events of the past. You can look around the corner into the future. You can enjoy the adventures of traveling, too—all while sitting in your favorite easy chair.

By reading you can take part in many different kinds of lives. But let's face the facts. If reading is a slow and difficult task for you, you won't do much of it. By improving your skill, you can do more reading in less time with greater understanding.

Reading will give you more fun out of life. Good reading will help you see the point quickly in stories like the one that follows. Have you ever heard someone say on a stormy night, "I wouldn't send a dog out on a night like this"?

A Knight's Night Out

Sir Galahad jumped off his horse and ran into the inn. "I have an urgent message for the king," he told the innkeeper. "My mount is tired and spent. Can you lend me a horse?"

"I have no horse," replied the innkeeper. Then he pointed to a huge dog and said, "This is the only animal I possess."

"Very well! I'll take him!" Galahad exclaimed.

"Oh, sir!" cried the innkeeper. "I can't let you have him. I wouldn't send a knight out on a dog like this!"

In this lesson you have examined seven reasons why you should try to improve your reading. Of all these reasons, doing better schoolwork probably seems the most important to you.

Over the past few years many thousands of students have been given the SRA *Youth Inventory*. Forty-three percent of these students said they would like to know how to study better. Some 56 percent said they had difficulty staying calm when they recited in class. And 53 percent said they had trouble keeping their minds on their studies.

These problems would not have seemed so great if the students had learned how to read better. Better reading would have improved their study habits, and better study habits would have increased their confidence when it came time to speak in class. Greater confidence would have helped them to speak with ease and success.

Practice Reading 2

In a book, magazine, or newspaper that you like, practice reading for speed and comprehension. Make a record of this reading in Chart 3 on page 8 of the progress folder.

2
article

A secret for two²

by Quentin Reynolds

Montreal is a very large city, but it has some very small streets. Streets, for instance, like Prince Edward Street, which is only four blocks long. No one knew Prince Edward Street as well as did Pierre Dupin. Pierre had delivered milk to the families on the street for thirty years.

During the past fifteen years the horse which drew the milk wagon used by Pierre was a large white horse named Joseph. When the big white horse first came to the Provincial Milk Company, he didn't have a name. They told Pierre that he could use the white horse. Pierre stroked the softness of the horse's neck and he looked into the eyes of the horse.

"This is a kind horse, a gentle and a faithful horse," Pierre said, "and I can see a beautiful spirit shining out of the eyes of the horse. I will name him after good St. Joseph, who was also kind and gentle and faithful and had a beautiful spirit."

Within a year Joseph knew the milk route as well as Pierre. Pierre used to boast that he didn't need reins—he never touched them. Each morning Pierre arrived at the stables of the Provincial Milk Company at five o'clock. The wagon would be loaded and Joseph hitched to it. Pierre would call as he climbed into his seat and Joseph would turn his head, and the other drivers would say that the horse would smile at Pierre. Then Jacques, the foreman, would say, "All right, Pierre, go on," and Pierre would call softly to Joseph, "Go on,

my friend," and this splendid combination would stalk proudly down the street.

The wagon, without any direction from Pierre, would roll three blocks down St. Catherine Street, then turn right two blocks along Roslyn Avenue; then left, for that was Prince Edward Street. The horse would stop at the first house, allow Pierre perhaps thirty seconds to get down from his seat and put a bottle of milk at the front door and would then go on, skipping two houses and stopping at the third. So down the length of the street. Then Joseph would turn around and come back along the other side. Yes, Joseph was a smart horse.

Pierre would boast at the stable of Joseph's skill. "I never touch the reins. He knows just where to stop. Why, a blind man could handle my route with Joseph pulling the wagon."

So it went on for years. Pierre and Joseph grew old together, but gradually, not suddenly. Pierre's huge walrus mustache was pure white now and Joseph didn't lift his knees so high. Jacques, the foreman of the stables, never noticed that they were both getting old until Pierre appeared early one morning carrying a heavy walking stick.

"Hey, Pierre," Jacques laughed. "Maybe you got the gout, hey?"

"But yes, Jacques," Pierre said uncertainly. "One grows old. One's legs get tired."

"You should teach the horse to carry the milk to the front door for you," Jacques told him. "He does everything else."

2 From "A Secret for Two," by Quentin Reynolds, *Collier's*, by permission of Littauer and Wilkinson.

Pierre knew every one of the forty families he served on Prince Edward Street. The cooks knew that Pierre could neither read nor write, so they did not follow the usual custom of leaving a note in an empty bottle. If an additional quart of milk was needed, they would sing out when they heard his wagon wheels on the cobbled street, "Bring an extra quart this morning, Pierre."

Pierre had a remarkable memory. When he arrived at the stable he'd always remember to tell Jacques, "The Paquins took an extra quart this morning; the Lemoines bought a pint of cream."

Jacques would note these things in a little book he always carried. Most of the drivers had to make out the weekly bills and collect the money, but Jacques, liking Pierre, had always excused him from this task. All Pierre had to do was to arrive at five in the morning, walk to his wagon, which was always in the same spot at the curb, and deliver his milk.

One morning the president of the Provincial Milk Company came to inspect the early morning deliveries. Jacques pointed Pierre out to him and said, "Watch how he talks to that horse. See how the horse listens and how he turns his head toward Pierre. See the look in that horse's eyes. You know, I think those two share a secret. It is as though they both sometimes chuckle at us as they go off on their route. Pierre is a good man, but he gets old. Would it be too bold of me to suggest that he be retired and be given a small pension?" he asked anxiously.

"But of course," the president laughed. "He has been on this route now for thirty years, and never once has there been a complaint. Tell him it is time he rested. His salary will go on just the same."

But Pierre refused to retire. He was panic-stricken at the thought of not driving Joseph every day. "We are two old men," he said to Jacques. "Let us wear out together. When Joseph is ready to retire, then I too will quit."

Jacques, who was a kind man, understood. There was something about Pierre and Joseph which made a man smile tenderly. It was as though each drew some hidden strength from the other. When Pierre was sitting in his seat, and when

Joseph was hitched to the wagon, neither seemed old. But when they finished their work, then Pierre would limp down the street slowly, seeming very old indeed. Then the horse's head would drop and he would walk very wearily to his stall.

Then one morning Jacques had dreadful news for Pierre. The air was like iced wine that morning, and the snow glistened like a million diamonds piled together.

Jacques said, "Pierre, your horse, Joseph, did not wake this morning. He was very old, Pierre, he was twenty-five, and that is like seventy-five for a man."

"Yes," Pierre said slowly. "Yes, I am seventy-five. And I cannot see Joseph again."

"Of course you can," Jacques soothed. "He is over in his stall, looking very peaceful. Go over and see him."

Pierre took one step forward, then turned. "No . . . you don't understand, Jacques."

Jacques clapped him on the shoulder. "We'll find another horse just as good as Joseph. Why, in a month you'll teach him to know your route as well as Joseph did. We'll—"

The look in Pierre's eyes stopped him. For years Pierre had worn a heavy cap, the peak of which came low over his eyes. Now Jacques looked into Pierre's eyes and he saw something which startled him. He saw a dead, lifeless look in them. The eyes were mirroring the grief that was in Pierre's heart and his soul. It was as though his heart and soul had died.

"Take today off, Pierre," Jacques said, but already Pierre was hobbling off down the street, and had one been near one would have seen tears streaming down his cheeks and have heard half-smothered sobs. Pierre walked to the corner and stepped into the street. There was a warning yell from the driver of a huge truck that was coming fast and there was the scream of brakes, but Pierre apparently heard neither.

Five minutes later an ambulance driver said, "He's dead. Was killed instantly."

Jacques and several of the milk-wagon drivers had arrived, and they looked down at the still figure.

"I couldn't help it," the driver of the truck protested. "He walked right into my truck. He never saw it, I guess. Why, he walked into it as though he was blind."

The ambulance doctor bent down. "Blind? Of course the man was blind. See those cataracts? This man has been blind for at least five years." He turned to Jacques. "You say he worked for you? Didn't you know he was blind?"

"No . . . no . . ." Jacques said softly. "None of us knew. Only one knew—a friend of his named Joseph. . . . It was a secret, I think, just between those two."

Record your finishing time in the time record for Article 2. Then take the reading test.

Read each test item and choose the answer you believe is correct. Print your answers in the answer record on page 4 of the progress folder.

Reading Test 2

Getting main ideas

1. The main point of this story is that
   A. Montreal is a large city
   B. it is easy to deliver milk
   C. Joseph and Pierre depended on each other
   D. blind men can do many jobs
   E. horses are very smart

2. The author wrote this story to
   A. surprise you
   B. puzzle you
   C. inform you
   D. amuse you
   E. scare you

3. To accompany the main title, the best subtitle for the story would be
   A. Retirement
   B. A Special Friendship
   C. The Milk Company
   D. A Fine Horse
   E. A Smart Horse

4. Pierre didn't have to see to deliver milk because
   A. he did it early in the morning
   B. Joseph knew the route so well
   C. he'd been doing it so long
   D. he had a walking stick
   E. it was an easy route

5. Pierre didn't want to retire because he
   A. needed the money
   B. liked Jacques
   C. wanted to be near Joseph
   D. would miss the milk route
   E. liked to deliver milk

6. Pierre was hit by the truck because he
    A. didn't see it
    B. didn't hear it
    C. was too slow
    D. ran in front of it
    E. was looking the other way

7. Pierre arrived one day with a walking stick because
    A. he was tired
    B. his legs were weak
    C. he couldn't see where to walk
    D. it was a present to him
    E. his arms were weak

Choosing the best reason

8. The cooks on the milk route would call out if they wanted extra milk. Why didn't they leave notes?
    A. They were too lazy to leave notes.
    B. Paper for notes was hard to get.
    C. They wanted to see Joseph.
    D. They liked to talk to Pierre.
    E. They knew that Pierre couldn't read.

9. Joseph died because
    A. he was hit by a truck
    B. he wasn't well fed
    C. he worked too hard
    D. he was old
    E. the milk company didn't need him anymore

10. The president wanted to give Pierre a pension because
    A. Pierre had always done a fine job
    B. Pierre didn't do his work well
    C. they were going to use milk trucks
    D. Pierre was too old to work
    E. Jacques said not to do so

11. No one had noticed that Pierre had cataracts in his eyes because
    A. his hair was over his eyes
    B. he never looked at anyone
    C. he kept his eyes closed
    D. he wore dark glasses
    E. he wore a cap with a visor over his eyes

Getting deeper meanings

12. When Joseph died, Pierre said that he couldn't see Joseph again. He said that because
    A. he was retiring
    B. he was blind
    C. he was going away
    D. Joseph was dead
    E. Joseph was buried

13. It was important for Pierre to have a fine memory because

- **A.** he couldn't read or write well
- **B.** he had a very long route
- **C.** paper for notes was hard to get
- **D.** he was blind
- **E.** all milkmen have to have good memories

Understanding descriptive expressions

14. Pierre's *huge walrus mustache* was

- **A.** thin and long
- **B.** straight and short
- **C.** thin and full
- **D.** curly and long
- **E.** large and full

15. The cooks would *sing out* at Pierre. They would

- **A.** call out
- **B.** sing songs
- **C.** scream at him
- **D.** sing to him
- **E.** laugh at him

Recognizing the right words

16. Pierre's cap had a

- **A.** speak
- **B.** beak
- **C.** peak
- **D.** sneak
- **E.** tweak

17. When Joseph died, Pierre

- **A.** dabbed
- **B.** stabbed
- **C.** daubed
- **D.** sobbed
- **E.** cobbled

Knowing word meanings

18. The horse would go on, *skipping* two houses. He would

- **A.** trot fast up to the houses
- **B.** gallop up to the houses
- **C.** jump over two houses
- **D.** bump into two houses
- **E.** pass by two houses

19. Pierre would *boast* about Joseph. He would

- **A.** tell how slow Joseph was
- **B.** tell how wonderful Joseph was
- **C.** tell how dumb Joseph was
- **D.** tell how long his route was
- **E.** complain about the milk company

20. Joseph was a *gentle* horse. He was

- **A.** noisy and wild
- **B.** mean and noisy
- **C.** mean and quiet
- **D.** tame and quiet
- **E.** tame and mean

Follow the directions (Steps 8–13) on page 1 of the progress folder.

What is reading?

There are many definitions of the word *reading*. Although it is obvious that we need to learn to read silently as well as orally, some people stress oral reading. They tell you that reading is the act of saying or pronouncing letters and words. The idea is that if you can pronounce a word you can read it.

Many people disagree with this idea. They say that, important though pronunciation is, it is only part of reading. The main object of both oral and silent reading is to understand—to get meaning from printed material. Perhaps the most useful definition of reading is that it is a process by which we obtain meaning from printed materials.

But reading is a two-way action that involves both the printed material and the person who is reading. Reading, then, is a means of communication. *Successful* reading takes place when the author and the reader communicate clearly. And reading is *unsuccessful* when the writer's meaning is unclear or poorly understood.

There are several kinds of meanings to be derived from reading. The simplest of these is factual information. For example, an account tells the distance a balloonist travels. To see whether the reader has understood this simple meaning, you might ask: Did the balloonist go up ten thousand feet or five thousand feet? From the answer, you will know whether the reader has obtained this simple meaning.

There is, too, a kind of logical meaning that a good reader watches for in events that are reported. A good way to get at this kind of meaning is to ask, Why did this happen? What was the cause? The good reader also observes the order in which things happen. He notes the importance of each item referred to in a presentation.

There is another kind of meaning that you get by "reading between the lines." The writer does not usually say everything that might be said. He may not tell you outright how he feels about his topic. He may expect you to figure out, for example, that he is just joking. He may expect you to draw your own conclusions from the facts he presents. And he may expect you to understand that he thinks some person he is writing about is silly or unpleasant.

You can see that there is a great deal to reading. A good reader is a very active person. He has to concentrate or he will miss something important.

In this book we will test you mainly on the first kind of meaning—knowing the facts that are stated by a writer. But you will get other meanings too—meanings that cannot be checked as easily as the first kind.

Meaning is expressed in word groups

There is an important fact to remember in all kinds of reading. In getting the meaning of most materials you read, it is better to respond to several words as a unit—to read by word groups rather than word by word. Meaningful reading is like meaningful listening. As you listen to a speaker, you do not respond to each word he says. Instead you respond to groups of words—to ideas.

Of course, in some situations we may respond to a single word. Sometimes one word is enough to give a great deal of meaning. Suppose you are driving along a highway and come to a sign that reads "Stop." You immediately bring your car to a halt. After making sure that the road ahead is clear, you continue your journey.

Clearly, the word *stop* has a great deal of power. When you see it on an official highway sign, you know it was put there by someone in authority. It was put there because traffic experts believe it dangerous for cars to go ahead at full speed. If you don't obey the sign, you may be arrested and fined. Or you may have an accident.

Sometimes, then, a single word has a great deal of meaning. But usually words have far greater meaning when they are used with other words.

Note how the meaning builds up in the following word group:

The . . .
The little . . .
The little white . . .
The little white dog . . .

Not until you get to the word *dog* do you have meaning. *The little white dog* is a word group. When you see *a* or *the*, you know that a word group is coming. The word group above is built around a noun (*dog*).

There are two other kinds of word groups to watch for. A second kind is built around a verb. Here is an example:

The dog was . . .
The dog was barking.

The word group *was barking* gives the reader some meaning.

The third kind of word group starts with little words like *of, in, at, near, by*. Notice how this word group builds up meaning:

at . . .
at the . . .
at the door . . .

The best way to get the meaning of a sentence is to read word groups. You cannot get the meaning easily by reading one word at a time. Let's put the word groups together to see how this works:

The little white dog—was barking—at the door.

It is better to read words in groups like these than to try to read them one at a time. After you have learned to read very well, you will be able to combine word groups as you read:

The little white dog—was barking at the door.

Meaning is both enriched and made specific by the addition of words. Notice how the addition of adjectives can sharpen the meaning of a sentence:

The sea is calm.
The blue sea is calm.
The dark blue sea is calm.

Seeing word groups

Exercise 5

Copy these sentences on a sheet of paper. As you write the sentences, divide them into word groups.

Example: The math teacher—was looking—into the room.

1. The school band was practicing in the hall.
2. An elderly lady helped the truck driver to his feet.
3. A weather-beaten face appeared in the dim light of the entrance.
4. The science teacher had been talking about the solar system.

Turn to the answer key to see how these sentences might be divided.

Getting meaning
from a paragraph

In many kinds of reading, the meaning is relatively easy to find. For example, a paragraph should have a main idea. This idea is often stated by the writer in a very simple form and is easily and quickly grasped by the reader. But sometimes it is not stated. You have to figure it out for yourself, as in the following paragraph. Here the main idea is not so obvious.

Read the paragraph and do the exercise that follows.

Exercise 6

The largest unexplored region in the world is not located at the poles, in Alaska or Tibet, or beneath the oceans.[1] It lies above us, in the atmosphere. Seventy-five times as deep as the deepest ocean, and

1 From pp. 15–16, *How About the Weather?* by Robert Moore Fisher. Copyright 1951 by Robert Moore Fisher. Reprinted by permission of Harper & Row, Publishers, Incorporated.

ninety times as high as the highest mountain, the air overhead extends roughly 500 miles aloft (estimates range from 300 to 700 miles). Ninety-seven percent of this space is unexplored by man himself.

Choose the statement that best expresses the main idea of the paragraph you have just read:

1. The atmosphere over our heads extends 300 to 700 miles above the earth's surface.
2. The most extensive unexplored area of our planet is its atmosphere.
3. The atmosphere is seventy-five times as deep as the ocean.

The correct answer to Exercise 6 is shown in the answer key at the back of the book.

How did you learn to read?

When you entered the first grade, you probably used correctly and knew some of the meanings of at least twenty-five hundred words. But when you saw these words on the printed page, you could recognize few if any of them. When your teacher started to teach you to read, she may have had you and your classmates tell a story about something you had done or about a place you had visited. She may have written out your simple story in large letters for you to read. Later she may have printed some of your words and phrases on cards. You then learned to recognize these words and phrases as she flashed the cards quickly. She may have had pictures on the back of the cards to make sure you got the right meaning of each word or phrase.

Soon you began to read. Your teacher helped you to pronounce each word correctly, and she gave you some rules to follow so that you could pronounce some of the new words by yourself. Intonation was stressed too. She then helped you to see when the rules worked and when they did not work. As you read more and more, you learned the names of living things, of objects, of actions. And you learned to recognize the important words that connect ideas—words such as *and, but, because.* You

also learned the little words such as *of, it, in, on,* and *under* that serve to hold small groups of words together. Gradually you became familiar with the most frequently used combinations of word patterns. Soon you were reading on your own.

Later you learned that long words can be divided into syllables and that the syllables at the beginning and end of some words are called prefixes and suffixes: *un-, in-, -ance, -ly,* for example. You learned that most of these prefixes and suffixes affect the meaning of a word. We shall learn more about them in Lesson 12.

As your reading improved, you were able to get the meanings of some new words by reading groups of familiar words that went with them. The sense of these familiar groups of words is called the *context.* We shall learn more about context in Lessons 12 and 13.

Learning to read a new language

Exercise 7

In order to get a clearer idea of one way to read new words and phrases, try to understand the French sentences that are illustrated on the next page. These pictured sentences appear on facing pages in a self-teaching textbook.

When reading these pictured sentences, look first at the picture in the upper left-hand corner, then at the picture next to it, then at the picture in the lower left-hand corner, and so on until you get to the picture at the lower right-hand corner. Notice that the circles and lines tell you whether the speaker is saying "here" or "there." In each picture it is the man who is speaking to you. Do not try to translate the sentences word for word, but see if you can say *in English* what the stick figure man is saying *in French.*

After you have figured out the meaning of the French sentences, see if you can match the words in List I with the words in List II. Write the numerals 1 to 12 on your paper. Look at the first word in List I. It is *c'est.* Look at the words in List II. Find the word that means "c'est." Write the letter that precedes that word.

Figure 1[2]

List I	List II
1. c'est	**A.** am
2. elle	**B.** are
3. est	**C.** it's
4. ici	**D.** he *or* it
5. il	**E.** they
6. ils	**F.** here
7. je	**G.** I
8. là-bas	**H.** she
9. lui	**I.** is
10. moi	**J.** there
11. sont	**K.** him *or* he
12. suis	**L.** I *or* me

The correct answers to Exercise 7 are shown in the answer key.

When reading these French sentences, you had to compare the words and the pictures *carefully*. You had to study the whole sentence of words and pictures to understand what the sentences said. After a time you were able to understand how each of the words worked with the others in the sentences. It was in much the same way that you learned to read English. The principal difference was that you understood spoken English before you learned to read it.

If you enjoyed this taste of learning a new language, you may want to look at other books in the "Language Through Pictures" series and listen to some of the records that go with them.

What do dictionaries say about reading?

According to the *Thorndike-Barnhart Comprehensive Desk Dictionary*, the definitions of *to read* are (1) "to get the meaning of writing or printing" and (2) "to speak written or printed words."[3] As an example of the first definition, you read silently while you are getting meanings from this lesson. As an example of the second definition, you read orally while you are reading aloud to the class your written report of a special project.

2 Copyright 1950 by English Language Research, Inc. Reprinted by permission of Washington Square Press, 630 Fifth Avenue, New York, from *French Through Pictures*, by I. A. Richards, M. H. Ilsley, and Christine Gibson.

3 From: *Thorndike-Barnhart Comprehensive Desk Dictionary*. Copyright 1951 by Thorndike-Barnhart Dictionaries, Inc. Reprinted by permission of Doubleday & Company, Inc.

Reading is a two-way action

We have already said that reading is a means of communication that begins with the writer. Suppose you are reading an article by a man who has discovered something important about the planet Mars. He is an astronomer and has studied Mars for many years. Words like *icecap* and *polar region* are frequently used in his work and have great meaning for him.

Now, this astronomer has discovered something that he wants everyone to know. He is going to write not for other astronomers but for the general reader. He will therefore pick words that everyone is likely to know rather than technical words. If he is a careful writer, he will explain the terms *icecap* and *polar region*. To explain them he will try to describe them in terms of the average person's experience.

Suppose, now, that you are reading the astronomer's report. You do not bring a blank mind to this reading. You know something about planets. Perhaps you know that Mars comes fairly close to the earth every two years. And you may have heard something about canals on Mars.

You have had experience with many of the words the writer uses. You may have seen a picture and heard the word *canal* used to name a waterway. Or you may have walked along a canal yourself.

But if the astronomer wants to talk to you about the canals on Mars, he must explain unusual things about them—for example, their enormous size. Otherwise you will not get his meaning. And he must also try to relate these facts to things he thinks you already know.

The astronomer in his writing will try to make you understand what *he* means by *canal*. But you, too, will have something to do. You have to figure out what the writer means by the word. It is not safe just to give it your own meaning.

This, then, is what makes reading a two-way action. The reader has to try to get the meaning the writer is trying to express.

The following excerpt illustrates in an amusing way how the meanings of words can change according to our experience. It shows too, that words have no meaning in themselves, and depend on our interpretation of them to become meaningful. Have you ever considered that work can be play, and play can be work?

Exercise 8

Tom Sawyer[4]

"Say—I'm going in a-swimming, I am. Don't you wish you could? But of course you'd druther *work*—wouldn't you? Course you would!"

Tom contemplated the boy a bit, and said:

"What do you call work?"

"Why, ain't that work?"

Tom resumed his whitewashing, and answered carelessly:

"Well, maybe it is, and maybe it ain't. All I know is, it suits Tom Sawyer."

"Oh come, now, you don't mean to let on that you like it?"

The brush continued to move.

"Like it? Well, I don't see why I oughtn't to like it. Does a boy get a chance to whitewash a fence every day?"

That put the thing in a new light. Ben stopped nibbling his apple. Tom swept his brush daintily back and forth—stepped back to note the effect—added a touch here and there—criticized the effect again—Ben watching every move and getting more and more interested, more and more absorbed. Presently he said:

"Say, Tom, let me whitewash a little."

Tom considered, was about to consent; but he altered his mind.

"No—no—I reckon it wouldn't hardly do, Ben. You see, Aunt Polly's awfully particular about this fence . . . it's got to be done very careful. . . . If you was to tackle this fence and anything was to happen to it—"

"Oh, shucks, I'll be just as careful. Now lemme try. Say—I'll give you the core of my apple."

"Well, here— No, Ben, now don't. I'm afeard—"

"I'll give you all of it!"

Tom gave up the brush with reluctance in his face, but alacrity in his heart. And while [Ben] . . . worked and sweated

---

4 From *The Adventures of Tom Sawyer*, by Samuel L. Clemens.

in the sun, the retired artist sat on a barrel in the shade close by, dangled his legs, munched his apple, and planned the slaughter of more innocents. There was no lack of material; boys happened along every little while; they came to jeer, but remained to whitewash. . . .

Tom said to himself that it was not such a hollow world, after all. He had discovered a great law of human action, without knowing it—namely, that in order to make a man or boy covet a thing, it is only necessary to make the thing difficult to attain. If he had been a great and wise philosopher, like the writer of this book, he would now have comprehended that Work consists of whatever a body is obliged to do, and that Play consists of whatever a body is not obliged to do. And this would help him to understand why constructing artificial flowers or performing on a treadmill is work, while rolling tenpins or climbing Mont Blanc is only amusement.

Now see how well you got the meaning of the story. Choose the correct answer for each item below. Write the answers on your paper.

1. The boys helped Tom Sawyer whitewash the fence because
   A. they enjoyed slapping the brush against the fence
   B. he made it seem like a privilege rather than a chore
   C. he allowed only a few boys to work

2. The author states that Work consists of
   A. that which you do every day
   B. whatever a body is paid for
   C. whatever a body is obliged to do

The correct answers to Exercise 8 are shown in the answer key.

Reading is active learning

Have you ever heard someone say of a fellow student, "When he reads, he soaks up ideas" or "He is thirsty for knowledge; he absorbs ideas quickly"? Does this mean that he is just taking it easy?

Perhaps you have had the experience of being interrupted in reading a good book by a telephone call. Your friend asks, "What are you doing?" You say quickly, "Oh, nothing. Just reading." Can you read without doing something?

As a matter of fact, if you are reading with understanding, you are active, not passive. You may be reading an exciting story just for pleasure. Or you may be reading a book to get information to use in class. The purpose of your reading determines how you read—slowly to get details or rapidly to get big ideas.

But in every case, if you are getting something from the printed page, you are reading actively. You are doing something.

Sometimes when you are looking at a book or a magazine, you are not *really* reading. Some people can actually go through the motions of pronouncing to themselves every word on a page while their thoughts are far away. But they are not reading. Just saying the words is never really reading. If you let your mind wander or if you doze off for a few seconds, you are not getting the meaning. If you are not getting the meaning, you are not reading successfully.

To improve your reading, you must be an active reader. You must give close attention to what the author has written. And you must do some thinking about it. What the writer says will recall your own experiences and other things you have read. You will make comparisons. You may jot down notes and questions. Active reading is reading in which you do something. You bring something to the reading, and you take away something from it. From some books you will gain a great deal.

Reading is a lifetime activity

Someone once said that in the first three grades you *learn to read* and that in later grades you *read to learn*. What this meant was that in the primary grades you learned certain reading skills—to recognize words, to get the meanings of new words, and to understand short sentences and stories. In the middle and upper grades you used these reading skills to study other subjects.

Today, however, reading experts believe that you should *learn to read* and *read to learn* all through school and college and into adult life. They agree with the great philosopher-poet Goethe. When Goethe was eighty years old, he wrote: "Learning to read is a lifetime process. I have been at it all my life, and I cannot yet say I have reached the goal." And they also agree with the psychologist Edward L. Thorndike. He found that a person does not have to stop learning when he leaves school or college. Instead, he wrote, a person can keep on learning throughout his life. And one thing he can learn is how to read better.

You can sharpen your reading skills by thoughtful practice all through school—and after your school years are over.

How do oral reading and silent reading differ?

While you were learning to read, you did more oral than silent reading. You read aloud in order to associate the printed form with the sound you already knew.

There are good reasons for learning to read in this way. When you first entered school, you could recognize thousands of words when they were spoken. Your reading problem was to tie the words you knew by sound to the printed symbols that you did not know. Sounding the words helped you. Sounding new words as you meet them may still help you master them quickly.

But by the time you had reached the middle grades, you were reading a great many words that you had never heard. Just pronouncing an unfamiliar word is not enough to get its meaning. You have learned a little about getting meaning for a word from the words with which it is used. And there are other ways of getting meaning that we will study in Lessons 12 and 13.

As you came along in school, you did more silent reading because silent reading suited your reading purposes better. But you continued to do some oral reading. Instead of learning to read, you were reading to learn geography, science, and other subjects. You had much more reading to do, and you had to read faster. In addition, you had to learn to adjust your reading rate to the kind of material you were reading.

Here are two ways in which silent reading is superior to oral reading: You can · read much faster when you read silently, and you can adjust your speed more easily to the types of materials you are reading.

To compare your oral reading speed and your silent reading speed, read the following two paragraphs. Have someone keep time for you. *First*, read the paragraphs silently and write down the number of seconds required to read each paragraph. *Second*, read each paragraph orally and write down the number of seconds required. Which took less time, the silent or the oral reading?

It is an overnight trip on the train from New York to Detroit. The distance of five hundred miles between these two cities may be traveled with ease. No one would give a second thought to what to put in the overnight bag, or how strongly the Pullman is constructed.

But suppose that Detroit were five hundred miles up in the air. Then trouble begins. If your Pullman weren't well heated, even the warmest clothes would be useless, for you might pass through temperatures of a hundred degrees below zero. If it weren't properly air-conditioned, you'd be overcome later by temperatures close to boiling. Moreover, if the car weren't well sealed and pressurized, you would lose consciousness before rising 25,000 feet.[5]

Although you read these paragraphs silently before you read orally, you probably found that it took you twice as long to read them aloud. In general, as you have just seen, you can read much faster silently than you can read orally—perhaps more than twice as fast.

Most students learned to read orally at first. Some of them have carried over their oral reading habits to their silent reading. When they are reading silently, they may pronounce each word almost as if they were reading it aloud. Their lips,

[5] From pp. 15–16, *How About the Weather?* by Robert Moore Fisher. Copyright 1951 by Robert Moore Fisher. Reprinted by permission of Harper & Row, Publishers, Incorporated.

their tongues, and their throat muscles sometimes move as they say the words to themselves. These movements slow down their speed of reading to something like the speed of oral reading. These students cannot read as much as they should, and they cannot adjust their rate of reading to different kinds of materials.

Even though you may do 75 to 90 percent of all your reading silently, you will find many occasions for reading aloud. At times you will want to read well orally in order to get your ideas across. You will read with emphasis. You will read word groups together. You will vary the loudness of your voice and its rise and fall as you do in normal speech.

You may need to read aloud a paragraph from your textbook. You may be asked to read a composition or a report that you have written. There will be times when you will want to read aloud a story, a poem, or a part in a play. If you can read accurately and smoothly, your audience will understand you. And you will find that oral reading can be a most enjoyable experience.

In reading, your eyes move from left to right along a line of print. When they reach the end of a line, they quickly move to the left to the beginning of the next line, just below.

You may think that in reading a line your eyes move smoothly from left to right. But that is not the case. Instead your eyes move with a *stop-go-stop-go-stop-go* movement.

When your eyes stop for a fraction of a second, they focus on a word or on a group of words. In that instant your mind gets the meaning of what you are seeing. When your eyes are moving toward the next stop, your mind is not getting meaning from the printed page.

While your eyes are focusing on a single word, they may also be taking in the words that are near it—one or two words on the left and one or two words on the right. That is, your eyes may be grasping the meaning of a group of words.

If you are a poor reader, *your eyes stop on every word like this. You read very slowly. And you often have trouble understanding what you are seeing. If you are a good reader, your eyes stop near the center of a group of* words—say, two or three words or even five or six words. And you get the meaning of the whole word group at once.

When a person, even a good reader, meets a reading passage that is hard to understand, he goes back again to reread. He may go back a sentence or a whole paragraph to try to get the meaning. This kind of rereading is essential to everyone. But there is another kind of rereading that is unwise and harmful. This is the kind of reading in which the reader's eyes go back over words he has read even in the simplest material. This is a bad habit, called *regression*, which greatly slows down a person's reading rate and actually decreases his chance of understanding.

What can you do about oral reading habits and eye-movement skills?

If your eye movements are not efficient, or if you have carried over oral reading habits to silent reading, you are not reading at your best. There are several things you can do to improve your reading, but you will have to make a conscious effort to do them. Discovering your bad reading habits is the first step toward correcting them.

You can cut down or stop lip movements or whispering while you are reading. Some students have trained themselves by placing fingers on their lips or throats as they read. This makes them aware of muscle movements, and if they are aware of them, they may stop them.

You can improve your eye movements in reading. The length of your eye span may be limited by the shape of the lens of your eyes or by muscle weakness. If so, an eye doctor can help you. But if your narrow eye span is just a matter of habit, you can correct it yourself. One of the best ways of doing this is to begin reading easy material and gradually increase your reading speed. Another good idea is to look for and read word groups.

If your eyes go back too often over words you have read, you can train yourself out of this habit. You can train your eyes to move steadily from left to right with a full sweep back to the beginning of the next line.

For practice in improving your reading, read the following paragraphs as rapidly as you can, but make sure that you understand what you read. You will test your understanding when you have finished.

As you read, have another student watch your eyes. Let him place a large mirror, about the size of this page, on the left side of the page you are reading. Let him observe your eye movements in the mirror and notice the number of stops you make for each line and the number of regressions. Then have him read the same page and observe his reading. Good readers will make few stops and few regressions.

Exercise 9

Mud Pies and the Weather[6]

Mud pies are difficult to cook. You can put one under a broiler, but it won't cook thoroughly. The upper crust may be burned to a crisp. However, because heat is not easily carried through the pie, the filling inside stays raw and muddy.

But if you set a dishpan of water in the broiler in place of the pie, the results are different. Water cooks easily. As the surface is warmed by the flame, the heat is carried slowly throughout the water. As a result, the water at the bottom becomes about as warm as that on the surface.

This experiment shows some important things about the weather. Suppose, for instance, that the mud pie were the continent of North America, the dishpan of water the oceans around it, and the gas flame the sun. When the sun rises, what happens? The surface of the earth, like the upper crust of the mud pie, warms rapidly. All the heat it receives from the sun is absorbed within the first two feet of topsoil. But the huge dishpan of water, the ocean, warms little. The sun's rays are

6 From pp. 27–28, *How About the Weather?* by Robert Moore Fisher. Copyright 1951 by Robert Moore Fisher. Reprinted by permission of Harper & Row, Publishers, Incorporated.

distributed through a large volume of water. All of this water must be heated before the temperature of the water at the surface changes much. By midafternoon, therefore, the surface of the land may have risen ten degrees. That of the ocean may be less than one degree higher.

After sunset the process is reversed. The earth cools quickly, since all its heat is close to the surface and escapes easily. The ocean, on the other hand, remains at about the same temperature. The heat it gives off during the night is an infinitesimal part of what it has stored up in its depths. As a result, the twenty-four-hour surface temperature change may equal twenty degrees for land, but one degree for water.

A comprehension test

Write the numerals 1 to 4 on your paper. Read the following statements. Write **T** for each true statement, and **F** for each false or partly false statement. You may reread the paragraphs.

1. Heat moves through a mud pie much more easily than through a dishpan of water.

2. If you get chilly at the beach after dark during the summer, you can usually get warm by going in the water.

3. Heat flows into the surface of a body of water much more slowly than it does into the surface of a body of land.

4. The difference between the noon temperature and the midnight temperature is much less in the Middle West of the United States than it is in the middle of the North Atlantic Ocean.

The correct answers to Exercise 9 are shown in the answer key.

On a separate paper, write a short paragraph that answers the question "What is reading?"

Then write a statement telling your opinion of your present reading habits and abilities.

Practice Reading 3

In a book, magazine, or newspaper that you like, practice reading for speed and comprehension. Make a record of this reading in Chart 3 on page 8 in the progress folder.

3
article

A, B, and C — the human element in mathematics[7] by Stephen Leacock

The student of arithmetic must master the first four rules of his art. Then he must strive with many sums and fractions. After these, he finds himself confronted by an unbroken expanse of questions known as problems. These are short stories of adventure and industry with the end omitted. Though betraying a strong family resemblance, they are not without a certain element of romance.

The characters in the plot of a problem are three people called A, B, and C. The form of the question is generally of this sort:

"A, B, and C do a certain piece of work. A can do as much work in one hour as B in two, or C in four. Find how long they work at it."

Or thus: "A, B, and C are employed to dig a ditch. A can dig as much in one hour as B can dig in two, and B can dig twice as fast as C. Find how long, etc., etc."

Or after this wise: "A lays a wager that he can walk faster than B or C. A can walk half as fast again as B, and C is only an indifferent walker. Find how far, and so forth."

The occupations of A, B, and C are many and varied. In the older arithmetics they contented themselves with doing a "certain piece of work." This statement of the case, however, was found too sly and mysterious, or possibly lacking in romantic charm. It became the fashion to define the job more clearly and to set them at walking

matches, ditchdigging, regattas, and piling cordwood. At times, they became commercial and entered into partnership, having, with their old mystery, a "certain" capital. Above all they revel in motion. When they tire of walking matches, A rides on horseback, or borrows a bicycle and competes with his weaker-minded associates on foot. Now they race on locomotives; now they row; or again they become historical and engage stagecoaches; or at times they are aquatic and swim. If their occupation is actual work, they prefer to pump water into cisterns, two of which leak through holes in the bottom and one of which is watertight. A, of course, has the good one; he also takes the bicycle, and the best locomotive, and the right of swimming with the current. Whatever they do they put money on it, being all three sports. A always wins.

In the early chapters of the arithmetic, their identity is concealed under the names of John, William, and Henry, and they wrangle over the division of marbles. In algebra they are often called X, Y, Z. But these are only their Christian names, and they are really the same people.

Now to one who has followed the history of these men through countless pages of problems, watched them dallying with cordwood, and seen their panting sides heave in the full frenzy of filling a cistern with a leak in it, they become something more than mere symbols. They appear as creatures of flesh and blood, living men with their own passions, ambitions, and aspirations like the rest of us.

[7] Reprinted by permission of Dodd, Mead & Company and The Bodley Head Ltd. from *Literary Lapses*, by Stephen Leacock.

A is full-blooded, hot-headed and strong-willed. It is he who proposes everything, challenges B to work, makes the bets, and bends the others to his will. He is a man of great physical strength and phenomenal endurance. He has been known to walk forty-eight hours at a stretch, and to pump ninety-six. His life is arduous and full of peril. A mistake in the working of a sum may keep him digging a fortnight without sleep. A repeating decimal in the answer might kill him.

B is a quiet, easy-going fellow, afraid of A and bullied by him, but very gentle and brotherly to little C, the weakling. He is quite in A's power, having lost all his money in bets.

Poor C is an undersized, frail man, with a plaintive face. Constant walking, digging, and pumping has broken his health and ruined his nervous system. His joyless life has driven him to drink and smoke more than is good for him, and his hand often shakes as he digs ditches. He has not the strength to work as the others do; in fact, as Hamlin Smith has said, "A can do more work in one hour than C in four."

The first time that ever I saw these men was one evening after a regatta. They had all been rowing in it, and it had transpired that A could row as much in one hour as B in two, or C in four. B and C had come in dead fagged and C was coughing badly. "Never mind, old fellow," I heard B say, "I'll fix you up on the sofa and get you some hot tea." Just then A came blustering in and shouted, "I say, you fellows, Hamlin Smith has shown me three cisterns in his garden and he says we can pump them until tomorrow night. I bet I can beat you both. Come on. Your cistern leaks a little, I think, C." I heard B growl that it was a dirty shame and that C was used up now, but they went and presently I could tell from the sound of the water that A was pumping four times as fast as C. After that, owing to a long absence from home, I lost sight of them.

Now it chanced one day that I stumbled upon old D, in the little garden in front of his cottage, hoeing in the sun. D is an aged laboring man who used occasionally to be called in to help A, B, and C. He was eager to talk about his old friends. "Did I know 'em, sir?" he answered.

"Why I knowed 'em ever since they was little fellows in brackets."

From the garrulous old man I learned the melancholy end of my former acquaintances. Soon after I left town, he told me, C had been ill. It seems that A and B had been rowing on the river for a wager, and C had been running on the bank and then sat in a draught. Of course the bank had refused the draught and C was taken ill. A and B came home and found C lying helpless in bed. A shook him roughly and said, "Get up, C, we're going to pile wood." C looked so worn and pitiful that B said, "Look here, A, I won't stand this, he isn't fit to pile wood tonight." C smiled feebly and said, "Perhaps I might pile a little if I sat up in bed." Then B, thoroughly alarmed, said, "See here, A, I'm going to fetch a doctor; he's dying." A flared up and answered, "You've got no money to fetch a doctor." "I'll reduce him to his lowest terms," B said firmly. "That'll fetch him." C seems to have sunk rapidly. On the evening of the next day, it was clear that the end was near. I think that even A was affected at the last as he stood with bowed head, aimlessly offering to bet with the doctor on C's labored breathing. "A," whispered C, "I think I'm going fast." "How fast do you think you'll go, old man?" murmured A. "I don't know," said C, "but I'm going at any rate." The end came soon after that. As his soul sped heavenward, A watched its flight with melancholy admiration. B burst into a passionate flood of tears and sobbed, "Put away his little cistern and the rowing clothes he used to wear. I feel as if I could hardly ever dig again."—The funeral was plain and unostentatious. It differed in nothing from the ordinary except that, out of deference to sporting men and mathematicians, A engaged two hearses. Both vehicles started at the same time, B driving the one which bore the sable parallelopiped containing the last remains of his ill-fated friend. A on the box of the empty hearse generously consented to a handicap of a hundred yards, but arrived first at the cemetery by driving four times as fast as B. (Find the distance to the cemetery.) As the sarcophagus was lowered, the grave was surrounded by the broken figures of the first book of Euclid.

Record your finishing time in the time record for Article 3. Then take the reading test.

Read each test item and choose the best answer. Print your answers on page 4 of the progress folder.

Reading Test 3

Getting main ideas

1. The author's purpose in writing this article was to

A. point out the difference in people
B. amuse and interest you
C. explain arithmetic problems
D. tell about his friendship with A, B, and C
E. interest you in mathematics

2. Stephen Leacock was a famous Canadian

A. actor
B. scientist
C. fisherman
D. humorist
E. lumberjack

3. In asking you to think of A, B, and C as real people, the author expects you to

A. use your imagination
B. solve the problems
C. believe the impossible
D. lose your interest
E. make up your own problems

Understanding important details

4. C loses every bet because he is

A. a late starter
B. helped by B
C. helping A
D. trying too hard
E. weak and frail

5. Besides A, B, and C, the author mentions X, Y, and Z. But he says these are

A. friends of A, B, and C
B. different characters
C. really the same people
D. cousins to A, B, and C
E. different problems

6. To finish the story, D is introduced by the author as an old friend and

A. the only survivor
B. occasional helper
C. village gossip
D. funeral director
E. hunting companion

Understanding descriptive expressions

7. ". . . the sable parallelopiped containing the last remains of his ill-fated friend" means

A. the problem
B. a regatta
C. the cistern
D. the coffin
E. the hearse

8. The phrase "or after this wise . . ." means

A. either or else
B. after this happened
C. or in this manner
D. or the very end
E. later perhaps

9. "B and C had come in dead fagged" means they had come in

A. raring to go
B. in a dead heat
C. opposite directions
D. completely exhausted
E. from the funeral

10. ". . . and C is only an indifferent walker" means that C

A. doesn't know how to walk
B. isn't very good at walking
C. hates to walk
D. falls down quite often
E. walks in a strange way

Remembering key details

11. The author first saw A, B, and C

A. after a regatta
B. after the ball
C. in his backyard
D. mowing the lawn
E. running a race

12. The author states that A might be killed by

A. his friends B and C
B. working too hard
C. a parallelopiped
D. a minus fraction
E. a repeating decimal

13. A name mentioned by the author is

A. Hamlin Smith
B. Hamlin Jones
C. D. S. Carter
D. Collin Smith
E. Farmer Jones

14. At one point, B offers his exhausted friend C

A. two aspirins
B. a hot lemonade
C. a leaky cistern
D. a cup of coffee
E. some hot tea

41

15. D says that he has known A, B, and C since they were little fellows

    A. in knee-pants
    B. in the same school
    C. in his hometown
    D. in brackets
    E. about so high

Getting word meanings

16. "They *wrangle* over the division of marbles" means that they

    A. wrestle
    B. argue
    C. dally
    D. think
    E. debate

17. "His life is *arduous*" means that his life is

    A. dull
    B. active
    C. difficult
    D. boring
    E. exciting

18. "Poor C had a *plaintive* face" means he looked

    A. pretty
    B. envious
    C. complaining
    D. sad
    E. plain

19. "He must *strive*" means that he must

    A. make great effort
    B. walk very fast
    C. never argue
    D. find his way
    E. make a long jump

20. They entered into partnership, "having a certain capital." The word *capital* means

    A. element
    B. business
    C. money
    D. need
    E. idea

Follow the directions (Steps 8–13) on page 1 of the progress folder.

How you can remember what you read

Has this ever happened to you? You have been given a homework assignment in social studies. You go over the assigned pages carefully in the evening. Everything seems perfectly clear and understandable. But the next day in class, you cannot remember enough of what you have read to answer questions about it.

This happens to everyone, even to the best students. It happens to adults when they try to tell someone the details of a news story they have read.

There is nothing much more discouraging than to forget something you have just read carefully. This lesson will give you some ideas and some methods that will help you retain what you read.

How do you remember best?

To get a picture of the way your memory may act, let's imagine that you are riding with your family on a country highway. It has been a long drive, and you are sleepy. You close your eyes and fall into a comfortable doze. Suddenly you hear the screech of brakes. You are awakened violently by being thrown forward out of your seat.

Automatically, you open your eyes and stretch out your arms to protect yourself. What happens next?

Almost at once, you think: *What happened? Why? How?* Your first reaction, in other words, is to try to make sense out of the situation.

You do this all the time. A change of any kind in how you feel, what you see, or what you hear demands an explanation. And here is the important point: *No matter how baffling the situation may be, you do explain it to yourself.* You may change your explanation many times. But you do

figure out the situation at once. Everyone does this over and over again.

Now let us suppose that it is one year later. You are trying to tell about the incident in your car. You do not remember all the details. But those you do remember make a perfectly sensible story. At home that evening you say, "Remember the time I was sleeping in the car? Dad was driving and—"

Your father interrupts. "Why, I wasn't driving. Your mother was driving." And your mother agrees. Now you are baffled. Here was an important event, but somehow you got the details mixed up. The important thing is this: *Even though your details were wrong, you had arranged them into a logical and sensible story.* We make sense, or try to, out of the details we can recall.

But you can remember the details better if you try. In fact, you may be pretty accurate in telling about things that happened in the past. If you are, you have probably organized the details and checked them several times.

How can you improve your memory in reading?

Now let's apply to reading what we have been saying about memory. If you make sense out of what you read, you have a better chance of remembering it fully and accurately. You give your memory a job that it can handle more easily.

Let's look again at the phrase "make sense out of what you read." What does it mean "to make sense"? Whole books have been written on this subject. But here it is enough to mention only one or two points.

You make sense out of what happens before your eyes by deciding:

1. What are the causes and reasons for what happened?
2. In what time order did events occur?
3. Where are things located? What is their position?

You make sense out of your reading in the same way. You ask *why* and *how*. You make sure what happend first, second, last. And if the position of people and objects is important, you ask, *Where are they?*

In short, you *organize* what you read. You do this to understand it. You do this to remember it.

Experiments have shown that it is easier to remember something you understand. This can be demonstrated by an interesting experiment.

Memory experiment

At the beginning of a class period, your teacher will write six of the eight nonsense syllables on the chalkboard. They will be written in a different order than they appear here.

lem	mep	zapl	moj
abo	tek	pah	nov

You will have exactly one minute to memorize the syllables. Then they will be erased. You must remember them in the order in which they were written. Ten minutes before the end of the period, your teacher will give you a signal and you will have one minute to write the syllables. The teacher will then appoint someone to collect the papers, correct them, and tell the class how many students got all the syllables in the right order.

On the next class day, your teacher will write a short sentence on the chalkboard at the beginning of class. It will be the first sentence from one of the lessons in this book. Again you will have a minute to memorize the sentence before it is erased. Before the class ends, you will be given one minute to write down the sentence. Again the teacher will appoint someone to collect the papers, correct them, and tell the class how many students wrote the sentence correctly.

Compare the results of the two tests. Was it easier to remember sense or nonsense syllables?

Now let's get back to the main line of our thought about memory problems in reading. It is easier to remember what you read if it makes sense to you. You make sense of what you read by seeing and relating causes and reasons, time order, and space order.

There are two main types of memory used in reading and studying

When you are trying to remember something word for word, you use *rote memory*. This is the way you learn a poem you are to recite or a part in a play your class is to give. It is the way you learn some of the facts you must know in science or social studies. You want to learn the words so well that you can recall them when you need to, in exactly the right order.

When you are reading something to get its basic meanings, you use *meaningful memory*. In reading a chapter of a text or reference book, you try to understand its meanings and fix them so well in your mind that you can recall them at will. In this kind of memory you do not use the exact words of the writer. You are interested only in the ideas he is trying to express. You may use some of his words, but you use your own words too.

Both *rote memory* and *meaningful memory* can be improved.

Suggestions on reading to remember

Reading to remember is much different from reading for pleasure or for other purposes. It is slower. It takes more time because you must go back over the things you want to be able to recall. In reading to remember, you make a conscious effort. You fix your attention on particular words and sentences. Here are a few suggestions to help you use your effort and attention efficiently:

1. *Read in the way that best suits your purpose.* If you want to learn to recite "The Charge of the Light Brigade," you should

read the poem through carefully and then memorize it line by line. If you are reading a magazine article to prepare a report on rockets, look for the main ideas and the important details. Then restate them in your own words.

2. *Try to develop an interest in what you are reading.* If you are interested in what you read, you are more likely to remember it. If you are not interested in it, you will not give the material the attention required for remembering.

You must remember that your interests are not fixed and unchanging. When you were a baby, your main interests were eating and sleeping. Now you have many interests, and these you have learned. You will learn many others as you go through life.

You can develop an interest in what you read, particularly in your school studies. There is one fact that will help you. The more you learn about something, the more interested you will become in it. You can start a new interest just by making up your mind to do so.

Once you have a new interest started, you will seek firsthand experience. You will observe closely everything that bears on the subject. You can get books and magazines from the library that will give you far more information than your textbooks contain.

If you are studying science, you can read the magazines *Popular Mechanics* and *Popular Science*. Or you can ask your librarian for books for young people about animals, rockets, spaceships, or whatever topic you may be studying in class.

If you are studying geography, you will read about the continent of Asia sooner or later. In the library you will find a number of fascinating books and magazine articles about exploration and adventure in Asia. Roy Chapman Andrews, Lowell Thomas, Richard Halliburton, and others have written exciting books about their experiences.

But is this geography? Yes, indeed it is. Anything that bears on how and why people live where they do, anything that describes how the land looks and what it contains, is geography. The more you read of travel and exploration, the more you will understand your geography course and the more interested you will become in the whole field of geography.

3. *Pay close attention to what you are reading.* You will remember what you read only if you concentrate on it. Try to avoid disturbances and interruptions. When you are working on a study assignment, try to get all the way through it before breaking off.

4. *Recite to yourself.* If you are going to memorize a poem, begin by reading it all the way through. Try to feel the rhythm, or meter, of a poem. This helps to set the word pattern for each verse in your mind. As you read, try to get the writer's meaning. Remember that it is easier to memorize something that makes sense.

Read the poem through again, so that you begin to see the writer's whole idea or story. Then read the first verse aloud. Look away from the page and say the verse aloud; then look at the page to see whether your recital was accurate. Think of the meaning of the verse; then recite it again.

Go on to the second verse and memorize it. Then say the two verses together and notice how they are related. Learn each verse of a stanza separately, but say each new verse with the verses that you have already learned. Finally, practice the whole poem from beginning to end several times.

If you are reading a textbook chapter to understand and remember the main ideas, read the whole chapter through from beginning to end. Try to get the important meanings that the chapter presents. Then try to state what the chapter means to you—in your own words. Ask yourself questions about different parts of the chapter and answer these questions. If you are uncertain about what the chapter means, ask your teacher to help you.

Repetition will help. Recite the main ideas of your textbook chapter to your parents and friends. Ask them to hear you recite the poem you are memorizing.

5. *Write it down.* If you write down something that you want to remember, you bring more of your senses to bear upon it. It will be fixed more firmly in your memory. In addition, by writing down important ideas gathered from your reading, you give yourself a handy way of referring to

them later. Making notes and outlines of your reading will help you to review.

If you make notes, do not try to write down everything—all the details as well as the main ideas. Notes that are too long will be too hard to remember. It is desirable to read an assignment all the way through first, noting only important facts. You will probably want to reread the passage and take notes again during the second reading. By the time you have read the whole assignment, you begin to see which details and ideas are most important. These are things to put in your notes. Rereading will help you find important details you may have overlooked.

6. *Review helps.* Go back now and look over the first pages of this lesson. Bear in mind that when you try to recall something, you are seldom able to remember all the details. You may rebuild past events into a sensible explanation or story, but the recall may not be wholly accurate. You are likely to give incorrect explanations if you do not check up on your memory from time to time.

The best way to make sure your memory is accurate is to review what you want to remember. When you have finished a topic in your classes, review your notes and the text chapter. For good measure, review quickly the topics covered in earlier weeks.

A few minutes spent in review from time to time during a course will keep it all fresh in your mind. You will see new connections between one topic and another. Most important, your review for final tests and examinations will be much easier.

In this kind of review you can skim chapters of the book and also your own notes. Read only the main headings or topic sentences. If you come across something you do not understand, take time to read the whole passage again carefully. If you still do not understand it, ask your teacher for help. By following this procedure, you will reach the end of a semester with confidence. There will be a minimum of items that you cannot handle well in an examination.

In all of your reviewing, reread and study the main ideas in your materials. Be sure you understand them. Give special attention to the points you do not know and to the difficult passages. Use your study time for things you do not know rather than things you know. If you have a great many details to remember—dates and names, for example—make lists of them and memorize them by rote.

Memory experiment

Exercise 10

The exercise below calls for meaningful memory. The ideas in this article are of importance to everyone. If you remember them, they may save your life, or someone else's life, someday.

First Aid[1]

"Accidents will happen," it is said. They shouldn't—but they do.

There may be many times in your life when you will come face to face with an accident. Out alone or with the gang, you may come upon a serious automobile smashup. Some summer day you may have to save a person from drowning. In camp, a green tenderfoot may cut himself with an ax or get stung by a hornet. On a hike you or your pal may develop a blister or sprain an ankle. And at home some member of the family may have a fall, or a child down the street may swallow some poison.

In each case you might be the only person who could give the necessary first aid.

What is first aid?

First aid is very definitely given *at first* in case of injury or sickness. That word *first* suggests that there is more to follow: the aid given by a person who has many years of training for the job—the doctor. Never play at "doctoring." If a case is at all serious, get a doctor.

To do a good first-aid job, you must realize that there is more to first aid than stopping bleeding or bandaging a wound. The way you act in an emergency has a

---

1 "First Aid," reprinted from the *Boy Scout Handbook* by permission of the Boy Scouts of America.

great bearing on the patient's recovery. The *confidence* you show because you know what to do, the *common sense* you display in doing first things first, your *calmness* and *cheerfulness*—all these will make your patient feel that everything is being done that can be done and will help put his mind at ease.

Most of the accidents you will come upon will be minor ones where you can take your time to plan and to act. But someday you may be up against one of the "hurry cases" where life is at stake, where you have to know what you are doing and move with the utmost speed.

These are the "hurry cases":

1. Blood is spurting or gushing from a deep wound—it must be stopped immediately.
2. Breathing has ceased—it must be started again by artificial respiration.
3. Poison has been swallowed—it must be made harmless.

JUMP TO THE JOB! A second saved may mean a life saved.

Severe bleeding

A car crash, a railroad accident, carelessness with an ax or a power tool! You rush to the scene, and there is a victim with blood spurting from a wicked-looking gash!

Grab at the wound with a bare hand and PRESS—HARD! Stop that blood! Then use your free hand to reach for your neckerchief or handkerchief or to tear a piece off your shirt—or, if someone is near, call for a cloth folded into a pad or for a pad of sterile gauze. Let go of the wound for the split second it takes you to slap the pad on it; then press again. Finally, tie the pad firmly in place with some kind of bandage. If the pad gets blood-soaked, don't remove it. Just put another pad on top of the first, and another bandage. Then call a doctor or a hospital!

Artificial respiration

A drowning person is pulled out of the water . . .

A mechanic is dragged from under a car that had its motor running . . .

A child is pulled away from an electric wire . . .

In each of these cases, breathing may have stopped. Yet the victim's life can be saved if someone gets to work right away giving artificial respiration. That someone could be *you*.

The most effective method of artificial respiration is mouth-to-mouth breathing. With this method, you breathe air into the victim's lungs through your own mouth.

Rescuers who cannot use the mouth-to-mouth method can use the back-pressure–arm-lift method. Scouts should know both. But whichever method you use, *do not quit!* Let the doctor decide when to stop.

When the victim's breathing starts, time your efforts to match his efforts to breathe for himself. Keep him lying down and make him warm with blankets or other coverings. Get him under a doctor's care during the recovery period.

Poisoning by mouth

One-third of all accidental deaths among children are caused by poison. It is unbelievable what things children will swallow: kerosene, turpentine, insecticides, rat poisons, ammonia, lye, furniture polish, nail-polish remover, pills and tablets from the medicine cabinet, weed killer from the garden supplies, battery fluid from the garage.

Your first thought if you find yourself up against a case involving poison is this: Dilute it! DILUTE IT! Water! WATER! Have a child drink half a glass of water immediately, an adult a full glass. Then more water. Or milk if you have it. Look around quickly to see what poison was swallowed and get a call in for a doctor, giving the name of the poison. If the instructions on the poison container tell what antidote to use, send someone for it immediately and use it quickly.

Shock

Every serious accident is accompanied by shock—a sudden lowering of the vitality caused by pain and fear and loss of blood. The more serious the injury, the greater the shock.

A shock victim is very weak. His face gets pale, his skin cold and clammy, his breathing shallow. He shivers from chills; he may even vomit. He seems dazed, does not know what is happening around him. In serious cases he may lose consciousness entirely. Shock may come immediately with the accident or soon after, or may even be delayed for several hours.

DON'T WAIT FOR SYMPTOMS TO SHOW—head them off! Take for granted in any injury that the patient will suffer from shock, and take care of it.

Keep the patient lying down. If he has a head injury, keep him level; otherwise raise his feet on a packsack, a log, or whatever else you may have.

In cool weather, put enough blankets, coats, or layers of newspapers over the patient to protect him. If the weather is hot, do not cover him. The idea is not to make him warm, but to prevent him from getting cold.

If your patient is conscious, let him sip a little water. If he is unconscious, do not attempt to force liquid between his lips—it may choke him.

Now close your book. Write the heading "First Aid" on your paper. List six main ideas in the article and then compare your list with the list given in the answer key at the back of the book.

Memory experiment

Exercise 11

Most Americans know parts of the first stanza of our national anthem, and a great many people know the whole stanza. But Americans seldom sing all four stanzas. In fact, many people do not know there are four stanzas. In the following exercise you will use both meaningful memory and rote memory. You will learn all four stanzas of "The Star-Spangled Banner." Before you start to memorize, you will read a brief history of the song. The story is interesting. With this background in mind, it may be easier for you to memorize the song. You will test youself on the meaning of the difficult words it contains. Then you will find out how well you understand each stanza of the poem.

History of the Song

The words of "The Star-Spangled Banner," our national anthem, were composed by a man being held by the British. In 1814, after burning Washington, D.C., the British sailed down Chesapeake Bay toward Baltimore. Only Fort McHenry stood in their way. For an entire day and night the fleet stood offshore and fired its shells at the fort. The early dawn lighted a scene of smoke, fire, and destruction. Through the swirling mist of smoke, the battered remains of the fort could hardly be seen. The British waited anxiously to see the results of their bombardment.

Among the anxious onlookers was Francis Scott Key, a young Washington attorney. He and another man had been sent by the U.S. government to effect the release of a prisoner being held on the ship. The British agreed to free the man, but would not let the Americans leave until after the attack on Fort McHenry. Key and his companions watched the bombardment from the beginning to the end. Through the long night they stood watch at the rail, wondering if the fort could hold out. At last, in the hazy dawn, they could see Fort McHenry. And there, high above the walls, they could see the tattered ensign still waving defiantly in the breeze.

The sight so inspired Key that he was able to write the greatest part of his poem before he arrived ashore. He completed it that evening in Baltimore and had it printed the following day. It was set to an old English song and immediately became popular. After many years as an unofficial anthem, "The Star-Spangled Banner" became our national anthem in 1931 under a law passed by Congress.

The Star-Spangled Banner

by Francis Scott Key

Oh, say can you see by the dawn's early
    light
    What so proudly we hailed at the
      twilight's last gleaming?

Whose broad stripes and bright stars,
    through the perilous fight,
    O'er the ramparts we watched were
      so gallantly streaming?

And the rocket's red glare, the bombs
    bursting in air,
      Gave proof through the night that
      our flag was still there.
Oh, say does that star-spangled banner
    yet wave
      O'er the land of the free and the
      home of the brave?

II

On the shore, dimly seen through the
    mists of the deep,
      Where the foe's haughty host in
      dread silence reposes,
What is that which the breeze, o'er the
    towering steep,
      As it fitfully blows, now conceals,
      now discloses?
Now it catches the gleam of the morning's
    first beam,
      In full glory reflected now shines
      on the stream:
'Tis the star-spangled banner! O long
    may it wave
      O'er the land of the free and the
      home of the brave!

III

And where is that band who so
    vauntingly swore
      That the havoc of war and the
      battle's confusion,
A home and a country should leave us
    no more?
      Their blood has washed out their
      foul footsteps' pollution.
No refuge could save the hireling and
    slave
      From the terror of flight, or the
      gloom of the grave;
And the star-spangled banner in
    triumph doth wave
      O'er the land of the free and the
      home of the brave!

IV

Oh! thus be it ever, when freemen shall
    stand
      Between their loved homes and the
      war's desolation!
Blest with victory and peace, may the
    heav'n rescued land
      Praise the Power that hath made and
      preserved us a nation.

Then conquer we must, for our cause it
    is just,
      And this be our motto: "In God is
      our trust."
And the star-spangled banner in
    triumph shall wave
      O'er the land of the free and the
      home of the brave!

A comprehension test

Now let's see whether you understand the stanzas you have just read. Write on your paper the numerals 1 to 4 for the four stanzas. After each numeral, write the letter of the paragraph below that explains the meaning of the stanza.

A. Where are the British soldiers that were determined to defeat us? They have retreated or died.

B. During the night we could see the flag flying in the flashes of light from the bombs and rockets. Now, in the dawn, will the flag still be there?

C. People who love freedom are ready to fight for it. God has helped us to set up and to keep our nation; we believe in Him. Because we are fighting for the right, we shall win the war and shall then live in peace.

D. We saw the American flag as it faintly appeared and then disappeared—again and again. Finally, as the sun begins to shine, we see that the flag is still there. It is waving clearly and brightly in the breeze.

A vocabulary test

Write the numerals 1 to 20 on your paper. Look at the list of words below. The words at the left are from "The Star-Spangled Banner." If the word or phrase on the right has the same meaning as the word or phrase on the left, write the letter **S.** If it has a different meaning, write the letter **D.**

1. slave—freeman
2. ramparts—earthworks
3. mists of the deep—ocean fogs
4. havoc—destruction
5. conceals—discloses
6. banner—flag

7. beam—gleam
8. spangled—glittering
9. foul—polluted
10. haughty host—modest army
11. bravely—gallantly
12. perilous—safe
13. twilight—bright light
14. terror—flight
15. triumph—victory
16. hailed—greeted
17. reposes—awakes
18. vauntingly—boastfully
19. fitfully—steadily
20. gloom—trust

Correct answers to Exercise 11 are shown in the answer key.

Memorize all four stanzas of the song

Because you have studied the meanings of the more difficult words and thought about the meanings of the verses, it will be easier for you to memorize this song. Try to learn the whole song. First read aloud all four stanzas. Then read the first verse. Try to say it aloud without looking at the page. Then look back to check your mistakes. When you have mastered the first verse, learn the second. Now combine the first two verses. When you have mastered all the verses of the first stanza, go on to the second. Continue in this way until you have learned the whole poem.

Practice Reading 4

In a book, magazine, or newspaper that you like, practice reading for speed and comprehension. Make a record of this reading in Chart 3 on page 8 of your progress folder.

As you read the next selection, try to remember the most important points. Write down these points on your paper.

Record your starting time in the time record on page 4 of the progress folder. Then read the selection. Read as fast as you can, but make sure you understand what you are reading.

4

article

Jungle zoo without a cage[2]

by John Barkham

As the car swung around the curve in the road, the driver jammed on his brakes. The lion sitting in the middle of the road opened a lazy eye and swished his tail. But he didn't move—nor could the car.

Soon a lioness, followed by two cubs, padded silently from the bush. The lioness made for the car. She rose on her hind legs to stare into it. Three of the four passengers were frozen with excitement. The fourth passenger was taking the finest movies he had ever made.

This was not Hollywood. But this is an example of what may happen any day in South Africa's Kruger National Park. This park is the greatest game refuge on earth. It is the home of hundreds of thousands of animals. They are the remaining members of the large herds that once covered all of South Africa. They live as nature meant them to—never hunted by men with guns.

In Kruger Park the blood-red law of the jungle rules. The animals can, and do, prey on each other. But no man may hunt them.

The park is about the size of the state of Massachusetts. It is in a wooded bush-land two hundred miles long and forty miles wide. It has some twelve hundred miles of dirt roads. Within the park area there are thirteen fenced-in camps where visitors can safely stay overnight. Half an hour after sundown the gates of each camp are locked for the night, and no one may leave or enter the camps until dawn.

2 Reprinted from *Coronet*, June 1951. Copyright 1951 by Esquire, Inc.

During the night the silence is broken by a roar from a lion that has made its kill. Other lions answer. The barks and yelps of hyenas and jackals follow. Baboons chime in. Birds fly screeching into the night.

In the morning, as the tourist drives his car through the park, he sees lions by the roadside calmly eating their kill. He sees large herds of antelope—perhaps twenty thousand in an hour—grazing quietly. He passes a group of eighteen-foot giraffes nibbling at treetops. And everywhere great herds of gnus and zebras are cropping the grass.

In one day the visitor can see at least fifty kinds of game, birds, and reptiles. He can see them as no explorer ever did, for the animals do not seem to notice the people around them. It is a strange fact that animals do not connect the scent of automobiles with that of human beings. A car is not good to eat and it is not dangerous, so animals ignore it—and the people inside.

Were the car's driver to step out and pet the kittenlike cubs playing in the road, however, it would probably be the last thing he ever did. At once the mother lion would catch his scent and go into action.

Getting a flat tire inside the park is also dangerous. When it happens, the best thing to do is wait for a ranger to tow the car to the nearest camp. Some years ago a man tried to fix a flat tire. He learned that the park lions weren't as tame as they seemed to be.

He was lying on a roll of bedding, jacking up the car. An approaching ranger called quietly: "There's a lion looking at you—get into your car!" Man and lion leaped at the same moment. But it was the bedding roll the lion wanted. He dragged it off and had a wonderful time tearing it to ribbons.

Apart from man, the lion fears only the lowly porcupine. When a lion gets quills into his paws, it generally means great pain and death, since hunting becomes impossible. But guns and quills aside, Leo here is king. Every visitor brings back his own lion story, confirmed, like as not, by his camera.

One will tell you of having waited half an hour in his car while a lion blocked the road, listening drowsily to the purr of the motor. Another will tell of a group of lions lying on their backs with their paws drooping in the air just like tired cats.

This writer has watched lion cubs learning to kill. Papa set off a herd of antelope in their direction. As the animals thundered by, the cubs leaped and missed. Then Mama showed them how.

But danger is always present. For example, there is the story of ranger Harry Wolhuter. Late one afternoon he was patrolling the park on horseback. A lion brought down his horse. He then knocked out the ranger with a blow on the head. When the ranger came to, the lion had him by the shoulder and was dragging him into the bush for dinner. Wolhuter, in great pain, remembered he had a knife in his belt.

What happened next is told in the ranger's own words. "I decided to stick my knife into his heart. I began to feel carefully for his shoulder. This was difficult because my head was pressed against the lion's mane. I had to reach with my left hand, holding the knife across his chest, to reach his left shoulder.

"However, I managed it and, knowing where his heart was, I quickly struck him twice. The lion roared and I struck again, this time into his throat. Blood spurted out all over me. The lion released his hold and slunk off into the darkness."

Weak from pain and loss of blood, Wolhuter dragged himself up a nearby tree. He strapped himself to a branch with his belt and waited there until he was rescued by the morning patrol. The mounted lion skin now hangs over his fireplace. And rangers no longer patrol the park on horseback.

Lions are not the only park animals that are dangerous to man. The rhinoceros and the buffalo generally keep to the thick bush. However, they have been known to charge a car and damage it. Elephants enjoy turning over cars. Visitors are warned to stay at least fifty yards away from these animals.

One large elephant became angry at a car that followed him. He turned and sat on its hood. After flattening the wheels and the motor, he walked off without a glance at the car's frightened passengers.

At a dam next to the park, a troop of elephants were giving themselves showers with their trunks. Then an old bull started to squirt the sloping wall of the dam. Soon he had a mud slide. He climbed up to the top of the slide; then, sitting on his hams, he slid down. He hit the water with a great splash. He was so pleased with his game that he started all over again.

Before long the other elephants copied his game. Each of them made a slide and slid into the water. They played this game for more than an hour. Then they marched off, waving their trunks in high good humor.

The park has its snakes, but they keep to the deep bush. The visitors see very few of them. One morning ranger Wolhuter was taking his dogs for a walk near his camp. He saw them run into a clump of bushes, barking loudly.

"I saw that they had found a huge python. I shot the snake. I looked around to see if all my dogs were there. A fox terrier was missing. Then I saw a large bulge in the snake. Thinking this might account for the dog's absence, I slit the snake open.

"Sure enough, there was my dog. At first I thought he was dead. But in a few moments he shook himself and stood up, as good as new."

Kruger Park is full of such wonders. But the biggest wonder to visitors is the fact that there is no fence or boundary of any kind around the park. None of the animals are restricted in any way.

"Why," visitors always ask, "do the animals stay here? Why don't they just walk out of the park?"

The answer is simple. Game is hunted in all areas next to the park. Any beast that strays outside the park is soon shot.

"What keeps them inside," the rangers explain, "is the unseen ring of rifles all around them."

Record your finishing time in the time record for Article 4. Then take the reading test.

Read each test item and choose the answer you believe is correct. Print your answers in the answer record on page 4 of the progress folder.

Reading Test 4

Getting main ideas

1. The animals do not stray out of the park because
   - A. the fence keeps them in
   - B. the rangers are on patrol
   - C. they find it easy to get food
   - D. they are safe where no hunting is allowed
   - E. they are all tame

---

2. It is safe for visitors to stay in the park at night because
   - A. the animals are not dangerous
   - B. the visitors stay in their cars
   - C. the animals are locked up
   - D. there are fenced-in camps for visitors
   - E. the rangers protect the visitors

---

3. The lions are not afraid of the visitors' cars because
   - A. they are used to them
   - B. the cars don't get close to them
   - C. the cars don't carry a human scent
   - D. the cars make no noise
   - E. never before have they seen cars

---

4. The rangers no longer use horses because
   - A. a man can walk deep into the woods
   - B. the woods are too thick
   - C. they now have roads in the park
   - D. cars are faster
   - E. the lions attack horses

Remembering key facts

5. The park is about the size of
   - A. Massachusetts
   - B. Texas
   - C. ten city blocks
   - D. Mexico
   - E. Canada

---

6. Apart from man, the lion fears only

A. the rhinoceros
B. the giraffe
C. the elephant
D. the porcupine
E. the snake

7. The elephants in the park are dangerous because

A. they are bad-tempered
B. they often fight
C. they enjoy turning over cars
D. they are so large
E. they keep to the thick bush

Drawing conclusions

8. By the *unseen ring of rifles*, the ranger meant the rifles of the

A. visitors
B. rangers
C. hunters in the park
D. hunters outside the park
E. soldiers

9. The *law of the jungle* means that

A. all animals rule
B. the animals live as in the jungle
C. the largest animals rule
D. there is no jungle law
E. the animals learn laws

Choosing the best reason

10. When a lion gets quills in its paws, it almost always dies because

A. hunting becomes impossible
B. the wounds become poisoned
C. it bleeds so much
D. the other animals attack it
E. the quills are poisonous

11. Ranger Wolhuter strapped himself up in the tree in order to

A. signal other rangers
B. watch the lions
C. get some sleep
D. see better
E. be safe from the lions

12. The visitors see few snakes because snakes

A. keep to the deep bush
B. are hard to spot
C. stay away from roads
D. are afraid of people
E. keep low in the grass

Understanding descriptive expressions

13. When the lion *opened a lazy eye*, he

A. opened and closed his eye
B. winked quickly
C. stared
D. looked tired
E. slowly opened his eye

14. When the passengers were *frozen with excitement*, they

A. were very cold
B. stayed in the car
C. stayed very still
D. moved on quickly
E. jumped with surprise

15. When baboons *chime in*, they

A. make a ringing sound
B. join in the noisemaking
C. run into the woods
D. come close to the visitors
E. live in the park

Knowing word meanings

16. When the lion *slunk* off into the darkness, he

A. crept
B. jumped
C. ran
D. leaped
E. dived

17. The park is a game *refuge*. It is a

A. trap
B. forest
C. hunting ground
D. cemetery
E. shelter

18. Everywhere zebras are *cropping* the grass. They are

A. killing it
B. eating it
C. hunting it
D. carrying it
E. walking on it

Recognizing words that stand for sounds

19. When the lion *swished* his tail, the visitor heard a

A. thumping sound
B. booming sound
C. brushing sound
D. snapping sound
E. cracking sound

20. The visitors heard birds *screeching* into the night. They heard

A. whistling
B. screaming
C. drumming
D. chirping
E. whining

Follow the directions (Steps 8–13) on page 1 of the progress folder.

How you can get main ideas

Have you ever been lost in a strange city? If you have, you can recall how every street corner seemed to look the same. One big building looked just like another. You were lost because you had no guidelines or signs to lead you back to your starting point.

You can get just as lost in your reading as you can in a big city. Readers who do not know how to find the writer's guidelines will come to the end of a piece of reading with no idea of where they have been. One word looks just as important as another. One sentence seems to have the same importance as another.

A careful writer always gives his reader guidelines. He tells the reader where he is going, and at each step of the way he shows how far he has gone. By following these guidelines, the reader can make his way easily from beginning to end.

Sometimes the writer says, "Here are several ideas, but the most important is this one." Sometimes he gives a great many details and then says, "Here is what these details show." Sometimes he says, "Here is what I believe, and here are my reasons." These are reading clues that the efficient reader will note and follow carefully.

A well-written paragraph and a well-written book both have basic plans. The reader's job is to search out and discover these plans. If he does, he will not get lost along the way.

But some writers do not say outright what their objective is. Some paragraphs do not have a topic sentence to summarize their meaning. Some books present a great many ideas and leave it to the reader to organize them.

In either case, whether the writer has furnished signposts and guidelines or not, the reader has to be careful or he will get lost. He always has to look for the main idea.

What is a main idea?

If we were talking about the main street of a town, we would mean the most important street. We would not be saying that the town has no other streets. Nor would we be saying that it has no other important streets. We would be saying simply that we were talking about the one most important street where the most people walk, work, drive their cars, and do their shopping.

When we talk about the main idea of a paragraph, we mean the most important idea in the paragraph. But we mean more than that. The main idea of a paragraph is the one big idea around which the paragraph is built.

If a writer has stated this idea, the reader can see where he is going. In the two paragraphs below, the main idea is printed in italics. As you will see, this idea is at the beginning in the first paragraph and at the end in the second paragraph. Of course, the main idea *may* appear anywhere in the paragraph.

1. *There are many quaint superstitions about bees.* The natives of Suffolk, England, believe that if a marriage occurs in your family you must go and tell the bees about it or they will become fretful. The custom of telling the bees about your personal affairs is known as "telling it to the bees." In other quarters it is said to be unlucky to have a stray swarm of bees settle on or in your dwelling. I should think so.[1]

2. The first time you drive a car on a public highway, you will probably be nervous. You mistrust your own judgment and cling desperately to the wheel. You

---

[1] From *How to Get from January to December*, by Will Cuppy. Edited by Fred Feldkamp. Copyright 1951 by Fred Feldkamp. Reprinted by permission of Holt, Rinehart and Winston, Inc.

fumble for the controls and are afraid to take your eyes off the road. The other cars seem to be rushing by at breakneck speed. You needn't be upset, though. *You are merely experiencing something that every other driver has gone through.*

You can see that the italicized sentences *sum up* the paragraphs. The main sentence ties all the other sentences together. *It provides something in common* for these other sentences.

You can see the importance of finding the main idea—the unifying idea in a paragraph. But sometimes the writer does not supply this unifying idea. When this happens, the reader has to state it for himself. The unifying idea need not be a sentence that sums up a paragraph. It can be the point of the story, the reason for telling the story in the first place. The reader has to find out what the point of the story is. And this is what the writer is really talking about. Here is an example of such a story:

When Jascha Heifetz made his triumphant debut in New York many years ago, in the audience was Mischa Elman, the celebrated violinist, as well as the distinguished pianist Josef Hofmann. The hall was crowded and it was a fine spring evening. The concert progressed and the audience was spellbound by the genius of Heifetz. As the program continued, Elman became increasingly nervous and fidgety, running his finger frequently around the inside of his collar and mopping at his forehead with a handkerchief. In the pause between two selections he leaned over and whispered to Hofmann, "Awfully hot in here, isn't it?"

Hofmann smiled and whispered back, "Not for pianists."[2]

This rather amusing anecdote tells of the reactions of two musicians at a concert. What is the writer trying to say? Could you sum it up or give the point of the story? How would this do?

2 From the book *New Treasury of Stories for Every Speaking and Writing Occasion*, by Jacob M. Braude. © 1959 by Prentice-Hall, Inc.

The superb quality of Heifetz' performance made the violinist nervous and warm, while the pianist could sit back and enjoy the concert.

Exercise 12

Write the numerals 1 to 4 on your paper. For each of the following paragraphs, copy the sentence that most nearly expresses the main idea.

1. All day long the storm had battered the northern Michigan mainland. At Charlevoix the waves were exploding like bombs against the piers of the Lake Michigan channel entrance, hurling spray almost to the top of the lighthouse tower and clear across the foghorn installation. Huge combers went spilling over the breakwater. Out on the lake the waves had lost their whitecaps; they were whipped into flying mist. One of the red gale flags hoisted above the Coast Guard station along the breakwater had been ripped into tatters by the wind. An occasional gust of snow rattled the windows of the houses as if they had been hit by buckshot.[3]

2. At 5:30 P.M. the serpentine length of the bulk carrier seemed to be riding the twenty-foot waves as ever. But at 5:31 P.M. First Mate Elmer Fleming and Captain Bryan, both on watch in the pilothouse, heard an unusual thud. They spun around and looked down the six-hundred-foot deck toward the stern. The stormy day was darkling into sunset but the deck lights were glowing and, at the end of this string of lights, the two officers saw the aft section of the boat sag. They realized the *Bradley* was in mortal danger.[4]

3. Not many years ago, men learned what coral really is. Now we know that the substance we call coral is composed of the skeletons of innumerable tiny marine animals. Flourishing in all the world's warm waters, these creatures have built thousands of reefs, atolls, and islands, including one of the greatest structures ever

3 From *Great Lakes Shipwrecks and Survivals*, by William Ratigan. Copyright 1960 by William Ratigan, by permission of Wm. B. Eerdmans Publishing Co.

4 *Ibid.*

built by living beings—the Great Barrier Reef of Australia.[5]

4. Good habits are as hard to break as bad habits. Although we usually think of them as being "bad," habits can also be "good." We shake our heads at some of the things we do, and vow to break the habit. But we rarely say to ourselves, "That was a good thing I did. I should develop that habit." These good habits can become a part of us, and we would find it difficult to change our ways. Sometimes a good habit will replace a bad one.

The sentences that express the main ideas in Exercise 12 are shown in the answer key.

Stories and articles have main ideas too

The kind of article you read in a magazine usually has one big idea—the idea that made the writer want to write it. A chapter in a textbook may have several big ideas. The ideas may have nothing in common except that they all pertain to the same topic—to conversation, to World War I, or to the weather, for example.

The chapters in your textbooks cover a great deal of ground very rapidly. Whole books have been written about topics covered in twenty pages in your texts. Since there is so much to say about each topic, it is almost impossible to write a textbook chapter about one big idea.

Most textbook chapters are divided into sections. Usually each of these sections has one main idea. Sometimes it is stated; sometimes you have to find it out for yourself. There is an easy way to do this. Suppose you are studying a section that has eight paragraphs. It will not be hard to find the main idea of each paragraph. Write them down in order. Look for the idea they have in common. Then see how that idea has grown and developed through the passage. Check to make sure that nothing in the passage is contrary to the main idea you have written down.

Finding the main idea of a passage

Exercise 13

Here is a section from an interesting booklet called *Discovering Your Real Interests.*[6] It is much like a section in a textbook. Read it to get the main idea of the whole passage. But as you read, look for the main idea of each paragraph.

Write on your paper the topic sentence of each of the six paragraphs. Then write, in one sentence, the main idea of the whole selection.

The topic sentences are shown in the answer key.

1. Opportunities in the world of work are unlimited. Pick up any newspaper or magazine and you will find articles that say—

Needed: more scientists

Urgent: more teachers

Help Wanted: secretaries, librarians, tool and die makers

Opportunities Unlimited: public service, engineering, law, medicine

The number of professional and technical jobs is expected to zoom upward, and the number of managerial, sales, service, and clerical jobs to climb, too, in the next ten years. (How old will you be by then?) Skilled jobs as well will increase sharply; and semiskilled jobs will hold their own. Only unskilled and farm jobs will be fewer in proportion to the total number of workers; but even in these fields there will continue to be some employment.

2. With all this opportunity, the question is: Which jobs or job fields interest you most? If this question makes you wonder where you will fit in best and have the most fun on the job, you are like most of the rest of your age group. But the world of work is in the future, and you have some decisions for tomorrow morning. Perhaps you are puzzled by such school choices as these: More foreign languages or more history? The school newspaper or the

---

5 From *The World We Live In*, by Lincoln Barnett and the editorial staff of *Life*. Courtesy, Life Magazine. © 1956, Time Inc.

6 From *Discovering Your Real Interests*, by Blanche B. Paulson. Copyright 1961 by Science Research Associates, Inc.

dramatics club? An advanced placement course or volunteer work in a hospital after school?

3. When the ancient Greeks had knotty problems to solve, they appealed to the oracle at Delphi, whose wisdom and knowledge were considered supreme. The oracle's most famous bit of advice was: Know thyself. Of course, this did not tell the puzzled Greek how to get out of his immediate difficulty, but it did tell him what he should do to find the answer to his problem.

4. Ever since those days at Delphi (and before them too, of course), people have been trying to find the answers to personal problems by understanding themselves. Although he may never have uttered the question aloud, each person who has thought about himself at all has asked, Who am I? The Delphian advice is good today, and it will go on being good advice.

5. In the year 2000 (how old will you be then?) it may be that spaceships will be mass-produced as airplanes and compact cars are today, but people will continue to retain their individuality, and each person will ask the same questions of himself: What interests me most? Who am I? When we have the answers to these questions, we will find that a good many other questions have been answered also. We will know what we want to do, how we can best contribute to life, and what will give us the deepest satisfaction. We will get along better with our families, friends, and employers, because we will be getting along better with ourselves.

6. Who you are is a composite of all your characteristics: your abilities and skills, your physical self, your successes and failures, your ambitions and fears, your ideas, and your interests.

How to get the main idea of a story

You may believe that a good short story does not have a main idea. After all, a story is an account of action. How can a series of actions or events have a central idea?

It is true that if a train hurtles off the tracks, killing passengers, there is no main idea. There is never a main idea in an event itself.

But when someone writes about events, he may put a main idea into his story. He will choose from the many details of the event just those that are related to his idea. In this way a writer pulls the story together so that it makes an impression on the reader.

Sometimes a writer states his idea. Sometimes he lets his reader discover it for himself. But you can be sure that any carefully written story has a main idea. It is the reader's job to think about the story to see how the author has organized the details and worked out his idea.

The subject of a story—its main idea —is never just the action of the story. It is the meaning that the writer has given to the action that counts.

Exercise 14

The following article tells about some recent events which have a dramatic meaning. See if you can discover the sentences that express this meaning. There are several difficult words in this selection that are printed in italics. You can probably get their meanings from context, but write down a definition for each word and check it with a dictionary to be sure that you are right.

Understanding Life's Chemical Code[7]

1. In 1942, scientists showed that atoms, of which all matter is made, can be destroyed. Moreover, they showed that when matter is destroyed, energy is created —huge amounts of energy. This knowledge was used to develop atomic and nuclear weapons which can be used to destroy all life on earth.

---

7 From "The Fine Structure of the Gene" by Seymour Benzer, "Messenger RNA" by J. Hurwitz and J. J. Furth, copyright 1962 by *Scientific American*; "Biologists Hopeful of Solving Secrets of Heredity This Year" by John A. Osmundsen, copyright 1962 by *The New York Times*. Reprinted by permission.

2. Twenty years later, scientists became hopeful of discovering how life is created, how living things grow and how they multiply. Extremely important breakthroughs were reported early in 1962. The secrets that were being discovered had until then been hidden inside the living cell. The reports showed how the nucleus of a cell controls the ways in which chemicals coming into the cell are put together to make the huge, long-chain molecules called *proteins*—the molecules which are the building blocks of life. Hidden from sight in the nucleus of every cell is a *system*, which controls the ways in which the cell does its work and which also describes the exact *structure* of the cell. It is this detailed and exact description which makes it possible for cells to divide and make copies of themselves.

3. Every cell contains complicated chemical factories which do their work according to strict sets of rules. What are these rules? How are they "written down"? And in what language are they "written"?

4. Teams of scientists in different parts of the world—in the Americas, in western Europe, and in Russia—have been discovering *clues* to the answers to these questions for more than twenty years. Because of the combined efforts of biologists, chemists, physicists, mathematicians, physicians, radiologists, and others, mankind is beginning to understand nature's chemical language.

5. The discoveries which are being made are extremely important. It now seems possible that mankind may gain the knowledge that will make him able to control cancer, to correct certain *defects* that are inherited, to improve the chemical structure of living things, and even to create forms of living matter. These are the scientific breakthroughs which will be in the news for the next twenty years. They may well force the spectacular reports of space probes and manned space flights from the front pages of our daily newspapers.

The main idea of this story is expressed in the sentence: "Because of the combined efforts of biologists, chemists, physicists, mathematicians, physicians, radiologists, and others, mankind is beginning to understand nature's chemical language."

A vocabulary test

Did you get the meanings of the italicized words in the story? Write the numerals 1 to 5 on your paper. Write the letter of the correct meaning of each of the following words.

1. *proteins*
   A. things that change their shape
   B. bricks
   C. huge molecules made by living cells

2. *system*
   A. a being
   B. a plan or set of rules
   C. a force

3. *structure*
   A. size
   B. arrangement of parts
   C. shape

4. *clues*
   A. hints, guides
   B. false leads
   C. problems

5. *defects*
   A. advantages
   B. flaws or imperfections
   C. characteristics

The correct answers to Exercise 14 are shown in the answer key.

Practice Reading 5

In a book, magazine, or newspaper that you like, practice reading for speed and comprehension. Make a record of this reading in Chart 3 on page 8 of your progress folder.

As you read the following selection, apply what you have learned in this lesson. Try to find the main idea of each paragraph and of the story as a whole.

Record your starting time in the time record on page 4 of your progress folder. Then read the selection. Read as fast as you can, but make sure you understand what you are reading.

5

article

The lonesome bear[8]

by Harrison Kinney

My brother George and I were selling candy in our backyard. George went off to find the gang and tell them to come and be our customers. I was sitting on the ground eating a chocolate bar. Suddenly I looked up and saw a brown bear walking through the apple orchard. He came up and sniffed at the candy.

"You'd better go away," I told the bear. "My brother George will get mad if you eat his candy."

The bear just sat down and stared at the candy. Neither of us moved, but I went on eating my chocolate bar. After a while George and his gang came up the driveway. When they saw the bear they stopped.

"You get away from that bear," George yelled to me. "He'll kill you with one swing of his paw."

"No he won't," I said, patting the bear on the head.

"Give him some candy to eat and maybe he'll go away," George shouted.

So I put an open box of marshmallows in front of the bear. He slid into a crouch and began chewing them.

One of the boys said to George, "The state pays a twenty-five-dollar bounty for bears. Why don't you keep him and get the money?"

Because this seemed like a fine idea, we decided to put the bear in the icehouse. As this wasn't used, no one knew we had a bear in it.

---

8 From "The Lonesome Bear," by Harrison Kinney, by permission of Constance Smith Associates.

The night the bear got out of the icehouse, my aunt was visiting us. She was given my bed. I slept on a couch in my parents' room. It was a hot night, so the doors were open.

Although I still don't know how the bear escaped, I do know that everyone was sleeping when he came into my parents' room. First the bear tried to crawl under my couch, but he didn't fit. He just banged the couch against the wall. Then he snorted loudly and lay down.

My father sat up in bed. "Are you making all that noise, Son?" he asked.

"No, sir," I said. "I think it's the bear."

"All right," said my father, lying down again.

After a few minutes my father sat up in bed again. "What did you say that noise was, Son?" he asked quietly.

"I think the bear is sleeping under my bed," I said.

My father sat in the darkness for a time, thinking this over. Finally he turned on the table lamp beside his bed. This awakened my mother.

"What is it?" my mother asked.

My father got out of bed and came over to the couch. He kneeled down and looked at the bear.

"He eats marshmallows," I said.

Father stood up. "We must all remain calm," he said. "I don't think anybody is in danger. There's a bear in our room."

My mother began weeping softly.

"He won't hurt you," I told her.

My father asked me where the bear came from and I told him. My mother went to sleep with my aunt. My father and I pulled the couch off the bear. The bear sat up and yawned.

"I never saw a bear like this that liked to be around people," said my father. "His coat isn't shaggy like a wild bear's. I think he's tame."

"Can we keep him?" I asked.

"This is a very friendly bear, Son. Maybe we can keep him until his owner shows up."

The next day my father and I went to the courthouse to get a license for the bear. They didn't have any licenses for pet bears.

Then one day the sheriff came. "Look, Stephen," he said to my father, "you've got to get rid of that bear. Do you know where he is?"

"In the icehouse," said my father, looking worried.

"He's sitting in my car," said the sheriff. "He won't get out."

My father and I followed the sheriff to his house next door. The bear's head and front paws were sticking out of the car window.

"Go get the marshmallows, Son," said my father.

"Yes, sir," I said.

When the bear saw the marshmallows, he climbed out of the sheriff's car and sniffed at the box.

"I have enough to worry about without a bear loose in town," said the sheriff. "You'll have to get rid of him. You've heard about the bank robberies north of here. We're expecting them to take a crack at the Farmers Trust any day now. If I have to chase bank robbers I don't want a bear in my back seat breathing down my neck."

"We'll take him back to the woods this Saturday and lose him," said my father a little sadly.

When Saturday came my father and I got ready to go fishing. When we opened the car door for the bear, he made happy woofing sounds in his throat.

"He likes to ride in cars, I guess," said my father.

"He'll never be able to ride in cars if we leave him in the woods," I said.

"He won't mind," said my father. "He'll forget."

The bear sat and watched us as we fished. Then he wandered into the woods.

"You mustn't feel badly about the bear, Son," said my father as we walked back to the car. He blew his nose on a large handkerchief.

It was dusk when we started for home. When we were on the highway, the lights of a car behind us threw the shadow of a bear on our windshield.

"Is the bear in the back seat, Son?" my father asked quietly.

I turned and looked in the back seat. The bear sat with his back to us, looking out the rear window.

"I think it's the bear," I said.

In June the circus came to town. My father wired the manager that he could have the bear if he called for it. A few days later the man came. "I knew it was Henry," he said when he saw the bear. "We lost him last summer up this way." He got the bear into his car and drove away.

A few weeks later, we found the bear sitting on the front porch.

"Look at the dust on his fur," said my father. "He must have walked twenty miles."

I put the bear in the icehouse. Later that morning I discovered the bear had again escaped. I couldn't find him, so I went downtown to tell my father that the bear was loose.

A block from the Farmers Trust building I saw the bear come out of an alley. He headed for a car that was standing in front of the bank. The car's motor was running and its front door was open. The bear entered the car, crawled over the front seat, and sat on the floor in the back. While I was looking at him through the car window, two men carrying guns and sacks ran from the bank and jumped into the car.

"The bear's in there," I told them.

They didn't hear me. They drove away fast as the burglar alarm went off outside the bank.

I went to see my father. "The bear got in a car and the people drove away and didn't see him," I said.

My father buried his face in his hands.

We drove slowly home. When we got there, we saw a group of people standing on the lawn near a parked car.

"The bear is sitting in the sheriff's car," I said.

"Those bank robbers didn't even get out of town," the sheriff happily told my father. "When the driver saw your bear sitting on the back seat, he drove into a ditch. They're in the prison hospital."

"The bear likes to ride in cars," I said.

"He didn't get hurt a bit," said the sheriff. "We're going to give him part of the reward. And Judge Holt doesn't see why the town can't give this bear a special license."

"By George!" said my father. "That's good of the judge. He's a good bear. We won't let him loose again."

I shook the bear awake and led him to the icehouse.

Record your finishing time in the time record for Article 5. Then take the reading test.

Read each test item and choose the answer you believe is correct. Print your answers in the answer record on page 4 of the progress folder.

Reading Test 5

Getting main ideas

1. The main point of the story was that the bear liked

    A. to be near people
    B. to be with other bears
    C. to chase after robbers
    D. to ride in automobiles
    E. to eat a lot of marshmallows

---

2. The bear in this story is best described as

    A. The Friendly Bear
    B. The Homely Bear
    C. The Happy Bear
    D. The Tricky Bear
    E. The Wandering Bear

---

3. In this story the author mainly tries

    A. to puzzle you
    B. to amuse you
    C. to surprise you
    D. to inform you
    E. to frighten you

Understanding important details

4. When his gang came back and saw the bear, George was most afraid that the bear would

    A. run away
    B. sit down
    C. steal the candy
    D. kill his brother
    E. break into the house

---

5. When the boy's father discovered the bear in his bedroom, he was

    A. upset and worried
    B. happy and delighted
    C. excited and pleased
    D. angry and afraid
    E. surprised and calm

---

6. The sheriff knew who owned the bear because the boy and his father had

   A. told the sheriff about the bear in their house
   B. seen the bear in the sheriff's car
   C. tried to get a pet license for the bear
   D. telephoned the sheriff about the bear's real owner
   E. asked the sheriff to put the bear in jail

Remembering key facts

7. The bear very much liked each of these things except one. Which one did the bear *not* like?

   A. Being near the boy and his family
   B. Eating marshmallows
   C. Going on automobile rides
   D. Being kept in the icehouse
   E. Being patted on the head

8. When the boy and his father took the bear to the woods to lose him, how did the father show that he liked the bear?

   A. He opened the car door for the bear.
   B. He gave the bear a freshly caught fish.
   C. He told the bear to go catch the robbers.
   D. He let the bear climb a tall tree.
   E. He blew his nose on a large handkerchief.

9. According to the circus manager, the bear's name was

   A. Candy
   B. Henry
   C. George
   D. Stephen
   E. Elmer

10. The name of the boy who told the story was

   A. Elmer
   B. George
   C. not given
   D. Henry
   E. Stephen

Choosing the best reason

11. The bear seemed to like the boy and his family because the bear always

   A. came back
   B. liked candy
   C. sat in cars
   D. wandered away
   E. left the circus

12. The bank robbers drove their car into the ditch and were captured because

   A. the bear's manager caught up with them
   B. the bear in the back seat frightened them
   C. the bear tried to seize the steering wheel
   D. the sheriff had the bear chase them
   E. the bear under the front seat scared them

64

13. In the end, the sheriff and the judge gave the bear a reward and a license because the bear was

A. a good friend
B. a tame animal
C. a nice pet
D. a funny trickmaker
E. a brave hero

Looking for proof

14. The bear helped the sheriff capture the robbers mainly because the bear

A. thought the robbers had candy in their sacks
B. liked to ride in the back seat of cars
C. wanted to win the reward and the license
D. ran after the robbers' car
E. escaped from the family's icehouse

Putting things in order

15. Here are five events that appeared in the story. Which of these events happened first?

A. Bear returned to boy.
B. Boy fed bear.
C. Bear came up to boy.
D. Boy lost bear.
E. Boy kept bear.

Knowing word meanings

16. When the boy's brother George went to find *customers*, he was looking for persons who would

A. sell him chocolate bars
B. swear at the bear
C. buy his candy
D. pay him to see the bear
E. eat some of his marshmallows

17. The boys decided to keep the bear to get a bounty for it. As the word is used here, a *bounty* means

A. a large and valuable gift for doing something good
B. a word of praise for being kind to a dumb animal
C. a collar and chain for holding an animal in one place
D. a government reward for catching or killing a harmful animal
E. punishment for doing something wrong

18. The boy and his father went to the courthouse to get a license for the bear. As the word is used here, a *license* means a permit

A. to keep an animal in a city
B. to fence in or tie up an animal
C. to shoot or trap an animal
D. to allow an animal to go anywhere
E. to hold an animal exhibit

Recognizing the right words

19. Because the bear was tame, his coat was *not*

A. haggy
B. baggy
C. saggy
D. shagy
E. shaggy

20. Just before the bear ate some candy, he

A. snuffed it
B. sifted it
C. snorted it
D. sniffed it
E. snubbed it

Follow the directions (Steps 8–13) on page 1 of the progress folder.

05892

How to read for details

What do we mean by "details"? Perhaps you have heard something like this: "We interrupt this broadcast to bring you a special bulletin from our newsroom. An airplane has fallen into the stands at the new stadium. No *details* have been reported." What facts can you imagine might be reported as details in such a tragedy?

You may have read an editorial like this in your daily newspaper: "The mayor's plan for solving our parking problem sounds fine. But so far he has given us only general statements. Before the citizens of this community can make up their minds about it, they need more *details*." What do you think details of a plan to solve a parking problem might be?

Or perhaps you have read a news story like this: "Two scientists returned to civilization today after ten months in the upper Amazon wilderness. They brought with them a detailed description of a fabulous lost city that flourished in that region twelve hundred years ago." What sort of *details* might be included in such a description?

What kinds of details do we meet in reading?

Do you remember Ichabod Crane in *The Legend of Sleepy Hollow,* that wonderful tale by Washington Irving? The author says that the schoolmaster looked like a crane, one of those tall birds with long thin necks.

"The name of Crane was not inapplicable to this person. He was tall, but exceedingly lank, with narrow shoulders, long arms and legs, hands that dangled a mile out of his sleeves, feet that might have served for shovels, and his whole frame most loosely hung together."

Details may be phrases used to describe

Note the phrases in the description of Crane:

tall, but exceedingly lank
with narrow shoulders
hands that dangled a mile out of his sleeves
feet that might have served for shovels

Details may be single words used to describe

Irving goes on to tell more about Ichabod Crane's unusual appearance. "His head was small, and flat at top, with huge ears, large green glassy eyes, and a long snipe nose." Note the single words that give details of Crane's appearance:

small	green
flat	glassy
huge	long
large	snipe

Details may be words, phrases, or statements used to explain

In the following paragraph, the first sentence makes a general statement. The other sentences are details used to explain the first sentence.

It may well be that the horrifying new weapons of war have brought an end to warfare among nations. No nation can attack another without being attacked in return. Even if a surprise attack were possible, hidden weapons would be able to launch a counterattack. There is no sure way of destroying jet bombers and guided missiles before they do their damage. Even if a bomb drops twenty miles away from a city, the entire city will be destroyed. Missiles are even more accurate than bombs. No nation can start a war without being destroyed itself.

Noting details

Exercise 15

Here is a famous old poem by an English poet. He speaks as an old man sick, weary, and tired of life. He is looking back to the carefree, happy days of his boyhood. He gives details to show what he enjoyed as a boy.

I Remember, I Remember

by Thomas Hood

I remember, I remember
The house where I was born;
The little window where the sun
Came peeping in at morn;
He never came a wink too soon,
Nor brought too long a day;
But now I often wish the night
Had borne my breath away!

I remember, I remember
The roses, red and white,
The violets, and the lily cups—
Those flowers made of light!
The lilacs where the robin built,
And where my brother set
The laburnum, on his birthday—
The tree is living yet!

I remember, I remember
Where I was used to swing,
And thought the air must rush as fresh
To swallows on the wing;
My spirit flew in feathers then,
That is so heavy now.
And summer pools could hardly cool
The fever on my brow!

I remember, I remember
The fir trees dark and high;
I used to think their slender tops
Were close against the sky;
It was a childish ignorance,
But now 'tis little joy
To know I'm farther off from heaven
Than when I was a boy.

Write on your paper the twelve details the poet remembers. There are three in the first verse, seven in the second, one in the third, and one in the last.

The details are listed in the answer key.

Details may be reasons given to explain a belief or action

Here is a paragraph that begins with a statement of what the writer believes about man's ability to live in outer space. It is followed by five reasons for his belief. Each of these reasons is a detail.

It is doubtful that men will be able to step outside a spaceship in outer space and live to tell about it. There is no oxygen in space, and without oxygen men die quickly. Ultraviolet rays in the sun's light would soon cook a man to a cinder if he were exposed to them. The lack of air pressure in space would tend to make his blood vessels burst. Dangerous cosmic rays would bombard his body. Since he has no weight in space, he would not be able to move around by his own strength.

Why it is important to note details in reading

Exercise 16

Details are words, phrases, or statements used to explain or describe. Reading is a two-way street. If the writer must use detail in order to be understood, the reader must notice and visualize detail in order to understand.

Detail is important, too, in remembering and using general ideas. Suppose you have been reading an article about the early American clipper ships. The article speaks of Nat Palmer as one of the greatest captains of that era. Later you try to tell someone how great Palmer was. "Why?" your friend asks. "What did Palmer do?" If you cannot support your statement, you may feel embarrassed. You are not likely to make the statement again, and gradually the story of Nat Palmer will fade from your memory.

Now read this paragraph about Palmer and note the details that back up the general statement "Nat Palmer was one of the greatest [captains] . . ."

During a period when daring and adventurous sea captains were almost common, Nat Palmer stands out as one of the greatest. He spent his boyhood on a fishing boat, and at age fourteen shipped out as a professional seaman. About three years later he commanded the forty-seven-foot sloop *Hero*, not much larger than a modern trailer truck. With a mate and four men, he sailed nine thousand miles to the Antarctic to hunt seals. His job was to locate seal rookeries for a fleet of large ships. In his small ship he defied the bitter cold and strange waters to discover unknown islands abounding with seals. He did quite a bit of exploring in the Antarctic, and Palmer Peninsula is named after him. He designed some of the first clipper ships, and commanded many of them in their record-breaking runs to China.

Write the numerals 1 to 3 on your paper. The paragraph above mentions five things about Palmer. Write three of the things that made Palmer "one of the greatest captains of that era." You may read the paragraph again.

The correct answers are shown in the answer key.

What clues help you find important details?

A good piece of writing may have a great many details. But these details are not equally important. Some are there to help you imagine or visualize a scene. Some details help set a mood. They are not all worth remembering. How can you find the most important items?

Careful writers use a number of devices to call the reader's attention to details they want him to notice. If you know these clues and watch for them, you will read far more efficiently and you will find it easier to remember what you have read.

Watch for examples

Whenever you see the words *for example*, or *for instance*, or *to illustrate*, read carefully. The writer is giving you an explanation that he thinks you need in order to understand his ideas.

Watch for numbering

Some writers help you locate details by saying *first . . . second . . . third. . . .* These words will help you locate important details and give them your special attention.

Watch for negative words

There are many ways of saying no in English. Everyone knows that *no* and *not* are negative words. But not everyone watches for these words carefully enough. *Neither*, *nor*, *hardly*, and *scarcely* are also negative words to watch for.

Exercise 17

In Lesson 5 you read the following paragraph. How carefully did you read it? Try again and pay particular attention to the negative words.

If we were talking about the *main* street of a town, we would mean the most important street. We would not be saying that the town has no other streets. Nor would we be saying that it has no other important streets. We would be saying simply that we were talking about the one street where the most people walk, work, drive their cars, and do their shopping.

Read each statement below and decide whether it is true or false. Write your answers on your paper.

When we speak of the main street of a town, we mean—

1. The town has no other important streets.
2. The town has other streets.
3. The town has other streets just as important.

The answer is shown in the answer key.

Watch for words that tell "how many"

When you say "*All* the girls in the class," you mean *every* girl. If you do not mean every girl, you have to use some other word. You can say "*nearly* all" or "*almost* all." Or you can say "*most* of the girls in the class." If you want to be more specific, you might say "*half* of the girls in class." If the number is less than half, you might say "*some* of the girls." If the number is really small, you might say "*a few* of the girls."

All and *every* are definite. *Always* is another word that is definite. The opposites of these words are *none* and *never*. All of these words tell you something definite.

Words such as *some, a few, most, several,* and *many* are not definite. Just how many they mean depends upon the situation in which they are used.

Getting the meaning of quantity words

Exercise 18

Write the numerals 1 to 5 on your paper. Read each item below and choose the answer you believe is correct.

1. Seven of the thirty-five U.S. Presidents have died in office. Which expression best describes this number?
    A. Many
    B. A few
    C. Several
2. Babe Ruth hit sixty home runs in the 1927 season. Few players have hit more than fifty home runs in a season. which word best describes Ruth's sixty home runs?
    A. Some
    B. Many
    C. Several
3. "At midnight a few people were still standing outside the door, waiting for the general to appear." *A few* means
    A. 6 or 7
    B. 100
    C. 35 or 40
4. "After walking twenty-two miles, we still had several miles to go to reach the cabin." *Several* means
    A. 25 miles
    B. 1 or 2 miles
    C. 5 or 6 miles
5. "There are eighty-nine members in the senior class; forty-seven are going to college next year." Which is the best expression to describe the forty-seven college-bound students?
    A. A few
    B. Some
    C. A majority

The correct answers are shown in the answer key.

Punctuation marks give clues to important details

Try saying these words without a pause and see what happens:

I went over to Jim's house after his uncle had gone we had a good time.

Read the words again, but pause after the word *gone*. Read it once more and pause after the word *house*. Do you hear the difference?

When you are speaking, you pause and let your voice drop to show your listener which words go together. If you ran right along in a single tone without pausing, no one would understand you because your meaning would not be clear.

When someone is reading what you have written, he cannot hear your voice drop, or hear you pause. You must make something take the place of your voice. Writers use punctuation marks to help the reader to see which words go together. Periods, commas, colons, and other marks do two things. *First*, they combine words and word groups that belong together. *Second*, they separate words that do not belong together.

Punctuation marks are therefore clues to meaning. They point out important details.

1. *Italics* are used to call the reader's attention to especially important words and ideas.

2. *Dashes* are used to set off explanatory details. The dash says, "The words that you see from here to the next dash explain *what you have just read*." Dashes direct the reader's attention backward. When you see two dashes, think of them as arrows like this:

Several punctuation marks ←— commas, dashes, quotation marks ←— give clues to meaning.

3. *Colons* are used, too, to call the reader's attention to details that explain. They direct the reader to watch *what follows*. Think of a colon as an arrow pointing forward.

There were three reasons for Lincoln's success: intelligence, the desire to learn, and great energy.

4. *Quotation marks* are used in several ways. Their most important use is to show the exact words of the speaker. See what happens when the quotation marks are used in this sentence:

I can't believe the doctor said that Tom is going to die.

"I can't believe," the doctor said, "that Tom is going to die."

5. *Commas* are used both to combine words that belong together and to keep apart those that do not belong together. Read over this group of words:

The circus will be here Monday and Tuesday it will leave for Chicago.

Will the circus be here two days or one? You can figure out the answer by going back and rereading, but it is a waste of time to reread something that should be clear the first time. Where would you place the comma to make the meaning clear?

Now try these sentences to see how important commas can be:

While we were eating the neighbor's dog came over to beg.

Just as I finished painting my husband came in.

6. *Semicolons* are used to join statements that express closely related ideas.

Alice was in trouble; she had lost her purse.

In the following story, two paragraphs have punctuation marks and two do not. After you read them, discuss in class (*a*) how the punctuation marks in paragraphs 2 and 4 help the reader; (*b*) what marks are needed to make paragraphs 1 and 3 easy to read.

1. The years 1896 1897 and 1898 were discouraging the magic shows put on by Houdini and his wife Bessie brought in very little money

2. Then one day, Houdini suddenly said, "We're going to Europe, Bess." Bess stared.

3. We'll get bookings when we get there he quickly added all the big agencies here grab imported talent well we will be imported they'll want to hire us all right you wait and see

4. Houdini arrived in England with his scrapbook under his arm, a list of agents in his pocket, and high hope in his heart. But for some reason, the moment Houdini began to quote notices describing his hand-cuff escapes as "marvelous," the agents quickly dismissed the Houdinis.[1]

Punctuation marks are like street signals and highway signs. A capital letter at the start of a sentence is like a green light; it means "Go ahead." A period, question mark, or exclamation mark is like a red light or an eight-sided yellow sign; it says "Stop." A comma is a sign to slow down. A pair of dashes is a sign to look back. A colon tells you to look ahead.

If you are a skilled reader, you see and react to punctuation signals automatically. You know what these signs mean so well that you do not have to stop and think about them. In this you are like a skilled driver. He sees and obeys road signs automatically, without having to study them. Road signs give a driver details on how to drive. Punctuation marks help you find important details in your reading.

How to read a passage for details

Exercise 19

In reading a passage for details, you look for answers to one or more of the following questions: What? Who? When? Where? Why? How?

---

1 Condensed and adapted from *The Great Houdini: Magician Extraordinary*, by Beryl Williams and Samuel Epstein, published by Julian Messner, Inc. Copyright 1950 by Beryl Williams and Samuel Epstein. Reprinted by permission of Julian Messner, Inc.

Read rapidly through the story that follows and look for answers to these questions—Who? What? When? Where? How?

Be Prepared![2]

"Be Prepared!" is the motto of the Boy Scouts of America. What this motto means was clearly shown by the Oklahoma scout whose little sister was in great danger.

On a cold winter morning the scout's mother lighted the fire in an open gas heater in the upstairs bedroom. She wanted to warm up the place where her two youngest children were dressing.

While the small girl was getting dressed, this child stepped too close to the heater. In an instant, her clothing caught fire and was in flames. She screamed loudly with fear and pain. Her mother could do nothing because she was so horrified.

The father and his son ran up the stairs and into the room. The boy quickly picked up a rug from the floor. He wrapped this rug closely around the body of his sister. Within a few seconds he put out the flames. By doing this, he kept his sister from getting more serious burns, burns that might have killed her.

In his scout troop, the leader had trained this thirteen-year-old boy in first aid. That is why he knew exactly what to do. Because he was prepared, he saved his sister's life.

_____

Write the numerals 1 to 18 on your paper. After each numeral, write one of these six words: *Who, What, When, Where, Why, How.* You will choose the word that tells what each of the following details shows in the story.

1. On a cold winter morning
2. the scout's mother
3. lighted the fire
4. in an open gas heater
5. in the upstairs bedroom
6. She
7. wanted to warm up the place
8. where her youngest children were dressing
9. While the small girl was dressing
10. this child

2 "Be Prepared," reprinted from the *Boy Scout Handbook* by permission of the Boy Scouts of America.

11. stepped
12. too close to the heater
13. She
14. screamed
15. loudly with fear and pain
16. Her mother
17. could do nothing
18. because she was so horrified

The correct answers are shown in the answer key.

Now read the story again. In order to take the test in Exercise 20, you must read each paragraph carefully for details. This is the kind of reading you will do over and over again in your school studies.

Reading a paragraph for details

Exercise 20

The fourth paragraph in the story contains a number of facts. Answer the questions below from memory. Read each test item and choose the answer you believe is correct.

1. In the story, which two persons ran up the stairs to the bedroom?
   A. The mother and the little girl
   B. The mother and the father
   C. The father and the scout
   D. The mother and the scout
   E. The father and the doctor

2. In which order did these events occur? Write down the letters in the correct order.
   A. The scout picked up a rug from the floor.
   B. The scout ran up the stairs and into the room.
   C. The scout put out the fire in his sister's clothing.
   D. The scout wrapped the rug around his sister's body.

3. In the fifth paragraph you learned that the scout had been trained in first aid
   A. by his father
   B. by his family's doctor
   C. by his classroom teacher
   D. by his best friend
   E. by his troop leader

The correct answers are shown in the answer key.

How to read an article for details

Exercise 21

In a well-written article, each paragraph contains important details. Before reading for details in the following article about the American porcupine, answer the following questions. Write your answers "yes" or "no" on your paper. This test is in two parts.

Part 1

1. Do porcupines move very fast?
2. Will a porcupine chase a larger animal?
3. Does a porcupine throw its quills?
4. Can a porcupine kill a wolf?
5. Should you kill a porcupine?

Keep these questions and your answers in mind as you read.

The American Porcupine[3]

You can't teach a porcupine new tricks. And you can't make it hurry. In fact, the tree porcupine of North America is very stupid. It is also very slow on its feet. It walks with a clumsy shuffle. But it is an animal to let alone. If its quills could speak, they would say "Danger! Do not touch!"

The porcupine was certainly given the right name. It comes from two Latin words—*porcus* meaning "pig" and *spina* meaning "thorn." The American tree porcupine has some thirty thousand "thorns," or quills. The quills are fairly small, about an inch and a half in length. Yet they are barbed darts that can wound and even kill an enemy.

The porcupine will not attack another animal. But if attacked, the porcupine will fight back, in its own strange way. As the porcupine walks along, its quills lie along its back and tail. If an enemy comes near, the porcupine at once takes an "on guard"

position. It arches its back; this makes its quills stand up. And it whirls about quickly so that its back and tail are aimed at the enemy.

Some people believe that the porcupine shoots its quills as an Indian shoots his arrows. But what really happens is this: Suppose that a wolf attacks a porcupine. The porcupine turns its back, but it does not run away. Instead it backs slowly toward the enemy. Then it suddenly lashes out with its short clublike tail. Its tail strikes quickly at the right time and place— usually the mouth of the wolf. The porcupine drives a dozen or more quills deep into the flesh of its enemy. If the wolf grabs the porcupine by the neck or body, it gets a mouthful of quills.

Whether the flick of the porcupine's tail or the closing of the wolf's jaws causes the quills to go into the wolf's flesh, these quills are very painful. For this reason, after the wolf is stuck by the first quill, it has usually had enough. It lets the porcupine go on its way unharmed. Then the wolf tries to take out the quill with its teeth or with its paw. This is difficult and here is why.

If you look at a porcupine quill, you will see that it is about the same size and shape as a round toothpick. However, at one end, the quill is blunt. At this end the quill is attached loosely to muscles just under the animal's skin. At the other end the quill is very sharp. A little below the tip at this end, the quill has a large number of tiny barbs. These barbs can be seen only under a miscroscope.

While a quill is on the porcupine, the barbs near its tip lie flat. But when the quill is in the flesh of the mouth, nose, or paw of a wolf or other enemy, the quill's barbs "explode"— that is, open up rapidly. The quill easily pulls loose from the porcupine's skin and it sticks fast in the enemy's body. Like a barbed fishhook, the quill is hard to remove. It can be pulled out only by tearing the flesh. If it is not removed, it automatically works its way farther and farther into the body.

Porcupine quills have killed wild animals such as wolves, coyotes, foxes, mountain lions, and lynxes. When these animals could not remove the quills from their mouths, they slowly starved to death.

---

[3] Reprinted by permission of Hawthorn Books, Inc., from *The Animal Kingdom* (Frederick Drimmer, editor in chief), Volume I: *Mammals*, by George C. Goodwin. Copyright 1954 by the Greystone Press.

During most of the summer the porcupine feeds on green plants. It is especially fond of clover and alfalfa. Because this animal does not hibernate, in the winter it feeds completely on bark. It peels the bark from the trunks or the branches of evergreen trees. Sometimes a porcupine girdles a tree. It strips off the bark in a band that goes all around the trunk. This, of course, kills the tree.

Some states have laws protecting porcupines. According to these laws, a person is not allowed to kill a porcupine. For hundreds of years the Indians have had an unwritten law. "Never kill a porcupine unless you have to," the Indians said. "If you are ever lost in the woods and are starving, a porcupine may save your life."

Part 2

Write the numerals 1 to 8 on your paper. Read each test item and choose the answer you believe is correct.

1. In defending itself against an enemy, the porcupine
   A. walks backward toward the enemy
   B. runs forward to escape the enemy
   C. climbs a tree to be above the enemy
   D. rolls over on its back
   E. aims its quill-covered head at the enemy
2. The porcupine uses its quills
   A. to attack another animal
   B. to get fresh meat
   C. to girdle a tree
   D. to frighten an enemy
   E. to protect its life
3. The porcupine gets its quills into the flesh of an enemy by
   A. throwing the quills
   B. allowing the enemy to bite its neck
   C. standing on its hind feet
   D. lashing its tail
   E. shaking its whole body
4. In size and shape, a porcupine's quill is most like
   A. a knitting needle
   B. a fishhook
   C. a harpoon
   D. a razor blade
   E. a round toothpick
5. A porcupine quill sticks in a wolf's mouth because the tip of the quill
   A. has a hook in it
   B. has a hole in it
   C. has barbs in it
   D. is very sharp
   E. sinks in very deep
6. The porcupine's quills can cause a wild animal to die from
   A. bleeding
   B. exhaustion
   C. starvation
   D. thirst
   E. poisoning
7. When a porcupine girdles a tree, it eats
   A. a long strip of bark up and down the tree
   B. a band of bark all round the trunk
   C. a large number of branches and twigs
   D. a big root just below the ground
   E. many seeds on the ground near the trunk
8. American Indians had an unwritten law that said you should kill a porcupine only if you are
   A. stuck by a quill
   B. helping to protect a dog
   C. trying to save a tree
   D. starving to death
   E. attacked by the porcupine

The correct answers are shown in the answer key.

Practice Reading 6

In a book, magazine, or newspaper that you like, practice reading for speed and comprehension. Make a record of this reading in Chart 3 on page 8 of your progress folder.

Record your starting time in the time record on page 4 of the progress folder. Then read the selection. Read as fast as you can, but make sure you understand what you are reading.

6
article

Terror in the woods[4]

by Earle Doucette

One November afternoon last year in Maine, a searching party came to the end of a tragic trail. At their feet on the forest floor was the lost hunter for whom they were looking. The hunter was dead.

The cause of death was overexertion. Yet the man had been healthy. He was last seen only five miles from where he was found. He had been lost for only eight hours.

Clearly the hunter had fallen into the panic that overcomes many who are lost in the woods. Woodsmen call this becoming "bushed." When bushed, even well-balanced persons will often do surprising things.

Some, like the dead hunter, run madly through the forest, trying to get out. They stumble over fallen trees. They get up, shaken and bruised. They then rush on even faster. At last their bursting hearts quit and they drop.

In others the shock of being lost soon brings on a condition that is like amnesia. The victim walks aimlessly through the woods. When found, he cannot remember his name or anything else about himself. Still others suffer from hallucinations; they think they are being chased by wild beasts.

The dead hunter had carried a compass, candy bars, matches, warm clothing, a rifle, even a belt ax. He could have been lost a week without serious harm—if he had kept his head. But when he was found, he was without rifle, ax, even outer clothing.

Hampered by them in his mad rush, he had thrown them away, even though the weather was below freezing.

More often than not, a bushed person will throw away the very things that would keep him alive. One lost hunter, found dead in the woods, had thrown away his gun and coat and shoes. Four of his friends had become lost while looking for him. They also threw away their guns before making their way to safety.

Deputy Commissioner Earle Bradbury of the Maine Department of Inland Fisheries and Game tells of an experience. Bradbury said two wardens were searching for a lost hunter who was suffering from a kind of amnesia.

"The man's tracks in the snow led toward a wide, paved highway. The tired wardens were sure they would find him there. But they found he had crossed the road without seeing it and had gone into the deep woods on the other side.

"When at last they saw their man, they shouted to him. To their amazement, he started running away from them.

"Catching up, they had to fight with the crazed man before they could quiet him. And then they had to carry him out of the woods—he wouldn't walk."

A few years ago a hunter became lost near Maine's Moosehead Lake. He thought he was being chased by men bent on killing him. From a trapper's deserted cabin, he was ready to shoot his would-be rescuers. For several hours they reasoned with him. Finally he came to his senses and ran toward them with tears of relief on his cheeks.

The most tragic case on which Maine wardens have worked is hard to believe. Warden Supervisor Charles Harriman was in charge of a searching party that finally caught up with a lost hunter. Except for socks, he was naked. He had torn off the rest of his clothing. In his hand was his hunting knife. He was so afraid of being lost that he had killed himself.

Can anything be done to stop such needless suffering and loss of life? Harriman, one of the most woodswise men in the North Country, has this to say:

"It should be drummed into sportsmen's heads that a person lost in the woods who remains calm will be safer than if he were at home dodging traffic. If he acts according to prearranged plans when hunting with others, or if he tells someone just where he is going when he is hunting alone, he will hardly ever be in the woods longer than overnight before he is found.

"But suppose he is lost two, three, or four days. He can find enough fuel. He can shoot birds and animals for food. But even though a man has nothing to eat for a week, what of it? It won't hurt him seriously.

"The idea that anything in the forest will harm a man is childish. Can't people stop believing fairy tales? Thousands of us—wardens, guides, woodsmen—are in the woods all the time. Many times, when weather permits, we just roll up in a blanket when night comes.

"No one has ever been attacked in our North Woods. I have had animals come near me only twice. Once a mouse tried to build a nest in my pocket while I slept. Another time a chipmunk filled one of my boots full of prune pits during the night."

Those who get their living in the woods greatly admire the Boy Scouts. No one in Maine can remember a scout, or anyone who ever has been an active scout, becoming bushed. Their training seems to give them self-reliance.

One November day in 1938 an early blizzard roared down on Maine's forests. Thousands of hunters were marooned. That night, with the blizzard raging, Warden Supervisor Daniel Malloy trudged through the forest, seeking a hunter who hadn't shown up.

"I had traveled three miles when I saw a campfire," he said. "It was built in front of a little lean-to. In this shelter, snug as a bug, was a boy about twelve years old.

"I expected to be greeted with shouts of joy. But the youngster was madder than a hornet. Seems that he was out rabbit-hunting when the storm overtook him. So, mindful of his scout training, he had done exactly the right thing.

"He planned to make his way back home next morning. All he had on his mind was the hope that his experience would win him a scout award. And then I had come along, threatening to spoil the whole thing.

"Soon afterward I found the man I was looking for. He was wandering around babbling, near exhaustion. Strange, isn't it? In one night I had run across a little boy who had used his brains and a big man who hadn't!"

A group of hunters in strange territory should spend the first evening with a guide, getting to know the area. In what direction do the brooks and streams run? Where are the landmarks? Where are the deep swamps? Are there any camps in which a person could stay in case of a storm?

Before each day's hunt the group should understand where each member will hunt and what he will do if he becomes lost. Shall he stay where he is when he becomes lost? Shall he make for some predetermined road or stream? Once having agreed on plans, all hands should stick to them. Many a hunter has been shot because he disregarded plans and wandered into another hunter's line of fire.

The safest thing for a lost person to do, especially if it is getting late, is to build a fire and a lean-to, then stick it out there until he's found. The road or stream he would try to reach may be farther away than he thinks. Stumbling around in the dark trying to find wood to burn is no fun.

So remember, if you are lost in the woods, you won't lose your life until you lose your head. Your only possible enemy, besides yourself, is exposure to the elements. And if you are smart, you will carry a small ax (not a knife) for cutting wood. You can keep warm even if the weather is below freezing.

Once, deep in the woods, a trapper came across an old Indian sitting beside a fire. Since the reservation was far away, the trapper greeted the old brave with the question, "Chief, what's the matter? You lost?"

For a while the chief thought about the strange words of the white man. Then he grunted and answered: "No, Indian chief not lost. Wigwam lost."

I think he had something there.

Record your finishing time in the time record for Article 6. Then take the reading test.

Read each test item and choose the answer you believe is correct. Print your answers in the answer record on page 4 of the progress folder.

Reading Test 6

Getting main ideas

1. The safest thing for a person lost in the woods near nightfall is to
   - A. build a crude flag
   - B. build a fire and a lean-to and wait
   - C. climb a tree and look for a trail
   - D. head for the nearest stream
   - E. yell for help

---

2. A person lost in the woods won't lose his life, the author says, unless he loses his
   - A. ax
   - B. shoes
   - C. knife
   - D. drinking water
   - E. head

---

3. Hunters in strange woods should spend the first evening with the guide
   - A. making trail markers
   - B. telling stories
   - C. building a campfire
   - D. cleaning guns
   - E. getting to know the area

---

4. The idea that anything in the woods will harm a man is said to be
   - A. based on facts
   - B. proved every day
   - C. childish
   - D. true of the woods of Europe
   - E. occasionally valid

Remembering key facts

5. The most tragic case on which Maine wardens have worked was a lost hunter who killed himself with
   - A. a hunting knife
   - B. an overdose of medicine
   - C. a rifle
   - D. a revolver
   - E. poison

---

6. No one in the state can remember a boy scout who got

A. shot by another hunter
B. a merit badge for hunting
C. bushed
D. marooned
E. lost in the woods

7. A mouse once tried to build a nest in the warden's

A. shoe
B. bedroll
C. pocket
D. lunch box
E. hat

8. All the events in the story took place in the state of

A. Maine
B. Vermont
C. New Hampshire
D. Montana
E. Minnesota

9. One hunter was so confused that he crossed, without knowing it,

A. a snake-filled swamp
B. a raging mountain stream
C. a burning bridge
D. a bog of quicksand
E. a wide, paved highway

10. In the 1938 blizzard thousands of hunters were marooned. During the storm the warden found in the woods

A. an Indian chief
B. an Indian squaw
C. a twelve-year-old boy
D. a crazed trapper
E. a lost airplane pilot

Drawing conclusions

11. The purpose of this article is to

A. inform you
B. frighten you
C. puzzle you
D. amuse you
E. surprise you

12. A person lost in the woods should, above all else, be

A. excited
B. worried
C. amazed
D. calm
E. amused

13. Boy Scout training helps those who enter the woods because it teaches them to

A. earn merit badges
B. think of others
C. be kind to animals
D. know the names of birds
E. look after themselves

14. The author tells the story of the old Indian, the fire, and the wigwam to show that
    A. an Indian knows how to build a fire
    B. a man is not lost if he knows where he is
    C. even Indians get lost in the woods
    D. the Indian knew where his wigwam was
    E. Indians should not leave their reservation

15. The author tells the story of the boy scout lost in the woods to show that even a young boy can use his
    A. compass
    B. rifle
    C. ax
    D. brains
    E. hunting knife

Knowing word meanings

16. *Landmarks* are signs that help a hunter
    A. keep away from posted land
    B. fool wild animals
    C. avoid deep swamps
    D. find his way in the woods
    E. wipe out his trail

17. A *bushed* hunter is one who suffers from
    A. hunger
    B. panic
    C. loneliness
    D. bruises
    E. exhaustion

18. When a lost hunter has *hallucinations*, he may
    A. have extra rations with him
    B. make good use of them
    C. have remembered to bring a compass with him
    D. think he is being chased by wild beasts
    E. not be lost at all

19. If a hunter has a plan that is *prearranged*, the plan has been arranged
    A. before he actually starts to hunt
    B. after he starts to hunt
    C. the day after he leaves the woods
    D. while he is leaving the woods
    E. just before he leaves the woods

20. *Terror* is to *panic* as *crazed* is to
    A. happy
    B. mad
    C. found
    D. lost
    E. exhausted

Follow the directions (Steps 8–13) on page 1 of the progress folder.

7
lesson

How to read to follow directions

All of us frequently need to follow written directions. Some directions are easy, but others are hard to understand. We need help to understand them better.

More and more, Americans are making their homes comfortable and livable with do-it-yourself kits and pamphlets. Carpenters are too busy to work on small jobs. It costs too much to get decorators to do over the living room. There is no shop in town where you can take the metal table to be repaired. So you must do it yourself. It costs less; it gives you a sense of achievement—and you get things done.

Directions differ greatly in detail. But all directions are alike in two respects. (1) There are parts, objects, materials, or symbols that you must recognize and identify. (2) There is a definite order in which the steps of a process must be followed. Here are some suggestions that will help you follow directions:

1. Make sure that you have the right directions. If you are planning to make divinity, make sure you are reading the directions for that candy, or you may end up with a batch of taffy.

In school you are given assignments either orally or in writing. In either case, make sure that you know exactly what you are to do. Write the assignment down word for word. Then check it to see that you have not left out any details.

Before you leave the classroom, make sure you know what you are to do. Are you just to read a number of pages? Or are you to read them and make an outline, list the important topics, work up some questions, or write a paragraph? Just exactly what is your responsibility?

Sometimes you are given assignments several days or weeks in advance. Make sure you know exactly when and in what form your work is to be finished. Are you to give an oral report or a written report? If it is to be written, must it be written in ink?

2. Before you start following any set of directions, make sure you know what they mean. If unfamiliar materials or tools are called for, ask someone about them. You will save time in the end.

In any trade, technical terms are very exact; if the directions call for a Stillson wrench, a plain monkey wrench will not do. If the directions tell you to use a lacquer thinner, turpentine probably will not work. If a recipe calls for half a cup of milk, it is a standard measuring cup that is meant, *not* just any coffee cup you have at hand.

3. Read the directions all the way through. Suppose you are reading directions for replacing a washer in a leaky faucet. If you read the directions all the way through, you will get a picture of the whole operation. You will see why each step must be taken at the particular time specified. You will be less likely to slight some part of the job that is small but nevertheless important.

If the directions are long, you may have to read them several times to get the whole picture in mind, and you will want to proceed step by step, rereading each step before you start it.

4. Follow the directions in the order they are given. If the directions are long, read over the first step. Take this step and reread the directions to make sure you have left out nothing. Read the directions for the second step. Carry them out and check your work. Do one thing at a time and do it in the order called for. Don't try to anticipate or read ahead. Don't read the final step and then assume that you know what the other steps must be. You may overlook the most important step in the instructions and spoil your work.

Reading to follow directions

Exercise 22

Read the directions below for preparing chili. It is delicious and can be made easily.

How to make chili

1. Assemble the ingredients

2 tablespoons oil or margarine
1 onion, chopped
1 clove of garlic, chopped
1½ pounds of ground beef
1 #303 can of tomatoes (approximately 2 cups)
1 cup water
1 #303 can of kidney beans
1 tablespoon (or more) chili powder
2 teaspoons ground cumin seed
1 tablespoon (or more) salt
½ teaspoon pepper

a large pan with a close-fitting lid

2. Cook the chili

Step 1. Heat the oil in the pan over a high fire.
Step 2. Add the onions and garlic. Stir them for a minute or two.
Step 3. Add the meat. Stir it until it is brown.
Step 4. Add the tomatoes and water.
Step 5. Cover the pan and cook over a low fire for one hour.
Step 6. Add the beans, chili powder, cumin, salt, and pepper. Cover and cook for 45 minutes.
Step 7. Add more seasonings to taste.

Next weekend, try to get permission to make chili for your family or friends. *First*, read the recipe all the way through. *Second*, get the ingredients all together. *Third*, get out the pan and measuring spoons you will need. Be sure you have regular measuring spoons. *Fourth*, follow the steps in cooking.

The chili can be served as soup or it can be served as "chili mac." If you want to make "chili mac," cook a half pound of spaghetti according to the directions on the box. Use the chili as a sauce over the spaghetti. Test yourself on how well you understand the recipe.

Write the numerals 1 to 5 on your paper. For each item below, write **T** if the statement is true; write **F** if the statement is false.

1. Several pots and pans are needed to make chili.
2. The tomatoes are added after the meat is browned.
3. After the cover is put on, the fire should be turned lower.
4. After the mixture has cooked for one hour, the remaining ingredients are added.
5. The chili can be served in two different ways.

The correct answers are shown in the answer key.

Reading to follow directions

Exercise 23

Sometimes you read directions to find out how to conduct an experiment. The following experiment explains some principles that Edison discovered when he was experimenting with the electric light. You should read the experiment to understand what each step involves and to learn what the results prove.

Experiment[1]

Get a flat cork or a disk of thin wood or a piece of plastic foam or sponge. You can slice such a disk from an ordinary bottle cork or pry the lining from a pop-bottle cap. In the center of your disk, attach a little birthday cake candle. A good way to fasten the candle in place is to let a little of the melted wax drip onto the disk and then push the bottom of the candle against it. The dried wax will hold the candle. Float the little candle in a shallow pan of water (a pie plate will do). If the candle boat is topheavy and upsets, cut off the bottom half of the candle and try again with just the top part.

1 From *Edison Experiments You Can Do*, text by Marjorie Van de Water. Copyright 1956, 1958 by Science Service, Inc. Copyright © 1960 by Thomas Alva Edison Foundation.

When the boat is floating, light the candle and turn a drinking glass, bottom side up, over the burning candle. Push the glass down until the rim is against the bottom of the pan. You will notice that the candle goes to the bottom too. At first the water will not go into the glass. This is because the glass is filled with air and there is no room for water.

But the burning of the candle uses up the oxygen in the air. As the oxygen is used, the water will rise in the glass and the little candle boat will bob up with the water. When the oxygen is all gone, the flame will go out.

This experiment shows two things: First, the burning of the candle uses up the oxygen that is in the air in the glass. But, more important for the understanding of the incandescent electric light, it also shows that when there is no oxygen in the glass the flame goes out. This means that a glowing filament will not burn itself up in a glass bulb in which there is no oxygen.

This fact, basic to the incandescent light, was not known to Edison when he began to work on his lamp. He found it out by a long series of experiments.

First he baked strips of paper until they turned to carbon. Then he passed an electric current from a battery through the carbon strips to find out how much current it would take to make them glow. The strips burned up instantly.

Then he mounted the carbon strips in a glass jar and pumped out the air with a hand vacuum pump. This produced a partial vacuum, but a very poor one. The strips glowed for a few minutes, but then they burned up.

Edison tried a large number of other materials for his lamp, hoping to find something that would not be destroyed so rapidly. He used hard-to-melt materials such as boron, ruthenium, and chromium. None of them worked as he wanted them to. He did not try tungsten, the filament so widely used today, because at that time tungsten was available only as a very hard metal and was almost unworkable; it could not be made into filaments.

Of all the metals Edison tried, platinum turned out to be the most promising. So he began an extensive series of experiments with various platinum-iridium alloys, trying to find the right combination.

Today a vacuum is still used in some incandescent light bulbs to keep the filament from burning up. Most bulbs of twenty-five watts or less are vacuum bulbs. Bulbs of forty watts or higher are kept free of oxygen by another method: they are filled with a gas that does not support burning

---

Did you understand the directions and the explanation in this article?

1. For this experiment you need, besides a pan of water and matches, three things. They are (1) _____ (2) _____ (3) _____

2. Put these steps in the proper order:
   A. Put the glass over the candle.
   B. Light the candle.
   C. Assemble the materials needed.
   D. Float the candle boat.
   E. Attach the candle to the cork or sponge.

Complete these sentences:

3. The candle goes out after it has burned up all the_____in the glass.

4. A glowing filament will not burn itself up in a glass bulb in which there is no_____.

The correct answers are shown in the answer key.

Reading to follow directions

Exercise 24

If you have never slept in a tent outdoors, you have missed a pleasant and exciting experience. Each year, more and more families are taking camping vacations. Many areas in our state and national parks have large camping sites for the convenience of the vacationing family. In camping out, you do not have the comforts of home, but you do have experiences that you will remember and tell about for a long time.

Anyone who plans to camp out must know the best place for pitching his tent. To find out how to choose a good place, read the article that follows. After you read it, you will take a short test on it.

How to Choose a Good Campsite[2]

Before putting up your tent, you will want to find a campsite that has as many good points as possible. Here are the things to look for:

1. Slope. Pitch your camp at a place where the land slopes so that rainwater will drain off. However, be sure that the land is level enough for comfortable sleeping. Try to find a place where the soil will absorb any rainwater. Find ground that is soft enough to drive tent pegs into, but stay away from ground that is soggy or damp.

2. Air and wind. Put up your camp so that its back is toward the prevailing winds and storms. Place it in a clearing where the sun can dry the ground and where the air can ventilate your tent. Avoid low spots where fog collects and where mosquitoes bite. Camp on high ground but not on the highest point, where lightning may strike.

3. Water and wood. If possible, camp at a place where you can easily get water and wood. Before drinking any water, be sure that it is pure. Before cutting any wood, be sure that you have permission to do so. Whenever you can, use dead wood, not live wood, for your campfires.

4. Layout. Allow space around and between all the tents. Place the camp kitchen and the eating area at a place that is convenient for the whole camp.

5. Safety. Watch out for dead trees, dead branches on live trees, and leaning trees. During a windstorm these may be blown down onto your camp. In mountainous country, look uphill for boulders that a heavy rain may start rolling toward your camp. Do not put your camp too near a riverbank. During a heavy rain the river may overflow and wash away your tents.

6. Comfort. If you plan to sleep on the ground, find a place that is free from rocks. Before putting up your sleeping tent, be sure that you have a spot where you can clear away all sticks and stones. If you sleep on a small pebble, it may seem to be a large boulder before morning.

Test yourself on how well you understood this article. Read each test item and choose the answer you believe is correct. Print your answers on your paper.

1. Pitch your camp on land that
    A. does not slope
    B. slopes gently
    C. slopes steeply
2. If the prevailing winds are from the west, place your tent so that it faces
    A. south
    B. west
    C. east
3. Before drinking any water, be sure that it is
    A. pure
    B. clear
    C. cold
4. Pitch your tent
    A. in an open place
    B. under a tree
    C. along a riverbank
5. If you expect to sleep on the ground, make sure that the ground is free of
    A. grass and leaves
    B. moss and weeds
    C. sticks and stones

The correct answers are shown in the answer key.

Read to follow directions

Exercise 25

In this exercise you will read a long article about an exciting sport and science—diving and underwater archaeology. The article is divided into seven short parts. For each part there is a test. In this exercise you are given directions to follow. Study the directions and try to understand why they are given. This will help you learn ways to study that you can use in your school assignments.

Direction 1. Learn the meanings of the ten terms listed below. Look these words up in a dictionary. They are not explained in the article. You will miss some of the excitement if you do not know what they mean. Write the words and their meanings in your notebook.

abyss	extinct
deceptive	eliminates
legend	equalize
bathyscaphe	caisson
exploitation	contemporary

---

2 "How to Choose a Good Campsite," reprinted from the *Boy Scout Handbook* by permission of the Boy Scouts of America.

Sometimes the difficult words in an assignment are explained in the textbook. In some books the meanings are given in footnotes. In other books they are given in a glossary. Sometimes your teacher writes them on the chalkboard. Before you start reading an assignment, glance over any list of words that is given to you. See whether you can find clues to their meaning in the words themselves.

Direction 2. Look over the following list of words. How many of them do you know now? Watch for these words as you read the selection. You can get their meaning from the words used with them.

agility	nourishment
murky	endurance
competent	plummet
archaeologist	transparent
excavated	aquarium
ponderous	submerged
enable	insulating
inverted	bathysphere
replenish	buoyant

Direction 3. Read the whole article quickly for enjoyment. By reading it all the way through, you will get a general idea of what the whole article is about. Disregard the interruptions as you read the whole story first. You will be able later to see how the various parts fit into the whole. In this reading do not stop for the tests that follow each part. But when you come to the end of the article, take the short test that follows.

Direction 4. After you have taken the short test at the end of the selection, turn back and reread Part 1. Take the test that follows. Then go on to Part 2, read it, take the test. Continue in this way until you have finished rereading all seven parts.

Conquest of the Depths[3]

Part 1. Through the looking-glass

Come, put on your swim mask and fins and compressed-air tank, and dive with us through the looking-glass into the sea.

Down we go into the cool blue waters to a strange new world. Just as the image in a mirror is reversed, so life in the water is different from life on land. The water is a world without shadows and without a horizon. Of the 197,000,000 square miles of the earth's surface, a little over seven-tenths is covered with water.

Here we find animals that look like plants and are solidly rooted. We see plants that float about freely. There is no gravity. Our bodies are weightless. Our lungs take on a new function. Inhaling a great chestful of air, we soar toward the surface. Exhaling, we drift slowly downward. We sit, stand, lie back, and relax. A flick of our fins sends us gliding forward as silently as the fish that watch us curiously in the murky distance.

The senses that we find so necessary for existence in our natural-air environment seem strangely inadequate. Our eyes deceive us and distort the size and nearness of things. Without our masks we would be almost blind. Diving to the bottom, thirty feet below, we find our ears to be more of a nuisance than a blessing. In them we feel the pressure of the water as a pain that can be relieved only by swallowing or blowing sharply through the nose. We strain our ears for a familiar sound, but around us is an eerie silence, broken only by the gurgle of exhaust bubbles from the regulator of our air tank.

Near us the sunshine from the upper world has made everything glow in a pure light, but at a distance of a few yards everything fades away in a blue haze. Below is a sandy floor strewn with rocks and seaweed, and until we come along it is absolutely motionless. Beyond us the bottom slopes away in the black abyss. Not until we are thoroughly accustomed to our new existence in this underwater world will we attempt to explore at greater depths. Even the most experienced divers find these depths cold and forbidding. At twenty fathoms (120 feet) we would discover a world made up of an infinite number of shades of blue. Photoflash pictures have shown that vibrant color exists at this depth, but it cannot be seen, for the seawater acts as a filter, absorbing all but the blue rays of light. If we were to cut ourselves on a jagged piece of coral, even our blood would look blue.

We could lose track of our directions

---

3 Condensed from *Ships, Shoals and Amphoras*, by Suzanne de Borhegyi. Copyright © 1961 by Suzanne de Borhegyi. Reprinted by permission of Holt, Rinehart and Winston, Inc.

and not know which way was up, but a cool head would tell us to follow the direction of our air bubbles. No, the depths are not for wandering. In time we will explore their mysteries, but for the moment we are quite content to soar up and back to the sunlight.

Above us we see the thrashing arms and legs of a swimmer. How tiring his exertions seem to us now! We pity him, and delight in our own freedom and ease of movement. We actually feel more akin to the fish around us than to this churning, splashing foreigner from dry land. With a bit of a shock we realize that we have changed. With the self-contained breathing apparatus we have temporarily become amphibians.

Test on Part 1

1. What proportion of the earth's surface is covered with water?
   A. One-half
   B. Five-sevenths
   C. Seven-tenths
2. Under water, we can hear the gurgle of exhaust bubbles from our air tank. Other than that, our ears hear
   A. animal noises
   B. nothing
   C. the splash of water
3. Seawater acts as a filter and absorbs all rays of light except
   A. red
   B. blue
   C. green
4. If we lost track of directions, we could tell which way is up by the
   A. way the seaweed grows
   B. rays of light from the sun
   C. direction of our air bubbles

Part 2. Three kinds of underwater divers

Skin diver is the proper term for a diver who does not use self-contained breathing equipment. His time under water is limited to the expiration of one chestful of air. *Helmet diver* refers to a diver who uses the traditional diving suit with its weighted boot and metal helmet, and lifeline and air line connecting them with the surface. The diver who uses self-contained breathing apparatus is known as a *scuba diver*. The term *scuba* is an abbreviation for the words self-contained underwater breathing apparatus.

Man has gladly and eagerly accepted the challenge of the deep. Every year more and more men and women join the ranks of scuba divers. However, the ease with which one learns to swim with breathing equipment is deceptive. The underwater world is not without its dangers. No one but a competent swimmer should attempt to dive. Even then, a complete course in the use of underwater breathing equipment is an absolute necessity. Those who are qualified must be constantly on guard for the unexpected. In the water fear, panic, and foolhardiness are the most likely killers. And, of course, no one should ever dive alone. Understanding and accepting these limitations must be the first step in conquering the deep.

Once we train ourselves to pass with ease through the watery looking-glass, we find a new world waiting to be discovered. We feel the thrill of adventure that comes with the sense of exploring the unknown. The sea has its sinister aspects, but it can also be exquisitely beautiful. It offers rare opportunities for sport and scientific exploration. It also hides many of the secrets of man's past.

For as long as man has lived on earth he has made good use of its many rivers, lakes, and seas. He drank the water, ate the fish and shellfish, and adorned himself with pearls, coral, and shells. He found it easier to travel by boat along a water route than to cross deserts, swamps, and mountains. At different times and places he even imagined the waters to be populated with gods, and he worshiped them. Whenever he lived on or near the shore he left clues to his past in the water. Archaeologists— men who study man's ancient, unwritten history—have long been aware of this. It is not surprising that with the invention of various kinds of underwater breathing apparatus has come a new method of investigating the history of man: underwater archaeology. The science is young, but in its short life it has caught the imagination of scores of divers.

Test on Part 2

Read each of the following items. If the statement is true, write the letter **T**; if the statement is false, write the letter **F**. Write your answers on your paper.

1. Skin divers do not use self-contained breathing equipment.
2. Helmet divers do not wear diving suits.
3. *Scuba* means "self-contained underwater breathing apparatus."
4. Underwater archaeology is a young science.

Part 3. Man discovers the sea

There is a legend that Alexander the Great descended in a diving bell and remained for several days to watch the activities of the sea creatures. He saw a sea serpent, so the story goes, that was so long it took four days to pass before his observation chamber. Today we do not believe in sea serpents, and we question the ability of anyone, even the mighty Alexander, to stay under water for such a long time in a diving bell. Still, it makes a good story and it would not be surprising to learn that Alexander, who supposedly cried when he had no more lands to conquer, had designs on the sea.

On February 15, 1954, the French naval engineer Pierre Wilm and his companion, Lieutenant Commander Georges Houot, looked out the window of their bathyscaphe and saw the bottom of the Atlantic Ocean at a depth of about two and a half miles (13,287 feet). They saw no sea serpents, but they did see a large-headed six-foot shark and a sea anemone.

The story connecting the ancient legend and the modern scientific miracle is the epic of man's conquest of the deep. Actually the story begins long before Alexander. It goes back to the dawn of prehistory, when glaciers covered most of the Northern Hemisphere.

The real exploitation of the sea began at the end of the last ice age, about ten thousand years ago. As the glaciers began to melt and the climate became warmer, many of the large animals, such as the mammoth and the woolly rhinoceros, became extinct. Others, like the reindeer, followed the glaciers and the cold weather to the north, where they have lived ever since. Forests grew up to cover the ground and give protection to new kinds of animals, such as the elk, the deer, and the wild pig. They were much harder to catch than the massive slow-moving ice-age mammals. European man found food hard to come by.

As a result he took to living along the shores of lakes and seas, where he could fish and hunt for clams and oysters. We know that in many regions shellfish were his major source of food. Archaeologists have excavated huge piles of the discarded shells that marked his prehistoric "kitchens." It was about this time that man invented such useful items as the fishhook, the canoe, the harpoon and line, nets, and fish traps.

We do not know when man first learned to swim and dive for shellfish. At first he must have found them in shallow water and in tidal pools. Nevertheless, to gather the oysters, clams, scallops, and other shellfish that he relished, he would have had to dive for them in deeper water, too.

Even when other types of food became more plentiful, man continued to dive. He made the discovery that the sea was a source of beauty as well as nourishment. Instead of discarding all of the shells, he kept the largest and prettiest for use as containers and oil lamps. Later he strung them on cords for necklaces and bracelets. Within the rough gray oystershell he found one of the loveliest of all gems, the pearl. The finest saltwater pearls have always come from the Persian Gulf, where they are found at depths of between thirty and sixty feet. Such a depth strains a naked diver to the limit of his physical endurance, and yet men dived for these pearl oysters at least forty centuries ago.

The ancient divers of the Mediterranean and the Persian Gulf, like those in primitive regions today, dived without the aid of equipment of any kind. Apparently they were able to descend to depths of sixty feet and more. Possibly they weighted themselves with heavy stones in order to plummet to the bottom with no waste of precious time. Or they may have dived with empty lungs, exhaling sharply before beginning their dive and then kicking hard for the bottom, just as the Pacific islanders do today. Their biggest problem was to hold their breath long enough to get to the bottom and do their job. To do this required a lifetime of training.

Today the most seasoned divers average between one and a half and two minutes under water on one breath. However, some almost unbelievable records have been made in recent years. In 1913 a Greek sponge diver descended to a depth of two hundred feet to tie a line on the lost anchor of an Italian battleship. Another diver is recorded as having held his breath for four minutes and forty-five seconds, but this was in shallow water without moving. In Japan, women pearl divers descend many times a day to depths of 145 feet.

Test on Part 3

1. As the glaciers began to melt, many of the large animals
    A. became extinct
    B. became smaller
    C. went south to a warmer climate
2. Man's first step in gathering food from the sea was
    A. the invention of the bow and arrow
    B. learning to swim and dive
    C. collecting food that the sea deposited near the shore
3. After eating shellfish, ancient man
    A. discarded all the shells
    B. ground up the shells
    C. used the shells for containers and decorations

Part 4. Goggles and masks

The second step in man's conquest of the deep came with the invention of various kinds of equipment that increased the efficiency of his dive and his time under water. The date that goggles were first used is not certain. But long before glass was known, divers made lenses of thin slices of tortoise shell, which when highly polished were transparent. Today the one absolutely indispensable item in diving is the watertight mask. There is a good reason why an eye covering was one of the first and most important of man's underwater inventions.

If you stand at the edge of a swimming pool you can see every detail on the bottom, even though the pool may be ten or eleven feet deep. The moment you put your head under water, however, your vision is cut to one or two very blurred feet. This is because your eye is constructed for sight in a world of air. There must be an air space in front of your eyes before they can focus on an image. This can be accomplished with either watertight goggles or a mask. Goggles, however, had two main defects: more

often than not the two lenses caused the diver to see double; and they collapsed painfully against the face under the pressure of a deep dive.

The idea behind today's masks, which consist of one large glass plate that covers the nose as well as the eyes, did not develop until the late 1930s. The single glass plate eliminates the problem of double vision. The diver is able to equalize the pressure of the water during a deep dive by exhaling air into the mask. Even though the mask makes objects appear larger and nearer than they are, it opens man's eyes to the wonders of the underwater world by giving it the appearance and clarity of an immense aquarium.

Test on Part 4

1. Man's second step in conquering the deep was the invention
    A. of equipment to increase his efficiency under water
    B. of tortoise-shell goggles
    C. of a mask consisting of one large glass plate
2. Before glass was known, divers made lenses or goggles of
    A. tortoise shell
    B. snail shell
    C. plastic
3. Today's masks make objects under water appear
    A. larger and nearer than they are
    B. farther away and smaller than they are
    C. a different color

Part 5. Snorkels and helmets

Another object that has come to be closely associated with the modern skin diver is his rubber breathing tube, or snorkel. The idea of the breathing tube occurs in nature. There is a species of fly that spends the first stage of its life under water as a maggot. It breathes by means of a tail-like projection that is nothing more or less than a breathing tube. Elephants have also been observed snorkeling. Although it is difficult to imagine that these ponderous beasts can swim, they have been seen completely submerged except for the trunk, which is held above water for breathing. The Greeks knew about elephants, and possibly got the idea of a breathing tube from watching them in water. At any rate, they made great use of breathing tubes, as did the Romans centuries later. Like many another invention, it was developed as an aid to warfare.

Almost everyone has read of an exciting escape during which the hero hid from his enemies in shallow waters by breathing through a reed. Reeds were probably the first breathing tubes. Not only did they enable the swimmer to hide from his enemies; they also enabled him to engage in one of the oldest and most effective of military tactics, the sneak attack. As early as the time of Alexander the Great, swimmers carried messages into blockaded ports, destroyed enemy defenses, and bored holes in enemy ships. Occasionally they were met by enemy swimmers, and there are records of several early underwater battles.

The earliest known diving helmet made use of a breathing tube that was kept afloat by an attached inflated bladder. It was probably invented early in the sixteenth century, but we have no record of whether it was ever used. Such a device would have been absolutely useless at depths of more than four or five feet. Below five feet the pressure is so great that air cannot be drawn down through the tube, nor the exhausted air blown out.

The snorkel used today is essentially the same as that used in ancient times, except that reed has been replaced by rubber. It is useful only for skimming along the surface, but it does permit the swimmer to breathe while his face is under water.

The trademark of the modern skin diver is his rubber foot fins. These fins add about 40 percent more power to the foot stroke and make it possible for the diver to move easily without having to use his hands. Although not as old as the mask and snorkel, various versions of hand fins and foot fins were designed by Leonardo da Vinci in the sixteenth century and Benjamin Franklin in the eighteenth century. The kind used today was first patented by the Frenchman Louis de Corlieu in 1933.

Test on Part 5

1. The idea of the breathing tube
   A. appears in nature
   B. does not appear in nature
   C. is not practical

2. The snorkel that is used today
   A. cannot be used more than five feet below the surface
   B. is useful only for skimming along the surface
   C. can be used at great depths
3. Rubber foot fins add about how much power to the foot stroke?
   A. 20 percent
   B. 40 percent
   C. 60 percent
4. Various kinds of foot fins were designed as early as
   A. the twelfth century
   B. the seventeenth century
   C. the sixteenth century

Part 6. Carrying air below the surface

The ancients of the Mediterranean must be given credit for taking the third step toward conquering the deep. They were the first to experiment with methods of carrying a supply of air below the surface. The Greeks have been credited with inventing the diving bell. According to the Greek philosopher Aristotle, diving bells were used very successfully during Alexander the Great's siege of the Phoenician port of Tyre in 333 B.C. With them his swimmers were able to destroy underwater obstacles intended to prevent the Greek fleet from entering the harbor. These bells were also used by Greek sponge fishermen.

The principle of the diving bell is simplicity itself. Plunge a glass, mouth down, into a container of water and you will see that air is trapped inside the glass. The Greeks submerged huge pottery vases and suspended them from their ships or floats. The divers, at work under water, could pop up under the inverted cones as often as they needed for a fresh supply of air. The only way to replenish the air in the diving bell, however, was to haul the whole heavy contraption to the surface.

There was a gap of over two thousand years before an English astronomer, Sir Edmund Halley (known for the comet that bears his name), finally invented a means of carrying air from the surface down to the diving bell. Two thirty-six-gallon barrels filled with air were attached to the diving bell by an arrangement of counterweights and pulleys. Each barrel had a hole in the bottom and an air hose extending from the top. So long as the air hose hung lower than the hole on the bottom, the water pressure prevented the air from escaping. To transfer air from the barrel to the inside of the bell, the diver lifted the open end of the hose to the top of the bell and the air flowed in. The continuous raising and lowering of the barrels kept the divers supplied with fresh air.

The next step was to substitute a hose and pump for Halley's barrels. This was accomplished in 1771 by John Smeaton, an English civil engineer. Further improvements were made, until the simple device invented by the Greeks had become the huge caisson used today in excavating and in laying foundations for bridges, subways, and tunnels. The modern version of the diving bell is a large chamber into which compressed air is pumped. The men who work in these caissons are known as sandhogs. The strange sickness that sometimes attacks them became known as caisson disease, or the bends.

Edmund Halley can also be credited with the invention of the first functional diving helmet. It was a combination of diving bell and helmet suit. The diver wore a wooden helmet, which was linked by a pipe to a submerged air-filled tub. The diver soon exhausted the air in the tub, however, and had to come to the surface for a new supply. The breakthrough came in June 1797, when the German scientist Otto Klingert constructed a tin helmet with pipes leading to the surface. For the first time, air was forced down through the pipe to the mouthpiece of the helmet by a pair of bellows. In 1819 a German scientist working in England, Augustus Siebe, adapted Klingert's idea to a diving suit with a removable metal headpiece attached to a waterproof jacket. Compressed air entered the helmet by an intake valve. The excess air flowed down into the jacket and escaped around the waist. The trouble with this suit was that the diver could not bend over without getting water into his helmet. In 1837 Siebe solved the problem by inventing the closed diving suit, with both intake and outlet valves in the helmet. The idea was so successful that it became the model for all later helmet suits.

Those who have followed Captain Nemo's adventures in Jules Verne's classic *Twenty Thousand Leagues Under the Sea* usually credit the author with a rich but unscientific imagination. Actually the underwater breathing apparatus that he described was far from imaginary. It was invented in 1863. The diver carried on his back a tank that was filled with air forced down through a pipe. It was quite possible for a diver using this contraption to detach the pump line and walk about freely, as long as the air supply in the tank held out. This device was introduced to the sponge divers of the Aegean in 1866. It was used with such success that it is surprising that it never became popular. The reason probably lies in the fact that the Siebe suit, invented earlier, had more and better publicity.

In 1879 an independent underwater breathing apparatus was devised that used pure oxygen. Its inventor was an English merchant seaman by the name of Henry Fleuss. The diver carried a tank of oxygen on his back. This was connected to his rubber face mask by two breathing tubes. The air in the system was used over and over again. The exhaled air simply passed through a bag containing caustic potash, which absorbed the waste carbon dioxide. It was replenished with oxygen and was again ready for use. A type of oxygen "rebreathing" unit was used with great success by U.S., British, and Italian frogmen during World War II. Since no air escapes, there is no telltale trail of bubbles on the surface. When divers began experimenting with this device at depths below thirty feet, however, they found that oxygen under pressure causes frightful convulsions and even death.

The direct ancestor of the modern compressed-air diving lung was invented by Commandant Yves Le Prieur of the French navy. The bottle of compressed air was strapped on the side of the diver. The air, which passed through an air pipe to a full face mask, was released by means of a hand valve.

In 1943 Captain Jacques-Yves Cousteau hit upon a means of improving the Le Prieur apparatus. He asked the French engineer Émile Gagnan to devise a fully automatic regulator that would feed the proper amount of air to the diver regardless of his position. Gagnan made his regulator from a plastic valve, the kind used on the gas tanks of French wartime automobiles. Cousteau and Gagnan patented the device, which became an integral part of the now famous aqualung. With it man was really free for the first time to explore the underwater world.

Test for Part 6

1. The third step in conquering the deep was
   A. carrying air below the surface
   B. discovered by Edmund Halley
   C. the invention of the diving helmet
2. Diving bells were used as early as
   A. the sixteenth century
   B. the fourth century
   C. the fourth century B.C.
3. The principle of the diving bell is
   A. not fully understood
   B. complicated
   C. simple
4. The first functional diving helmet was invented by
   A. Edmund Halley
   B. John Smeaton
   C. Otto Klingert
5. Oxygen under pressure
   A. is used up quickly
   B. leaves a trail of bubbles
   C. causes convulsions and death

Part 7. Diving suits and bathyscaphes

Another of the problems man faced in the water was that of keeping himself warm. This is because water, being a better conductor than air, quickly drains off body heat. The warm-blooded aquatic mammals are equipped by nature with an insulating layer of blubber. Man had to devise his own insulation.

Any form of body covering is a help, but the best protection is afforded by an exposure suit. There are two types, wet and dry. The dry suit is made of thin rubber and must be watertight. Woolen clothing is usually worn underneath for additional warmth. The wet suit, made of foam neoprene, gets its name from the fact that a small amount of water enters the suit. This water is quickly warmed to body temperature. Since neoprene is an excellent insulator, the diver is as comfortable as if he were swimming in a warm bath.

A completely different type of diving suit, invented in 1923, was made entirely of metal and had movable arms and legs. It was strong enough to withstand the water pressure of moderate depths, with the result that the air pressure inside the suit could be the same as at the surface. It was a clumsy contraption and the diver's movements were limited, but in it a man could work as deep as three hundred feet for an hour or more and still ascend rapidly to the surface with no ill effects.

Exploration at even greater depths was begun by the American naturalist William Beebe. He designed a research ship called a bathysphere, which was a hollow steel ball able to endure tremendous pressure. It was suspended by a heavy steel cable from a ship on the surface. In it, in 1934, Beebe reached a depth of 3028 feet off the coast of Bermuda. From his little observation window he viewed weird deep-sea creatures never before seen by man.

Further explorations were made in the bathyscaphe designed by the Swiss physicist Auguste Piccard, who had earlier become famous by ascending in a balloon to a height of 53,152 feet. Piccard made his first descent in the bathyscaphe in 1948. In fact, the bathyscaphe operates on the same principle as a balloon; it is completely independent of the surface, having no cable line.

Gas in a balloon makes it lighter than air. Bags of sand were carried during early balloon ascensions to weight the balloon and control its rate of ascent. To make the balloon rise, some of the sand was thrown overboard. In order to descend, gas was released from the balloon, making it less buoyant.

It is a high-grade gasoline carried in a large tank above the observation chamber that makes the bathyscaphe much lighter than water. Iron shot held to the bottom of the bathyscaphe by a powerful electromagnet gives it weight. All that is necessary to make the depth ship rise once again to the surface is to release the load of iron shot.

In January 1960 another bathyscaphe, the *Trieste*, with Jacques Piccard and U. S. Navy Lieutenant Don Walsh aboard, plunged 35,800 feet (over six miles) into the Marianas Trench near Guam.

Jacques-Yves Cousteau has written that "the aqualung is primitive and unworthy of contemporary levels of science." Lieutenant Commander Houot and Pierre Wilm have described the bathyscaphe as a "prototype, a blind, clumsy, limping monster." We are only at the frontier of the underwater world. As this book is being written, scientists are designing new and better kinds of equipment with which to continue their explorations. The last chapter in man's conquest of the deep will be an exciting one and as challenging as the conquest of the moon and the planets.

If you have just read the article for the first time, skip this test on Part 7 and take the test on the whole article, which follows.

Test on Part 7

1. Water quickly drains off body heat because it is
    A. a better conductor than air
    B. a slower conductor than air
    C. a better insulator than air
2. Exposure suits are of two types,
    A. wet and dry
    B. wool and metal
    C. wool and rubber
3. Piccard, who designed the bathyscaphe, was already famous for his
    A. invention of the metal diving suit
    B. flights in balloons
    C. invention of the foam neoprene suit

4. The bathyscaphe carried high-grade gasoline
    A. to make it lighter than water
    B. for power
    C. to make it heavier than water

Test on the whole article

Read each test item and choose the answer you believe is correct. Print your answers on your paper.

1. The main idea of this article is
    A. that man knows nothing about the sea
    B. that man cannot learn any more about the sea
    C. that man can adapt to the underwater world
2. When we swim under water, we find that our senses are
    A. adequate
    B. sharper than on land
    C. inadequate
3. Cousteau wrote that "the aqualung is primitive and unworthy of contemporary levels of science." This means that the aqualung is
    A. not safe and should be used as little as possible
    B. out of date and cannot be of any value
    C. only the beginning and that science should invent more efficient tools

Practice Reading 7

In a book, magazine, or newspaper that you like, practice reading for speed and comprehension. Make a record of this reading in Chart 3 on page 8 in your progress folder.

Read Article 7 and take the reading test. Then follow up your answers to the test. Reread each test item that you answered incorrectly. Then, in the article, find and read the statement or statements that give the correct answer to the test item.

7
article

Whales — the world's largest animals[4]

"There she blows!" the men in the fast catcher boat probably shouted in Japanese when they sighted the big blue whale.

In January 1949 a group of twelve whaling ships from Japan were hunting near the Balleny Islands in the Antarctic Ocean. These ships had a total of 1300 men in their crews.

When the catcher boat was near the blue whale, its gunner shot the first harpoon. It hit, sinking deep into the whale's body. To escape, the whale dived under water. After two hours of fighting, the whale tired, and the gunner killed it with another harpoon. The catcher boat then towed the whale tailfirst to the factory ship.

At the factory ship an engine pulled the whale up to the deck. There eighty men cut the whale into pieces. They weighed each piece. The tongue alone was three tons. The heart was half a ton. In the rooms below deck other men removed oils from the whale fat. From this one whale the men drew 133 barrels of oil and sixty tons of red meat. The meat alone was enough to make 800,000 "whaleburger" sandwiches. The men also took vitamin oil from the whale's liver. From leftover bones and meat they made fertilizer.

This blue whale was one of the largest ever caught. It weighed 150 tons, or 300,000 pounds—more than the total weight of

the population of a small city of 3000. The whale was ninety feet long—about as tall as a ten-story building. If its jaws had been opened and set on end, a grown elephant could have walked through them. This was truly "a whale of a whale."

Whales are the largest animals in the world. In fact, they are the largest animals that ever lived.

Whales, however, differ greatly in size. Largest of all is the blue whale. The male reaches a length of about one hundred feet. Next-largest is the finback whale, about eighty feet long. The Greenland whale, the Atlantic right whale, the Southern right whale, and the sperm whale are about sixty feet long.

The humpback whale and the sei whale are fifty feet from head to tail. The narwhal, the whale with the long tusk, is fifteen to twenty feet long.

But all whales are alike in many important ways. They are warm-blooded. They breathe air. And they are mammals. The female whale brings forth her young alive. She also suckles and cares for her baby.

Every whale has a rounded and streamlined body. It has a broad, flat tail that is horizontal, not vertical as is that of a fish. In swimming and diving the whale mainly uses its tail. At the front of its body it has two paddle-shaped limbs called flippers. It uses them to balance and to steer itself.

Beneath its skin the whale has a thick layer of fatty tissue known as blubber. This blubber keeps the whale warm when it is in near-freezing waters. It supplies the

4 Reprinted by permission of Hawthorn Books, Inc., from *The Animal Kingdom* (Frederick Drimmer, editor in chief), Volume I: *Mammals*, by George C. Goodwin. Copyright 1954 by the Greystone Press.

whale with food when it is in food-scarce waters. And it keeps the whale from being crushed by water pressure when it dives.

A large whale can live as long as fifty to sixty years. Because of whale hunters, however, its average life span is usually short—about twenty years.

How does a whale breathe?

A whale must breathe air and stay in water to keep alive. If it gets its lungs full of water, it drowns from lack of oxygen. While a whale is in the water, the water helps to hold up its heavy body so that it can breathe easily. But when a whale is on land, its heavy body presses in on its lungs so that it cannot breathe in enough air.

The whale has on top of its head an opening called a blowhole. It always breathes through its blowhole. It cannot breathe through its mouth.

The lungs hold a large amount of air. Because of this, a whale can stay under water for as long as forty-five minutes. A man can stay under water for only about three minutes.

The whale's body heats the air in its lungs and fills the air with moisture. When the whale forces this warm damp air out through its blowhole, this air hits the colder outside air, forming a column of white water vapor. This column, called a spout, is what whaling men look for. When they see such a spout, they cry, "There she blows!"

What are the two main kinds of whales?

Whales are divided into two main kinds—the toothed whales and the whalebone whales.

A toothed whale has cone-shaped teeth. It uses these teeth to catch and hold food—squids, fish, and other sea animals. It swallows its food whole. It has a large mouth and throat. Among the toothed whales are the sperm whale, the narwhal, and the killer whale.

A whalebone whale has whalebone instead of teeth. Whalebone, sometimes called baleen, is not bone; it is a strong horny material.

In its large mouth the whalebone whale has hundreds of long thin whalebone blades. They hang in two long rows on each side of the mouth. The edges of these blades have stiff bristles. Inside, the whale's mouth looks somewhat like the thick wool of a sheep.

When the whalebone whale feeds, it swims along with its big mouth open. The bristles of its whalebone blades catch plankton—very small sea animals and plants. Then the whale closes its mouth and pushes its huge tongue against the whalebone blades. These blades are a strainer. They let the water out but hold the plankton in. Then the whale swallows this food.

The whalebone whale's throat is no larger than a man's fist. By constantly eating, this whale is able to get the large quantity of food that it needs. A large whale eats about a ton of food a day.

What is the killer whale?

All of the larger whales are mild and gentle animals except when they are harpooned. The strong killer whale, however, is one of the fiercest and most dangerous of all wild animals. Like a pack of wolves on land, a school of killer whales hunts in the sea. They will attack, kill, and eat a seal, a walrus cub, a big fish, or even a larger whale.

What is the sperm whale?

One of the best known of all whales is the sperm whale, or cachalot. Moby Dick was such a whale.

The sperm whale is peace-loving most of the time. When this animal has been wounded, however, it has used its body or its tail to crush a small whaleboat. And with its mighty head, it has pushed in the side of a large wooden whaling ship.

The sperm whale's head has a large pocket filled with a white oily material. Scientists believe that this pocket is a cushion that protects the animal from the great pressures far under water. The sperm whale goes down as deep as 3000 feet; there the pressure is 1400 pounds to the square inch.

For many years men have hunted the sperm whale to get the valuable oil from its head. Fine sperm oil is used to lubricate watches and sewing machines, for example.

Should whales be protected?

For hundreds of years men have hunted whales. In some places they have killed so many whales that certain kinds have been in danger of extinction.

As men have found better ways to hunt whales, they have increased the yearly catch. To protect whales, a number of nations have worked out rules for whale hunting. Whalers are allowed to catch only so many whales each year. They are not allowed to kill a calf, or a cow that has a calf. Such rules may save the world's largest animals from extinction.

Record your finishing time in the time box. Then take the reading test.

Read each test item and choose the answer you believe is correct. Print your answers in the answer record on page 4 of the progress folder.

Reading Test 7

Getting main ideas

1. An important idea in this article is that
   - A. there are no rules for whale hunting
   - B. whales should be protected by hunting rules
   - C. no one knows very much about whales
   - D. only a hundred or so whales are now living
   - E. only the Japanese know how to hunt whales

2. The author says
   - A. there is only one kind of whale
   - B. whales differ only in size
   - C. there are several kinds of whales
   - D. whales differ only in color
   - E. whales differ only in eating habits

3. This article was written to
   - A. frighten you
   - B. inform you
   - C. puzzle you
   - D. amuse you
   - E. surprise you

4. The tongue of the blue whale can weigh as much as
   - A. thirty-three hundred tons
   - B. thirty pounds
   - C. three tons
   - D. thirty ounces
   - E. thirty tons

5. The heart of the blue whale weighs
   - A. more than the tongue
   - B. as much as the tongue
   - C. as much as the tail
   - D. more than the tail
   - E. less than the tongue

6. The ship on which workers remove oils from the whale fat is known as the

    A. fat ship
    B. home ship
    C. oil ship
    D. factory ship
    E. light ship

7. One of these statements about whales is *not* true:

    A. They are warm-blooded.
    B. They are mammals.
    C. They live for about a hundred years.
    D. They breathe air.
    E. They suckle and care for their young.

8. The hole on the top of a whale's head is known as the

    A. blowhole
    B. air hole
    C. hatch
    D. nose hole
    E. vent

9. The column of white water vapor a whale makes is known as a

    A. spout
    B. snout
    C. crout
    D. lout
    E. bout

10. The oil from a sperm whale is used to lubricate

    A. tanks
    B. trucks
    C. airplanes
    D. watches
    E. motorboats

11. To balance and steer itself, a whale has

    A. keels
    B. oarlocks
    C. flippers
    D. rudders
    E. gears

12. A whalebone whale's throat is no larger than a man's

    A. head
    B. body
    C. eye
    D. little finger
    E. fist

Choosing the best reason

13. A whale drowns if its lungs are full of water, because of lack of

    A. oxygen
    B. blubber
    C. plankton
    D. sperm oil
    E. food

14. When a whale is on land, its heavy body presses in on its lungs so that it cannot

    A. move
    B. use its flippers
    C. form a column of white water vapor
    D. roll over
    E. breathe

15. A whale can stay under water for forty-five minutes, because of the size of its

    A. tail
    B. flippers
    C. tongue
    D. lungs
    E. head

Knowing word meanings

16. The *blubber* of a whale is

    A. its large head
    B. the thick layer of fatty tissue
    C. its outer skin
    D. the oil it gives
    E. its broad, flat tail

17. A *harpoon* is

    A. a small whale
    B. a spear
    C. a man who hunts whales
    D. the heart of a blue whale
    E. the outer skin of a whale

18. We speak of a *pack of wolves* and a

    A. brood of whales
    B. flock of whales
    C. covey of whales
    D. party of whales
    E. school of whales

Noting word relationships

19. *Elephants* are to the *land* as *whales* are to

    A. the sea
    B. a harpoon
    C. a whaleboat
    D. the Japanese fleet
    E. a factory ship

20. A *deer* is to a *bullet* as a *whale* is to

    A. a gunner
    B. a squid
    C. a whaleboat
    D. a walrus
    E. a harpoon

Follow the directions (Steps 8–13) on page 1 of the progress folder.

How to think about what you read

"I like to ask myself questions and then answer them," said one young lady.

"Why?" asked her friend.

"I can be sure of hearing good questions and getting intelligent answers," was the reply.

Although this young lady set too high a value on her own ability, she was doing something that every good reader must do. Part of good reading is asking questions such as these:

How can the writer say this? Didn't he just say the opposite a few pages back? Is the writer really proving his point, or is he just giving an opinion?

Good reading is an active process

The experts do not agree on how many different reading skills there are. Some have mentioned as many as fifty skills. This is probably too high an estimate, but it suggests that when you read you are *doing* a great many things.

Let's say that to begin with you recognize words on a page. Then you put these words together into groups. When words like *that*, *this*, *these*, and *they* are used, you connect them with the words for which they stand. You recognize punctuation marks and use them as clues to the author's meaning.

If you are reading well, you sort out general statements from those that give details. You follow the time order in a narrative. You note the author's clues so that you see his organization—his first, second, third points.

In reading even the simplest passage, you are doing a great many things. You are being very active. If you are to read effectively, you must be alert. Your mind is not a container into which words, facts, and ideas are thrown.

Exercise 26

A writer may frequently make a comparison to help his readers. He may say, "His mind is like a sponge." The reader's job, then, is to fill in the details. He must ask himself, "What is a sponge like? How can a person's mind be like a sponge?"

These comparisons can be subtle. The reader must search out the exact meaning of each. Using the word *sponge*, the following story illustrates some clues the writer might use. The alert reader will be able to complete the picture by filling in the details that the writer has implied.

"Hello," said Harry into the phone. "I wonder if I could come over for dinner?"

He waited for a moment, then added, "Fine, I'll be right over."

He put down the phone and dashed madly into the bathroom. There was no time for a shower, so he took a quick sponge bath.

When he arrived, the hostess was preparing the dough for bread. Harry started to press a finger into the spongelike loaf, but the hostess chased him out of the kitchen.

In the living room he found one of the children playing with a toy cannon. Lying beside the cannon was a long-handled sponge.

"What's this for?" asked Harry.

"That's the sponge," said the boy, snatching it from him.

The host came downstairs and went into the kitchen.

"Boy, what a sponge that Harry is!" he said to his wife.

A writer depends a great deal on his reader to supply the missing parts of his story. The above shows concentrated use of the word *sponge*. It illustrates the many possible ways a writer can suggest word pictures. You, as the reader, must develop the picture.

Harry first calls and invites himself to dinner. He is sponging off his friends. This suggests the kind of person he might be. In a hurry to get a free meal, Harry takes a quick sponge bath. The spongelike dough suggests two pictures. One is of the appearance and texture of the dough. The other suggests a hostess who does not mind the extra effort of baking her own bread. Another glimpse of Harry's manner is shown when he pokes a finger into the dough. The little boy has a sponge attached to a stick, with which he pretends to clean his toy cannon. The sponge cleans the barrel of the cannon after each shot. The host expresses his opinion of Harry by calling him a sponge.

In such ways a writer communicates with his reader. But you must help him.

Most of the above references are familiar to all of us. The sponge is an animal. It is among the most primitive of animals. It has no brain, no nerves. It cannot move; it is fastened to a rock or to the bottom of the ocean. It soaks up its food by absorbing substances from the water that passes through it.

The good reader reads to answer questions

Part 1

Some of the questions a good reader answers are elementary. They are so simple, in fact, that he may not even be aware of asking them. The following questions are of this sort.

On your paper, write "yes" or "no" to each of the following questions.
1. Is the sponge an animal?
2. Is the sponge a water animal?
3. Is the sponge intelligent?
4. Does the sponge move from place to place?

Test questions that can be answered "yes" or "no" are often the simplest kind.

A more difficult and important kind of question is the one that seeks out reasons and causes. To answer questions of this sort, you have to tie together two or more details from your reading. You have to organize what you know and what you are reading. Can you write your answers to these questions?

Part 2

1. Why doesn't the sponge have to work for its food?
2. If you cut a sponge with a knife, it feels no pain. Why?
3. No sponge ever tries to swim away from a sponge diver. Why?

The correct answers are shown in the answer key.

A third kind of question deals with likenesses and differences. We can explain or describe new things, new experiences, new people, new facts, and new events by showing how they are like something we already know. In 1947, for example, when the first reports of unidentified flying objects were made, the observers said the objects were "shaped like saucers." When the pilots of an Eastern Airlines plane met a strange flying object in the sky, they said it was "shaped like a cigar."

The good reader is able to find the facts he needs

In reading to answer a question, you often have to go through a great many facts that have little or no bearing on what you are looking for. You have to size up the details, pass by those that are not related to your problem, and select those you need. In this way you are looking for likenesses and rejecting differences.

You will use this skill in solving practical problems in arithmetic—problems of everyday life. You will also read for details in many kinds of schoolwork.

Exercise 27

Read the problem below. You will note a number of details you must attend to and others you should disregard in order to answer the following questions.

How much change did the clerk give me? Was the change correct?

Answer the questions. Then write the number of each statement that helped you find the answer.

1 Last Saturday I went into town to buy groceries. **2** At the store, I pushed one of the carts around and loaded it with what I needed. **3** Some of the things I bought were a pound of coffee (87 cents), a pound of bacon (53 cents), and a quart of milk (21 cents). **4** At the checkout counter I watched closely as the clerk entered each item on the cash register. **5** When he finished, he handed me the sales slip; it read $11.43. **6** Because I needed extra money, I made out a check for $20.00. **7** The date was October 2. **8** I handed the check to the clerk and he gave me the following in change: two pennies; one nickel; one half dollar; three one-dollar bills; and one five-dollar bill.

The correct answers are shown in the answer key.

The good reader questions what he reads and compares it with his own experience

As readers, we are bombarded from all sides by stories of fact, fiction, and fantasy. It is sometimes difficult to separate one from the other. Your newspaper lists thousands of facts in reporting daily happenings around the world. Magazines contain lengthy reports on items of general interest. The books you read vary from textbooks to science fiction and stories of fantasy.

In fiction or fantasy you accept the author's flights of imagination. You may find the story dull or exciting, but you know that it is only a story. It may be based on historical facts or an authentic experience. The author, however, shapes the facts to make his story more interesting.

You may read other books and articles that claim to be true. The author may list facts and figures to prove his story. To the uneducated, the printing of these facts in a book or article is proof enough.

"It must be true. I read it in a book," you will sometimes hear people say.

The good reader brings a questioning mind to his reading. If you read with care, you question many of the statements you read in books and magazines. You put some reports in a "doubtful column" and wait for more facts. You question them because they do not fit in with your previous experience.

We have already mentioned "unidentified flying objects" and we will discuss them later in the chapter. But here is some background information for you.

A few years ago the newspapers carried many stories about "UFOs" (unidentified flying objects). People all over the United States reported seeing strange objects flying in the sky at night. Some were described as cigar-shaped; others were said to be shaped like saucers. Most of them glowed with a strange light.

Opinion was divided as to the existence of these UFOs. The nonbelievers scoffed at the idea that spaceships from another planet were visiting the earth. They demanded proof. The people who believed in flying saucers formed organizations to compare and investigate all reports. Their investigations made them only more certain that the UFOs were spaceships from another planet. They wrote and published books and articles to prove their theories.

Airline pilots, who can be considered trained observers, reported that they had seen UFOs. When the arguments pro and con had reached their climax, the government decided to investigate. All the information was gathered together, checked out, and evaluated. The final report stated that as yet there was no actual proof of the existence of the reported flying saucers. Since then, there have been very few reports of UFOs.

If you were following these arguments in the newspapers and books, how would you test the truth of these stories? First, you might say that never in your experience have you seen a flying saucer. And you probably do not know anyone who has seen one. But then, there are many things you have not seen—an atom, for example.

Second, you might say that until more definite proof is offered, you will reserve your opinion. You might go on to ask questions like these:

1. Why is it that no one has seen these

flying saucers land on the earth?

2. Why have they been seen only at night?

3. Could natural phenomena, such as the northern lights, cause people to think they have seen flying saucers?

In asking questions such as these and in questioning a report, you are doing critical thinking.

Check what you read against your experience. Suppose you are reading for the first time that water expands when it freezes. You begin thinking how cold it it was last winter. You remember how the milk froze on the back porch and pushed up the cap of the bottle. It suddenly occurs to you that there must be water in milk. How will you find the answer?

If you read carefully, you draw from your memory to explain new facts and ideas you meet in reading. And the other way around: you use what you read to explain things that have happened to you in the past.

Bringing your experience into reading

Exercise 28

Late in life P. T. Barnum, the circus man, made a speech in the town of his birth, recalling his boyhood days. He said:

"I am surprised to find that I can distinctly remember events which occurred before I was four years old. . . .

"Rainwater was caught and used for washing, while that for cooking and drinking was drawn from wells with their old oaken bucket and long poles and well sweeps.

"Fire was kept overnight by banking up the brands in ashes in the fireplace, and if it went out one neighbor would visit another about daylight the next morning with a pair of tongs to borrow a coal of fire to kindle with. . . . Homemade soft soap was used for washing hands, faces, and everything else. The children in families of ordinary circumstances ate their meals on trenchers [wooden plates]. As I grew older, our family and others got an extravagant streak, discarded the trenchers,

and rose to the dignity of pewter plates and leaden spoons.

"Our dinners several times each week consisted of beef, salt pork, and vegetables, all boiled together in the same big iron pot.

"In the pot with the salt pork, potatoes, turnips, parsnips, beets, cabbage, and sometimes onions was placed an Indian pudding, consisting of plain Indian meal, mixed in water, pretty thick, salted, and poured into a homemade brown linen bag which was tied at the top.

"When dinner was ready, the Indian pudding was first taken from the pot, slipped out of the bag, and eaten with molasses. Then followed the beef and vegetables."[1]

A vocabulary test

In this selection there are clues to the meaning of many words and expressions that we now take for granted. If you have ever heard these expressions before, perhaps they have more meaning for you now. The next time you hear them, they will mean more if you recall this reading experience.

Read each test item and choose the answer you believe is correct. Print your answers on your paper.

1. The *old oaken bucket* was used
   A. to catch rainwater
   B. to lift water out of a well
   C. for cooking dinners
2. To *bank up a fire* means to
   A. make it burn rapidly
   B. soak it with water
   C. cover it so that it will burn slowly and evenly
3. The *brands in ashes in the fireplace* are
   A. pieces of burning wood
   B. irons used for branding
   C. pieces of unburned wood
4. ". . . our family got an *extravagant streak*"
   A. eager
   B. apparent
   C. unthrifty

The correct answers are shown in the answer key.

---

1 Quoted in *Barnum*, by M. R. Werner, Harcourt, Brace & World. Reprinted by permission.

Drawing conclusions

In your reading you will occasionally come upon reports containing a great many facts without any conclusion as to what these facts means. This is true of many government reports. It is often true of newspaper stories. Indeed, some newspapers pride themselves on presenting the facts without expressing an opinion, so that the reader can make up his mind for himself.

The question the reader has to answer is "What do all these facts mean?" or "What general explanation will cover them all?" In drawing a conclusion, you must be sure that (1) you have enough facts; (2) the facts really support the conclusion; and (3) you have taken into account the important facts.

Exercise 29

Suppose that in several different articles you have come across these facts:

1. If you watch a sailing ship going away from shore on the ocean, the ship becomes smaller and smaller, then the hull is hidden, and finally the top of its mast disappears.
2. If you see the shadow of the earth on the moon during an eclipse, the shadow is curved.
3. Because a television beam goes in a straight line, you have trouble getting a picture fifty miles from the TV station.

From these facts, which of the following conclusions can you correctly draw?

1. The sun is much brighter than the moon.
2. The moon and the earth go round the sun.
3. The earth is shaped like a ball.
4. The sun bends a television beam.
5. A TV station is much taller than a ship.

The correct answer is shown in the answer key.

The good reader knows how to evaluate an opinion

If someone says "This ruler is warped," you can pick up the ruler, look at it, and test its straightness.

If someone says "Babe Ruth hit sixty home runs in 1927," you can go to the *World Almanac* or some other reference book and check the facts.

These are statements of *fact*. They can be tested by going to the records or by examining the object in question. Scientists check statements of fact by performing experiments in their laboratories.

But suppose someone says, "I think we should lower the age for voting." Or someone tells you, "All high school students should be required to take driver training."

You cannot test these statements by experiments with test tubes, or by looking up facts in almanacs. These statements are opinions. They are someone's judgment of a situation.

We cannot test opinions in the same way we test statements of fact. But we can evaluate them. We can ask three questions about them: Who says so? Why does he say so? How does he know?

Who says so?

- Is the speaker an authority on the subject, or is he talking from a superficial knowledge?
- Is the speaker well known?
- Is he a person with a reputation for honesty and wisdom? Has he been right in similar situations before?

Why does he say so?

- Is he interested in getting people to know the truth?
- Is he trying to get people to do something from which he will benefit?
- Is he just trying to attract attention to himself?

How does he know?

- Is he guessing?
- Does he have facts that other people do not have?
- Has he had special experiences that other people have not had?
- Has he studied the problem more than other people have?
- Does he have special sources of information?

Identifying opinion

Exercise 30

Here is a report on a baseball game as it might appear in a school newspaper. The reporter is a student at the school. Each of the sentences is numbered for easy reference. First read the report all the way through, disregarding the numbers. Then do the exercise that follows.

1. Last Saturday was the day of the big game between Eastview High and Lakeside High. **2.** The entire student body had hoped for a sunny day. **3.** They were all disappointed. **4.** It was a cold, cloudy day. **5.** The game got off to a slow start, and the first three innings were scoreless. **6.** In the fourth inning Ted Clay got on base with a single to left field. **7.** He is one of the best hitters on the team. **8.** Al Nester drove him home for the first run with a three-base hit. **9.** Following him, Hank Neely hit into a double play. **10.** The umpire called him out, but we think he was safe. **11.** Everyone in the stands booed the umpire. **12.** Eastview held its one-run lead up to the ninth inning. **13.** Then Lakeside's Al Levy got lucky. **14.** He hit a line drive and stopped at third base. **15.** You could feel the tension in the air as the next batter came up. **16.** After two strikes he ended the ball game with a home run to left field. **17.** Final score: Lakeside 2, Eastview 1.

Write the numerals 1 to 17 on your paper. Read again each of the above sentences. Write **F** for each sentence that is a statement of fact. Write **O** for each sentence that expresses an opinion.

The correct answers are shown in the answer key.

Evaluating Opinion

Exercise 31—Part 1

Read the newspaper story below. The *story* was written in 1955 by the United Press, a news service agency. The *headline* was written by the *Chicago Sun-Times*.

2 Adapted from the *Chicago Sun-Times*, October 26, 1955. Copyright 1955, by the United Press International.

Study Calls Flying Saucers a Myth[2]

WASHINGTON (UP)—The Air Force wound up an eight-year study of flying saucers by concluding there is no such thing.

Air Secretary Donald A. Quarles said Tuesday an investigation of almost 5000 "saucer" sightings produced "no evidence of the existence of the popularly termed flying saucers." He made public a 216-page book summarizing the inquiry.

The flying saucer study, called Project Blue Book and dating to mid-1947, showed that the Air Force is now able to identify as balloons, aircraft, astronomical bodies, or other objects all but 3 percent of the so-called flying saucers. The 3 percent are listed as "unknown."

[*Out of 4316 citings reported to the Air Force from 1955 until 1962, only about 84 have not been identified as familiar objects, astronomical bodies, mirages, or optical illusions.—Editor.*]

Read each test item and choose the answer you believe is correct. Print your answer to each item on your paper.

1. Who wrote the headline for the story?
   A. Air Secretary Quarles
   B. United Press
   C. *Chicago Sun-Times*
   D. Project Blue Book

2. Secretary Quarles said that there was no evidence of flying saucers because
   A. he didn't want people to report strange flying objects
   B. he wanted to hide the fact that the Air Force could not explain all of them
   C. nearly all the sightings had been explained and no evidence had confirmed the existence of flying saucers

3. Secretary Quarles knew about the so-called flying saucers because
   A. he had seen them himself
   B. the Air Force, of which he was the civilian director, had studied reports of flying saucers for eight years
   C. he had talked to everyone who reported seeing flying saucers

The correct answers are shown in the answer key.

Exercise 31—Part 2

It is important for every reader to realize that two people having the same facts may have quite different opinions about what they mean.

For example:

1. The air chief marshal of England has been quoted as saying that unidentified flying objects are real and that they come from outer space.

2. Colonel Ruppelt, who was in charge of Project Blue Book for three years, has written:

"Personally, I don't believe that 'it can't be.' I wouldn't class myself as a 'believer,' exactly, because I've seen too many UFO reports that just appeared to be unexplainable fall to pieces when they were thoroughly investigated. But every time I begin to get skeptical, I think of the other reports, the many reports made by experienced pilots and radar operators, scientists, and other people who know what they're looking at. These reports were thoroughly investigated and they are still unknown."[3]

3. Major Keyhoe, formerly of the U.S. Marines, has studied reports of flying saucers for more than twelve years. At one time he was permitted to see a great deal of the evidence gathered by the U.S. Air Force. Major Keyhoe believes that the unidentified flying objects are real and that they come from outer space.

Here are three expert opinions that differ from the opinion of Secretary Quarles.

For each item, choose the answer you believe is correct and print your answers on your paper.

1. When a reader meets conflicting opinions, it is best for him
   A. to take sides at once
   B. not to make up his mind at all
   C. to keep on looking for facts

2. Which of these probably had the most facts to base his opinion on?
   A. Colonel Ruppelt
   B. Secretary Quarles
   C. Major Keyhoe
   D. You can't tell from the article.

The best answers are shown in the answer key.

When the experts disagree, delay making up your mind. If you must choose, make your decision a temporary one. Be ready to change your mind when more facts come in. Choose the opinion that seems to be based on the most facts, that fits with your own experience, that seems least likely to be based on someone's own personal interest.

The good reader organizes what he reads

At times, both in school and out, every reader has to read through a large number of pages to get the facts that are important for him. He may be looking for the answer to a question. He may be trying to find out his duties in the civil defense organization. He may be reading directions. He may be trying to discover the time order in which things happened.

To succeed at his task, the reader must be able to organize the information he has read. To do this, he can make a list of things to do or remember. He may write down the time order in which things happen. But in every case it is important to recognize and record the most important things to keep in mind.

Exercise 32

Here is an article about an interesting topic. Read it carefully and do the exercises that follow.

Training for a Dog's Life[4]

by Jack Celli

Rags, our Skye terrier, is both servant and pal. He brings me my bedroom slippers at night, fetches the newspaper in the morning, and likes to carry small packages when the family shops. When we tell him

---

3 From *The Report on Unidentified Objects*, by Edward J. Ruppelt. Copyright 1956 by Edward J. Ruppelt, reprinted by permission of Doubleday & Company, Inc.

4 From *"Training for a Dog's Life,"* by Jack Celli, by permission of *Boys' Life*, published by the Boy Scouts of America.

to *come*, he does—on the double. He responds with the same cheerful obedience to the commands "Sit," "Stay," "Heel," and the like.

Of course, there are better-trained dogs than Rags—dogs that do flips, walk on their hind legs, open and shut doors. But as far as basic training goes, Rags knows the dos and don'ts—and a few tricks besides.

You can train your pooch, and without shouting at him like a sergeant drilling recruits. A dog can get the bad conduct habit early in life. So teach him the word *no*—but don't overuse it. When he responds to commands, tell him he's a good dog and pet him.

If he barks or howls too much, tell him "No, no." If this fails, tap him lightly on the flanks with a loosely rolled-up newspaper.

Your pet can become a pest by jumping on people, especially when his paws are muddy. When scolding fails, raise your knee just as he jumps so that it hits him in the chest, knocking him off balance. Or hold his front paws when he jumps, and step *lightly* on a rear foot.

After Pooch is six months old, introduce him to the collar, adjusting it so that it won't slip over his head—but not so tight it causes discomfort. After he gets used to the collar, snap on a six-foot leash and let him play with it.

The leash is your *lead*, which controls the dog in all obedience training.

Place the dog at your left side with his head even with your knee. Hold the leash close to the dog's collar if necessary.

Walk, calling "Heel" in a determined voice. If he lunges ahead, pull him back to the proper place at your knee—but slacken tension in the leash immediately. Repeat the command "Heel."

If he runs ahead again or lags behind, pull him back to your side. Talk to him as encouragement, and pet him when he responds to the command. Never let him stop or strain against the collar.

He should be heeling in a week if you train him for fifteen-minute periods once or twice daily. Don't let him heel leash-free until you're sure he's ready for it. In some large cities you must keep him on a leash.

After he learns to walk by your side, teach him to *sit*. With the leash in your right hand, press down on his hindquarters with your left hand until he sits. Be sure he sits by your left side. Hold him there for a while; then say "Heel" and walk on.

Once he learns the meaning of *sit*, make him sit as soon as you stop walking. Try turning quickly to the right or left when walking — and stopping abruptly. Practice patiently until he heels and sits without hesitating. A week's work, and he should catch on.

Next, with your dog at heel, teach him the command "Down." Hold one end of the leash in your right hand and step on the leash with your left foot. At the same time say "Down" and motion down with your left hand while pulling up with the right. This will force his head down. If his rump sticks up, force it down with your left hand.

After practicing this operation for a while, try it without the leash. Just motion with your hand and say "Down."

Next, teach him to *stay*. Sit him at heel, and then say "Stay." Hold out your hand, palm toward him, warning him not to move. Gradually back away, saying "St-a-a-ay" in a quiet but firm tone. Be patient and when he does stay, even for a few seconds, praise him. A few days training and you can walk away without his moving—if he's an intelligent dog.

The simplest, most important thing you can teach your pet is to come when you call. As a pup he obeyed only when he felt like it. Now you want him to respond— and no nonsense.

Fasten a twenty-foot rope to his collar, order him to stay, and back off from him. Say "Come" quietly and firmly. At the same time pull steadily on the rope. Don't let him hesitate. Never give a dog a chance to disobey. Soon he'll think obedience is his only choice.

If he resists your pulling, yank on the rope. After practicing awhile, try slackening the line and calling. If he comes, praise him.

Practice this for several days; then try it without the rope. Give the command in the same tone. If he runs away, don't follow him. Make him come to you by coaxing or walking away.

Make your dog's basic training fun for him. Play with him before and after each session; always praise him enthusiastically when he performs well. Don't expect too much from him.

After his basic training is completed, try teaching him tricks.

He may become the family's feature attraction—just as Rags is in the Celli household.

The following exercises are designed to test your ability to organize information. They are based on the article you have just read.

Record your answers on your paper.

Part 1. Suppose that you are planning to train your own dog. Make a list of the equipment that you will need. To make this list, you may need to read the article again. To save time, you should skim it, looking for the training aids you must have.

Part 2. According to the article, you should teach commands in a certain order. The commands that you should have your dog obey are given below.

Write the commands in the order in which you should teach them to your dog. The commands are Come, Down, Heel, No, Sit, Stay.

Part 3. If your information about dog training is well organized, you will use certain principles of teaching. To make sure you understand these principles, read the statements that follow.

Write **T** if the statement is true. Write **F** if the statement is false.

1. You want your dog to learn to obey your command promptly and cheerfully.

2. If your dog does not obey you, shout at him.

3. When your dog obeys you, always pet him and say "Good dog."

4. Whenever your dog refuses to obey you, hit him with a stick or step hard on his back feet.

5. In training your dog, always be firm but kind.

6. Always try to make sure that your dog understands exactly what you want him to do.

7. In training your dog, teach him to obey commands both at your left side and at your right side.

8. To teach your dog the command "Sit" or "Down," use your hand to press his body toward the ground.

9. Teach your dog to obey commands first without a leash and then with a leash.

10. Play with your dog before and after each training period; make learning fun for him.

The correct answers for the three parts of the exercise are shown in the answer key.

The good reader asks for proof

In every field scholars and scientists are making astonishing new discoveries every day. The wonders they uncover are often almost beyond belief.

There once was a time when reports of new discoveries and inventions were viewed with suspicion until they were proved true beyond all possible doubt. The first reports that the Wright brothers had flown a plane seemed so fantastic that newspaper editors refused to print the story.

But so many strange things have been proved true that many people today seem willing to accept any scientist's statement as a fact. This is no more sensible than the old attitude of believing nothing.

The sensible thing for the modern reader is to require proof. If the facts support the new idea, the reader may accept it. If facts are not given, the reader may accept the writer's *opinion* temporarily but keep his eye open for facts that may come later.

Strangely enough, old beliefs held by people long ago have a way of turning up from time to time in our day. Some of these beliefs are mere superstitions. Some of them are incorrect conclusions from observations.

One of the old beliefs that appeared time after time in history was the idea that huge monsters lived in the sea. The sea serpent, some people said, could swallow a man whole or crush a wooden sailing ship.

Was this just a superstition? Was it based on fact? What do you think?

Read the following story carefully and take the test that follows.

Exercise 33

Are There Sea Serpents?[5]

by A. E. Hotchner

"Yes," says Dr. Anton Bruun, a leading Danish scientist. He has laboratory proof now, but he'll be happy when he catches a real live monster.

COPENHAGEN—The old sea serpent, with its bulging green eyes and its saw-toothed back, has once again raised its threatening head. This time, however, it is being talked about by natural scientists, particularly by oceanographers. For years scientists have pooh-poohed the idea that there are serpents in the sea. But the well-known oceanographer Dr. Anton Bruun has dropped a depth bomb that has really stirred up scientific waters all over the world.

The International Congress of Zoology was held in Copenhagen in 1955 and attended by five hundred scientists from all over the world. At this meeting Dr. Bruun made an important announcement. After years of research, Dr. Bruun said, he had decided that great sea serpents do actually live in the Atlantic and Pacific oceans.

Six-Foot Mystery

Dr. Bruun first became interested in sea serpents when he learned about a strange fish that the Dana deep-sea expedition of 1930 caught in the South Atlantic. After this six-foot fish was pickled, scientists identified it as the larval form of an eel, an eel that was never observed before or since.

"This specimen," Dr. Braun says, "had 450 vertebral plates. The largest eels we know about have only 150 plates. This means that if that fish had grown to adult size, it might well have been as big as any sea serpent from the pages of science fiction. Fishes weighing several tons, such as bask-

ing and whale sharks, are not uncommon. If their flesh were put into the long shape of the eel, it would be a monster indeed."

To prove that some fish do look like sea serpents, Dr. Bruun pointed to the oarfish. It lives in tropical and semitropical seas. This fish is long and silvery. Its fins in back look like oars. Its front fins are a bright red, making the fish look like a real fire breather. Near Australia, a twelve-foot oarfish was caught; other specimens have been known to reach a whopping forty feet.

Could Be Real

After Dr. Bruun studied the Dana fish, he began to do some more thinking. He remembered the many reports of sea serpents that scientists believed were imaginary. Some of these serpents, he said to himself, might have been actual serpents. To look into this, he began a long study of the reports. As a result of this study, he decided that two hundred of the reports were probably true. From these reports, he concluded that six of the cases reported were real sea monsters. "In these six cases," Dr. Bruun said, "the serpents observed cannot be reasonably related to any creature now known to zoology."

Here are Dr. Bruun's six cases:

1. Along the New England coast, in 1819, a number of sea captains reported a hundred-foot monster with "hunches on its back." A study of these reports leaves no doubt that for more than a year a strange, enormous fish was living in the New England waters.

2. There were twenty-four well-founded reports of a sea monster observed along the Norwegian coast about 1845.

3. Off the Cape of Good Hope on August 6, 1848, the commander of the *Daedalus* (a Royal Navy corvette) observed a sea monster. Here is part of his official report to the Admiralty:

"Discovered an enormous serpent with head and shoulders kept about four feet constantly above the surface of the sea; there was at least sixty feet of animal. It passed rapidly but close under our lee quarters."

Later that same year, the commander of the American brig *Daphne* reported a

5 Reprinted from *This Week* magazine. Copyrighted 1955 by the United Newspapers Magazine Corporation.

similar monster observed from forty yards away. The commander fired at it, but it escaped.

4. In 1877 Captain H. L. Pearson, commander of Queen Victoria's yacht, described a monster observed off the coast of Sicily.

5. In 1942 F. W. Kemp, officer of the Provincial Archives, and Major W. H. Langley, of the British Columbia legislature, saw an immense monster off the coast of Vancouver. This beast stayed in the vicinity for some time and was observed by three ships' captains and a pilot. The monster was sixty feet long and greenish-brown. It had flippers, and its back was serrated near the tail.

6. The most celebrated of all the monsters was seen off the shore of Loch Ness, Scotland, in January 1933. The Loch Ness monster received worldwide publicity. Reporters from the London *Times* obtained twenty-two well-authenticated statements from witnesses, and a photographer from the *Daily Mail* actually got a picture of the beast.

"These are not sketchy reports made by superstitious fishermen of the Middle Ages," Dr. Bruun points out, "but precise accounts by responsible, experienced naval officers and sea captains who could not possibly be fooled by dolphins or floating logs."

No matter what objections disbelievers raise, Dr. Bruun has an answer. To the objection that animals of the sea are so thoroughly known that there is no chance that an unknown thing still exists, Dr. Bruun says:

"New creatures are constantly being discovered. Within recent years a whole school of small whales, never seen before, was stranded on a Scottish coast. For years a straight horn, nearly five feet long, was on display in Florence. Naturalists remained puzzled by it until Captain Varian discovered a giant sable antelope in Angola. How often is a sperm whale observed, or a ribbonfish, or the great white rhino of East Africa? Very, very seldom, I can assure you. The ocean is a big place and there are many, many unknowns still in the sea."

Catch One

"Of course, there is only one way to prove my theory," Dr. Bruun adds, "and that's to catch a sea monster and put it on display. In my opinion, no one has ever caught a sea serpent because it requires a special fishing technique. I have no doubt that such a monster could be caught, and that is what I'm going to do—organize an expedition and go after one. I shall fish for it on the continental slopes of tropical and subtropical West Africa and Pacific Central America. The food-rich waters off Ecuador and Peru have already yielded many giant game fishes of record size. No one has ever fished five hundred to one thousand fathoms. I will fish at that depth with baited hook on a cable towed behind the ship.

"Since my expeditions always bring back surprising trophies," Dr. Bruun says, "why should the unfished deeper waters not yield the prize trophy of them all: the Great Sea Serpent, a mystery turned into reality?"

Comprehension test

For each test item, choose the answer you believe is correct. Print your answers on your paper.

1. According to Dr. Anton Bruun, the oceanographer quoted in the story, sea serpents
    A. exist but have not yet been caught
    B. do not actually live in the oceans today
    C. never existed and do not exist today

2. For years, according to the story, scientists have pooh-poohed the idea that there are serpents in the sea. *Pooh-poohed* means that these scientists believed the idea was
    A. *worthless*—that is, not worth studying or thinking about
    B. *interesting*—that is, worth looking into for a while longer
    C. *proved*—that is, proved by the information already collected.

3. While discussing sea serpents with the author, Dr. Bruun talked about a real specimen of each of the following sea animals except one. Of which one did Dr. Bruun *not* have a specimen?
    A. An oarfish
    B. A Dana eel
    C. A sea serpent

4. In talking about the Dana eel, Dr. Bruun said that he believed this deep-sea creature might grow into a fish many feet in length. To support this belief, he pointed to
   A. the large number of plates in its vertebra
   B. the oarlike fins at the rear of its body
   C. the plentiful foods in its home waters

5. Dr. Bruun supported his belief in the existence of real sea serpents by citing six cases, including that of the Loch Ness monster. These cases, he said, were based on a careful study of the reports made by persons
   A. who had good imaginations and who wrote interesting stories
   B. who were good observers and who gave true reports
   C. who were trained scientists and who carried on experiments

6. To indicate that sea serpents may exist even though they have not yet been caught, Dr. Bruun referred to other animals that were
   A. constantly being discovered
   B. very plentiful and not killed off for many years
   C. dead and buried but not dug up for many years

7. According to Dr. Bruun, no fisherman has caught a sea serpent because he has *not*
   A. used the right bait
   B. believed this animal existed
   C. fished deep enough

8. Dr. Bruun stated that he would try to catch a sea serpent in parts of the ocean that are
   A. warm and food-scarce
   B. warm and food-filled
   C. cold and food-filled

9. Near the end of the article, Dr. Bruun is quoted as saying something that shows he thought he would catch a sea serpent on his next fishing trip. This something was:
   A. "My expeditions always bring back surprising trophies."
   B. "I have no doubt that such a monster could be caught."
   C. "New creatures are constantly being discovered."

The correct answers are shown in the answer key.

The class may hold a discussion of the question, "Are there sea serpents?" During the discussion, draw two columns on the chalkboard. In the left-hand column, list the points of evidence that tend to prove the existence of sea serpents. In the right-hand column, list the points of evidence that tend to disprove the existence of sea serpents. After the discussion, hold a referendum on the question. Have each class member write his answer, "Yes," "No," or "?" (for uncertain) on a small slip of paper. Then count the number of each of the three answers and report these numbers to the class.

Practice Reading 8

In a book, magazine, or newspaper that you like, practice reading for speed and comprehension. Make a record of this reading in Chart 3 on page 8 of the progress folder.

8
article

Elastic metal[1]

by Elizabeth Rider Montgomery

Do you realize how often you travel on rubber? Perhaps you wear rubber heels on your shoes. When it rains, you undoubtedly wear rubbers or rubber boots. When the weather is nice, you may go for a ride in your father's car: again you are traveling on rubber, for the car could not go far without rubber tires. And the very pavement you ride over may be made of rubber!

We use rubber so often in our daily lives, and in so many ways, that it is very important to us. But a hundred years ago rubber was scarcely used at all, because no one knew how to keep it from melting in warm weather and becoming stiff and hard in cold weather. In those days people preferred getting their feet wet to wearing rubbers, for if the sun should come out the rubbers would stick to their shoes and to the street; and if it should freeze the rubbers would be too stiff to get off. So you see that the man who learned how to make rubber remain firm yet elastic at all temperatures did a wonderful thing for the world.

One evening in 1839 some friends stopped in to see Charles Goodyear. As usual they found him standing over a red-hot stove, stirring something in a big kettle.

"Come in," he cried. "I think I'm on the track of the secret of rubber at last."

"Oh, Charles!" laughed a friend. "You have been saying that for years. You have mixed rubber with everything under the sun, and still it is the same old story:

either heat or cold ruins it. Aren't you convinced by now that rubber can never be made usable?"

"No, John," answered Charles firmly. "On the contrary, I am certain there is a way to make the use of rubber practical, and I intend to find it." Carefully he lifted the kettle from the stove and set it on the floor to cool.

"But, Charles," objected another friend, "you can't afford to keep up this experimenting any longer. Think of the money you have spent on rubber and chemicals to mix with it. Think of the time you have wasted that you could have been using to earn money. Think of your family, Charles, and how destitute they are. We came tonight to try to persuade you to go back to your hardware business where you can at least earn a living. You can't afford to go on with this crazy experimenting."

"I can't afford to quit," Goodyear said. "There is a way to make rubber usable. Someone is going to discover it, and I intend to be the one. I shall succeed. I know it. And then I shall be able to take good care of my family and pay all my debts."

He bent over the kettle and lifted a small amount of the rubber mixture on a spoon. As he looked at it, his annoyance disappeared. His boundless enthusiasm for his rubber experiments again took hold of him.

"But look!" he cried. "This is the best method I have ever tried. See! I am mixing sulfur with the rubber gum. It is not quite right yet. Something is still lacking. But the rubber so treated does not get so stiff with cold, or so very sticky with heat. It is better than any I have yet found."

He took up the cooling bit of rubber from the spoon and held it up.

"See, this is firm and yet it is elastic. I can hold it up over the hot stove, like this, and still it does not become sticky. Of course if it becomes really hot it melts."

"Let me see it," asked John, reaching across the stove.

Goodyear started to put the bit of rubber in his friend's hand, but instead—he dropped it on the stove!

"Well!" he cried. "I guess that piece of rubber is ruined now. If there is one thing I have learned, it is that heat ruins rubber. I'll get you another piece." And he dipped the spoon into the kettle again.

While the second spoonful of the mixture was cooling, he took the poker and raked from the red-hot stove top the rubber that he thought was ruined.

Then his friends, watching him, were amazed at what they saw. Charles picked up the bit of rubber and looked at it closely. He fingered it, pulled it, pressed it, with an unbelieving look on his face. Then he began to dance around the room, shouting like a madman!

"Charles!" they cried. "Charles! What is it? Try to calm yourself." But Goodyear kept on with his wild antics.

"Poor man," thought his friends. "All these years of work and worry have been too much for him. He has lost his mind."

But Charles Goodyear was shouting, "I have the secret at last! I can make rubber that will not melt! Look! Look!"

They looked at the piece of rubber in his hand—the rubber that had fallen on the hot stove.

"See! It didn't melt! Instead, it charred like leather on the edges. In the center it is perfectly cured. I just said that if there was one thing certain it was that rubber is ruined by heat. But that isn't true! If the heat is great enough, the rubber is cured! By mixing rubber with sulfur and heating it very, very hot, I can make practical rubber. Rubber can now be used for everything—except for food!"

Still doubting, his friends shook their heads. So many times Charles had thought he had found the secret of rubber curing. This was just another of his dreams that would melt away with daylight.

But Goodyear did not notice. He had thought of something else. "I must see if cold affects this heat-cured rubber," he cried. "I'll put it out in the snow." And out of the house he dashed.

For the rest of that evening, Charles Goodyear was like a madman. Forgetful of his guests, he made experiment after experiment to test his new discovery. And he was happy indeed when he had satisfied himself that he really had found the secret of making rubber usable.

Although he still had ahead of him months of work perfecting the process (discovering the proper degree of heat for a decided hardness), the secret of vulcanization that Goodyear stumbled on that night repaid him for all the years of fruitless experimenting. Rubber treated by his process could be made soft and pliable but without stickiness, or it could be made hard and durable, an elastic metal. Since Goodyear's vulcanization process made it possible to make rubber of every degree of hardness, so many uses have been found for rubber that his prediction has really come true: rubber is used for almost everything these days, except food!

Rubber was named by Dr. Joseph Priestley of England, the discoverer of oxygen. A friend in America sent Priestley a ball of crude rubber. This was in 1770. When the good doctor found that the ball would rub out pencil marks, he broke off small pieces and called them "rubbers."

Goodyear named his process of combining rubber and sulfur by heat "vulcanization," after the Roman god of fire, Vulcan. In 1844 Goodyear secured patents for his discovery. He received medals at the London Crystal Palace Exposition of 1851 and the Paris fair of 1855. He never grew rich from his invention, even though he lived to see his discovery put to five hundred different uses in 1860.

Although Goodyear used sulfur with the rubber gum, many other compounds are added today. As much as 60 percent of sulfur may go into hard rubber, whereas as little as 1 percent may be used in thin elastic goods.

The United States makes more rubber products today than the rest of the world combined. In addition to natural rubber, which it uses, this country also makes synthetic rubber. But it was Charles Goodyear, back in 1839, whose experiments showed the world the great possibilities in elastic metal.

Record your finishing time in the time box. Then take the reading test.

Read each test item and choose the answer you believe is correct. Print your answers in the answer record on page 4 of the progress folder.

Reading Test 8

Getting the main ideas

1. The man who first cured rubber was
   - A. Charles Goodrich
   - B. Charles Firestone
   - C. Charles Goodyear
   - D. Charles Sieberling
   - E. Charles Atlas

2. The inventor was trying to make rubber that would not
   - A. wear out
   - B. melt
   - C. burn
   - D. curl
   - E. skid

3. In making rubber, the inventor mixed gum with
   - A. sulfur
   - B. coal tar
   - C. olive oil
   - D. cottonseed oil
   - E. gasoline

4. Success came when he dropped the mixture
   - A. in the sink
   - B. in a barrel of tar
   - C. in boiling water
   - D. on the stove
   - E. on ice

5. The inventor proved that rubber can be cured with
   - A. cement
   - B. freezing
   - C. friction
   - D. sand
   - E. heat

Remembering key facts

6. His friends thought his experimenting was
   - A. crazy
   - B. breaking the law
   - C. worth continuing
   - D. wonderful
   - E. magic

7. The inventor's friends wanted him to return to

   A. schoolteaching
   B. banking
   C. the hardware business
   D. farming
   E. selling lumber

8. The inventor said rubber would one day be used for everything—except

   A. food
   B. shelter
   C. clothing
   D. tires
   E. toys

9. To see if cold hurt cured rubber, the inventor put it in

   A. a block of ice
   B. the snow
   C. a mountain brook
   D. the refrigerator
   E. the icy rain

Reading with a keen eye

10. Rubber was first cured in

   A. 1539
   B. 1739
   C. 1639
   D. 1839
   E. 1439

11. The stove on which Charles Goodyear stirred the mixture was

   A. deep blue
   B. pure white
   C. red-hot
   D. pearl-gray
   E. stone-cold

Drawing conclusions

12. We admire the inventor because he

   A. was good to his friends
   B. was kind to his children
   C. owed no debts
   D. refused to quit
   E. loved animals

13. The inventor had failed in the past because he

   A. stirred too much
   B. did not heat the mixture enough
   C. did not cool the mixture
   D. did not freeze the mixture
   E. heated the mixture too much

14. This selection was written to

   A. amuse you
   B. inform you
   C. frighten you
   D. surprise you
   E. puzzle you

Putting things in order

15. Here are five events that happened in this selection. Which one happened first?

    A. The inventor shouted, "I have the secret at last!"

    B. The inventor's friends urged him to quit.

    C. He dropped some of the mixture.

    D. He placed the cured rubber outside to cool.

    E. The inventor stirred something in a kettle.

Knowing word meanings

16. "I think I'm on the track of the secret of rubber at last." As used here, *on the track* means

    A. ready to give up

    B. sad about

    C. far away from

    D. happy about

    E. close to

17. Four of the five words shown here have been correctly divided into syllables. One has been incorrectly divided. Which one?

    A. rub/ber

    B. im/por/tant

    C. e/las/tic

    D. lift/ed

    E. hundr/ed

18. "Kept on with his antics." *Antics* means

    A. animals

    B. thoughts

    C. snakes

    D. actions

    E. friends

19. Big words often contain smaller words. One of the five words shown here does not contain a smaller word. Which one?

    A. wonderful

    B. madman

    C. kettle

    D. coatless

    E. shouting

20. "His prediction has really come true." As used here, *prediction* means

    A. statement about the future

    B. bad luck

    C. increase in pace

    D. promotion

    E. good luck

Follow the directions (Steps 8–13) on page 1 of the progress folder.

How to read at the right speed

Until 1954 no one had run a mile in less than four minutes. Then in that year three men broke through the four-minute barrier. In one race, both Ralph Bannister and John Landy finished in less than four minutes!

When these men set out to beat the mile-run record, they studied the race as though it were a science problem. They studied breathing, the action of their muscles, and the way their hearts worked.

They broke up the mile into quarters. For each quarter they set a rate, a rate that would leave a little extra kick for the last fifty yards of the race. Then they practiced. They learned to pace themselves so well that they could tell within a half second how fast they were running each quarter.

The two-mile race is run at a different pace. Since it is longer, the runners take the quarter miles at a slower pace. Sprinters who run the 100- and 220-yard dashes plan each of these races in quite a different way.

In track races, runners suit their pace to the job they have to do. In this respect, good reading is like good track work—reading speed must be adapted to the kind of job there is to do.

What is the right reading speed?

An automobile can move at any speed from 2 or 3 miles an hour to more than 100 miles an hour. It can go 19 or 20 or 56½ miles an hour. But the best rate for driving depends on the road, the amount of traffic, and the speed limit.

In heavy traffic within city limits, the right speed might be 25 miles an hour. On an open highway, it might be 50 miles an hour. An experienced driver learns to drive at the speed that will get him to his destination with the least nervous fatigue.

A good reader follows a similar plan. He usually has three reading speeds that he follows for three different general purposes. He has one rate for *skimming*, another rate for *pleasure* reading, and still another for *study*.

The right reading speed for anyone depends upon his purpose. If he is looking through a reference book to find material for a report, he may read rapidly. He reads at the same rapid pace to find out an author's general point of view—which side of an argument he favors, for example.

He will not read quite so fast if he is reading a story for entertainment. If he is trying to discover a writer's ideas, or if he is reading directions or looking for an answer to a problem, he will read at his study rate.

In each of these situations the reader has a different purpose. He adapts his rate to his purpose. But he also adapts it to the difficulty of his material. He studies a science lesson more slowly than a history lesson if the science is harder. No one races a good car over a bumpy road even though it is out in the country with no other car in sight. And reading a science lesson may sometimes be like driving a car over a bumpy road.

The right speed for you is the fastest speed at which you can understand the material and satisfy your reading purpose.

How much do you have to understand?

An experienced reader may go through a detective story at the rate of 600 words a minute. He can read at this rate because there are not many things he has to understand in order to follow the story. He must know the characters and the details of the crime. He must catch the clues to the solution of the story.

But suppose the reader is signing a contract to perform a job or to buy a house. How much must he understand? To avoid trouble, he must understand every word in the contract before he signs it. In the same way, a lawyer must understand every word in a law or a court decision. If he misses even one small word, he may lose his case.

In reading a poem, you must get the writer's ideas, but you must also read to *feel* the rhythm and to enjoy the words and figures of speech the poet has used.

Your effort to understand what you read will vary according to your purpose and the kind of material you are reading.

Choosing the right speed

Here is a list of purposes for which you might read:

- To find the answer to a question.
- To get a writer's opinion on some problem.
- To find out why something happened.
- To find out how to do something.
- To entertain yourself.
- To find a specific fact you are looking for.
- To find out how, where, when, and why someone did something.

Make three columns on your paper. In the first column, copy the items below. In the second column, write the purpose for which you might be reading each item. In the third column, write "Skim," "General," or "Study" to show the right rate for reading this kind of material for the purpose stated.

1. Headlines in a newspaper
2. *World Almanac*
3. Article in the *World Almanac* on a topic you are studying in science class
4. Application blank for a job
5. Comic strips of a newspaper
6. Editorial in your school paper
7. History assignment
8. Math problem
9. Manual telling how to operate a new electric stove

How fast do you read now?

The speed of a car is measured in miles per hour. Reading rate is measured in words per minute. How many words do you read a minute when you are reading stories? newspapers? your science textbook?

Before going on with your study of reading, you ought to find your present reading rates for various kinds of material. The exercise below will give you some idea. Do not be content with a single score on each kind of reading. You should average the scores on several different readings.

You can check your rate with your own exercise materials. Here is how to do it:

1. Count the number of words in the passage. For this example, let's say it is 340 words.

2. Write down the time at which you start in minutes and seconds: 9:30:15, for example. That is, 30 minutes and 15 seconds after 9 o'clock.

3. When you finish, write down the time: 9:32:30, for example.

4. Subtract your starting time from your finishing time. In this example, it is 2:15. You have read the passage in 2 minutes and 15 seconds.

5. Change this figure to seconds: 2:15 = 135 seconds.

6. Divide the number of words by the number of seconds: $\frac{340}{135} = 2.51$ words per second. (Carry the division to two decimal places.)

7. Multiply by 60 to get the number of words per minute: $2.51 \times 60 = 150.6$ words per minute. We can put this operation into a formula:

$$\text{Rate} = \frac{\text{number of words read}}{\text{number of seconds used in reading}} \times 60$$

You can make up your own speed tests from time to time to see how you are doing. Get a friend to help you check the time you take in reading. Then have him ask you questions on the passage to see how much you understand and whether you are able to explain what you have read. Never try to increase your speed without checking your understanding.

You can keep a record of your rate by using this simple chart:

Time Box

Finishing time	
Starting time	
Total time used	
Number of words	
Rate: words per second	
Rate: words per minute	

Check your reading rates

Exercise 34

Choose someone to work with you. Time him as he reads each of the following passages. Then have him time you. Help each other in figuring out your rates. All the selections are about the same length; the number of words for each is given. But each of the selections presents a different kind of material, and you will read each one for a different purpose. Keep a record of your rates on the five selections and also a record of your scores on the short tests that follow.

Part 1.

Every able-bodied American boy is subject to call by the armed forces. Both while he is on duty and after, the government will give him opportunities to increase his education. One of the best of these opportunities is in the new Air Force Academy. Your reading purpose is to find the answer to this question: *How can a young man get into the Air Force Academy?* The selection is 387 words in length.

The United States Air Force Academy [1]

The United States Air Force Academy, the nation's newest service academy, is located at the foot of the Rocky Mountains near Colorado Springs, Colorado. Established in 1954, the academy occupied temporary quarters on Lowry Air Force Base in Denver until the fall of 1958, when the move was made to its permanent campus.

Most of the graduates of the academy have gone on to Air Force pilot training. A percentage of each class has entered institutions of higher learning for graduate work in technical and professional fields. The Air Force Cadet Wing is authorized to have an enrollment of 2500 cadets.

Nominations to each class open each year on June 1 and close on January 31. To qualify, an applicant must be at least seventeen and not yet twenty-two on July 1 of the year he enters the academy; must be a male citizen of the United States, morally and physically fit; and must never have been married.

A resident of the United States who meets the eligibility requirements may apply for a nomination by writing to a U.S. senator from his state or the U.S. representative from his congressional district. In such a letter the applicant should state briefly his qualifications, parents' names, place of residence, and educational background. Approximately 85 percent of the vacancies in each class are reserved for congressional nominees.

A congressman may nominate one principal and ten alternate candidates designated by his preference. If the principal candidate qualifies on the entrance examinations, he will be selected. If he does not pass the examinations, the first qualified alternate will be chosen. Should a senator or representative prefer, he may authorize the Air Force Academy to select the best-qualified young man from his eleven candidates. The Air Force also selects the best-qualified of alternate nominees to fill vacancies.

All candidates are required to take the following examinations, usually scheduled from December through April: physical aptitude; the College Entrance Examination Board tests; and the Air Force medical examination.

Cadets spend four years at the Air Force Academy engaging in scientific and liberal arts studies along with military training. Upon graduation they receive a bachelor of science degree and a second lieutenant's commission in the regular Air Force. Those physically qualified may elect

---

[1] From "The United States Air Force Academy," *World Almanac,* 1962.

to undergo a complete course in pilot training after graduation.

Read each test item and choose the answer you believe is correct. Print your answers on your paper.

1. The first step for a young man to take in getting into the academy is
   A. to send an application to the U.S. Air Force Appointments Branch in Washington
   B. to get someone in his local city government to nominate him
   C. to write to a U.S. senator from his state or to the U.S. representative from his congressional district

2. Which one of the following meets the entrance requirements?
   A. Tom Jones: age 18; unmarried; born in Seattle; applied for admission February 22
   B. Bill Edwards: age 20; unmarried; born in New York City; applied June 15
   C. John Brady; age 20; divorced; born in Salt Lake City; applied August 1

3. All candidates must take which of the following examinations?
   A. the College Entrance Examination Board tests and a high school physical examination
   B. a reading test; the College Entrance Examination Board tests; and a medical examination
   C. physical aptitude test; the College Entrance Examination Board tests; and the Air Force medical examination

Part 2

Sooner or later you will have to perform the citizen's duty of reporting his income to the federal government. It may be sooner than you think, as you will discover in reading this selection. If you make a mistake in filing this information, you may have to pay a penalty. This selection is from the instructional pamphlet that the Internal Revenue Service gives to every taxpayer. *Your reading purpose is to make sure you know every detail.* There are 360 words in this article.

How to File Your Income Tax Return

Who must file a tax return

Every citizen or resident of the United States—whether an adult or a minor—who had $600 or more income in 1962 must file; if sixty-five or over, $1200 or more.

A person with income of less than these amounts should file a return to get a refund if tax was withheld. A married person with income less than her (his) own personal exemption(s) should file a joint return with husband or wife to get the smaller tax or larger refund for the couple.

Earned income from sources outside the United States.—To determine whether an income tax return must be filed, income must be computed without regard to the exclusion provided for income earned from sources outside the United States. If you received such income and believe it is excludable for income tax purposes, complete Form 2555 and attach it to your Form 1040.

Members of armed forces

Members of the armed forces should give name, service serial number, and permanent home address.

When and where to file

Please file as early as possible. You must file not later than April 15. Mail your return to the District Director of Internal Revenue for the district in which you live. U.S. citizens abroad who have no legal residence or place of business in the United States should file with Director of International Operations, Internal Revenue Service, Washington 25, D.C.

Where to get forms

As far as practical, the forms are mailed directly to taxpayers. Additional forms may be obtained from any Internal Revenue Service office, and also at most banks and some post offices.

How to pay

The balance of tax shown to be due on line 16, page 1, of your return on Form 1040 must be paid in full with your return if it amounts to $1 or more. Checks or money orders should be made payable to Internal Revenue Service.

Attachments to the return

Insofar as possible, you should fill in all required information directly on your return. If schedules are attached, they should conform in arrangement and detail with the official schedules, and totals should be entered on the return form.

Read each item below and choose the answer you believe is correct.

1. You do not have to file a return
   A. if you are an alien
   B. if your income is less than $600
   C. if you are under 21 years of age
2. The law requires you to file a return
   A. unless all your tax has been held out of your wages by your employer
   B. unless you have paid your whole tax in advance
   C. to see whether you owe more than you paid or have money due you from the government
3. Checks and money orders for whatever you owe should be made out to
   A. Internal Revenue Service
   B. the superintendent of documents
   C. your bank
4. You can get copies of the tax forms from
   A. the high school principal
   B. the superintendent of documents
   C. the Internal Revenue Service office, banks, and post offices
5. If you are a U.S. citizen living in a foreign country and employed by the United Nations,
   A. you have to pay an income tax
   B. you do not have to pay an income tax
   C. you pay tax only in the country in which you live

Part 3

In reading this stirring poem, you will enjoy the swinging rhythm—the rhythm of troops marching. But you will also want to understand what is happening, and you will want to get the poet's ideas. Note, for example, that at the start the regiment's band is playing the slow dead march. At the close it is playing the fast quickstep march. Files-on-Parade is Kipling's name for a private. The color sergeant is the sergeant in charge of the regiment's flags. As you read this poem, remember that *you have two reading purposes: enjoyment of the poem's songlike rhythm, and understanding of the tragic story.* There are 339 words.

Danny Deever[2]

by Rudyard Kipling

"What are the bugles blowin' for?" said
　　Files-on-Parade.
"To turn you out, to turn you out," the
　　Color-Sergeant said.
"What makes you look so white, so white?"
　　said Files-on-Parade.
"I'm dreadin' what I've got to watch," the
　　Color-Sergeant said.
　　For they're hangin' Danny Deever,
　　　　you can 'ear the Dead March play,
　　The regiment's in 'ollow square—
　　　　they're hangin' him today;
　　They've taken of his buttons off an'
　　　　cut his stripes away,
　　An' they're hangin' Danny Deever in
　　　　the mornin'.
"What makes the rear-rank breathe so
　　'ard?" said Files-on-Parade.
"It's bitter cold, it's bitter cold," the
　　Color-Sergeant said.
"What makes that front-rank man fall
　　down?" says Files-on-Parade.
"A touch of sun, a touch of sun," the Color-
　　Sergeant said.
　　They are hangin' Danny Deever, they
　　　　are marchin' of 'im round.
　　They 'ave 'alted Danny Deever by 'is
　　　　coffin on the ground:
　　An' 'e'll swing in 'arf a minute for a
　　　　sneakin', shootin' hound—
　　O they're hangin' Danny Deever in
　　　　the mornin'!
"'Is cot was right-'and cot to mine," said
　　Files-on-Parade.
"'E's sleepin' out an' far tonight," the
　　Color-Sergeant said.
"I've drunk 'is beer a score o' times," said
　　Files-on-Parade.
"'E's drinkin' bitter beer alone," the Color-
　　Sergeant said.

---

2 "Danny Deever," from *Barrack Room Ballads*, by Rudyard Kipling, by permission of Mrs. George Bambridge, Doubleday & Company, Inc., The Macmillan Co. of Canada, Ltd., and Methuen & Co. Ltd.

They are hangin' Danny Deever, you
  must mark 'im to 'is place,
For 'e shot a comrade sleepin'—you
  must look 'im in the face;
Nine 'undred of 'is county an' the regi-
  ment's disgrace,
While they're hangin' Danny Deever
  in the mornin'.
"What's that so black agin the sun?" said
  Files-on-Parade.
"It's Danny fightin' 'ard for life," the
  Color-Sergeant said.
"What's that that whimpers over'ead?"
  said Files-on-Parade.
"It's Danny's soul that's passin' now," the
  Color-Sergeant said.
  For they're done with Danny Deever,
    you can 'ear the quickstep play,
  The regiment's in column, an' they're
    marchin' us away;
  Ho! the young recruits are shakin', an'
    they'll want their beer today,
  After hangin' Danny Deever in the
    mornin'.

Read each test item and choose the
answer you believe is correct.

1. Danny Deever was hanged because
   A. he was a deserter
   B. he had shot and killed another
      soldier
   C. no one liked him
2. The color sergeant said that the rear
   rank was breathing hard because of
   the cold and that the front-rank man
   was overcome by the heat. These
   statements show that
   A. the front rank must have been
      standing in the sun and the rear
      rank in the shade
   B. the color sergeant didn't know the
      temperature
   C. the temperature was not the real
      reason the men were breathing
      hard and falling in a faint
3. The color sergeant feels that
   A. although it is an awful thing to
      hang a comrade, Danny Deever
      had done an awful thing
   B. the punishment of Danny Deever
      was too harsh
   C. the men should not have been
      compelled to watch the hanging

Part 4

In the first years of the United States,
England seized its ships and forced American sailors into the English navy. President
Jefferson thought he could make the English
stop these actions by cutting off all trade
with them. The Embargo Act of 1807 for-
bade anyone to sell goods to England or to
buy goods from that country.

This selection is the kind of reading
you might do in preparing a report for your
class. *Your reading purpose is to get the
general idea and to remember details that
support* this idea. There are 403 words.

The Embargo Act of 1807[3]

Long before 1809, the embargo began
to be felt, and felt seriously. In the large
shipping towns business of every kind fell
off, and soon utterly ceased. The ropewalks
were deserted. The sailmakers were idle.
The shipwrights and draymen had scarcely
anything to do. But the greatest sufferers
of all were the sailors.

In Boston one hundred of them bearing
a flag went in procession to the Government
House demanding work or bread. The
governor told them he could do nothing for
them, and they went off.

At New York the Common Council
thought for a time of employing the sailors
to grade the streets, cut down the hills, and
fill up the deep swamps and lots. But a
better agreement was finally made with the
officer in command of the Navy Yard. The
sailors were to sign articles to remain in the
service of the United States during their
own pleasure and to do such work as the
commanding officer should prescribe.

In Philadelphia a band of seamen with
a flag paraded the streets, drew up before
the State House, and sent a committee in
to see the mayor. The mayor assured them
he had no power to grant relief, told them
such conduct was highly improper, and
advised them to seek help from the Chamber of Commerce. This group soon had the
sailors at work making canvas, rope, coarse
mats, oakum, and gaskets.

---

3 Adapted from *History of the People of the United
States*, by J. B. McMaster.

To enforce the embargo in the seaports and on the large bays was a matter of no great difficulty. But to enforce it on the Canadian border was all but impossible.

On the border, smuggling was bold and impudent. In Vermont a favorite way was to load a dozen sleds or wagons and drive toward Canada. A hill with steep slopes and close to the boundary line would be selected. A rude hut would be put up on the summit. The hut was made so that when a stone was pulled from the foundation, the floor would fall, the sides topple over, and the contents be thrown on English ground. When the hut was thus built, the sleds would be unloaded and the barrels of potash, flour, and pork would be stored in the hut. Then someone would remove the stone, which would cause the hut to collapse and send the barrels rolling down into Canada. Once there, they became English property and were quickly carried off.

Print your answers to these items as you have done on Parts 1, 2, and 3.

1. The embargo was felt most seriously by
    A. sailors who were thrown out of work
    B. merchants who could not get English goods to sell
    C. people living in towns who could not get food supplies
2. In New York and Philadelphia the sailors who lost their jobs
    A. were given food and clothing by the government
    B. starved to death
    C. were given other jobs
3. People living along the Canadian border
    A. loyally supported the Embargo Act
    B. broke the law by smuggling
    C. were not affected by the Embargo Act

Part 5

During the next few years you will be reading a good deal about vocations. Until you find a field that interests you, you will want to read widely and explore many possibilities. In this kind of reading your purpose is to get a general idea of various fields. When you have found one that interests you, you will read to get all the details you can. *Read this selection to get the general idea.* There are 356 words.

Job Opportunities for Women as Food-Service Managers[4]

As restaurant operation becomes more of a science, the value of the trained home economist is becoming recognized. Many food-production managers today are college graduates who majored in home economics, foods and nutrition, or in management. They use a scientific approach to problems of food production. A woman in this work can apply the principles of chemistry, bacteriology, nutrition, accounting, psychology, and many other academic subjects.

Opportunities for trained women far exceed the supply and include key positions in both large and small restaurants. They are well paid in these jobs. The restaurant owner will find in the future that his customers are becoming more demanding. He will need a restaurant manager able to provide satisfactory food service and experienced in selling, employee relationships, and food-cost control.

In the restaurant business human relationships are assuming a more important place. A wise supervisor can keep employees working steadily and happily by careful planning. Skill in keeping the goodwill of the customers is another part of the restaurant manager's job.

One woman, who is general manager of a huge restaurant chain, says that there is a good future in the restaurant industry for college-trained women. But to succeed they must have a desire to grow professionally and personally. Women supervisors need physical stamina, since they are on their feet most of the time. They need to be accurate and to have an appreciation for detail.

A college degree is not necessary, although it will help a woman with a flair for restaurant management to go farther in a shorter period of time. However, there are opportunities for high school graduates and for those with even less education if they acquire the proper skills and techniques on

---

4 Adapted from *The Outlook for Women*, published by the U.S. Department of Labor.

the job. Occasionally people who begin in low-level jobs reach a high degree of success in the restaurant industry.

As long as restaurants are needed, the home economist will find opportunities. There are always customers for a restaurant where good food is served in clean, pleasant surroundings. The home economist with good training, enthusiasm, vision, and the capacity for hard work will find satisfaction in this field.

Print your answers to these items as you have done on the previous tests.

1. A woman who goes into the restaurant industry
   A. must have a college education
   B. will go farther and faster with a college education
   C. cannot expect to learn the necessary skills on the job
2. Opportunities for women in the restaurant industry
   A. are at their peak right now
   B. will be greater in the future
   C. are declining
3. To be successful in restaurant management, a woman needs
   A. luck in finding the right job
   B. physical stamina, accuracy, and the ability to handle details
   C. physical charm, a desire to run other people, and the ability to handle details

The correct answers to Exercise 34 are shown in the answer key.

How do your reading rates compare on the five articles you have just read?

Write the numerals 1 to 5 on your paper. Go back to the beginning of each selection and find the reading purpose that was stated. Jot down that purpose for each selection. Then write down your reading rates. Did you read at the same speed or at different speeds for different reading purposes?

A survey might be made of the class reading rates. How many students read the first selection at the fastest rate? the second? the others? Discuss the class survey with your classmates. If you were to read these selections again, would you read any of them at a different rate? Did you make

mistakes on the tests from careless or too rapid reading?

You can improve your reading speed

For many years experts have been studying the reading habits and abilities of people of all ages. They have found that few people read as efficiently as they could. They have discovered that most people do not read as fast as they should. People tend to slip into a reading rate that makes little demand on their energies.

This is not a bad thing to do—unless the speed that you find easy and comfortable is far below your reading ability. If you are not reading comfortably at the best rate you are capable of, you will not read as much as you should.

There are so many things to do in the world today that everyone has to set aside a definite time for reading. Few people today have the long, lonely winter evenings or dull, empty weekends that were common fifty years ago. There is only so much time in your life for reading. To make the most of it, you must learn to read efficiently. That means you must learn to read at your best rate.

You can train yourself to read the newspaper faster and still get all the important news. You can train yourself to read books faster and read more of them with greater enjoyment. You can learn to study more efficiently and do even better in your schoolwork than you do now.

Reading is like other skills. You have to keep working to improve it. In order to improve your reading, you must read— read—read. And you must think about *how* you are reading.

Once more you must be cautioned. It is a good thing to be able to read rapidly. But there is no point to rapid reading if you do not understand what you read or if you cannot remember it. Efficient reading is fast reading *with* understanding.

Exercise 35

Try to read the article below at a rate faster than your usual *general* rate. Read with close attention and watch for ideas and important details. When you have finished, you will check your understanding of the article.

Copy the time box shown on page 116. Record your starting time.

Why Don't Athletes Do Better?[5]

by Ernest La France

They could—if they trained more carefully.

Roger Bannister ran the mile in 3 minutes 58.8 seconds to beat John Landy at Vancouver in August 1954. He might have run it in 3:50 flat.

Bob Feller has thrown a baseball at a speed of 98.6 miles an hour. He might have thrown it 100 mph.

Ford Konno of Ohio State swam 220 meters in 2 minutes 3.9 seconds. He might have done it in 2:00.

Sam Snead beat Ben Hogan 70-71 in the 18-hole golf playoff of the 1954 Masters Tournament at Augusta, Georgia. Both might have beaten the par of 72 by scores that were perhaps in the mid-60s.

Does this sound impossible? Not according to a study of athletes now being made by a Canadian research organization called Sports College. Located in Toronto, Sports College is a nonprofit service that was started in 1944 by the YMCA and the Canadian Broadcasting Corporation to help raise sport and physical fitness standards. It has spent nine years testing 2700 athletes of all kinds, studying their performances, and working out ways they can be improved.

From their research studies, the men at Sports College have learned many important things about athletes. The following paragraphs explain two facts they have learned.

1. With better training, athletes in all sports can improve nearly all their performances by about 25 percent.

2. Only 12 out of every 100 athletes have better than 75 percent of the physical development needed to do their best.

Most of the athletes tested should have had more training to develop three main

abilities—strength, flexibility, and relaxation. These abilities are required for good performances in many different sports.

A good athlete must have *strength*, as shown by power, speed, and endurance. More than half of the athletes tested by Sports College were surprisingly low in strength. Only one athlete in 17 could do twenty-five two-hand push-ups without difficulty. Only one in 75 could do a one-arm push-up. And only one in 82 could do a one-arm pull-up on a bar. Except for sprinters, middle-distance runners, and basketball players, the athletes rated much too low in speed—another measure of strength.

After testing individual athletes, Sports College men set out to study athletes during actual games. These men used stopwatches to clock the speeds baseball players needed for running and throwing. They learned plenty. For example, the average time a baseball player takes to run from first to second base (with a 5-foot lead) is 4 seconds. But the average time for a ball to move from the pitcher (including his windup) to the catcher and back to the second baseman is only 3.5 seconds. So the average player trying to steal second is an almost sure out—unlike the great Ty Cobb, who could run it in 3 seconds flat.

Sports College says that any baseball player can improve his running speed—especially his starting speed—by .3 to .4 seconds if he practices the ways of running that any good track sprinter knows and uses. In base running this makes a difference of 4 to 12 feet, the difference between being safe and being put out at second. In the field it means that the fielder starts more quickly, runs faster, catches more balls, and makes more put-outs. By exercising his wrist muscles, a baseball player can increase his throwing speed. On distances of 100 feet, nineteen players raised their throwing speed by nearly 5 miles per hour.

To build up his big-muscle strength, an athlete should do old-fashioned weightlifting. He should also exercise the muscles that he uses most in his chosen sport. For example, to strengthen the muscles most often employed in hitting the ball, a tennis player should swing a racket with books taped to it.

5 Adapted from *Parade*, May 15, 1955. Reprinted with permission of Parade Publications, Inc.

A good athlete must have endurance. This is the ability to keep playing hard and well throughout a game with little fatigue. Because of fatigue, the average basketball player loses 4 to 5 inches in his jumping ability during a game. And the average football player, at the middle of the game, cannot run 100 yards without feeling all tired out. For greater endurance, an athlete not only needs to strengthen his muscles by the exercises that have been suggested; he also needs to learn to relax and to breathe properly. Ways to do this will be discussed later.

To perform at his best, an athlete must have *flexibility*. This is the ability to keep his muscles useful in all the actions he must take during a game. If his muscles are flexible, he can stretch them when necessary and without injury.

If you as an athlete want to develop flexible muscles, you can take the following exercises. Stand with your feet wide apart. Reach down and grasp your ankles. Try to touch the floor with the top of your head. Next try to do it sitting down. Then try to do it standing with your feet four to six inches apart. Next, bend your knees, place your hands flat on the floor, and try to straighten your legs. Not easy—but even the trying helps you.

For good performance in a sport, an athlete must learn *relaxation*. This is the ability to play a game without feeling nervous tension. Such tension may come from the fear of losing or from the annoying shouts of spectators. The remedy is simple: *Think about the game—not about yourself.*

Relaxation is also the ability to play without muscle tension—that is, without having your muscles tighten up on you in the middle of a game. The remedy is simple: While you are *not* playing, tense your muscles and take a deep breath. Then relax and breathe out. Try this during the next game that you play.

By regular practice to develop strength, flexibility, and relaxation, Sports College points out, anyone can improve in any sport by at least 25 percent. .Worth a try, isn't it?

Write your finishing time in the time box. Then take the following test. Print your answers to each item on your paper.

1. According to the article, Roger Bannister ran the mile in slightly less than
    A. three minutes
    B. four minutes
    C. five minutes

2. The men at Sports College are trying
    A. to train themselves to become better athletes
    B. to find out how to train better athletes
    C. to build a winning football or baseball team

3. The tests and the other studies at Sports College show that with better training, athletes can improve their performances by about
    A. 25 percent
    B. 50 percent
    C. 75 percent

4. According to Sports College, the baseball player who wants to steal second base safely should train himself
    A. to run faster
    B. to slide for the base
    C. to fool the pitcher

5. To do his best in sports, an athlete should exercise regularly to increase not only his strength and speed but also his
    A. tension and relaxation
    B. worry and fatigue
    C. endurance and flexibility

6. If you cannot do the difficult flexibility exercises at first, you should
    A. try do do them anyway
    B. have someone help you do them
    C. not try to do them

7. If you are afraid of losing during a game or if you are upset by the shouts of the spectators, you should
    A. think of yourself, not the game
    B. tell the spectator to be quiet, not noisy
    C. think of the game, not yourself

8. A good way to relax your muscles during a game is to
    A. relax your muscles and then tense them
    B. tense your muscles and relax them
    C. relax and tense your muscles at the same time

There are 1000 words in this story. Figure your reading rate according to the directions in column 2 on page 115.

The correct answers are shown in the answer key.

Exercise 36

Read the story below at a rate faster than your usual rate in reading for pleasure. But while you are reading, pay close attention to detail and try to get the author's main ideas. When you have finished, you will check your understanding of the story.

Copy the time box shown on page 116. Record your starting time.

A Good Deed Daily[6]

by Rice E. Cochran

I first heard of Woody when Mrs. Ballard phoned me. "I want to tell you a story," she said. "You know that my little daughter came down with polio last month. And my son, John, has been visiting her at Orthopedic Hospital every night." I knew, because John Ballard was in my scout troop.

Mrs. Ballard kept on talking: "Lately John has noticed another polio patient in the hospital—a boy about thirteen. He just lies there, staring at the ceiling. John asked the nurses about him. They said his name is Woody Shreve. His parents are government workers in Alaska. They had to stay there while they sent Woody here for treatment—all with the help of money from the March of Dimes. The nurses also said that Woody is all alone, helpless and hopeless, and does not want to live. The doctors and nurses can't get him interested in anything. Well, as soon as John heard all this about Woody, he wandered over and got acquainted."

I began to feel rather privileged to know John.

"John found that Woody was a boy scout in Alaska," Mrs. Ballard said. "So now the two of them talk scouting every night, and Woody seems to have a little more zest for life."

"Fine, I'm glad," I said, wondering if I, as John's scoutmaster, could help.

6 From *Be Prepared!* by Rice E. Cochran, copyright 1952 by William Sloane Associates, Inc., by permission of William Sloane Associates, Inc.

"John was just asking if there was any way that Woody could be made a part of our troop. Remember, this boy can't move even a finger. But I thought perhaps you might find something—something that would give Woody a purpose in life. John begged me to talk to you about it. He said I could explain it better."

"There's a way to help Woody," I said, even though I was not sure. "I don't know what it is, but we'll find it."

A few days later I looked in at the hospital, and asked for Woody. "He's a little better since John made friends with him," the nurse told me as she led the way to Woody's bed. "Now he smiles and talks. He looks forward all day to John's visits."

When I first saw Woody, I felt a chill. I looked down at the boy's pale face. I saw his sticklike arms and legs beneath his pajamas. Woody lay very still. But he grinned at me, and I made myself grin back.

"You're Mr. Cochran, I bet," he said. "John said you might come, but I thought he was kidding me."

"I wouldn't have missed it," I said. "I've been wanting to meet you, so I could ask a favor. Our troop needs some help you can give us better than anyone else."

Woody tried to smile, as if I had told a rather poor joke.

"Remember the first-class requirement to send and receive messages in Morse code?" I went on. "Our guys are lousy on Morse. They need some one who knows the code and will practice with them. That's where you come in. You've got time on your hands. I want you to memorize Morse—*really* memorize it, till you can send and receive in your sleep."

Woody was interested. "I can do that. Only I'll have to find somebody to send to me, while I learn."

"John Ballard says he'll do that. It'll be a good way for him to learn. When you know Morse upside down and backward, then you'll be our troop expert on signaling. All our scouts can come here to the hospital to learn it from you. When they know it, you can O.K. them."

"All right. Let's see—I guess I can send by whistle at first. But maybe I can move my fingers soon, so then I can use a buzzer set, or a regular telegrapher's key."

"That'll be much better. Try to get

the use of your fingers as soon as you can. Now, let's see. You're going to work with this troop, so you ought to be an official member of it. We have a ceremony at our troop court of honor for taking in new members. Better plan to be at our next court."

We both seemed to feel that nothing was impossible. Woody nodded his head slightly—the first time I had seen him move—and said, "I can probably talk the nurse into letting me go."

"I'll talk to her, too. And I'll see about transportation for you. Now get busy on that Morse code."

John Ballard was a big awkward boy. He was more interested in basketball than in anything else. His grades at school were just fair. He would find that studying Morse code with Woody was hard mental work. But since polio attacked his small sister, John had been changing. While his parents spent every free hour with her, he had voluntarily done all the cooking at home, and much of the housework. John also had found time to visit the girl every night.

John's sister was lucky. She recovered from polio quickly and completely, and returned home. Even so, John kept going to the hospital to see Woody. After Woody was a master of Morse signaling, John dropped in for a visit every week or so.

When I suggested that Woody go to our court of honor, the doctors and the nurses were delighted. "It'll be a bit of trouble to move him from his bed onto a stretcher, into an ambulance, into the church, and back again—but it's worth doing," the doctor told me. "To kids, a hospital seems like a jail. One evening away from it might work wonders." The doctor soon talked with the owner of an ambulance. The owner gladly furnished his ambulance free.

When Woody appeared at our court of honor, he had to lie flat on his back on the stretcher. But when he found himself in this never-never land, he was really thrilled. The parents and most of the scouts met Woody for the first time that night. When many of them tried to talk to him, their voices were quiet and shaky.

The time came to present Woody with the troop insignia—a cloth badge that showed the troop's number. Four scouts lifted Woody's bed onto the stage. As the scoutmaster, I laid the badge on his blanket, because Woody could not lift his hand to take it.

But Woody could move his fingers. With them, he pulled his hand like a crippled spider across the blanket. Finally he grasped the troop badge. As Woody's hand traveled, he gritted his teeth. It probably cost him something, but he was smiling.

In the weeks that followed, there were many visitors at Woody's bedside in the hospital. Scouts came and went almost every night. They drilled with him on the dots and dashes which every boy must know to be a first-class scout. Woody felt more and more that he was important to the troop. He made progress. From moving his fingers, he moved his hands, and then his arms. "I'll get well," he told the other scouts. "I'll start going to troop meetings pretty soon."

Woody did. Two months after the court of honor, he was sitting up in a wheelchair. One of the fathers in our troop went to the hospital each meeting night. He lifted Woody out of bed and carried him downstairs. He put the boy into his automobile and drove to the church. He next helped Woody to get into a folding wheelchair and into the troop meeting. After the meeting, the father drove Woody back to the hospital.

Woody took a regular part in our meetings. At first the muscles of his back were very weak. Whenever he tried to move, he fell sideways or forward in the wheelchair. Someone always helped him to sit up again. But Woody kept trying. One night he could bend to the side or front and then pull himself straight again.

As the scouts grew more used to Woody's wheelchair, they began riding on it with him. They pushed the chair like a coaster wagon across the floor. They rapidly turned the chair down and around like an airplane. Woody loved it, so I never interfered. However, I prayed all the time that there would not be an accident.

"Woody's case looks like a miracle," the hospital doctor told me one day. "When Woody Shreve came here, there was no hope whatever that he would walk again. Now there's hope. He's already done more than we thought possible."

Two years later Woody walked. He had to use crutches and heavy braces on his legs, but he walked. After a while his parents wrote the hospital and arranged to take him back to their home in Alaska. In the end Woody left and we never saw him again. But before he left, something remarkable happened.

After Woody began to attend our troop meetings, he listened carefully to all our first-aid and lifesaving instructions. When he could use crutches, he began coming to our troop swims. He watched the rescue drills and even learned to swim a little himself.

During his last summer in our town, Woody hung around the beaches. Lifeguards got to know him, and told him stories of their daily warfare with the water.

One autumn afternoon Woody with his crutches was standing on the dock. Suddenly the wind turned over a sailboat. The six persons in the boat were spilled into the water about fifty yards from shore. All of them were poor swimmers and all were struggling. Four grabbed the overturned boat, but the two weakest swimmers were unable to paddle their way back to it.

There were no other boats nearby. Only one lifeguard was on the beach. He jumped into the water and swam fast. Saving these six persons was really a tough job. On his first trip the lifeguard brought the two weakest swimmers to the dock. He swam back and caught two more swimmers just before they lost their hold on the boat. Then the guard made two more trips to get the stronger swimmers. They had been able to hang on while waiting for help.

While all this was going on, a big crowd gathered on the dock. As the guard pushed each drowning person upward out of the water, some people in the crowd lifted him to safety. Just after the guard delivered the sixth and last person, the crowd pressed more closely around the half-drowned victims who were stretched out on the dock.

No one except Woody noticed the lifeguard. The guard was exhausted. He could not pull himself out of the water. He could barely keep his head above the waves. He was sinking helplessly within two feet of the dock. Woody knew exactly what to do. He had watched our scouts (including the boys who couldn't swim) practice a simple thing called "the extension rescue." Woody threw himself flat on the dock. He held out his crutch to the guard. The guard grasped the crutch feebly, and Woody pulled him in. It was easy and quick. But the guard said later that he owed his life to Woody Shreve. That day Woody did a boy scout deed that was extra special. Probably an assist[7] should also be credited to John Ballard.

Write your finishing time in the time box. Then take the following test. Print your answers on your paper.

1. The author first found out about Woody Shreve, who had polio, from John Ballard's
   A. mother
   B. sister
   C. father

2. At first, because Woody was so helpless and hopeless, he did not want
   A. to join the scout troop
   B. to see John
   C. to get well

3. When John got to know Woody, they talked mostly about
   A. polio
   B. scouting
   C. Alaska

4. Woody was seriously crippled by polio; he could not even move his
   A. lips
   B. fingers
   C. tongue

5. John's mother told the author that she thought the most important thing he could do for Woody was to help him get
   A. an iron lung for breathing
   B. a wheelchair for traveling
   C. a purpose in life

6. When the author first saw Woody in the hospital, he forced himself to grin back at him. In doing this, the author
   A. looked sad outside but felt hopeful inside

---

7 *Assist* is a baseball term. For example, suppose that the shortstop catches a batted ball on the ground and throws it to the first baseman in time to put out the runner. The first baseman is credited with a put-out, the shortstop with an assist.

B. looked outside as he felt inside

C. looked cheerful outside but felt sorry inside

7. The author asked Woody to teach the scouts Morse code mainly because the author wanted to help the boy

A. get well

B. join the scout troop

C. pass the signaling test

8. By asking Woody to become an official member of the scout troop, the author helped the boy

A. remember the weakness of his fingers

B. forget the absence of his parents

C. get back his will to live

9. While his sister was ill in the hospital, John

A. did the housework for his mother

B. went on many scout hikes

C. stayed away from sick people

10. When the author suggested that Woody go to the troop meeting, the doctors and nurses felt that Woody should

A. wait until he was better

B. go for his own good

C. stay for only a few minutes

11. When many of the parents and scouts talked with Woody, their voices were quiet and shaky. This meant that they were very sorry that Woody was so

A. helpless

B. unhappy

C. tired

12. When Woody reached for the troop badge, he had

A. to ask another boy to hand it to him

B. to work hard and painfully to get it

C. to move his wheelchair in order to reach it

13. When Woody was able to attend troop meetings, he was taken from the hospital to the meeting place regularly by

A. the father of one of the scouts

B. the scoutmaster

C. John's mother

14. At troop meetings the boys would push Woody in his wheelchair rapidly around the room. At such times the author was afraid that in an accident

A. several boys would get hurt

B. he, the scoutmaster, would get hurt

C. Woody would get hurt

15. The hospital doctor said that Woody's progress from a helpless boy to a boy who might walk again was like a miracle. This miracle was due largely to

A. rest and relaxation

B. the efforts of the scoutmaster and scouts

C. the use of braces and wonder drugs

16. Woody learned lifesaving from

A. the lifeguard at the beach

B. the scout troop's instructor

C. his own father

17. The six persons who were on or near the overturned sailboat were in serious trouble mainly because they were

A. poor swimmers

B. too far from shore or from another boat

C. unable to yell to Woody for help

18. In rescuing the six persons who were holding on to the boat or struggling near it, the lifeguard first saved the

A. poorest swimmers

B. average swimmers

C. best swimmers

19. The lifeguard almost drowned because he had exhausted himself while

A. trying to keep the crowd back

B. showing Woody the way to rescue a drowning person

C. saving the people from the sailboat

20. According to the story, in what order did Woody get back the use of his muscles? Write the letters *A* to *F* in a column down the left side of your paper. At the right of each letter write the numeral that shows the order in which Woody was able to use certain muscles. For example, write the numeral 1 at the right of the letter *D*, "Speech muscles."

A. Leg muscles

B. Finger muscles

C. Arm muscles

D. Speech muscles

E. Back muscles

F. Hand muscles

There are 1940 words in this story. Figure your reading rate according to the directions on page 115. The correct answers are shown in the answer key.

How does your reading rate for "A Good Deed Daily" compare with your rate for the article "Why Don't Athletes Do Better?" Do you think your rate should be the same for the two selections?

Suggestions for a program to improve your reading rates

You can learn to read faster by pushing yourself to do so in regular practice every school day for a period of four weeks. To plan and carry out these practice readings, here are the steps to follow:

1. Get a good book, one that you are likely to read from beginning to end. It may be about animals or airplanes, or adventure, or science, or some other subject in which you are keenly interested. Your teacher or your librarian will help you find such a book.

2. Make sure that the book is about the right level of difficulty. The book should not be too hard for you. It may be fairly easy. If the book is easy and interesting, you are more likely to understand it, to enjoy it, and to finish it.

3. Plan to spend at least thirty minutes a day reading the book. Try to keep your daily date with the book until you finish it. You may want to read the book every day at the same time (perhaps 8–8:30 P.M.) and in the same place (say in your own room).

4. During the first part of each thirty-minute reading period, try to increase your reading speed. Time yourself or, better still, have someone else time you. If you have an alarm clock, set it to ring fifteen minutes after you start reading. At the end of the fifteen-minute period, count the number of lines that you have read and record this number on a separate sheet of paper.[8]

5. During the second part of each thirty-minute reading period, read your book at or near your ordinary rate just for enjoyment.

6. To check on your comprehension of the book, write a short summary once a week of what you read. Or have someone ask you questions about what you read, and answer them orally.

7. After you have read one or more books for twenty half-hour reading periods, compare your rate at the beginning of your training program with your rate at the end. The chances are that you will have made a very good gain in your reading speed.

---

[8] If you like arithmetic, you can learn to determine your reading rate for the fifteen-minute practice period. To do this, count the number of words in ten typical lines. Divide this number by 10 to find the average number of words per line. Next, multiply the number of lines that you read by the average number of words per line. The product is the number of words that you read during the fifteen-minute period. To determine your reading rate, divide this product by 15. The quotient is the number of words that you read per minute. After two or three times, you will find that it is easy to figure your reading rate.

Practice Reading 9

In a book, magazine, or newspaper that you like, practice reading for speed and comprehension. Make a record of this reading in Chart 3 on page 8 of the progress folder.

9
article

Midshipman aboard the Half Moon[9]

by Lowry W. Harding

John Hudson stood before the captain. He tried to look innocent. It was not an easy task, first, because he wasn't innocent, and second, because the captain always saw through everything anyway.

"You left the ship yesterday," said the captain, "and without permission." Captain Henry Hudson came directly to the point. He did not believe in hedging or beating about the bush, even with his own son.

The boy swallowed. "Yes, sir," he said, "I did."

The big man looked stern. But his eyes were kind, those wide dreamer's eyes in the gruff face. Who would not be proud of a boy who would stand and admit the truth? Captain Hudson pulled at his beard. "You knew that I had advised against leaving the ship for the crew's own good?"

"Yes, sir."

For a long moment there was silence. "Why did you go, boy?" asked the captain finally. "Did you not know that I have enough troubles without your adding to them?"

John nodded. Well enough he knew! He was only a midshipman and therefore not considered old enough to be of any importance. But he had eyes and ears. He knew how the crew had muttered against his father from the very day they had sailed from Holland. He remembered how they grumbled as the ship, the good *Half Moon*, sailed ever northward. He thought of how gleeful they had all been when Captain Hudson had been forced to turn back from his dream of finding a northern

route to India by way of the Americas. He remembered the ice, the great blocks of ice, which had threatened to crush the tiny vessel, up there in Hudson's Bay. Now they had come to this more southern point, hoping that it might be the long-sought passage to India. It was not, however. They had discovered that it was merely a wide river.

Yes, John knew. "I did not mean to cause any trouble, sir," he said.

"Then what did you mean to do?" the captain asked.

The young man was silent. He would not answer—could not, dared not. "I cannot say, sir."

Of a sudden Captain Hudson lost his patience.

"You must be disciplined," said the captain. "Were you not my son, I would merely warn you as I have done before. I would warn all the crew again. They may go ashore in large parties, with arms to defend themselves if they have to; but it is dangerous and foolhardy to go ashore alone. But now, you must be disciplined. You are my son. As such, you must set an example. You will report to the first officer. You must be under his direction, checking charts and copying the logbook, until we weigh anchor. You understand?"

"Yes. Yes, sir."

He saluted and fled. He knew that if he stayed another minute he would feel so sorry for his father that he would not be

[9] Condensed from *Reading for Servicemen*, by Lowry W. Harding. Published by the United States Armed Forces Institute, Madison, Wisconsin.

able to leave the ship again. And it was important that he be able to go ashore just once again. It was important most of all to Henry Hudson himself.

What his father did not know, what he dared not let his father know, was that he had not only seen Indians the day before—he had talked with them and bargained with them. They possessed something which John knew every member of the crew, including the captain himself, would give almost anything to have. They must have it, or many men might die. And John proposed to get it.

It seemed as if the afternoon would never end. Yet it finally did, in a golden haze of sun-gold. Carefully John eased over the rail, found the painter, and slid down the rope to the small boat. He rowed quietly ashore.

John's breath came in excited gulps as he beached his boat and hurried to the appointed meeting place. No one was there. John's hopes vanished; he began to wish that he had not come. There was still the chance of being caught when he reached the ship on his return.

What was that? John crouched. He peered through the gloom. Something had moved—of that he was sure. Was it some wild animal? Or was it an Indian? The Indians had been very friendly when he met them the first time. Maybe that was a trick. Maybe they were hoping he would bring several other men with him when he returned. The Indians might have planned to ambush them and kill or capture the strange white men from over there.

Four Indians came from behind as many different trees. "This is my time," thought John. Then he relaxed. He smiled in happy relief. One Indian had held out his arm, hand up and open. A sign of friendship! These were the Indians he had met before. They had kept their promise to meet him again. They, too, had been a little fearful and suspicious. It paid to make certain.

The Indians had brought their woven wicker baskets. Each was full, and John traded for all of them. The Indians stowed the sixteen baskets into the small boat. Then they helped John shove it off, and he headed back to the ship.

It was completely dark by that time.

John rowed swiftly toward the *Half Moon*. There were lighted torches on deck. Something must be amiss. With all his might John pulled on his oars. They must have missed the small boat! He rowed faster.

"Mr. Midshipman! Is that you?" It sounded angry.

"Y-yes, sir," John answered breathlessly. He was winded from his hard rowing.

He could see his father then, leaning over the rail, looking down for the small boat.

"We missed you," said Captain Hudson. "Where have you been?"

John explained as quickly as possible. He was beginning to think that his adventure was not to end in a blaze of glory.

"What is that you have?" asked the captain, as John's voice trailed off. He could not decide what to make of the story.

"Maize, sir," answered John.

"Maize. What's that?" asked Captain Hudson.

And the men of the crew, having gathered to watch the scene, echoed, "Maize? Never heard of it!"

"Yes, maize. Indian corn. It's better than our grain. It's sweeter. It tastes mighty good when it's roasted. It will cure scurvy, and I have enough for everyone," said John.

"Enough for the crew, too?" asked a fellow down near the rail.

"Enough," said John, "and to spare." He wasn't proud of his achievement anymore. He said wearily, "I got sixteen baskets."

"Sixteen baskets!" bellowed the captain. "How did you come by them?"

It was as if John had told them he had a boatload of gold. In fact, the fresh Indian corn was worth more to the men than gold. The men had been eating hardtack and salt meat-during the whole long voyage. Lack of fruit and green vegetables was taking its toll. Half of the crew was down with scurvy. Many of the others were sick. Teeth were falling out, bones were brittle. The Indian corn would be just what they needed. The lives of half the crew would be saved. All would live to sail home.

John explained how he had bought the Indian corn. The Indians admired the brass buttons on his coat. John had seen the Indian corn growing in a small clearing.

He knew that it would cure scurvy. He wanted as much fresh corn as he could get, but he would have no time to pick it. The Indians offered to trade a basket of corn for a brass button. John agreed. He had sixteen brass buttons. So he got sixteen baskets of Indian corn. There were several small fields of corn ashore, he explained. More silence followed John's explanation.

Finally the captain spoke.

"Come up, John, and join me in the cabin."

And suddenly John knew that he had passed his test. He would soon be a midshipman no more. He would be responsible for a watch on the quarterdeck, come another voyage.

Record your finishing time in the time box. Then take the reading test.

Read each test item and choose the answer you believe is correct. Print your answers on your paper.

Reading Test 9

Getting main ideas

1. John Hudson was punished for

   A. hitting one of the crew
   B. telling his father a lie
   C. losing the logbook
   D. leaving the ship without permission
   E. talking back to his father

---

2. John Hudson felt sorry for his father because

   A. the crew had mutinied
   B. he was hungry
   C. he was lonesome
   D. he was sick
   E. he had failed in the main goal of his voyage

---

3. Fresh food was badly needed because

   A. the crew could catch no fish
   B. the supply of salt pork and hardtack was running low
   C. many of the crew were sick with scurvy
   D. the food on the ship had spoiled
   E. the crew did not have enough to eat

---

4. John knew that the Indians had corn because

   A. he saw the corn growing in a clearing
   B. his father had told him
   C. the crew had told him
   D. they showed him a bushel of it
   E. he had read about Indian corn in his books

5. The Indians were
    - **A.** hostile
    - **B.** angry with John Hudson
    - **C.** planning to attack the ship
    - **D.** fascinated by John's brass buttons
    - **E.** not afraid of the white men

6. Henry Hudson called John to join him in the cabin
    - **A.** to punish him
    - **B.** to give him command of the ship
    - **C.** to praise him
    - **D.** to give him permission to go ashore again
    - **E.** to tell him a secret

7. Henry Hudson
    - **A.** gave his son special favors
    - **B.** was proud of his son
    - **C.** wished his son had stayed at home
    - **D.** treated his son badly
    - **E.** threw his son into the ship's prison

Reading with a keen eye

8. Henry Hudson had sailed
    - **A.** to study the icebergs in northern seas
    - **B.** to explore the rivers on America's east coast
    - **C.** to explore the North American continent
    - **D.** to find a northern route to India
    - **E.** to find gold and silver

9. The crew was
    - **A.** glad to be on this voyage
    - **B.** unhappy about the voyage
    - **C.** expecting to share in gold and silver
    - **D.** eager to fight the Indians
    - **E.** sorry that they had to turn back in the north

10. John Hudson's punishment was
    - **A.** to go without meals for two days
    - **B.** to help the cook
    - **C.** to wash down the decks
    - **D.** to be flogged before the crew
    - **E.** to check charts and copy the logbook

11. John Hudson traded
    - **A.** 16 brass buttons for 16 bushels of corn
    - **B.** a gun for the corn
    - **C.** six brass buttons for 16 bushels of corn
    - **D.** colored glass for the corn
    - **E.** the small boat for the corn

Choosing the best reason

12. Many of the crew had scurvy because

    A. they had no fresh fruit or vegetables
    B. they had no fresh water
    C. they did not keep clean
    D. they ate too much
    E. scurvy is a contagious disease

13. John Hudson went to meet the Indians alone because

    A. he knew their language
    B. the crew would run off into the woods
    C. he wanted all the glory himself
    D. he was afraid a large group of men might frighten the Indians
    E. there was room for only one man in the boat

14. When John landed a second time, the Indians were hiding because they

    A. wanted to surprise him
    B. feared that the crew would come along in a second boat
    C. did not want him to see them
    D. planned to kill or kidnap him
    E. had not brought the corn with them

Reading between the lines

15. The Indians were willing to trade corn for brass buttons because they

    A. did not know the value of corn
    B. did not like corn
    C. used brass buttons as coins
    D. needed brass buttons for their uniforms
    E. had much corn but nothing like the brass buttons

Getting word meanings

16. A ship's log is a written record of what happens on a voyage. A *logbook* is

    A. a book about lumber
    B. a book of maps and charts
    C. the book in which is recorded the events of a trip
    D. a record of snags and sunken logs that a ship meets on a river
    E. a book with wooden covers

17. The word *maize* means

    A. wheat
    B. fish
    C. brass
    D. basket
    E. corn

18. "Carefully John eased over the rail, found the painter, and slid down the rope to the small boat." In this sentence, *painter* means

    A. small boat
    B. rope for tying up a boat
    C. person who paints
    D. ship's side
    E. coat

19. "Then he relaxed. He smiled in happy relief." *Relaxed* means

- **A.** became less tense and stiff
- **B.** became tense
- **C.** jumped up and down
- **D.** called out in fear
- **E.** grew frightened

20. "The Indians might have planned to ambush them." *Ambush* means

- **A.** make a surprise attack from a place of hiding
- **B.** take prisoner
- **C.** knock someone down
- **D.** tie someone up
- **E.** run away and hide

Follow the directions (Steps 8–13) on page 1 of the progress folder.

How to read illustrations

Good illustrations increase our enjoyment and understanding of what we read. When we have photographs before us, we do not have to depend on our imagination to make pictures of people, places, and events. The photographs give us a good indication of what these things are like—if we read them with care.

In the same way, an artist's drawings help the reader visualize the characters and scenes in a narrative. Maps help us understand where far-off places are in relation to our own homes. Good historical maps help us follow a series of events. Diagrams help us understand the parts of a machine or process. And graphs help us pull figures together and interpret them.

Good illustrations are helpful because they make dramatically clear what it may take several paragraphs to say. But, like good writing, good illustrations must be studied and read carefully.

How do pictures help you understand something?

You have probably heard the saying: "A picture is worth a thousand words." But is this saying true? The answer is not as simple or as easy as it seems. Sometimes a picture gives you meanings that you cannot get by observing something directly or by reading about it. But a picture cannot give you all the meanings that words can give. For this reason, pictures usually have words to accompany them. By studying a picture and reading its accompanying words, you will learn more than from either words or pictures alone.

When a picture is shown in a magazine or newspaper, it may be referred to in three places—in the caption, or title; in the legend; and in the text. Usually the caption appears above the picture and gives you a general idea of what the picture is about. The information below the picture is the legend. On a map the legend is at the lower left or lower right corner. The legend of a diagram, graph, or picture gives you detailed information about the illustration. The legend of a map tells you the meaning of lines, dots, or other marks. It may also give you the scale, that is, the number of miles represented by one inch on the map.

How do you read a picture diagram?

Exercise 37

Note the title of the diagram on page 136. It reads: "Steppingstones into Space." Also note the legend. It reads: "Diagram of the earth's atmospheric zones showing U.S. altitude records of manned flights in 1961." Study the diagram. Note at the left the *scale of miles:* 25, 50, 75, 100, and so on. At the right, observe the different layers of the atmosphere. Nearest the earth is the troposphere, a narrow band. Above it is the stratosphere and then the ionosphere. Next, look at each object shown—Mount Everest, a rocket plane, a balloon, and a space rocket.

A test on reading a diagram

Read each item and choose the answer you believe is correct. Print your answers on your paper.

1. Which manned vehicle has reached the highest level above the earth's surface?
   A. Balloon
   B. Freedom 7 rocket
   C. Rocket plane

Figure 2[1]
Steppingstones into space

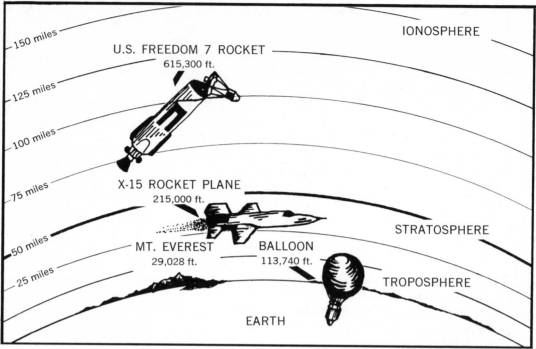

IONOSPHERE

150 miles

U.S. FREEDOM 7 ROCKET
615,300 ft.

125 miles

100 miles

75 miles

X-15 ROCKET PLANE
215,000 ft.

STRATOSPHERE

50 miles

MT. EVEREST
29,028 ft.

BALLOON
113,740 ft.

TROPOSPHERE

25 miles

EARTH

Diagram of the earth's atmospheric zones showing U. S. altitude records of manned flights in 1961

2. The balloon reached an altitude above sea level of about
   A. 50 miles
   B. 114,000 feet
   C. 29,000 feet

3. The rocket plane flew to a record height of:
   A. 158 miles
   B. 15 miles
   C. 40 miles

4. The Freedom 7 rocket is flying in the
   A. troposphere
   B. stratosphere
   C. ionosphere

5. As a rocket goes up, it passes through thinner and thinner air, that is, through air that has less and less oxygen and nitrogen in it. The rocket first goes through the troposphere, then through the stratosphere, and then into the ionosphere. According to the diagram, the boundary between the stratosphere and the ionosphere is about this distance above sea level:
   A. 5½ miles
   B. 50 miles
   C. 110 miles
   D. 160 miles

6. From recent developments, do you think that man will ever build rockets that are precise enough to put satellites around another planet?
   A. Never
   B. Very probably
   C. Uncertain
   D. Not for a thousand years

The correct answers are shown in the answer key.

How do you read a picture story?

Exercise 38

In a well-written and well-illustrated picture story, the pictures help you understand the words, and the words help you understand the pictures. Look at Figure 3, "Wilderness Ways—The Bumblebee." For reference purposes, the pictures have been given letters—A, B, C, and D.

1 "Conquest of Space," by permission of *The New York Times*. Updated from records published by National Aeronautics Association, Washington, D.C.

Figure 3[2]

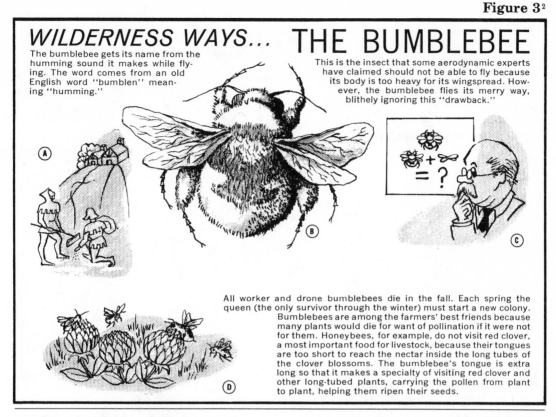

WILDERNESS WAYS... THE BUMBLEBEE

The bumblebee gets its name from the humming sound it makes while flying. The word comes from an old English word "bumblen" meaning "humming."

This is the insect that some aerodynamic experts have claimed should not be able to fly because its body is too heavy for its wingspread. However, the bumblebee flies its merry way, blithely ignoring this "drawback."

All worker and drone bumblebees die in the fall. Each spring the queen (the only survivor through the winter) must start a new colony. Bumblebees are among the farmers' best friends because many plants would die for want of pollination if it were not for them. Honeybees, for example, do not visit red clover, a most important food for livestock, because their tongues are too short to reach the nectar inside the long tubes of the clover blossoms. The bumblebee's tongue is extra long so that it makes a specialty of visiting red clover and other long-tubed plants, carrying the pollen from plant to plant, helping them ripen their seeds.

First, look only at the pictures; do not read any of the words. In Picture A two men are shown working in a field. They are watching an insect as it flies away; they hear its *hum-hum.* One man is cultivating the ground with a hoe. The other man is planting seeds; he takes them from the bag on his back. In the background are a farmhouse and a barn.

In Picture B a bumblebee is shown larger than life-size. Notice that the bee has a well-marked body and four small transparent wings, two on each side of its body. It also has six legs, two big eyes, and two whiskerlike antennae.

In Picture C at the upper right is a baldheaded man. His hand on chin indicates that he is thinking about something. He is studying a board on which six things are shown. From this picture alone, you cannot figure out what this board means.

In Picture D are some flowers. If you know flowers, you know that these are the blossoms of clover plants. Perched on or flying near these blossoms are four bees.

From these four pictures alone, you get little information about the bumblebee. You must read the paragraph that goes with each picture. As you read the paragraph, study the picture again. From Picture A and its text, you learn that the word *bumble* in *bumblebee* comes from the old English word *bumblen,* which meant "humming." The men, you may have guessed, are dressed in the clothing worn by English farmers during the Middle Ages.

From Picture C and its text you learn that men are still trying to solve this puzzle: The bumblebee has a very large body and very small wings, but it can fly. Although bees blithely ignore this handicap, experts pay close attention to it.

From Picture D and the paragraph to the right of it you learn a number of important facts about the bumblebee.

A test on reading a picture story

After you read these paragraphs, take the short test that follows. Print your answers on your paper.

1. If American farmers today were to give the bumblebee a name to indicate the

2 "Wilderness Ways . . . The Bumblebee," October 1955, by permission of *Boys' Life,* published by the Boy Scouts of America.

Figure 4

Courtesy of Morton Shapiro

sound it makes, they would call it a
- **A.** bumblingbee
- **B.** humblebee
- **C.** hummingbee
- **D.** bummingbee

2. Some experts in aviation claim the bee should not be able to fly because it does not
- **A.** have the right proportions
- **B.** understand the principles of flight
- **C.** fly with precision
- **D.** have a big enough body

3. If a farmer did not have any bumblebees in his summer pastureland, he would not have
- **A.** honeybees
- **B.** red clover for his cattle
- **C.** beeswax for his wife's sewing thread
- **D.** flowers for his honeybees

4. In a colony of bumblebees there are three kinds of bees: the *queen bee* (female bee that mates and lays eggs), *worker bees* (undeveloped female bees), and *drones* (male bees). The only kind of bumblebee that lives through the winter is the
- **A.** worker bee
- **B.** queen bee
- **C.** drone

The correct answers are shown in the answer key.

From your study of the pictures and of the accompanying text about the bumblebee, you quickly learned some important facts about this interesting and valuable insect. During this exercise, moreover, you learned how pictures and text together aid you in getting meanings.

How do you read a photograph?

Look at the picture on page 138. It is a picture of a model boat sailing in a quiet lagoon. You should know immediately that it is a model if you looked at the picture carefully. The hand showing in the picture makes it very obvious that the boat is a model. Write a caption or a legend for this picture that would tell what you think is happening.

Did you know that it is possible to fake a photograph? Probably you have seen extreme examples of faking in pictures taken at an amusement park where a friend's head peers out over a donkey's body? Faked photographs are used in many ways, and they are not necessarily bad. They are sometimes used in advertising or in publicity releases to create attention-getting pictures. Many governments use them for propaganda purposes.

The producers of science-fiction movies create detailed scenes showing monsters in space or on earth through the use of faked photography. Scientists may fake pictures of the surface of the moon so that future explorers will know what to expect.

It is possible for an expert to tell by microscopic analysis that a photograph has been faked. But it is not always possible for the average reader to know whether a photograph is genuine. Fortunately, most magazines and newspapers are very careful to use only photographs that they know are genuine.

The careful reader is always on guard to make sure that the photographs he looks at are real. But in addition he must make sure that the captions and legends accompanying a photograph really describe what the picture shows. The wrong legend may be placed under a picture; or if there are two pictures on a page, the legends may have been accidentally switched. Have you ever seen an example of this?

Books of pictures for which the legends are deliberately changed are often published. The humor resulting from the unexpected legends for these pictures has made these books very popular.

The best way to check a legend against the photograph it accompanies is to look closely at the photograph itself. You can get the main idea of a photograph just as you can of a paragraph. And you can look for details that will help you read the photograph as a whole.

One good clue to the meaning of a picture is the relative size of the objects portrayed. In the first picture, the hand was your clue. This led you to a closer examination of the boat itself. At that point, any landlubber would recognize that the boat was a model. But what if the hand had been removed from the picture as in Figure 5, or "cropped out," as the photographers say? And if the mast had been cut down slightly? Would you have recognized the boat as a model. Or would you have accepted it as a photograph of a contender for the America Cup? You can see now how

Figure 5

Courtesy of Morton Shapiro

important it is to study pictures carefully.

Knowing that the second picture was cropped, do you see any details that you might have missed? Could you have discovered that the picture was a miniature? What do you conclude about the importance of looking at all the details of a picture when you are deciding what it means?

How do you read cartoons?

Exercise 39

There are two main kinds of cartoons— comic cartoons and political cartoons. In both kinds the cartoonist shows a situation in which he makes fun of something or somebody. To add to the fun, he usually exaggerates—that is, he emphasizes some characteristic of the thing or person he is drawing. In a cartoon such as the one below, you look at the picture, read the accompanying words, get the point, and laugh aloud or chuckle to yourself.

Part 1

To check on whether you get the meaning of the cartoon, look at it again and record your answer to this item.

According to the cartoon, a customer has just said that

A. the waiter's service was terrible

B. the price of soup is too high

C. the soup tasted awful

Part 2

Look at the comic cartoon shown in Figure 7. Then answer the question below.

There is a saying that "an elephant never forgets." This cartoon is funny because the ridiculous-looking elephant

A. believes the saying is true

B. does not realize he has forgotten something

C. is worried about losing a wagon

In comic cartoons such as those just presented, the artist tries to make you laugh. His main purpose is to give you enjoyment. In a political cartoon the artist pokes fun at someone or at something. To make his point, he usually exaggerates. He takes sides for or against someone or something. He tries not only to make you laugh but also to get you to agree with him.

In a political cartoon the artist usually "gets into the fight" over a controversial issue—that is, over an issue that many people are talking about and debating.

Figure 6[3]

"Got a message for you!"

3 "Got a Message for You," by Sid Gordin, April 1953, by permission of *Boys' Life*, published by the Boy Scouts of America.

Figure 7[4]

MILLICENT

"Of course, elephants never forget! . . . What wagon?"

This issue may be which candidate would make a better President of the United States—a Republican or a Democrat. It may be whether or not the United States should aid underdeveloped areas such as parts of Africa and Asia.

Part 3

On the next page you see a political cartoon by Herbert Block, who signs himself Herblock. Cartoons of this kind are comments on some current national problem. In this cartoon Herblock is calling attention to the need for more schoolhouses.

The cartoon shows an old-fashioned wooden schoolhouse. It is labeled "U.S. School Construction Need." The schoolroom is crowded—so crowded that the children are being pushed out the windows. One boy is ringing a bell. This is the "Emergency Alarm," which is the caption of the cartoon. In the distance you can see the dome of the Capitol, where Congress meets.

What do all these details mean? Study the cartoon carefully. Then answer these questions.

1. The artist believes that
   A. children get pushed out of the windows of crowded schoolhouses
   B. American children go to school in wooden schoolhouses
   C. more schools are badly needed
2. The artist believes that
   A. only a few children go to school in overcrowded schoolhouses
   B. the need for more schoolhouses is so great as to be an emergency
   C. the need for more schoolhouses is not very great
3. The artist believes that
   A. the national government should do something about building more schools
   B. the national government should stay out of the school problem
   C. the Capitol should be used as a schoolhouse

The correct answers are shown in the answer key.

How well can you read graphs?

The graph is often the best means of presenting numbers and number relationships. If you have skill in graph reading, you can get the meaning of a graph at a

4 "Millicent," by Clyde Lamb, December 1953, by permission of *Boys' Life*, published by the Boy Scouts of America.

Figure 8[5]

glance. If you lack this skill, you can develop it. The following exercises will help you.

How do you read a circle graph?

Exercise 40

An author often uses a circle graph to show how the parts of something are related to the whole thing. To give yourself practice in reading such a graph, look at Figure 9 and take the following steps.

First, read the title of the graph: "How Americans Spent Their Income in 1959."

Second, read the footnote at the bottom of the page. You will note that the part labeled "Foodstuffs" in the graph includes food, liquor, and tobacco, and that this part amounts to about 27 percent (27.2). "Household, 27 percent" in the graph indicates two things: first, housing (rental or rental value), 12.9 percent; and second, household operation (cost of utilities, fuel, cleaning, equipment, etc.), 14 percent. Together these total about 27 percent (26.9).

Third, study the graph. For each part of it, note the kind of expense and the percentage number that goes with it.

5 HERBLOCK in the *Washington Post.*

A test on reading a circle graph

Write your answers to this test on your paper.

1. What percentage of their money did Americans spend on recreation?
   - **A.** 7 percent
   - **B.** .7 percent
   - **C.** .07 percent
2. What fraction of their income did Americans spend on foodstuffs?
   - **A.** More than a quarter
   - **B.** More than a half
   - **C.** More than a third
3. Americans spent about the same percentage of their money on each of these two things:
   - **A.** Foodstuffs and clothing
   - **B.** Household and clothing
   - **C.** Clothing and transportation
   - **D.** Transportation and recreation
4. If all the percentages in the circle graph represent one dollar (100 cents), how many cents did Americans spend on foodstuffs, household, and clothing together?
   - **A.** 47
   - **B.** 55
   - **C.** 76
   - **D.** 66
   - **E.** 88

The correct answers are shown in the answer key.

Exercise 41

How to read a bar graph

A bar graph is used to show amounts and quantities. It helps the reader make a quick comparison between one amount and another.

To practice reading a bar graph, look at Figure 10. To study this graph, take the following steps.

First, look at the graph and read the title: "Annual Mean Income in 1958 for Men 25 Years Old and Older with Different Amounts of Education."

To find the mean income for men who had one to seven years of elementary education, for instance, the incomes of all the men in this group were added together to get a total. This total was divided by the

Figure 9[6]
How Americans spent their income in 1959

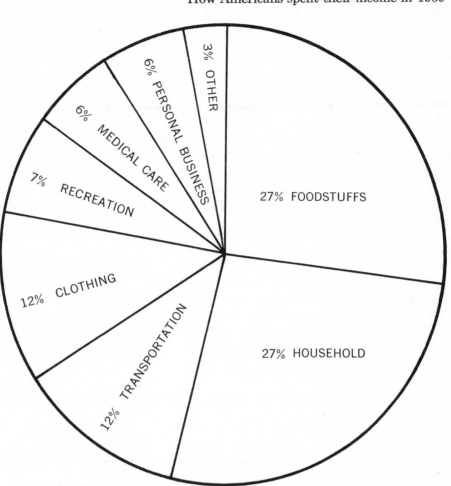

number of men. The result was their mean income; it was $2551 per year.

All the men studied were twenty-five years of age or older.

Second, look at the first column, headed "Amount of Education." The men were divided into groups according to the amount of education they had. One group had one to seven years of education; that is none of them had gone to school beyond the seventh grade. Another group had completed four or more years of college.

Third, look at the second column, headed "Mean Income." For each group of men the yearly mean income is listed. The group with one through seven years of schooling had a mean income of $2551 a year; the group with one through three years of high school had a mean income of $4618.

Fourth, just below the graph notice the

legend, "Income in thousands of dollars," and the rows of numbers—$1000, $2000, and so on. This row of numbers is called a scale; this scale is used to estimate the length of the bars.

Fifth, practice reading this bar graph. Cut out a narrow strip of paper. Make this strip so that it covers the column of numbers headed "Average Income."

6 SOURCE: U.S. Department of Commerce, Office of Business Economics, *U.S. Income and Output* (a supplement to the *Survey of Current Business*), July 1960. Taken from *Statistical Abstract of the United States, 1961*, p. 302. The percentages of total personal consumption expenditures are as follows: food, liquor, and tobacco, 27.2 percent; clothing, accessories, jewelry, and personal care, 12 percent; housing, 12.9 percent; household operation, 14 percent; medical care and death expenses, 6.3 percent; personal business, 6 percent; transportation, 12.4 percent; recreation and foreign travel, 6.7 percent; private education and research, 1.3 percent; religious and welfare activities, 1.4 percent.

While the strip of paper is still in place, look at the second group, "Elementary school: 8 years," and at the bar to its right. Notice where the right-hand edge of the bar is located. Look down one of the grid lines. It is near the figure $4000. Therefore the annual mean income of men with eight years of elementary school was about $3800. Write this figure on the strip of paper.

Now study the third group, "High school: 1–3 years," and look at the bar at its right. The right-hand edge of the bar is about halfway between two grid lines—the lines for $4000 and for $5000. The mean income for this group was about $4600. Write this figure on the strip of paper.

In the same way, estimate the mean income of each of the other groups and write these figures on the strip of paper. After you estimate the mean income of the last group, "College: 4+ years," compare your figures (as estimated from the bars) with the actual figures (those in the column headed "Mean Income"). If your esti-

mated figure is within $100 of the actual figure, your estimate is excellent. For example, an estimate of $9100 or $9300 for an income of $9206 is excellent.

Immediately after you have checked your estimates with the actual figures, look briefly at the footnote. Because the source is authoritative, the information is probably very reliable.

As you practiced reading this bar graph, you may have been unable to see the forest for the trees. You have been so concerned with the details of the graph that you may not have understood its purpose. To see whether this is so, take the test that follows.

A test on reading a bar graph

You may look back at the graph to answer the following test items. Write your answers to these items on your paper.

1. If you wish to increase your chances of earning a higher income as an adult,

Figure 10[7]

Annual mean income in 1958 for men 25 years old and older with different amounts of education

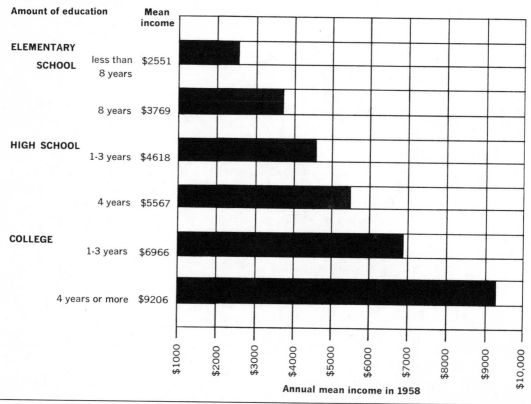

7 American Economic Association; *American Economic Review*. Taken from the *Statistical Abstract of the United States*, 1962, p. 119.

Figure 11 [8]

Estimated lifetime income, by years of school completed, for males 25 and over

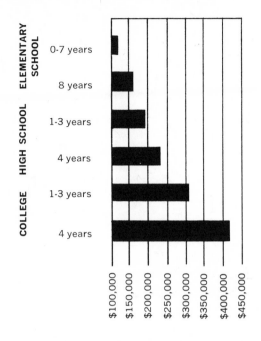

C. $4600
D. $5600
E. $7900

The correct answers are shown in the answer key.

Figure 10 illustrates that the more years of school or college you complete, the higher your yearly income tends to be. Figure 11 shows that the more years of education you have had, the higher your lifetime income will be. A lifetime of work is said to continue from age twenty-two until age seventy-five.

From Figure 10, you estimated the mean yearly salary of each group by studying the bar for that group. You then compared your estimated figure with the actual figure.

When you work with the graph of Figure 11, you will again make estimates of the amounts indicated by the length of the bars. Look first at the bar for the group of men who have had 0–7 years of elementary school. By referring to the vertical grid lines, you notice that the right-hand edge of this bar is more than $100,000 but less than $150,000. Write down $100,000, the smaller amount. Next, notice that the distance between $100,000 and $150,000 stands for $50,000. Notice that the bar covers about two-fifths of this distance. Two-fifths of $50,000 is $20,000. Add this amount to $100,000. The total is $120,000—an estimate of the lifetime income of the first group.

Exercise 42

Now take the following test. Find the answers by studying the bar graph in Figure 11. Write your answers on your paper.

1. The average lifetime income of eighth-grade graduates was about
   A. $200,000
   B. $150,000
   C. $170,000
2. The average lifetime income of high school graduates (twelve years of schooling) was about
   A. $220,000
   B. $240,000
   C. $280,000

you should, according to Figure 10,
   A. leave school as soon as you can
   B. stay in school through the eighth grade
   C. complete as many years in school and college as you can
2. On the average, if you become a high school graduate instead of an eighth-grade graduate, you will probably make *this* much more money each year when your income is highest:
   A. $1000
   B. $1800
   C. $1900
   D. $2500
   E. $3400
3. On the average, if you become a college graduate instead of a high school graduate, you will probably make *this* much more money each year when your income is highest:
   A. $1900
   B. $3600

8 American Economic Association; *American Economic Review*, December 1960. Taken from the *Statistical Abstract of the United States, 1962*, p. 119. Figures are based on Current Population Survey, a monthly sample survey conducted by the Bureau of the Census.

Figure 12[9]

Horses and mules and tractors on farms 1910-1954

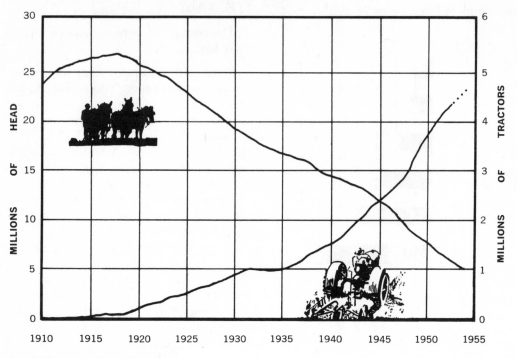

3. The average lifetime income of college graduates was about
   A. $410,000
   B. $440,000
   C. $420,000
4. During a lifetime of work, the college graduate had a lifetime income that was more than twice that of a man who left school in
   A. grade 9, 10, or 11
   B. grade 14
   C. grade 12
5. The difference between the lifetime income of the college graduate and the lifetime income of the high school graduate was about
   A. $120,000
   B. $140,000
   C. $180,000
6. On the basis of the information in Figures 10 and 11, does it pay to be educated?
   A. Yes
   B. No
   C. Uncertain

The correct answers are shown in the answer key.

How to read line graphs

If the writer wants to show you what has been happening to something over a period of years, he may use a line graph. By looking at the line graph, you can find out how many persons or things there were in a given year, say in 1950. You can also find out whether the number of persons or things has been going up or down year by year, or perhaps every tenth year (for instance 1910, 1920, 1930, 1940, and 1950).

Sometimes the writer presents two related things on the same line graph, as in Figure 12. To learn how to read this kind of graph, take the following steps.

First, read the title of the line graph. This graph is about "Horses and Mules and Tractors on Farms, 1910–1954."

Second, find out what the vertical and horizontal lines stand for. In this graph the vertical lines stand for dates: 1910, 1915, and so forth. The horizontal lines stand for two things. If you read from left to right, they stand for so many millions of horses and mules. Notice that the figures on the right are different. They stand for so many millions of tractors.

9 From *America's Needs and Resources*, the Twentieth Century Fund. Sources: Agricultural Outlook Charts, 1953, Bureau of Agricultural Economics, U.S. Department of Agriculture.

Figure 13[10]

Map of airways and standard time zones of the United States

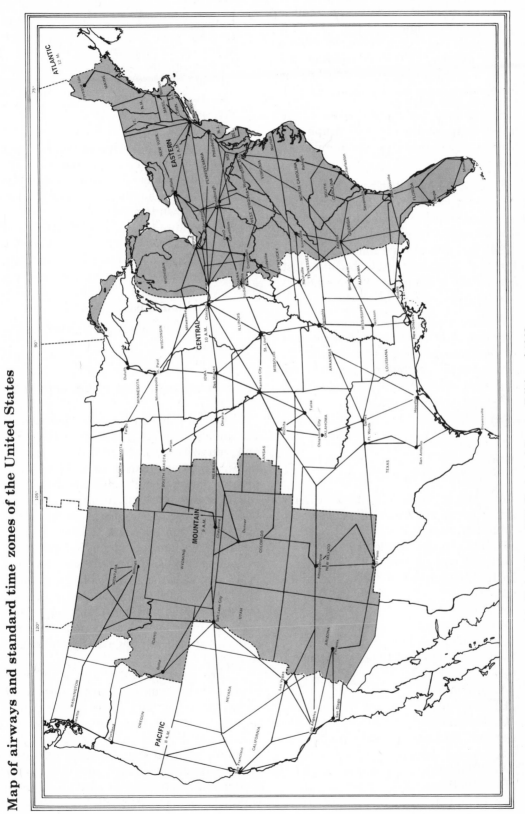

10 SOURCE: *Standard Time Zones of the United States.* U.S. Geological Survey. Edition of 1962.

If you want to know what was happening in 1925, you read up the fourth vertical line.

Third, read the vertical scale at the left. In this graph it indicates the number of horses and mules. In 1910 (the first vertical line) there were about 24 million of these animals. The line showing the number of animals crosses the grid line for 1910 at about 24 on the left-hand scale.

Fourth, read the vertical scale at the right, if there is one. In this graph the right-hand scale indicates the number of tractors.

Fifth, figure out what the heavy black lines in the graph mean. In this graph they are progress lines. They both start from the 1910 line and move to the right toward the 1955 line. The top line stands for horses and mules. You know this because just below the line is a picture of some horses. The bottom line stands for tractors.

Practice reading this graph. *To read the number of horses and mules you read the vertical scale at the left of the graph. To read the number of tractors, you read the vertical scale at the right.*

Exercise 43

Find the answers to these test items by studying the line graph in Figure 12. Write your answers to each item.

1. According to the graph, the peak number of horses and mules occurred about
   A. 1918, during World War I
   B. 1932, during the depression
   C. 1942, during World War II
2. In 1930 the number of horses and mules was about
   A. 10 million
   B. 14 million
   C. 18 million
3. In 1950 the number of horses and mules was about
   A. 7.5 million
   B. 12.5 million
   C. 17.5 million
4. Between 1930 and 1935 the number of tractors was about
   A. 1 million
   B. 5 million
   C. 16 million

5. About what year did the number of tractors reach 3 million?
   A. 1944
   B. 1948
   C. 1952
6. About what year was the number of tractors almost equal to the number of horses and mules?
   (Watch out for this one—it might fool you.)
   A. 1945
   B. 1949
   C. 1953
7. Which of the following statements best tells what this line graph shows?
   A. The number of horses and mules and the number of tractors go up or down together.
   B. Because the number of horses and mules has steadily decreased the number of tractors has increased.
   C. Because the number of tractors has increased, the number of horses and mules has decreased.

The correct answers are shown in the answer key.

How well can you read a map?

As you know, maps are diagrams of the earth's surface. Look at any large atlas, and you will see many different kinds of maps. There are maps that show political divisions (such as states and countries) and the location of cities, towns, rivers, and bodies of water. There are maps that show physical features or characteristics, such as elevation, normal rainfall and temperature, prevailing winds, natural resources, and types of soil. Other maps contain cultural information, such as the number of persons per square mile, movements of people from place to place over long periods of time, and the spread of languages from region to region.

Through a careful study of different kinds of maps, you can learn a great deal about the people and places in the region in which you live and in other regions throughout the world.

Not only do maps contain different kinds of information, but they are drawn to different scales and in several different ways. Some maps show the earth as if it were stretched out at the top and bottom so as to lie smooth on a flat surface. Some maps cut and separate sections of the earth's surface at the top and bottom, very much as you would have to cut and separate the skin of an orange to make it lie flat. Other maps show the surface of the earth as it would look if you were looking down on a particular point from out in space. These different ways of drawing the earth's surface are called projections.

Exercise 44

To test your skill in using a map, answer the ten questions that follow. First study the map on page 147 carefully, then refer to it to find your answer to each question. Don't guess; look at the map. Some of the questions are tricky.

1. How many time zones are shown on the map?
   A. 3
   B. 5
   C. 4
2. If a jet traveled from Washington, D.C., to Los Angeles in just three hours and if it took off at 7 A.M., it would arrive in Los Angeles at
   A. 9 A.M.
   B. 8 A.M.
   C. 7 A.M.
3. How many states lie partly in one time zone and partly in another?
   A. 12
   B. 8
   C. 20
   D. 5
4. Which of these pairs of cities is *not* in the same time zone?
   A. Boston and Milwaukee
   B. New York and Detroit
   C. Chicago and Minneapolis
5. If all cities are on standard time and it is 2 P.M. in Chicago, what time is it in Albuquerque?

A. 2 P.M.
B. 3 P.M.
C. 1 P.M.

6. On a nonstop flight a 704 jet left New York City at 10 A.M. (Eastern Standard Time) and landed at Los Angeles at 11:45 A.M. How many hours did this flight take?
   A. 1 hour and 45 minutes
   B. 3 hours and 45 minutes
   C. 4 hours and 45 minutes
7. A nonstop jet flight will leave Los Angeles for New York City at 10 A.M. The trip is scheduled to take five hours. At what time should it land in New York?
   A. 12 noon
   B. 6 P.M.
   C. 3 P.M.
8. The map shows more air routes east of Chicago than west of Chicago. This indicates that
   A. there are more cities connected by air routes in the east than in the west
   B. more people fly from west to east than from east to west
   C. people in the east travel more than people in the west
9. The network of airways that lines the map of the United States brings cities and people closer together as measured by
   A. time changes from zone to zone
   B. distance in miles from city to city
   C. flying time from city to city
10. North is at the top of this map. With this fact in mind, in which direction does an airplane fly when traveling from Minneapolis to Chicago?
    A. South
    B. Southwest
    C. East
    D. Southeast

The correct answers are shown in the answer key.

Practice Reading 10

In a book, magazine, or newspaper that you like, practice reading for speed and comprehension. Make a record of the reading (Chart 3, p. 8) in your progress folder. Read the following selection to determine your present reading rate, comprehension, and vocabulary.

Record your starting time in the time record on page 4 of your progress folder. Then read the selection. Read as fast as you can, but make sure you understand what you are reading.

10
article

Clipper ship boy[11]

by Louis Smith

New York in 1840 was a busy seaport. From there, ships sailed all over the world, trading for tea in China, spices in the South Seas, and goods in Europe. The sailor's life was a hard one, and the captain's or mate's word was law. In the following scene from Clipper Ship Boy, *David Staples, age fourteen, comes to New York with his Uncle Ben and visits the* Cathay Queen, *on which he will be sailing as an apprentice.*

You will find words in this story that might be new to you. Some you will understand from the context; others you might want to look up in your dictionary. Knowing which part of the ship is being described would heighten your appreciation of the story. Yards, for instance, are the long cross-poles to which sails are attached. Bulwarks are the railings of the ship.

Ben Staples stopped and looked behind him. A smile lit up his face and he chuckled. He set down the bag he was carrying. "Come along, David," he shouted. "Time enough to look later."

As David came up to him, he added, "It may be that you will have had your fill of ships sooner than you think."

"Oh, never," said David breathlessly. He shifted his bag from hand to hand and tried to match his steps to his uncle's long stride.

The cobblestone street was slippery underfoot. A slight mist hung in the air, its tiny droplets laying a wet coat over the stones. The buildings gleamed and dripped with the dampness. One beside the other in a solid wall, they seemed to lean on each other for support. Facing them across the street were the ships.

Brigs and barks, schooners and square rigs, they lined the wharf edge as far as David could see. Their sharp bows were snugged against the pilings, and their bowsprits formed an arch half over the street.

David craned his neck, twisting to look at the towering masts and yards outlined against the gray sky. Swaying slowly and gently with the roll of their ships, they looked down on the busy street as though impatient to be free of the land. Below them, the people scurried about their affairs, jostling each other as they pushed along in and out of the buildings. They had no time for dreaming or looking at ships. There was only the serious business of refitting the ships, finding a cargo, and rounding up a crew.

Ben stopped. He pointed toward the topmost yards of the ships. "What do you think, David?" he asked. "Will you be able to fist canvas up there?"

"Fist, sir?" asked David.

"Aye," said Ben. "Haul and fasten wet canvas."

"Yes, sir," said David. "At least, I think so."

His uncle slapped him on the shoulder. "It's only the first time or two that's bad. You'll be scurrying up the ratlines like a monkey in no time."

They walked in silence for a while. David's glance dropped to the street and the crowd moving around him. Horses, carriages, and wagons pushed their way along the cobblestones. Drivers shouted at one another as they guided their wagons through the crowded street. There were fat merchants in tall hats, puffing cheroots. Heavy gold watch chains hung across their paunches. The dandies twirled their canes daintily, their lace shirt fronts and cuffs sparkling white in the gray mist. David turned his head quickly to catch sight of an Indian who was wearing a tall hat with a feather standing straight up behind it.

The sailors were easiest to recognize, he decided. They walked along with a rolling gait, planting their feet wide with each step as though the cobblestones were the swaying deck of a ship. They wore duck trousers and pea jackets, and many of them had duffel bags slung over their shoulders.

"We'd better hurry," said Uncle Ben. "I don't want to miss Captain Gamble."

A light rain was starting to fall as they hurried past the many shops and lofts facing the street.

David read the signs over the shops: "Ship Chandler, Sailmaker, Merchant, Oriental Spices." He sniffed. There was a heavy smell of spices in the air. He sniffed again. And also a smell of tea.

"There she is," said Uncle Ben, pointing down the line of ships.

David searched ahead eagerly among the ships lining the wharves.

"That's the *Cathay Queen*. The three-master with the blue pennants."

David's eyes singled her out from the ships beside her. A sudden feeling of disappointment came over him. For some reason, he had expected the *Cathay Queen* to be the biggest ship in the world, much bigger than the ships they had passed. She lay bare-poled at the wharf, her black paint cut by a wide white stripe that circled her fore and aft.

As David came closer, his feeling of disappointment changed to one of pride. There was a sleek, rakish look about the *Cathay Queen* that sent a sharp thrill down his spine. He realized that she was to be his home for almost a year.

"There's the Staples house flag flying on the mainmast," said Uncle Ben.

They were alongside the ship now and walking on the narrow wharf that stretched along her side. David threw his head back and looked up at the flag. It was a bright blue. In a white oval in the center of the flag was a large *S*. Uncle Ben walked up the plank that led to the *Cathay Queen* and David followed him. As they stepped down on the deck, a short, fat man ran toward them.

"Good morning, sir," he said to Uncle Ben. "You caught me unawares. We were looking for your carriage."

"Good morning, Mr. Gruenther," said Uncle Ben. "We decided to walk. I thought David might enjoy seeing the sights. David," he added, "this is Mr. Gruenther, the first mate."

"So this is the young lad?" said Mr. Gruenther, looking down at David. "And you want to be a seaman?" His thick, bushy eyebrows lifted, and he shook his head slowly from side to side.

"Yes, sir," said David. He decided that he liked Mr. Gruenther.

"It's a hard life, lad," the first mate said. "But, it puts muscle on those bones." He turned to Ben Staples. "The captain is expecting you aft, sir. The lad can watch us at work here."

"Good. I'll be back shortly, David."

Ben walked aft, picking his way carefully across the wet and crowded deck. David watched him go, and then looked around curiously. Barrels and boxes were scattered about the deck in what seemed to be a great deal of confusion. Coils of rope and spare yards were lined against the bulwarks.

"Doesn't seem likely we'll be hoisting anchor in two weeks, does it?" asked Mr. Gruenther, following David's glance.

"I couldn't say, sir."

"Most of what you see is the last of the ship's stores. The biggest part of the cargo is snugged tight below."

"What are we carrying, sir?" David asked. He couldn't help but accent the word *we*.

Mr. Gruenther wrinkled his brow in thought. "Well, let me consider," he said. "We have about sixteen hundred skins of fur, two hundred piculs of cotton, three hundred and fifty piculs of ginseng, a great quantity of lead, and some odds and ends."

"What's a picul?" asked David.

"A picul is a Chinese hundredweight. About equal to a hundred and thirty-three pounds. And before you ask me," he went on, "ginseng is a medicinal herb highly prized by the heathens in China."

David was about to ask another question when Mr. Gruenther suddenly left him and strode across the deck toward a sailor who was seated on a small keg. The sailor's head seemed to be bent over his work, and he didn't notice Mr. Gruenther's approach. With a swift kick, the first mate knocked the keg out from under the man and sent him sprawling to the deck. The seaman's head hit sharply on the wooden planking but he was on his feet in an instant and stood facing the mate. In his hand he held the long thin sailmaker's needle with which he had been working.

"I've not disturbed your sleep, I hope," said Mr. Gruenther.

The man's hand tightened around the needle, and its sharp point swung around toward the first mate. Mr. Gruenther looked at the man for an instant, then threw his head back with a roar of laughter.

"You wouldn't be doing anything so foolish as that, now would you, Weasel?" asked the first mate when he had stopped laughing.

"As what, sir?" asked the sailor innocently. "It was in thought that my head was bowed, not sleep."

"That thick skull of yours never harbored a thought. You'll do your sleeping below on your off watch, Weasel."

"The name is Wetzel, sir."

But Mr. Gruenther was on his way back to David. He seemed to have forgotten the incident already as he came smiling up to the boy.

"We'll be as tight as a drum in a week. Gear stowed and canvas hung. You won't recognize the *Cathay Queen*, lad, when you see her riding her anchor next week."

Record your finishing time in the time box. Then take the reading test.

Read each test item and choose the best answer. Print your answers on page 4 of the progress folder.

Reading Test 10

Getting main ideas

1. The main purpose of the author is to describe

   A. Gruenther's treatment of Wetzel
   B. the way ships are loaded
   C. David's first visit to *Cathay Queen*
   D. the people on the waterfront
   E. the cargo of the *Cathay Queen*

2. In the early days of sailing ships seamen were

   A. treated very gently
   B. treated very harshly
   C. not very experienced
   D. not allowed on the upper deck
   E. always sleeping on deck

Choosing the best reason

3. Gruenther knocked the seaman off the keg because

   A. the keg was broken
   B. he needed it
   C. David was watching
   D. the man was asleep
   E. it was time for lunch

4. Uncle Ben said that David might become tired of ships because
   A. the ocean is not exciting
   B. there would not be enough food
   C. he would be beaten
   D. no one would speak to him
   E. he might not like a sailor's life

5. David was disappointed when he first saw the *Cathay Queen* because
   A. she was painted black
   B. the sails were not on the ship
   C. he had expected a giant of a ship
   D. she was anchored at the wharf
   E. the decks were crowded with ropes

6. Uncle Ben left David and went aft to
   A. see the sailors
   B. check the cargo
   C. see the captain
   D. get out of the rain
   E. see Mr. Gruenther

Reading with a keen eye
7. Mr. Gruenther was the
   A. third mate
   B. captain
   C. boatswain
   D. first mate
   E. second mate

8. The *Cathay Queen* was a
   A. steamship
   B. sailing ship
   C. coal-burning ship
   D. paddle-wheel steamer
   E. oil tanker

9. The Staples' flag flying over the ship was
   A. blue with a yellow oval center
   B. blue with a white oval center
   C. lowered to half-mast
   D. tattered and torn
   E. white with a blue oval center

10. The *Cathay Queen* was supposed to sail in
   A. two months
   B. two hours
   C. three weeks
   D. two days
   E. two weeks

11. David saw an Indian who was wearing

   A. a buckskin coat with fringes
   B. a sailor's uniform
   C. a tall hat decorated with beads
   D. a coonskin cap
   E. a tall hat with a feather

12. The *Cathay Queen* was painted black
with a

   A. wide white stripe
   B. high deck at her stern
   C. wide yellow stripe
   D. wide blue stripe
   E. narrow white stripe

13. As he walked along, David noticed

   A. the busy shipyards
   B. the smell of salt water
   C. a construction crew
   D. many frontiersmen
   E. the smell of spices

14. Mr. Gruenther's nickname for the
sailor was

   A. Sleepy
   B. Lazy
   C. Weasel
   D. Wetback
   E. Old Salt

15. The men twirling their canes were
called

   A. chandlers
   B. dandies
   C. dancers
   D. buccaneers
   E. merchants

Getting word meanings

16. To walk like a sailor is to walk with a

   A. deep slouch
   B. military bearing
   C. heavy step
   D. rolling gait
   E. light step

17. To push and shove through a crowded
street is called

   A. jostling
   B. jousting
   C. mending
   D. crunching
   E. jumping

18. A Chinese hundredweight is called a

    A. dragon
    B. pistol
    C. century
    D. picul
    E. portent

19. When a sailor is not on duty he is

    A. off shore
    B. on rations
    C. off watch
    D. sent aft
    E. off list

20. To haul and fasten wet canvas is to

    A. fist canvas
    B. freeze canvas
    C. keelhaul
    D. fight canvas
    E. walk the plank

Follow the directions (Steps 8–13) on page 1 of the progress folder.

11
lesson

How you can best read aloud

Do you read well aloud? Do other people understand and enjoy what you read to them? Do you yourself get pleasure and satisfaction from reading aloud?

When you read aloud, do you read in phrases that express thought units? Or do you read mechanically, word by word? Do you attempt to read with changes in your voice or do you read in a monotone? Do you get across to your listeners the feelings and moods expressed by the author? Or do you read everything in about the same way, without emphasis?

To check up on how well you read aloud, read each of the following short selections silently and then orally. After you have practiced, read them aloud to someone else.

Fighting Words[1]

by Patrick Henry

Is life so dear, or peace so sweet, as to be purchased at the price of chains and slavery? Forbid it, Almighty God! I know not what course others may take; but as for me, give me liberty, or give me death!

A Tall Tale[2]

Buffalo Bull Maxwell, head man of the Randsburg Desert Museum, reports a sad happening in Spring District. According to Buffalo, Larry Reynolds, the mechanic at Hardy Witt's garage, was bitten by a rattlesnake yesterday and in spite of everything they could do, the snake died within thirty minutes.

On Dormice[3]

If you overslept today, don't feel guilty. You might try meditating on the dormouse, a cousin of the house mouse.

Dormice are always sleepy. They know little or nothing of what goes on in the world, as they sleep for six months each year and about half the time during the remaining six months. Thus they are conscious only a fourth of the time and miss a lot of foolishness.

Dormice are prettier than house mice. Why wouldn't they be, with all that sleep?

Jim Bludso

by John Hay

Someone has just asked the speaker in this poem where Jim Bludso lives. If you like this verse, you will want to read the rest of the poem.

Wall, no! I can't tell whar he lives,
Bekase he don't live, you see!
Leastways, he's got out of the habit
Of livin' like you and me.
Whar have you been for the last three
    year
That you haven't heard folks tell
How Jimmy Bludso passed in his checks
The night of the Prairie Belle?

An Order to the Careless Driver[4]

During a safe-driving campaign in Connecticut, a South African suggested that

---

1 From a speech before the Virginia Convention, held in Richmond, Virginia, March 23, 1775.

2 From *Harry Oliver's Desert Rat Scrap Book.* Thousand Palms, California. Reprinted with permission.

3 From *How to Get from January to December*, by Will Cuppy, edited by Fred Feldkamp. Published by Holt, Rinehart and Winston, Inc.

4 From the *Chicago Sun-Times*, May 19, 1955.

every speeder be given this short but sharp lecture in Dutch dialect:

"Git offen dot acceleratoren der klodhopper booten mit, dumbkopf knuckelhead." (English translation: "Get off that accelerator, you plowman with heavy boots, you stupid, foolish person.")

You learned to read by reading aloud

When you were young, you did a great deal of reading aloud. In the first three grades you probably read aloud every day.

Before you started to school, you knew the meanings of several thousand words when you heard them. In the first grade in school you learned to recognize some of these words when you saw them in print.

Each time you came to a new word, such as *mother*, your teacher pronounced it while you looked at it. Then you looked at the word and pronounced it yourself. By looking at words closely, noticing their shapes and saying them aloud, you learned to recognize the appearance of more and more words that were already in your speaking vocabulary. You also developed some phonic principles to help you pronounce new words. By saying new words, looking them up in the dictionary, and using them in your writing and speaking, you gradually built up your vocabulary.

Then you discovered that in printed language, as in spoken language, words go together in groups. You stopped reading just word by word and began to read word groups that had meaning.

You still need to read aloud

As you climbed the grades of the school ladder, you did less and less oral reading and more and more silent reading. It is probable that as much as 90 percent of your reading is now done silently. To improve this reading, you have had to get rid of some of the oral reading habits that slowed down your reading rate. You had to stop saying the words aloud to yourself or whispering them, and you had to stop moving your lips, your tongue, and your throat muscles while reading.

It may well be that in getting rid of these habits you have gone too far. You may have done such a good job that you are no longer able to read aloud efficiently. But you still have many opportunities to read orally, and you will meet many situations in which you will have to do it well.

To see how often oral reading occurs, try making a list of the kinds of oral reading you have done during the past week. Your list may include activities such as these:

1. Reading aloud a newspaper headline or story to your family at home or to your class at school.
2. Reading aloud one or more sentences from your English, history, science, or other textbook to explain or prove something to your class.
3. Reading aloud the report you wrote for a course assignment.
4. Reading aloud a short story to the rest of your class.
5. Reading aloud a poem that you or someone else wrote.
6. Reading aloud a play or a part in that play.
7. Reading aloud to children in your family.

When you read aloud, you use many of the skills and habits of silent reading. In both kinds of reading, you have to recognize words quickly and group them into meaningful units. But oral reading requires special skills that are not needed in silent reading.

You can improve your oral reading

In oral reading you have two main purposes. First, you want to give information to your listeners. Second, you want to give them enjoyment. Sometimes one purpose is more important than the other. Often both of them occur together. For instance, you may read aloud to give your listeners some interesting historical facts. At the same time you want to stimulate their interest in the information and make them see how important it is. On the other hand, you may want to read a humorous story in an enjoyable way. But in addition to having fun, you want your listeners to get the point of the story. Without the facts that explain this point, they won't really enjoy the story.

How to prepare for oral reading

To get ready to read aloud, take the following steps.

Step 1. Choose the selection carefully. Look for something that will please you and interest your listeners. Look for a selection that is appropriate—something that relates to the topic your class is studying at the moment.

Step 2. Read the selection silently from beginning to end. Get the main idea and the important details in mind so that you will be able to make them clear to your listeners.

Step 3. Learn the meanings of the difficult words in the selection. Write these words and look them up in the dictionary. Write the meaning of the word *as it is used in the selection.*

Step 4. Learn to pronounce the words that are not familiar to you. The way the word is marked in the dictionary indicates where the accent falls and how the vowels and consonants sound.

Studies of poor readers show that they make many errors in pronunciation. They also tend to insert words that are not in the material and to repeat words. You will want to avoid such errors. Use the dictionary when you are uncertain about the pronunciation of a word. More information about using the dictionary will be given in Lessons 12 and 13.

If your selection contains dialect, read the words as they are spelled in the selection. When the speaker in Jim Bludso says "wall" he means "well," but you will say "wall" just as the speaker did.

Step 5. Practice reading the selection aloud. You can do this first by yourself and then ask one of your classmates or someone in your family to listen. Ask him to suggest ways in which you can read better. He may tell you that you are reading too fast or too loud or not loud enough. If the suggestions seem helpful, put them to work in your next practice.

How to read aloud

The best way to learn to read aloud is to read aloud again and again. The more oral reading you do, the better you will do it—and the more fun you will get out of it. As you work to improve your oral reading, these suggestions may be helpful:

Suggestion 1

Keep in mind *what* you are reading and *why* you are reading it. Suppose that you are reading from the book *Kon-Tiki*, a thrilling story about crossing the Pacific Ocean on a raft. You will want to give your listeners some of the facts about the voyage, but you will also want them to feel the excitement of it. You will read your selection in a fairly quiet voice, giving special emphasis to the exciting passages. You may want to stop at times to explain some of the necessary background—things mentioned in earlier chapters.

But if you are reading *The Highwayman*, by Alfred Noyes, you will read rapidly and make your readers feel the swinging pace of the lines.

Suggestion 2

Watch both your enunciation—the sharpness and clarity with which you say the words—and your pronunciation, the way you sound them. If you slur your words together, dropping word endings, you will miss a great deal of pleasure. Your audience may not understand your reading.

In reading aloud, some students make mistakes in pronunciation that confuse the listener. Such mistakes happen because the reader does not know he is mistaken or just has not taken the trouble to look up the pronunciation. Do you make any of these common mistakes?

1. Mispronouncing the first sound of a word: *wear* for *where*, *wat* for *what*, *wen* for *when*.

2. Changing one letter to another in the middle of a word: *ruther* for *rather*, or *set for sit*.

3. Leaving out middle letters or syllables: *libary* for *library*; *Febuary* for *February*; *artic* for *arctic*; *goverment* for *government*;

acrate for *accurate; reglar* for *regular; particlar* for *particular.*

4. Leaving sounds out of the last part of a word: *breath* for *breadth; strenth* for *strength; lenth* for *length; somethin* for *something; nothin* for *nothing; comin* for *coming; goin* for *going.*

You can correct such mispronunciations as these in several ways. *First,* ask your teacher, a friend, or someone in your family to listen closely as you read. *Second,* make a list of the words you mispronounce and practice saying them correctly.

A pronunciation exercise

1. Study the selection that follows. It contains many of the words commonly mispronounced. Have your teacher or a classmate listen as you read and have them note your mistakes.

Last February the other students in my social studies class asked me why I was going to the library. Here is the answer I gave them:

I am especially interested in Iceland. You know that this nation is just north of the Arctic Circle. But you probably do not know the exact length and breadth of this island. What is its climate? How are people able to live there? What is the nation's history? What kind of government does it have? These are some of the questions I want to answer. Being a very particular person, I want accurate and reliable information.

Write down the words you pronounced poorly. Study the words. Practice saying them alone. Then practice reading them in the selection. Get someone to listen to you.

2. Practice reading aloud the following tongue twisters.

• *Peter Piper picked a peck of pickled peppers.*

• *Sally saw six slick sleek slim slender saplings.*

• *All around the rugged rock the ragged rogue ran.*

Read these tongue twisters slowly at first, saying each word clearly and distinctly. Speed up your pace in later readings, until you can read the sentences rapidly and accurately.

3. Dr. Duncan Emrich, chief of the folklore section of the Library of Congress, has made a collection of tongue twisters. The following is among his harder ones. Try it.

Betty Batter bought some butter.
   "But," said she, "this butter's bitter."
So she bought some better butter,
   And she put the better butter
      In the bitter butter
And made the bitter butter better.

When you read too quickly, you may accidentally exchange or transpose letters, sometimes with amusing and surprising results. You may try to say "It was a crushing blow." But in your hurry the sentence may come out, "It was a blushing crow." This kind of error is called a spoonerism, after an Englishman who made this kind of mistake in public speeches. Bennett Cerf told of a radio announcer who got his tongue twisted and said this about a pretty movie star: "Her breath will take your beauty away."[5] There is also a story of an excited college freshman asking the secretary in the dean's office: "Excuse me, but is the bean dizzy?"

Suggestion 3

Relax and put yourself at ease. Remember that you have something interesting to read to your audience. Think of the selection you are reading rather than of yourself. With your mind on what you are reading, you will avoid embarrassment, stumbling over words, clearing your throat too often, awkward silences, and stage fright.

If you feel tense, you will look tense to others. If you hold your book too tight, if you screw up your face, if you stand on one foot and then on the other, or if you show other signs of nervousness, your audience will get nervous too. They will be distracted by what you are doing and

---

[5] Reprinted from *This Week* magazine. Copyright 1955 by the United Newspapers Magazine Corporation.

give inadequate attention to what you are saying.

If you feel tense, take several breaths before you start to read. Exhale slowly. Take one more deep breath just before you speak the first word. This practice will make you feel easy and sure of yourself. While you are reading, breathe deeply in and out again whenever you need to. But most important of all, think of the material you are reading and of the points you want to make—*not* of yourself.

Suggestion 4

Don't hurry through your reading. Your listeners will not run away. Don't read so fast that your words run together and are hard to hear. Watch your audience from time to time to see that they are listening.

Before you begin, wait for a second or two until your audience is quiet and attentive. If someone laughs at what you are reading, wait until he is quiet before going on. Actors call this *timing*. A good actor knows when to expect a laugh and waits for it to end before rushing on to something else.

Suggestion 5

Read word groups rather than word by word. In oral reading this is called phrasing. If you read thought units, you will help your listeners understand what you are reading. And you will read more smoothly and intelligibly.

Suggestion 6

Use pauses to punctuate your oral reading. When you come to a comma, slow down. When you come to the end of a sentence, make a full pause. You must pause at the end of a sentence if your listeners are to know where sentences begin and end.

Suggestion 7

Pronounce your words accurately and clearly. Put into effect the practice suggested earlier for enunciation and pronunciation.

While you are reading, speak up so that your whole audience can hear you. If you have any doubt whether people in the back of the room can hear you, ask them and speak accordingly.

Suggestion 8

Put some expression into your reading. If you are reading something exciting, make it sound exciting. You can do this by varying the loudness of your voice and the rate at which you read the words. Try to vary the pitch of your voice to fit the meaning. Less important words and phrases call for a downward tone. The important words and phrases deserve a rising tone.

Try this variation in tone and stress with the following story. Read all but the last word of the boy's answer in a high-pitched voice. Read the last word in a bass voice.

One day a father said to his teen-age son whose voice was changing: "What fish did you catch today?" The boy answered: "Three little fish and a chub."

Suggestion 9

Look at your listeners. Don't bury your nose in your book. On occasion, look up from your book and speak a phrase or two directly to the audience. You can do this without losing your place if you know the material you are reading well enough.

You read so much faster than you can speak that you can let your eyes go ahead of your voice. As you finish saying one word group, your eyes will take in the next. When they have done this, you can raise your head and speak the words while looking at your listeners. As you come to the end of the word group, your eyes drop again to the page to pick up your reading.

At times you may want to look at a particular person in the audience. Pick out someone in front, someone at the side, and someone at the rear. When you look at a particular person, not only he but others near him will probably have the impression that you are talking personally to them. There is no better way to keep the attention and interest of an audience.

Oral reading practice

In this exercise you will discover how your pronunciation is related to your understanding of what you are reading. In the story *Through the Looking-Glass*, by Lewis Carroll, Alice comes across a poem entitled "Jabberwocky." Here is the first verse:

'Twas brillig, and the slithy toves
    Did gyre and gimble in the wabe;
All mimsy were the borogoves
    And the mome raths outgrabe.

Read this verse twice—once silently and once aloud. Pronounce the words as well as you can.

If you are fairly good at oral reading, you may have pronounced all the words correctly. But even if you did, your listeners could not possibly get any meaning from what you said. In part, this was because you yourself did not know what the words meant.

Like you, Alice at first did not understand what the verse was about. Later, Humpty Dumpty explained to her what the words meant. Here is the conversation that took place. (A portmanteau is a suitcase that opens into two compartments.)

" '*Brillig*' means four o'clock in the afternoon—the time when you begin *broiling* things for dinner."

"That'll do very well," said Alice: "and '*slithy*'?"

"Well, '*slithy*' means 'lithe and slimy.' 'Lithe' is the same as 'active.' You see it's like a portmanteau—there are two meanings packed up in one word."

"I see it now," Alice remarked thoughtfully: "and what are '*toves*'?"

"Well, '*toves*' are something like badgers—they're something like lizards— and they're something like corkscrews."

"They must be very curious-looking creatures."

"They are that," said Humpty Dumpty: "also they make their nests under sun-dials—also they live on cheese."

"And what's to '*gyre*' and to '*gimble*'?"

"To '*gyre*' is to go round and round like a gyroscope. To '*gimble*' is to make holes like a gimblet."

"And '*the wabe*' is the grass-plot round a sun-dial, I suppose?" said Alice, surprised at her own ingenuity.

"Of course it is. It's called '*wabe*,' you know, because it goes a long way before it, and a long way behind it—"

"And a long way beyond it on each side," Alice added.

"Exactly so. Well then, '*mimsy*' is 'flimsy and miserable' (there's another portmanteau for you). And a '*borogove*' is a thin, shabby-looking bird with its feathers sticking out all round—something like a live mop."

"And then '*mome raths*'?" said Alice. "I'm afraid I'm giving you a great deal of trouble."

"Well, a '*rath*' is a sort of green pig: but '*mome*' I'm not certain about. I think its short for 'from home'—meaning that they'd lost their way, you know."

"And what does '*outgrabe*' mean?"

"Well, '*outgrabing*' is something between bellowing and whistling, with a kind of sneeze in the middle: however, you'll hear it done, maybe—down in the wood yonder—and, when you've once heard it, you'll be *quite* content. . . ."

Reading the verse from the nonsense poem "Jabberwocky" and reading Humpty Dumpty's explanation of the meaning of the unfamiliar words in that verse were important to you and your listeners to get the meaning of what you read and to give this meaning to others. As this nonsense verse has clearly shown, you may be able to pronounce words without knowing their meanings. But if you learn their meanings, you are able to read aloud with better understanding and with expression.

Oral reading practice

To give yourself more practice in reading aloud, try reading the newspaper story that follows. *First*, read the story silently and thoughtfully. As you read, write the words that you do not know on a separate sheet of paper. Look up the meaning and pronunciation of each word in a dictionary. Then read the story silently again. *Second*, read the story aloud. Try to make it sound interesting. Read the words group by group; for example, read: *"Do you remember the song 'The Big Rock Candy Mountain' . . . about a hobos' paradise? . . .*

"It's the place where . . . 'The sun shines ev'ry day . . . on the birds and the bees . . . and the cigaret trees . . . and the lemonade springs . . . where the blue bird sings.'"

Hobos' Heaven of Song[6]

by Ralph Friedman

Do you remember the song "The Big Rock Candy Mountain"—about a hobos' paradise?

It's the place where "The sun shines ev'ry day on the birds and the bees, and the cigaret trees, and the lemonade springs where the blue bird sings."

Well, there is such a mountain, a great yellowish hill that sweeps up above the canyon country of southern Utah. Right across the road from the hem of the mountain, a spur line of the Denver and Rio Grande ran out of track and here the wandering bindlestiffs built themselves a campground, or, as it is called in hobo parlance, a "jungle."

One night, about fifty-five years ago, a brakie on the D&RG had a dream—about a land where "the farmers trees are full of fruit and the barns are full of hay . . . where there ain't no snow, where the rains don't fall, the wind don't blow . . . ."

The brakie was Harry K. McClintock, who paid many a visit to the jungle, listening quietly as the "knights of the road" poured out their tales of woe and day-dreamed aloud of life in the lap of luxury.

In McClintock's dream, the symbol of "hobo heaven" was Big Rock Candy Mountain, where "all the cops have wooden legs, and the bulldogs all have rubber teeth; and the hens lay soft-boiled eggs."

McClintock never copyrighted what has become known as his version, and since then there have been numerous "Big Rock Candy Mountain" songs. On every railroad line and in every jungle, the Mc-Clintock ballad was sung. The words passed beyond the hobo camps and were heard in high-class vaudeville theaters, at social gatherings, and even in schools. Today the song is a part of American musical folklore.

After you finish reading the story, talk about it with other students in the class. Try to answer or discuss the following questions. How many students knew that there was a real Big Rock Candy Mountain? Can anyone think of other folk songs that are based on facts? The song about Casey Jones, for instance, is based on an actual railroading incident. Can someone describe a hobo jungle and tell something about the way its inhabitants live? Discuss and define the unusual words in the story, such as *bindlestiffs, brakie,* and *knights of the road.*

Oral reading practice

In the two previous exercises you practiced the oral reading of fairly short selections. In this exercise you will practice oral reading of a longer selection. "AA Is for Aardvark" is a humorous fictional story about a high school student and his schoolmates.

Read the story silently from beginning to end. As you read, try to make sure that you understand the most important points. These include an appreciation of the humorous remarks made by Herb Forrest, the young man who is supposed to be both the subject and the teller of the story.

AA Is for Aardvark[7]

by William B. McMorris

When you distribute 135 pounds over the frame of a 6 foot 3 politician, how unique can his athletic ability get?

Shorty Connors, my campaign manager, has an inventive mind. The campaign poster he was setting up on the Jackson High School campus proved it. The poster was made of paper tacked over a wooden frame shaped like a child's "ABC" block.

---

6 From "Songwriter's Big Rock Candy Mountain Is in Utah," by Ralph Friedman, *Chicago Tribune,* October 1962.

7 From "AA Is for Aardvark," by William B. Mc-Morris, by permission of *Boys' Life,* published by the Boy Scouts of America.

The contraption was placed on a spindle near the auditorium. When the wind blew, the block turned, slowly showing the letters on three sides that proclaimed:

AA is for Aardvark
AA is how students rate HERB FORREST
FORREST FOR STUDENT PREXY!

On the fourth side of the block was pasted a picture of an aardvark, a kind of South African anteater. Shorty had worked hard on that poster. It was a shame to waste it.

"Shorty," I said, "I'm quitting student politics."

For a minute he looked as if he didn't believe me. When the words finally added up, he bellowed like a wounded moose. Shorty is a member of an outing club. His lungs are in very good shape.

"Quitting!" he roared, letting his fancy poster fall on the ground. "You can't! Your petition is signed! The posters are already up! You're a cinch to win!"

Shorty was right. I was a cinch to become student-body president of Jackson High School. We had been building for this campaign for the past three years. Winning meant a lot to both of us. To me it would be the climax of three years of being class president. For Shorty it meant four straight years of successful and inventive campaign managing.

As important to us as it was, one thing was obvious. Unless I spent less time as a politician, I stood a good chance of losing something more important than any election. By that I mean the Bradford "Ripper" Walsh Scholarship to State University, which is offered each year to an outstanding student of Jackson High School.

This business of being "outstanding" in the particular way the scholarship demanded was forcing me out of student politics. As far as academic work and school service were concerned, I was eligible for the scholarship. My grades were good, and as class president three times I had plenty of service points. It was the scholarship's athletic clause that fouled me up.

Long before "Ripper" Walsh became a wealthy automobile dealer who gives away scholarships, he was the finest fullback State U. ever saw. This is why he expects the winner of his scholarship to be active in one approved school sport for at least one school year.

It's a reasonable request. That is, it's reasonable unless your name is Herb Forrest, you stand six feet three inches tall, weigh 135 pounds, and fall over things. This description fits me perfectly. As an athlete, I'm a good politician.

In my condition, it would take all my spare time to make any kind of athletic team. I had to give up something. It couldn't be homework. Student politics had to go.

I explained this to Shorty.

"You knew about this athletic business last year," he accused. "Why didn't you do something about it then?"

"Do you remember what I looked like last year?" I asked.

He did. I could tell by the look on his face.

Last year I was six feet one inch tall and weighed 115 pounds. During the summer vacation I went with my folks to the Canadian Rockies. We camped out a lot. I put on twenty pounds and two inches of altitude. Now I hoped it would be enough to get me on a team, any team.

"I guess you've got to quit," said Shorty, accepting defeat. "What are you going out for?"

"Football," I said.

"You're crazy," he said as he walked away, glumly shaking his head.

I squared my shoulders, what shoulders I owned, and headed for the gym and coach Buck Norwood's office. I soon found I was in no danger, despite Shorty's fears. The coach was polite but firm. He said he wanted no part of my suicide. I argued that I was an ideal height for an end position. He pointed out the fact that height would mean nothing after my 135 pounds had been broken in two.

It was three o'clock when I left the coach. By three fifteen I had reported to the tennis courts and (1) received one serve, (2) stuck my foot through a school tennis racquet, and (3) fallen over the net. The tennis coach suggested I go someplace else.

By four o'clock I had on gym shorts, sneakers, and headgear, ready to try out for the school boxing club. A freshman, two pounds lighter than I, floored me twice simply by feinting rapidly with his left hand.

At four thirty-five the tumbling instructor gave me ointment for mat burns received when I tried to master a backward somersault.

"Herb," he explained gently, "during the last four years you've gained height very rapidly. Your muscular strength and coordination just haven't caught up yet."

"You mean I'm a menace to navigation," I said.

"Only temporarily," he assured me.

That tore it. I headed for the showers. I changed clothes in the locker room while wondering gloomily who would get the scholarship I'd worked so hard to earn. That's when Shorty Connors stuck his grinning red-thatched head in the door.

"Hi, Champ," he said cheerfully. Shorty is always cheerful when he thinks he has solved a difficult problem.

"Don't make funny noises," I said. "It hurts when I laugh."

"Old buddy," Shorty said expansively, "I'm going to solve your problem."

"You're going to get me a fight with Sugar Ray Robinson," I said sarcastically.

"Better than that," he grinned. "It's so simple I wonder that my brilliant mind didn't seize the idea at once."

"Spare me," I groaned.

"The outing club I belong to," Shorty said, "it's school-approved. Join up with us."

"You think they'd have me?" I said dubiously.

"I will fix everything," he boasted. "What's more, since we only go out on weekends and holidays, you can still run for prexy."

I felt a surge of hope. It sounded good, almost too good. I was aware that Shorty's inventive genius sometimes took a strange twist. If I hadn't been so eager, I might have suspected he was up to something.

"It's great," I said. "What do you do in this club?"

"Oh, just climb Old Baldy and camp a little and things like that." Shorty passed it off casually, so casually I hardly heard him. Camping was okay by me anyway. "Show up at Mr. Frazier's house tonight at eight P.M.," Shorty said.

"Right," I said, like the dope I am.

At 8 P.M. sharp I knocked on the door of Mr. Frazier's house. Mr. Frazier is the Jackson High science teacher and, so Shorty told me, the adviser for the outing club. Mr. Frazier opened the door. He grinned at me, his teeth white against the tan he picked up in the summer while prospecting for uranium in Utah and Colorado.

"Hi, Herb," he said. "Come on in; you're late."

I was sure Shorty had said 8 P.M., but Shorty was already there as well as a dozen other kids, both boys and girls. I knew most of the crowd. You don't get to be class president three times without meeting a lot of people. And they all knew me, because you don't get to be class president three times without giving a lot of speeches where everyone can hear you.

"Shorty was telling us about your experiences in the Canadian Rockies," Mr. Frazier said.

"Oh, that. It wasn't much," I said.

"My, he's modest," one of the girls whispered.

Something was funny here, because my trip to Canada had been anything but adventurous. Something was mighty funny, but not as crazy as what happened next.

It was the club's first meeting of the year and they were scheduled to hold elections that night. That wasn't unusual, but when the members voted unanimously to elect me president, I was dumfounded. I could hardly make an acceptance speech, and that's saying something for a politician of three years standing like myself.

After the meeting broke up, Shorty stopped me outside. "How does it feel to be the new president of the Crag Crawlers?" he asked.

"Crag Crawlers?" I echoed.

For a minute Shorty looked embarrassed, but then he said, "Oh, that's just the name of the club," and then he hurried off. It seemed like a funny name for an outfit that only climbed Old Baldy, a mountain that has trails up every side of it—except, of course, the side where the cliffs are.

I didn't worry about names, however; I was too happy with the way things had worked out. I showed up at the foot of Old Baldy that weekend, bright of eye and clear of mind, and untroubled.

Frankly, it didn't look very exciting. Old Baldy is just a big bare hump that stands near some lesser humps. The only thing outstanding about Old Baldy is its palisades, or cliffs; otherwise, it's just another semidesert mountain peak.

Even the sky wasn't exciting. A few flat-looking clouds marred the sunshine that people in our part of the country come to expect every day. Clouds around here always go someplace else to rain.

Mr. Frazier came along with the main group of our club members. There were seven of us now, five boys and two girls. Mr. Frazier, with Shorty helping him, also brought along several coils of rope and a bunch of iron gadgets. Then we started out.

Mr. Frazier said he and I could climb together so that I could give him some hints on climbing technique like the ones I'd learned in the Canadian Rockies, while Shorty led the rest of the group.

I didn't see what I could tell Mr. Frazier about climbing Old Baldy. It was simply a case of putting one foot in front of the other. I couldn't see what use those ropes would be either. Boy, was I stupid.

But I felt too lucky being in this club to argue about details. After all, these kids elected me president without any questions; why should I gripe if they wanted to carry ropes to the top of Old Baldy. I just walked along behind Mr. Frazier, determined to keep up and just watching where I put my feet. In fact, I was so busy that I missed a sign that read: OLD BALDY PALISADES —HALF MILE.

I almost fell over Mr. Frazier when he stopped without warning and said, "O.K., gang, this is the spot."

We were at the foot of the cliffs that drop off one side of Old Baldy. Right in front of us was a ridge of rock that twisted up toward the cliffs like the spine of a gigantic dinosaur. About three hundred feet above, the ridge joined the cliffs that shot steeply skyward toward the summit.

The whole thing looked as forbidding as a brick wall topped with broken glass.

"Hey," I said weakly. "Hey."

"Looks pretty good," Mr. Frazier said to me. "I guess it doesn't compare with the Canadian Rockies, Herb, but you'll find it's good climbing."

"Gleep!" I said, and looked at Shorty, who was staring innocently away from me.

Things were just not right. All this talk about my mountain adventures and now this horrible mass of rock. Somebody had trapped me into this. I couldn't back out now, not with everyone watching. And it didn't take too much to figure out who the villain was. I was so lost in my thoughts about how to get even with Shorty that I didn't hear voices telling me to tie into one end of the climbing rope.

At last Mr. Frazier, rather impatiently I thought, tied one end of the climbing rope around my waist and settled the knot snugly over the spot my stomach had occupied before it squeezed itself into a fist and dropped into my right shoe.

"What's the matter? He looks scared." Whoever whispered that was right, and it made it even more certain that I couldn't back out. Now it was do or die. As if to emphasize that unhappy thought, a big cloud drifted across the sun and everything became dull and gray. Everything but my face, which was already that color.

"We'll go first," Mr. Frazier said. "That way we can help the others if they get in trouble."

Then he turned and nimbly scrambled up the ridge as if he were half rock lizard. Sixty feet above me he reached a wide ledge, anchored himself, pulled up the slack in the rope, and yelled for me to follow him.

Everybody was looking at me now, and I could tell what they were thinking. The big man on campus, the club president, the great mountain climber, let's see what he can do, that's what they were thinking. I grabbed a handhold timidly and pulled myself up a little way. O.K., Shorty Connors, I thought, when you come to the funeral, I hope you're sorry.

What happened next was a nightmare. I started up, and before long the kids below were thinking out loud.

"Look at him. He's using the rope to climb on."

"What's he trying to do now, step on his own hand?"

"This is the way they do it in Canada? Hah!"

"What a phony he turned out to be!"

I hauled my trembling body onto the

ledge where Mr. Frazier stood anchoring my rope. There I collapsed.

"You sick?" he asked.

"Very," I said.

Shorty led the rest of the group to the big ledge, and some new climbing arrangements were made immediately. They decided it would be safer to put me in the middle of a climbing rope where two or three guys could help pull me up and the two girls could direct me from below. In other words, I was just extra baggage; everybody made that quite plain, even though they didn't speak to me unless it was absolutely necessary. I was as good as booted out of this club already.

Shorty looked miserable. Evidently things hadn't gone the way he planned. I was a worse climber than even he had imagined. But right then I didn't care what Shorty thought. He had gotten me into this mess. If I lived through this climb, I would run for student prexy and I'd push a law through the student council to outlaw all campaign managers forever.

Then it hit me. The kids in this club thought I was a big blowhard. If word got out about this mess, I wouldn't have a chance to win the election, and I'd be booted out of this club for sure. I'd lose the election, the scholarship, and be laughed out of school besides.

"I don't know what you thought . . ." I began.

"Forget about it, Herb. It's O.K.," Mr. Frazier said. But I could see that it wasn't O.K. They all thought I had lied to them. I was ruined.

I was so miserable that I almost forgot to be scared as we continued the climb. Things couldn't have been worse. It would take a small miracle to salvage anything out of this mess.

At least I thought things couldn't be worse until I looked at the sky. It looked bad. The scudding gray-white clouds of the early morning had changed to massive dark ones that shouldered together and crowded out the blue of the sky. The wind came up, and wraiths of mist streaked along below the overcast. We were due for a storm.

"We'd better head for the cave," Mr. Frazier said. He looked worried. He had evidently figured like the rest of us that clouds in our part of the country didn't mean anything at all.

Moving as fast as they could, considering my creeping pace, the party headed off the ridge toward shelter. I could appreciate the teamwork of a mountaineering crew, even if I didn't enjoy the view. I could see how they protected each other with the climbing rope and how they functioned smoothly as a unit. This was a pretty fine athletic group I was about to become ex-president of.

When we reached the "cave," it turned out to be a broad ledge with an overhanging block above it. There was plenty of room for all of us to wait out the rain. It looked especially good to me, because anything was better than being on that cliff face. That's what I thought anyway, until the lightning struck.

It was close, too close. The flash was blinding, and the thunder exploded almost at the same instant the bolt hit. It was that near.

One of the girls screamed, and the other hid her face in her hands. I swallowed something that might have been my heart.

In the awful silence that followed, we sat frozen on the ledge. Then the second bolt struck somewhere above us. It was even closer.

Fear had come with the first flash. It had scared us good, but now there was blind panic. One of the girls jumped to her feet. Maybe she thought she could run away; I don't know. Anyway, she tottered at the lip of the ledge crying, when Shorty, as quick as I've ever seen him move, yanked her back again.

Mr. Frazier was white as chalk, and the girls sobbed hysterically. The wind howled and rain whipped under the overhang of our ledge with a sound like buckets of hurled gravel. I tell you, things were plenty shaky right then. And then I heard a voice speaking above the rain noise.

"Fellow students and faculty members of Jackson High School," it said. The voice was mine!

Everybody turned and looked at me as if I had lost my mind, and maybe I had. All I know is that I felt I had to do something, so I opened my mouth and that's what came out. Now what?

It's funny what your mind can come up with in times of stress. Mine turned up a campaign slogan, the one Shorty had worked so hard to develop into a poster. It was the one that started "AA is for Aardvark . . ."

"AA is for aardvark," I said, "but let us not stop there."

Everybody on the ledge still stared. The girls even stopped crying to watch what they must have thought was the final crackup of their club's ex-president.

"Webster says the aardvark is 'a burrowing African mammal that feeds on ants and termites.' Let us examine this definition," I said. "While it may be true," I continued, "that aardvarks eat termites and ants and burrow in the dirt, does it seem fair to pass the aardvark off in this summary manner? I say it does not!"

It wasn't very funny, but somebody snickered and the rest of the group smiled a little bit.

"Would you like to be known merely as a two-legged mammal that climbs mountains and eats hot dogs? Of course not! There is more to you than that, and I say it's true of the aardvark!

"Have you, in all your experience, fellow students, heard of an aardvark who was not kind to his mother? Who did not share his ants and termites with his playmates? Who refused to do all his homework? I for one have not."

Even the girls were giggling now. It wasn't so much what I said that struck them as funny. It was just the idea that anybody would be crazy enough to give a lecture on aardvarks while perched on that dizzy ledge in a thunderstorm.

I don't remember how the speech ended, but Shorty Connors took the cue. He told a shaggy-dog story that was so bad that the next guy was eager to tell a better one. The tension melted away. We were still scared, but the dangerous panic was gone. No one would do anything foolish now.

Before long, the freak thunderstorm disappeared as quickly as it had blown up. We had only to wait for the rock to dry a little before we would be able to finish the climb.

I didn't climb any better, and I was twice as scared on the last part of the climb, but everybody seemed glad to have me around anyway.

On the top of the mountain we gathered around, and Mr. Frazier said to me, "That took a lot of courage on that ledge, Herb. It was something a braggart couldn't have done. I have a feeling we've been misled about you," and he looked right at Shorty.

"I . . . I might have invented a few things about Herb," Shorty stammered.

I could see he felt pretty bad about the whole thing. After all, he was just trying to fix things for me. At the same time, I knew Shorty would have to be taught a lesson before he came up with any more bright ideas.

"Mr. President," Mr. Frazier said to me, "what do you think we ought to do about this character?"

"Does the president of this club have a right to levy fines?" I asked.

"Yes!" the whole group chorused.

"Well, Shorty," I said sternly, "for those little inventions you told about me, I fine you five thousand words."

"Words?" he said, puzzled.

"Yes," I told him, "a five-thousand-word essay. Subject: 'What the Aardvark Means to Me.'"

Even Shorty had to grin a little about that.

Exercise 45

A test of understanding

For each item below, choose the answer you believe is correct. Print your answers on your paper.

1. Shorty Connors used the word *aardvark* in Herbert Forrest's campaign for president because
   A. it appears first in the dictionary
   B. the aardvark is a very fierce and brave animal
   C. the letters *AA* stand for the very best
2. To get the university scholarship, Herb Forrest had only one thing still to do. He had to meet
   A. the citizenship requirement
   B. the athletic requirement
   C. the academic requirement
3. Before Herb tried to scale Old Baldy

with the Crag Crawlers, Shorty had probably told the club members that Herb had

    A. done dangerous mountain climbing in Canada

    B. taken advanced lessons in mountain climbing in Canada

    C. taught other students mountain climbing in Canada

4. Herb regained the respect of the other students because he

    A. won the election for student president

    B. punished Shorty for telling a lie about him

    C. gave an amusing speech to stop a panic

The correct answers are shown in the answer key.

The story is too long for one person to read aloud. It can easily be divided into ten parts, however, and each part assigned to two or three members of the class. This assignment will give each student a short enough passage to prepare carefully.

In preparing to read your part of the story, follow the suggestions given earlier in the chapter. Try out your passage two or three times before your turn comes to read in class. As the story is read, episode by episode, you will discover how much pleasure you can give and get by good oral reading.

Oral reading practice

To do a good job reading a poem to others, you must appreciate it yourself. You will know more about a selection if you find out something about the author, about his purpose in writing, and about the setting.

The Ballad of Reading Gaol is one of Oscar Wilde's most famous poems. Many years ago ballads were sung by wandering troubadours, sometimes to relate the events of a battle, sometimes to report some scandal of the court. Modern ballads are read or recited as stories in rhyme. Reading (pronounced *redding*) Gaol is the name of a famous English prison. The word *gaol* is simply the British spelling for our word *jail;* both words are pronounced the same

way. The poem tells of a convict who is doomed to hang for murder. Wilde describes his wistful looks toward the free blue sky, and questions everyman's guilt when he says "Yet each man kills the thing he loves." And he adds "It is sweet to dance to violins when Love and Life are fair . . . But it is not sweet with nimble feet to dance upon the air."

The Ballad of Reading Gaol

by Oscar Wilde

He did not wear his scarlet coat,
    For blood and wine are red,
And blood and wine were on his hands
    When they found him with the dead,
The poor dead woman whom he loved,
    And murdered in her bed.

He walked amongst the Trial Men
    In a suit of shabby gray;
A cricket cap was on his head,
    And his step seemed light and gay;
But I never saw a man who looked
    So wistfully at the day.

I never saw a man who looked
    With such a wistful eye
Upon that little tent of blue
    Which prisoners call the sky,
And at every drifting cloud that went
    With sails of silver by.

I walked, with other souls in pain,
    Within another ring,
And was wondering if the man had done
    A great or little thing,
When a voice behind me whispered low,
    "That fellow's got to swing."

Dear Christ! the very prison walls
    Suddenly seemed to reel,
And the sky above my head became
    Like a casque of scorching steel;
And, though I was a soul in pain,
    My pain I could not feel.

I only knew what hunted thought
    Quickened his step, and why
He looked upon the garish day
    With such a wistful eye:
The man had killed the thing he loved,
    And so he had to die.

Yet each man kills the thing he loves,
    By each let this be heard,

Some do it with a bitter look,
      Some with a flattering word,
The coward does it with a kiss,
      The brave man with a sword!

Some kill their love when they are young,
      And some when they are old;
Some strangle with the hands of Lust,
      Some with the hands of Gold:
The kindest use a knife, because
      The dead so soon grow cold.

Some love too little, some too long,
      Some sell, and others buy;
Some do the deed with many tears,
      And some without a sigh:
For each man kills the thing he loves,
      Yet each man does not die.

He does not die a death of shame
      On a day of dark disgrace,
Nor have a noose about his neck,
      Nor a cloth upon his face,
Nor drop feet foremost through the floor
      Into an empty space.

He did not wring his hands nor weep,
      Nor did he peak or pine,
But he drank the air as though it held
      Some healthful anodyne;
With open mouth he drank the sun
      As though it had been wine!

And I and all the souls in pain,
      Who tramped the other ring,
Forgot if we ourselves had done
      A great or little thing,
And watched with gaze of dull amaze
      The man who had to swing.

And strange it was to see him pass
      With a step so light and gay,
And strange it was to see him look
      So wistfully at the day,
And strange it was to think that he
      Had such a debt to pay.

For oak and elm have pleasant leaves
      That in the spring-time shoot:
But grim to see is the gallows tree,
      With its adder-bitten root,
And, green or dry, a man must die
      Before it bears its fruit!

The loftiest place is that seat of grace
      For which all worldlings try:
But who would stand in hempen band
      Upon a scaffold high,
And through a murderer's collar take

His last look at the sky?

It is sweet to dance to violins
      When Love and Life are fair:
To dance to flutes, to dance to lutes
      Is delicate and rare:
But it is not sweet with nimble feet
      To dance upon the air!

So with curious eyes and sick surmise
      We watched him day by day,
And wondered if each one of us
      Would end the self-same way,
For none can tell to what red Hell
      His sightless soul may stray.

At last the dead man walked no more
      Amongst the Trial Men,
And I knew that he was standing up
      In the black dock's dreadful pen,
And that never would I see his face
      In God's sweet world again.

Like two doomed ships that pass in storm
      We had crossed each other's way:
But we made no sign, we said no word,
      We had no word to say;
For we did not meet in the holy night,
      But in the shameful day.

A prison wall was round us both,
      Two outcast men we were:
The world had thrust us from its heart,
      And God from out His care:
And the iron gin that waits for Sin
      Had caught us in its snare.

Can you visualize an ancient troubadour singing this "news story" about a famous murderer to the local villagers? Did you find the ballad, or the "news," interesting? The complete ballad is much longer; and you might like to read the entire poem someday. The condemned man is neither sad nor weeping. He drinks in the sun as though it were wine. It is enough, says the balladeer, to make you think twice of the things we take so much for granted.

Oral reading practice

Walt Whitman is often called the poet of democracy. He knew and loved the common people. He had faith in their ability to build and run a great country. Whitman was born on a farm but moved to Brooklyn at an early age. He worked in printshops and newspaper offices. For a while he was editor of the *Brooklyn Eagle.*

Whitman used to tramp the streets and ride the ferries, meeting ordinary people and talking with them. To see more of the country, he went by steamboat, stagecoach, and rail to New Orleans. Later he served as a nurse in the Civil War.

In 1855 Whitman published a collection of poetry called *Leaves of Grass.* No one had ever seen poetry like this before. It had no clear-cut rhythm. It had no rhyme. Below is reproduced a portion of *Leaves of Grass.*

It is harder to read a poem like this than one like *The Ballad of Reading Gaol.* To do a good job, you will have to study the thought units. Read together the words that belong together in thought. As you practice reading these word groups, you will find that there is an underlying rhythm to the whole poem. You can make this rhythm clear by varying the length of your pauses between thought units.

I Hear America Singing[8]

by Walt Whitman

I hear America singing, the varied carols
    I hear,
Those of mechanics, each one singing his
    as it should be, blithe and strong,
The carpenter singing his as he measures
    his plank or beam,
The mason singing his as he makes ready
    for work, or leaves off work,
The boatman singing what belongs to him
    in his boat, the deckhand singing on
    the steamboat deck,
The shoemaker singing as he sits on his
    bench, the hatter singing as he stands,
The wood-cutter's song, the ploughboy's
    on his way in the morning, or at noon
    intermission or at sundown,
The delicious singing of the mother, or of
    the young wife at work, or of the
    girl sewing or washing,
Each singing what belongs to him or her
    and to none else,
The day what belongs to the day—at
    night the party of young fellows,

robust, friendly,
Singing with open mouths their strong
    melodious songs.

Oral reading practice

Junior Miss is a famous comedy that played for a long time on Broadway. It is about a family of four: parents and two teen-age daughters. It is a well-written and tasteful play. Many of the situations and lines will sound familiar to you. Fun is poked at adults as well as children. The following is a short excerpt from Act I of the play. You might enjoy reading the entire play. It is available at your public library.

Your appreciation and enjoyment of this short segment will be increased if you do the following.

Step 1. Note the stage directions. They will help you imagine the living room in which the play takes place, the appearance of the characters, and the properties for the play. Properties, more commonly called props, are the things used in the play—tables, telephone, newspaper, glasses are all props. "Stage L." means the left side of the stage from the actor's viewpoint. "Stage R." is on the actor's right. "Upstage" means the rear of the stage; "downstage" means the front of the stage. "U.C." means upper center—or the center of the stage near the rear.

Step 2. Read the play through silently and quickly from beginning to end to get the important ideas. Then reread the play to find the words that may be unfamiliar to you. Try to figure out their meanings from the way they are used. Here are a few of the words to make sure of:

foyer	decode
amok	superciliously
phlegmatic	ensemble
detached	

Step 3. As you read the play, you must keep several things in mind. First, try to get a mental image of the living room and the furniture. Second, as each character is introduced, try to imagine his appearance and his way of acting and moving. Third, as you read the dialogue or conversation, think how the words are spoken. What tone of voice is used? Is the person moving while he is speaking? To enjoy play

---

8 From *Leaves of Grass,* by Walt Whitman.

reading, you must read it at least once slowly. Allow time for pauses in the conversation; try to picture what the character is doing as he speaks and how he feels.

Junior Miss[9]

by Jerome Chodorov and Joseph Fields

Characters

Harry Graves, *the father*
Joe, *the elevator boy*
Judy Graves, *the younger daughter*
Fuffy Adams, *Judy's friend*
Grace Graves, *the mother*
Hilda, *the maid*
Lois Graves, *the older daughter*
Barlow Adams, *Fuffy's brother*
Haskell Cummings, *Barlow's friend*

Stage Directions

The scene of our play is the living room of the Graveses' home in Manhattan's upper sixties, just off Central Park. It is not a modern duplex affair, but an apartment in a post–World War I building that has reached the sand-blasting stage.

There is a foyer at stage L., leading into the room (the stage proper), with a door on the upstage wall opening into the outer hall and elevator. The living room is furnished in a comfortable but homely fashion. There are no fine pieces, but nothing of hideous taste to offend the eye. A sofa, a few easy chairs, and some not so easy, are the main articles of furniture.

At stage R. there is the suggestion of an archway, through which we see the entrances to the apartment's two bedrooms. Mr. and Mrs. Graves's bedroom is upstage, and adjoining it is the room occupied by their daughters, Lois and Judy.

The total effect is middle-class, of people who have a fairly steady struggle to maintain their position. It is eight o'clock in the evening in mid-December.

HARRY GRAVES is a good-looking sort of man of about thirty-eight, with the remains of an athletic physique. At the curtain's rise he is seated in a chair reading a newspaper. After a moment, the doorbell

(a buzzer) rings. He crosses L. and opens door. JOE is revealed, holding roller skates.

HARRY. Oh, hello, Joe — What can I do for you?

JOE. Mr. Graves, would you please ask Judy not to leave her roller skates in the lobby. (*Holds up skates.* HARRY *takes them.*) Mr. Streger, the janitor, slipped and went right across the foyer with an armful of garbage, and you ought to see the mess down there.

HARRY. That's awful, Joe—I'll see that it never happens again.

JOE. Thank you, Mr. Graves. . . . (HARRY *closes the door.*)

(HARRY *starts to cross R. as phone rings.*)

HARRY (*at phone*). Hello? Yes? Lois?— Hold the wire, please. (*Calls.*) Lois! (*Waits a moment.*) Lois! Phone!

LOIS (*from bedroom R.*). Take the message, will you please, Dad?

HARRY (*disengaging phone cord from skates*). She's busy right now. I'll take the message . . . . Wait a minute . . . what was that? (*Repeats slowly.*) Ralph is calling for her instead of Henry. . . . But he can't meet her in front of the gymnasium . . . . Can she go where? . . . Wait a minute . . . . Well, who is this—Ralph or Henry? . . . Charlie! . . . One moment—repeat that just a bit slower, will you, Charlie? (*Repeats.*) Henry has the grippe and his family doesn't think he ought to go . . . . Yes, I've got that . . . . She should call who? Oh, Ralph? And let him know if she wants to meet him because Merrill Feurback is going to call for her instead of Ralph . . . . Charlie, it gets a little involved . . . . Would you mind calling back later and explain it to Lois? Thanks, Charlie—do that. (*Hangs up annoyed and starts R.*)

GRACE (*from bedroom*). Harry! Harry! (*Enters from bedroom R.* MRS. GRAVES (GRACE) *is a very attractive young matron of thirty-five.*)

HARRY. Grace, you'll simply have to talk to Judy—she's running amok in this building.

GRACE (*as she sees skates*). Oh, did Judy leave her skates in the foyer again? (*Takes them from him and puts them on chair.*)

HARRY. Yes, and tell her to stop tormenting that elevator boy.

GRACE. It's not her fault. I think Fuffy Adams is a very bad influence on her.

HARRY. Oh, sure!

GRACE (*crossing down R*). Harry, you'd better get dressed. They'll be here any minute. And fix up a tray with some ice and glasses.

HARRY (*crossing to behind couch by arch*). What for? Aren't we playing at the Bakers'? . . . Hilda!

(GRACE *moves little table down R. closer to R. chair.*)

GRACE (*crossing to C.*). No, not Hilda—(*Crosses to get bottle.*) You—she's got enough to do.

(HILDA, *a phlegmatic Norwegian, comes into the room from foyer. She goes L.*)

HILDA. Huh?

HARRY. Never mind, Hilda. . . .

GRACE. Well, as long as you're here—Hilda, fix some ice and glasses on a tray.

HILDA. There is no more ice. . . .

HARRY. No ice? What happened to it?

HILDA. Miss Lois got it—

GRACE. Lois? What for?

HILDA. I don't ask anymore. (*Goes back into kitchen U.L.*)

(GRACE *looks to bedroom R.*)

GRACE. Lois!

LOIS (*off stage R., in muffled voice*). What is it?

GRACE. Come on out here!

HARRY. What the devil is she doing with the ice cubes?

(LOIS GRAVES *appears from her bedroom D.R., a turkish towel pressed to her face. She is a pretty girl of sixteen, slim and straight, wears a sweater and skirt and not quite high-heeled shoes. Her hair is held back by a circular comb.* LOIS *is a very sophisticated woman of the world with a permanently detached air.*)

LOIS (*through towel*). What is it, Mother?

GRACE (*alarmed*). What are you doing to your face?

LOIS. (*She shows them towel with ice cubes inside. Her face is red and blotchy.*) It's an ice pack.

HARRY. Ice pack? Got a toothache?

LOIS (*condescendingly*). No . . . . I rub it on to tighten the facial muscles and keep them from sagging.

HARRY. Good Lord! Sixteen years old and her face is sagging!

LOIS. Who was that on the phone, Dad?

HARRY. Charlie called in reference to Henry, Ralph, and Merrill.

LOIS (*annoyed*). Please, Dad—what was the message?

HARRY. I don't know. I couldn't decode it.

LOIS. Really, Dad!

GRACE. Now take that ice into the kitchen before it drips all over the carpet, and bring in some glasses. (GRACE *goes up R. to mirror.*)

(LOIS *goes into kitchen L., putting ice pack to her face. Crosses behind* HARRY.)

HARRY. Ice pack? Where the heck does she get those ideas?

(GRACE *crosses to him from mirror.*)

GRACE (*shrugs*). I read the same article in Harper's—only I need it.

HARRY. (*Takes her face in his hands, looking at it intently.*) Not a sag anywhere—don't let that streamlined daughter of yours make an old woman out of you!

(JUDY GRAVES *comes from her bedroom R., a thoughtful look on her face, carrying a school pad and a pencil stuck behind her ear. She is thirteen, tall for her age and heavily built. From her shoulders to her knees, she is entirely shapeless, which gives her a square broad look in spite of her height. Below her skirt, which is too short for her, her legs are hard, muscular and covered with scratches. Her dress, a soft blue one, smocked at the sleeves, is supposed to hang gracefully from the shoulders in a straight fold, but instead it is pulled, as though she had been stuffed into it. Her little round stomach bulges over a belt drawn tightly beneath it. On her fingers are a pair of cheap rings, and she wears three charm bracelets of a brassy color, and a locket and chain so tight around her neck it seems to strangle her. Her dark brown hair keeps straight below her ears, and is held in place by numerous bobby pins and two ready-made bows. She looks on as* HARRY *kisses* GRACE *tenderly.* JUDY *drops straight down R.C.*)

JUDY (*when almost down*). Daddy. . .

HARRY. Yes . . .

JUDY (*coming down to armchair*). Where were you born?

HARRY. Who wants to know?

JUDY. Miss Schwabacher.

HARRY. Miss Schwabacher?

JUDY (*sitting in armchair*). She's my

English teacher. I'm writing my autobiography. Everybody in our class has to. The best autobiography will be read out loud in assembly.

GRACE. I see— What do you want to know, darling? (HARRY *sits.*)

JUDY. Just outstanding events. I've thought loads about myself, but I want you and Dad for a sort of background.

HARRY. That's darn nice of you.

GRACE. You start, Harry—I've got to finish dressing. . . . (*She crosses to bedroom door and exits.*)

JUDY. Well?

HARRY. Well—as I say—I was born in Brooklyn—

JUDY. Oh! (*Reacts.*) Oh!

HARRY. (*He looks over at* JUDY.) Sorry, Judy, I wish it was Shanghai—then I went to Public School there until I went to Kent. (*Rises, for tobacco.*) Then when I got through Kent, I went to Yale. I met your mother at Smith, and a few years after the war I married her.

JUDY. Yes? Go on—

HARRY. That's about all. (*Crosses down to big chair.*)

JUDY. Gee, that's not much of a life.

HARRY. Well, I'm very sorry. Who do you want for a father—Rasputin?

JUDY. Fuffy's father had a very wild youth.

HARRY. Well, I'm having a very wild middle age.

JUDY. What about Mom? Anything happen to her?

HARRY. (*Crossing up to cabinet for tobacco.*) Well, she was born in Kansas City, Missouri. Your grandfather was vice-president of some wholesale drygoods store there.

JUDY. I wonder why he stayed in Kansas City? All the best people used to push on farther west.

HARRY (*annoyed*). He had a darned good business—a darned good business! He managed to send all his girls to Smith. (LOIS *enters L. with tray and glasses.*) So it's just as well for you that he didn't push on west. (*Up to cabinet.*)

LOIS (*looking at* JUDY *superciliously*). Now what'd she do?

JUDY (*flatly*). Charming Lois. . . .

(GRACE *comes out of her bedroom, fully dressed and looking quite smart. She has an emery board in her hand.*)

GRACE (*to* JUDY, *crossing to sofa*). Did you get all the facts you need?

JUDY (*dubiously*). Ye-es. . . .

GRACE. Why don't you read us the important part—the part about you?

JUDY. (*Sits.*) Okay . . . (*Reading.*) "My Life So Far" by Judy Graves. "It was exactly on the stroke of midnight, on the twenty-first of September, that I was born."

(HARRY *and* GRACE *exchange a look.*)

GRACE. How did you ever get it into your head that you were born on the stroke of midnight?

HARRY. You were born at six o'clock in the morning! And made plenty of trouble for everybody!

JUDY. Well, it's so flat, you've got to put some color into it. (*Reading again.*) "It was a wild stormy night and our family doctor fought his way through the terrible rain to reach the bedside of my mother, who hovered between life and death. . . ."

LOIS (*flatly*). "David Copperfield."

JUDY (*giving her a look*). Well, that ain't bad.

GRACE (*firmly*). You were born in a very nice little private hospital on Central Park West. It's been torn down since.

JUDY. Well, anyway— (*She reads.*) "I was a small, fat, healthy baby, and from the first objected to being called the image of any other member of the family because I knew I was different."

LOIS. (*A short, coarse laugh.*) The other members of the family were the ones who objected!

JUDY. Honestly, Mother . . .

GRACE. That'll do, Lois— Go on, Judy. . . .

JUDY (*reading, half smiling*). "At that time, my mother and father were a very affectionate couple. He used to call her his *enfant gâté*, which is French for 'spoiled child.' "

HARRY. (*Starts violently.*) Now listen—!

GRACE (*soothingly*). Just a minute, Harry. . . . (*To* JUDY.) What Dad was going to say, I'm sure, was that such things are . . . well . . . sort of family jokes. . . . And I'm sure your teacher doesn't want you to write about them.

JUDY (*marking pad*). "My sister Lois was born three years before I was, shortly after Mom and Dad were married and came back from Atlantic City."

HARRY. It was a year after!

GRACE. (*Hurriedly rises, going L., puts down emery board.*) It's all right, dear!

JUDY. "When I was six, Lois was forced to leave private school and attend public school. It was in 1933 when my father had suffered heavy losses, due to an unexpected failure in his business." (HARRY *slams magazine.*)

(HARRY *jumps up and strides the room silently, hands in pockets.*)

GRACE (*looking at him anxiously*). Judy, I hardly think that part is fair to Dad. Besides, it isn't considered nice for little girls to talk about money.

JUDY. Then I'll have to cut out the part about Dad starting (*Stands, crosses R.*) all over again as a junior clerk at twenty-five dollars a week.

HARRY. Lord!

(GRACE *crosses to behind* JUDY.)

LOIS. Mother, that'll spread through school like wildfire. I'll never be able to show my face to the senior body.

GRACE. (*Puts arm around* JUDY, *wheedlingly.*) Now, Judy, I'm sure we can think of something more interesting than that for your autobiography. I'll help you with it tomorrow. (*Moving to sofa.*)

HARRY (*grimly*). You better, or we'll all have to push farther west!

GRACE (*puzzled*). What?

HARRY. I'm going in to wash. . . . (*He starts for bedroom R.* LOIS *hurries ahead of him.*)

LOIS. Just let me finish up first, Dad, will you? I've got a date. I'll be out in a second. (*She goes into bedroom hastily.*)

HARRY (*calling after her*). Excuse me, princess.

(LOIS *slams door. There is a peculiar knock on L. door—two longs and three shorts.*)

JUDY. That's Fuffy's knock— Come in, Fuffy! (*She opens door.* FUFFY ADAMS *bounces in energetically.* JUDY *shuts door.*)

(GRACE *sits.* FUFFY *is the same age and height as* JUDY, *dressed in a very similar manner and overflowing with animal spirits. She is blond and not quite so lumpy.*)

FUFFY. (*Her own notebook is open to a page.*) Hi, Judy! Hi, Mrs. Graves! I just finished my autobiography—it's a killer-diller! Wanna hear it? (*Looks at* HARRY.)

(GRACE *is knitting.*)

HARRY (*eagerly*). Yes! I'd love to hear your autobiography, Fuffy!

GRACE. Harry. . . . (*To* FUFFY.) Have your parents heard it yet, dear?

FUFFY. No! I want to surprise them.

GRACE. Well, you'd better read it to them first.

JUDY. I'll let you read mine, Fuffy—

FUFFY. Okay.

GRACE (*warningly*). Judy!

JUDY (*hastily*). —after Mom and I fix it up.

(FUFFY *and* JUDY *whisper mysteriously, then giggle hysterically.*)

HARRY. (*Kills the laugh.*) Good Lord!

(*They stop. They don't know what to do.* FUFFY *glares at* HARRY.)

FUFFY (*archly*). I finished my Christmas shopping today, Judy. Bet you know what I got you!

JUDY. (*Grins.*) I got yours, too!

GRACE. Fine Christmas spirit! What do you do—tell each other what you're giving?

JUDY. Otherwise how can we be sure we'll get what we want?

(*Another whisper between* FUFFY *and* JUDY.)

FUFFY (*earnestly, crossing near* GRACE). Mrs. Graves, Judy and I have an important problem. Maybe you can help us out.

(LOIS *enters from her bedroom, leaves door open.*)

GRACE. What is it, Fuffy?

LOIS. Okay, Dad. You can have it now. . . .

HARRY (*heavily as he rises*). Thank you—very much. . . . (*He goes into bedroom.*)

FUFFY (*looking her over*). Hello, Lois— That's a gorgeous ensemble.

LOIS. (*Pained, hand under hair, walks on line to armchair.*) Please, Fuffy . . .

JUDY. (*Nudges* FUFFY. *Both imitate her gesture.*) Charming Lois.

(LOIS *sits in armchair.*)

GRACE (*hastily*). What did you want, Fuffy?

FUFFY. (*Sits on arm of sofa.*) It's about our escorts for Mary Caswell's dance on New Year's night.

LOIS. Escorts! Hah!

JUDY (*giving her a look*). It's formal.

LOIS. Pathetic! A dance for a lot of kids. You'll trample one another to death. Thank heavens, I don't have to go.

JUDY. You're too old.

FUFFY. Well, my brother Barlow is taking me—

JUDY. And if it's all right, his friend is going to take me.

LOIS. If what is all right?

JUDY (eyelids fluttering nervously). Oh, you know— If it's O.K. . . . He wants to meet me first . . . If he says he won't, Mrs. Adams is going to make Barlow take both of us.

LOIS. (Laughs scornfully. Rises and crosses R., gets emery board.) Huh! Before I'd be looked over like a prize pig or something!

(LOIS sits R. of table.)

JUDY (mildly). I don't mind. Barlow says he doesn't like girls.

LOIS. Who?

JUDY. This boy. His name is Haskell Cummings.

FUFFY. Barlow says he really doesn't mind girls so much if they're good sports. (To GRACE.) He was supposed to meet Judy in my apartment, but on account of the company—

GRACE. (Nods.) All right, they can come up here, but they can't stay—Judy's got to be in bed by nine thirty.

FUFFY. Oh, thanks loads, Mrs. Graves! You're super! (Turns to JUDY.) See, I told you she would.

JUDY. That's only because you asked her.

FUFFY (crossing to front door). I'll tell the elevator boy to send the men up here when they come. (Starts up. JUDY follows, opens door. FUFFY exits, closing door.)

LOIS. (Snorts.) Men! (Crosses up by cabinet.)

JUDY. (Scared, crosses L.) Gee, I didn't think they— Lois, maybe you could sort of . . . stay awhile . . . be here when they come?

LOIS. What are you afraid of?

JUDY. I dunno. I just am, that's all.

GRACE. (Smiles pityingly.) My poor baby!

(HARRY enters from bedroom with coat on, carrying GRACE'S coat.)

LOIS. I can't bear to watch this tender scene. I'll be in my room. (She goes into bedroom. Closes door.)

(HARRY helps GRACE into her coat and they go to door.)

GRACE. (Remembers, turns.) Judy!

JUDY. Yes, Mother.

GRACE. Give your little friends some ginger ale, and remember—I want you to be in bed by nine thirty. (HARRY and GRACE leave as FUFFY returns.)

(The girls sit down and look at magazines. The buzzer rings.)

FUFFY. (Looks at door in alarm and goes to it.) Oh, I'll bet that's Barlow and Haskell Cummings!

JUDY. (Following, gasps.) It is? Oh, Fuffy, let's not answer it—I'm in no humor to meet men now.

FUFFY. We've got to! Barlow knows I'm up here!

JUDY. But, Fuffy—I'm scared.

FUFFY. Scared? What's there to be scared of?

JUDY. Well, you know—men.

FUFFY. Well, you got to break the ice sometime.

JUDY. But—but suppose he doesn't like me? Honestly, Fuffy, I'd rather go to the dance with you and your brother.

FUFFY. Don't be silly. You've got to take the chance. (Grabs JUDY.) Just turn on everything you've got.

JUDY. What'll I do?

FUFFY. Leave it to me. All you got to do is to act blasé.

JUDY. Let's pretend to play cards or something. (Buzzer rings again.) It'll look funny if they find us just sitting here waiting! Beat you at double Canfield!

(She snatches twin deck of cards from R.C. table, starts dealing on it. FUFFY deals her deck opposite her on table. HILDA enters L. and crosses to the girls.)

HILDA. Don't move, ladies—you'll tire out those delicate little bodies. (She opens door L., revealing two boys about fifteen.)

(BARLOW ADAMS resembles FUFFY closely, and HASKELL CUMMINGS is a slender boy with thin hair that falls over his forehead and an interesting hooked nose. They look past HILDA, and come into the room. The girls are energetically playing cards, not noticing them at all.)

FUFFY. (Screams.) Oh, you rat! That was my ace!

JUDY. And a nine and a ten—and a jack! (Slamming down cards.) I can't move till you get something!

FUFFY. I'm bust, too!

HILDA (loudly). I'll see if the young ladies are at home. Excuse me, your highnesses, but you got callers. . . . (The girls look up, very elaborately surprised. HILDA exits U.L., closing door.)

FUFFY. Well! And an eight and a five. (BARLOW sneezes.) Don't come too near, Barlow, you've got a cold.

BARLOW. It's just a cold in the head. Mama says you're to come right downstairs as soon as you've finished with us.

HASKELL. Science has never proven that colds are catching. Particularly head colds.

JUDY. It hasn't?

HASKELL. Not to my satisfaction.

FUFFY. Oh, that's right. Haskell, you don't know Judy Graves, do you? Judy, this is Haskell Cummings.

JUDY. Hello. (Then, very cordially.) Hello, Barlow.

FUFFY. And that's game. Thirty-nine for you and only twenty for me. (To JUDY.) Judy's the champ at any card game. (Looks at HASKELL, giggles. She rises and goes to sofa, sits.)

JUDY (following her). Wow! I'm bushed!

(They sit there, waiting. After two or three false starts, HASKELL makes first move.)

HASKELL (flipping a dime expertly). I just took this away from young Adams at darts.

(They throw him a look, then look away in unison.)

FUFFY (nudging JUDY). I wish Mary Caswell would have games at her dance. Not silly games, you know, but real ones with cards.

JUDY. Me too. I've known how to play poker for years.

FUFFY. What's the sense of dancing all evening?

BARLOW (kicking at leg of table). Well, I said I'd go, but I didn't say I'd dance.

(They throw him a look.)

JUDY. As long as we have to go, we might as well have some fun. We had loads of fun at your party, Fuffy.

(They giggle.)

HASKELL. What happened?

JUDY. Oh, that's right—you weren't there. (Talking only to FUFFY.) Remember, we threw water out the window.

FUFFY. You're crazy, Judy. You'll do anything.

JUDY. I'll do anything when I happen to feel like it.

FUFFY. And you're the best basketball player at school.

JUDY (modestly). Oh, for heaven's sake!

HASKELL. Where do you go in the summer?

JUDY (trapped as FUFFY rises). Who, me?

HASKELL. Yeah.

JUDY (getting up). South Dorset, Vermont. We've been going there for years. Where do you go?

(FUFFY moves around behind HASKELL and gives go-ahead sign.)

HASKELL. Madison, Connecticut.

(FUFFY nods violently to JUDY.)

JUDY. I've been there. I visited my Aunt Julia there one summer. (BARLOW sneezes.) God bless you, Barlow.

BARLOW. Thank you.

HASKELL (poker-faced). Do you know Jane Carside?

(FUFFY signals again: nose-held business.)

JUDY. That drip!

(FUFFY follows her.)

HASKELL (lighting up). Drip is right. . . . I can't stomach that Jane Carside. . . . Where did you swim? At the Yacht Club or at the Country Club?

(FUFFY takes a swing at an imaginary golf ball.)

JUDY. At the Country Club.

HASKELL (hands in pockets). That's where I swim. (HASKELL turns brightly to FUFFY.)

FUFFY. Isn't that wonderful?

JUDY (laughing in relief, crossing in front of FUFFY). Well, isn't that the funniest thing? (She giggles again in excitement.)

FUFFY. Hey, look out—you'll get the hiccoughs.

JUDY. (Gasps.) Oh, don't! Every time you say that, I do get them, and—hic! (She draws in her breath.) I have got them! (Sits.)

FUFFY. (Cries, puts up on arm.) Hold your arms over your head and I'll get the vinegar! (HASKELL motions to stop her. She runs into foyer L. and off.)

(JUDY sits there, arms over head.)

BARLOW. (Nose business.) Try to stop breathing.

JUDY (after each hiccough). Excuse me.

. . . Excuse me. . . . Excuse me. (HASKELL *picks up magazine and hits her sharply over the head.*) Ouch!

(FUFFY *runs back, carrying vinegar bottle.*)

FUFFY. How are they?

JUDY (*looking at* HASKELL). They're gone. Haskell cured them.

FUFFY. That's the first time I've ever known Judy to have the hiccoughs and get over them like that.

HASKELL (*casually*). When they get the hiccoughs, the best thing to do is scare them.

JUDY. You're very scientific, aren't you?

HASKELL. Sort of.

BARLOW (*moving to door and opening it*). Well, we'd better get going.

JUDY. (*Rises.*) Wouldn't you like some ginger ale before you go?

BARLOW. We can't—we're late now for our weekly poker game.

JUDY. Well, thanks encore.

HASKELL (*straightening his tie*). I can almost always cure hiccoughs. (*Up to door.*)

(FUFFY *signals* JUDY. *The boys amble toward foyer L. and* FUFFY *high-signs to* JUDY *that she'll get the dope. They go out front door and hold a whispered conversation with* FUFFY *as she holds it open.* JUDY *stares at them, nervously biting her nails. After a long pause,* FUFFY *closes door and comes back into the room smiling.*)

FUFFY. It's all fixed! He's going to take you— He says you're a darned good sport and not a bit affected.

JUDY. I think he's nice, too!

A class discussion will increase your appreciation of the play. The following are suggested points for discussion.

A. Is the author making fun of teen-agers?

B. How do Judy and Lois feel about each other?

C. How does this family differ from your family?

D. Are the characters like anyone in your family?

E. Has the author exaggerated the boy-girl relationship in the play?

F. How do Lois and Judy feel about their father?

G. How do they feel about their mother?

H. How does Judy feel about Haskell?

I. Does the author make his characters seem like real people?

Plays, of course, are written to be acted out before an audience. Your class might enjoy acting out this scene from *Junior Miss*. It can be divided into two sections. The first section deals with five main characters: the Graves family and Fuffy. The second section is the scene played by Judy and Fuffy with the two boys. Hilda appears in both sections. Joe, the elevator operator, appears only in the first section.

Play reading is fun, and it increases your enjoyment of the play. By imagining the feelings and expression that a character might use, you can portray the part vividly. Many great actors have captivated audiences by the way they read scenes or speeches aloud. Sitting alone on a bare stage, they can bring to life a scene or passage from a book or play by the way they read.

Very few of us are great actors. But you can read aloud with expression and clarity. In acting out the scene from *Junior Miss* you can improve your ability to read aloud. Check your reading speed; the way you accent certain words; how your expression emphasizes the feelings of the character you are portraying. As we said before, play reading is fun.

Practice Reading 11

In a book, magazine, or newspaper that you like, practice reading for speed and comprehension. Make a record of the reading in Chart 3 on page 8 of the progress folder.

Read the article that follows and take the test based on it. After you complete this exercise, read the article again, this time aloud. When you read, try to read clearly, accurately, and with expression.

11

article

For the benefit of all[10]

by Ivan Ray Tannehill

Many of the people who help our government do its work are not in government jobs. They give their time freely as a service to all of us. We seldom hear about them, so that it is a fine thing when one of them is rewarded.

Not long ago a farmer named George W. Richards traveled to Washington from Minnesota. He came on the invitation of the United States government, which wanted to honor him for helping the Weather Bureau understand the weather.

This man was eighty years old. When he was a lad of twenty, the government had given him a rain gauge and a shelter box with thermometers. It had given him these instruments in exchange for a promise—that he would keep a daily record of the weather in his hometown of Maple Plain, Minnesota. For sixty years George Richards had kept his promise. Day in, day out, during all those sixty years he had recorded the weather in his hometown. He received no pay at all for this service. All he got was the satisfaction of doing something useful.

In Washington George Richards shook hands with high officials who had met to do him honor. He didn't realize that he was the important person there. But the government people looked at him with admiration and with something of envy. What a grand parade of weather this man with the pleasant smile and quick step had seen in sixty years! Violent storms had passed before him, great cold waves and blizzards, heavy rains, crashing hail, deep snow, blistering heat. Through it all he had faithfully kept the records. Every single day he had made a note of any ups and downs in the weather in Maple Plain, Minnesota. Put all together, his records gave the people of the whole country a very good idea of the climate in his part of America.

George Richards didn't think he had done anything wonderful. "I've enjoyed it," he said. "When you watch weather close like that, it's exciting."

This faithful record keeper wasn't the only person the government wanted to honor. Lots of other people had kept voluntary records for a very long, long time. Five others had kept them just as long as Richards had, but for reasons of health or business hadn't been able to travel to Washington.

For though most of us aren't aware of it, the United States has a small army serving it without pay. About five thousand men and women are keeping daily records of the weather in their own part of the country on a volunteer basis. Each is building up a local weather picture. Out of all these pictures we get a big picture of the climate in all parts of our vast country.

There was a time when the weather service knew much less about climate than they do today. That was back in 1870 when Congress first set up a national weather service. At that time a great many people were seeking homesteads in little-known parts of the West. They had to know what sort of climate they were moving into. Would they be able to raise wheat there? Or was the climate right for corn? What kind of houses would they have to build? Were the winters long and hard? Would settlers be likely to encounter drought?

So the government asked for volunteer record keepers. In time it got a staff of paid observers, too. For it's no fun to keep the records in all of the places the government wants to know about.

In Death Valley, California, for instance, the summer heat is nearly the worst in the world. Once it went up to 134°, the second-highest record in the world. At Greenland Ranch in Death Valley the average July temperature is above 100°. At the hottest time of day in the middle of summer it averages 116°. Here a volunteer observer kept records for years. In the hottest weather, he had to lie still on a wet sheet in front of a big fan. Today there is a resort there, a big air-conditioned hotel, and an airport.

On the summit of Mount Washington, in New Hampshire, paid observers suffer extremes of weather of a different sort. The wind up there reaches speeds unknown anywhere else in the country. The wind record there is 231 miles an hour. The weather station had to be tied to the solid rock of the mountain by steel cables; otherwise in these big winds the station might take off like a rocket ship. In winter the winds leave ice on the weather station like frost around the freezing unit in a refrigerator—only there are tons of ice. The wind gauge up on the ice-encrusted tower has to be heated by electricity to keep it from freezing stiff. The observers don't venture outside in winter unless they have to. They value their lives too much. Some daring men who have tried to climb the mountain in winter have been frozen in the bitter gales that sweep the slopes. The trails are marked here and there by their gravestones.

Besides being interested in climate, the weather service was very much concerned about the safety of ships. Storms on the Great Lakes and the seacoasts were wrecking hundreds of ships, and the government was determined to stop these losses. Storm warnings were badly needed. To get information about storms, the weather service established weather stations in all sorts of places. And it found the right people to stay and observe the weather.

It takes courage to stay in some of the places. One station stands off the northwest corner of the United States, on a rock called Tatoosh Island. The great storms sweeping eastward from the vast Pacific Ocean hurl wind, rain, and heavy seas at the lonely post. But lonely or not, the observer stays and keeps the records. Without his messages to the mainland many a ship would be wrecked on the rocky coast or sunk in the open sea.

Today the Weather Bureau is part of the Department of Commerce. For business, industry, and transportation have come to depend on the weatherman even more than farmers do. Especially has this been so since the development of aviation. Every year there are more planes in the sky. Every year more people travel by air and every year aviation makes greater demands on the weatherman.

Of course, for the pilot of an airplane the weather reports are more important than for anyone else—the distance he makes depends on the winds in the upper levels. He must know on what level he can make the best time, and how he can avoid dangerous conditions. But he gets many weather information services besides. Whether he is on the ground or in the air, teletypewriter and radio bring him news of the latest weather. He can get information and advice almost instantly. Then, too, many pilots make a habit of calling at a weather office to look at the maps and the latest weather reports along the route. They insist on fresh reports. Even from distant places a report is considered of little value by pilots if it is more than two hours old. For planes move swiftly, and the weather is difficult, yet weathermen meet its demands.

We know a great deal about weather today. We have traveled far since the days when people thought rain came down through openings in the sky or that lightning was a thunderbolt thrown by angry Zeus. We have gone way beyond predicting weather from old superstitious signs and sayings.

Weather prediction is pretty good now. Yet it could be better. Weathermen believe it will be a lot better. They hope—yes, expect—that electronic brains will one day take over a lot of the detail weathermen struggle with today. Telephone and radio already have solved some of their service problems. In the last few years electronic brains have been built that may solve the most difficult weather problems. Perhaps someday we will get our weather predictions from a machine.

Record your finishing time in the time box. Then take the reading test.

Read each test item and choose the best answer. Write your answers on page 7 of the progress folder.

Reading Test 11

Getting main ideas

1. This selection says that

A. no one knows much about the weather
B. daily weather reports are not true
C. the Weather Bureau values the help of amateur weather observers
D. the Weather Bureau is now run by the Army
E. amateur weather observers are not to be trusted

---

2. George Richards kept his promise for

A. thirty years
B. forty years
C. fifty years
D. sixty years
E. seventy years

---

3. Richards found his work

A. tiring
B. lonely
C. hard
D. exciting
E. easy

---

4. The author thinks we owe Richards

A. our thanks
B. nothing
C. ten thousand dollars
D. a trip to Europe
E. a thousand dollars

Remembering key facts

5. About five thousand men and women

A. attended the party for Richards
B. keep daily weather records for the Weather Bureau
C. write the Weather Bureau daily
D. are lost each year in Death Valley
E. have read this selection

---

6. In Death Valley during the hottest time of the day in midsummer, the heat averages

   A. 94 degrees
   B. 100 degrees
   C. 150 degrees
   D. 132 degrees
   E. 116 degrees

7. Pilots consider reports old if they are more than

   A. two weeks old
   B. two hours old
   C. two seconds old
   D. two minutes old
   E. two days old

8. The author thinks one day we will get weather predictions from

   A. machines
   B. Mount Washington
   C. the Department of Commerce
   D. pilots in fast planes
   E. Washington

9. People once gave the name "thunderbolt from Zeus" to

   A. lightning
   B. a tornado
   C. a hurricane
   D. a hail storm
   E. a snowstorm

Choosing the best reason

10. The Mount Washington weather station is held by steel cables to keep it

    A. dry
    B. off the ground
    C. from blowing away
    D. away from forest fires
    E. warm

11. Weather reports mean most to the

    A. airplane pilot
    B. bus driver
    C. locomotive engineer
    D. submarine commander
    E. taxicab driver

Reading with a keen eye

12. The Weather Bureau is now part of the

    A. Department of Defense
    B. Department of Labor
    C. Department of the Interior
    D. Department of Commerce
    E. Department of Agriculture

13. Congress first set up a national weather service in

    A. 1778
    B. 1800
    C. 1925
    D. 1900
    E. 1870

14. George Richards kept records in Maple Plain,

A. Maine
B. Minneosta
C. Montana
D. Massachusetts
E. Michigan

15. The wind reaches 231 miles an hour at the top of Mount

A. Sunapee
B. Rainier
C. Tom
D. Washington
E. McKinley

Knowing word meanings

16. Richards kept voluntary records. As used here, *voluntary* means

A. brief
B. careless
C. without pay
D. simple
E. daily

17. "The observers don't venture outside in winter unless they have to." This means they

A. don't ask to go out unless they have to
B. refuse to go out unless they have to
C. don't go out unless they have to
D. don't look outside unless they have to
E. don't talk about going outside unless they have to

18. The "ice-encrusted tower." In this phrase, *encrusted* means

A. built of ice
B. built on ice
C. filled with ice
D. once filled with ice
E. covered with ice

19. By *drought* we mean

A. rain
B. sleet
C. hail
D. frost
E. dryness

20. *Bitter* gales are winds that are

A. weak
B. strong
C. early
D. late
E. quiet

Follow the directions (Steps 8–13) on page 1 of the progress folder.

How you can read unfamiliar words

It has been estimated that there are more than 600,000 words in the English language. For anyone who wants to express his meaning exactly, few languages offer such rich resources.

The average student usually meets about 25,000 to 30,000 words in print. Perhaps he cannot use as many as half of them in his own writing. And in his conversation he may depend on only a few thousand of them. But when he meets these 25,000 or 30,000 words in print, he knows enough about them to get the general sense of what he is reading.

Do you know how big your vocabulary is? It is almost impossible for anyone to tell exactly the extent of his vocabulary. But suppose we make an estimate of 30,000 words. This sounds like a large number. Is it enough for you to get along with? You will take three tests in order to answer this question for yourself.

But before you take these tests, here are some thoughts to consider. Every school subject, every trade, every business has its own vocabulary. There are technical words in every field. And in addition, many trades, sciences, and businesses use common, ordinary words in special ways.

As long as you continue to grow mentally, you will have new experiences—in school and out. As long as you have new experiences, you will meet new words. What are you going to do about them? Or, to use another word, how are you going to *cope* with them?

Ideally, you should stop your reading, go to the dictionary, and look up a new word before reading further. But it is not pleasant to interrupt good reading for every new word. And many times there will be no dictionary within easy reach. To be sure, there is no good substitute for a dictionary. But there are other ways to get word meaning. This lesson will tell you about some of them.

Can you read the newspaper?

Does this sound like a silly question? Perhaps you feel that it is a bit insulting. You might even say that it is a gratuitous insult. And if you are curious about new words, you will go to the dictionary and look up the word *gratuitous.* You will find it a handy word to have around.

Vocabulary test

Here is a list of words and phrases that appeared in news stories on the front page in one issue of the *Chicago Daily News.* You could make just as long a list from the stories on the front page of any issue of any daily paper. How many of these words do you know?

Write the numerals 1 to 33 on your paper. Make a check for any of the italicized words below that you do not know. Be ready to explain in class the words you do know.

1. the *waning* summer
2. postwar *turmoil*
3. two *hectic* conferences
4. the *vantage* point
5. *stampeded* the conference
6. *glamorous* radicals
7. *idealists*
8. *native* radicalism
9. Moscow-*dominated*
10. *quasi*-military
11. *conspiracy*
12. *invalidating* a will
13. *blunt* finding
14. *judiciary*
15. *subject* to approval
16. dead of *natural* causes

17. *bulk* of the estate
18. *substantial* disagreement
19. *pelted* with tomatoes
20. to *restrain hostile sentiment*
21. *aspirations*
22. *apprehensions*
23. *untimely* death
24. a disputed *measure* in Congress
25. *tally*
26. *controversy*
27. the writer paid *tribute* to America
28. *coronary*
29. *hospitalized*
30. a *ceiling* on taxes
31. *curative* powers of a holy shrine
32. a chest *congestion*
33. *emerging* from a manhole

How much would you have understood of the front page of the *Daily News?* Count up the number of words you did not know. Compare your results with those of the rest of the class.

Exercise 46

Here is a story that appeared on the same front page of the *Chicago Daily News.*

Or Better Still, Bring the Body[1]

LISBON, Portugal (UP)—This city's funeral homes are taking standard Mardi Gras precautions. Until the pre-Lenten carnival is over, requests for funeral services must be made in person.

Telephone callers will be suspected as pranksters.

Write the numerals 1 to 6 on your paper. The terms below appear in the news story above. After each of them are three words or phrases. Copy the letter for the one word or phrase that is closest in meaning to each numbered term. The answers are shown in the answer key.

1. funeral homes
   A. homes where people have died
   B. undertaking parlors
   C. homes that have burned

---

1 From the *Chicago Daily News*, February 6, 1956. Reprinted by permission of United Press International.

2. standard
   A. regular
   B. special
   C. model
3. precautions
   A. suspicions
   B. measures taken beforehand
   C. warnings
4. pre-Lenten
   A. early
   B. beginning
   C. before Lent
5. carnival
   A. musical play
   B. period of merrymaking
   C. examination
6. pranksters
   A. jokers
   B. criminals
   C. people who are mentally ill

Perhaps you are saying, "I don't read the front page of the newspaper. I read only the comics." The words in the test below came from the comic strips in the same issue of the *Chicago Daily News.*

Exercise 47

Write the numerals 1 to 5 on your paper. Copy the letter for the word or phrase that is closest to the meaning of each italicized word.

1. a *canine*
   A. gun
   B. dog
   C. pertaining to a cane
2. an *unconcerned* citizen
   A. not interested
   B. not voting
   C. happy
3. her condition is *critical*
   A. dangerous
   B. complaining
   C. unhappy
4. *minor* injuries
   A. a bad wound
   B. small
   C. severe
5. a great *Thespian*
   A. dog
   B. actor
   C. native of Thessaly

How well did you do? Are you surprised to find that the comic strips use many unfamiliar words? The answers are shown in the answer key.

Get the meaning of spoken words

You have a great advantage when you are talking face to face with someone. If he uses a word you do not know, you can ask him what he means. You need not feel embarrassed to do this. Even the best-educated and most intelligent people sometimes stop a friend to ask him to explain a word. In fact, they may do it more often than people with less education and less experience, because they know how important it is to pin down the meaning of a word in discussion.

You can say something like this: "Would you mind explaining what you mean by 'critical condition'? The words may not mean the same thing to you as they do to me." Or you can say, "Let's define our words, so that we can be sure we are talking about the same thing."

If the other person says, "Well, a critical condition is a serious condition," you are not much better off than before. You may know by the way the speaker looks and by his tone of voice that a critical condition is bad. But just how bad? Keep on asking.

Keep on asking until you get an answer that is in terms of people, things, or events that you know. When the speaker says, "A critical condition is a dangerous one— the patient may not live through the night," you have a better idea of what he means. He is talking in terms of people and events that you know about.

Unfamiliar words in reading

When you come across an unfamiliar word in reading, there are three possibilities: (1) the word may not be important to the meaning of the whole sentence, and you can read right past it; (2) the word may be important, but you may be able to find enough clues to its meaning to understand the passage; (3) the word may be a key word in the sentence with no clues to its meaning.

If you can't find clues to a key word, there is only one thing to do. Put the reading aside and go to a dictionary for help. Fortunately, unless you are reading technical material in a field totally strange to you, this will not happen often.

You have probably come across first-aid articles entitled "What to Do Until the Doctor Comes." Knowing what to do about an accident may save lives. Knowing what to do about unfamiliar words may help you save time and avoid trouble. You ought to know "what to do until the dictionary comes."

Suggestion 1

Slow down and look for clues to meaning. You may find clues in the word itself or in the rest of the passage.

In 1955 this story appeared in the daily papers:

Survivor Tells 2-Day Desert Ordeal[2]

TWENTYNINE PALMS, Calif. (AP) —The grim story of a searing two-day ordeal on the Mojave Desert that cost the lives of two men was told by one of the two survivors.

Real estate developer Chester Bunker, 67, from his hospital bed, recounted Sunday how a surveying trip that was "just going to take half a day" turned into a desperate battle against heat and thirst after their Jeep broke down.

"It was the worst thing I've been through in twenty years on the desert," said Bunker, one of the founders of Twenty-nine Palms and other communities in this area, 120 miles east of Los Angeles.

He estimated temperatures were between 120 and 130 degrees last Wednesday and Thursday afternoons.

"Yet we woke up shivering from cold Friday morning," he related.

By "we" Bunker meant himself and Lyle W. Robertson, 49, hardware-store owner and rancher, who were rescued by air observers Friday.

2 From the *Chicago Sun-Times*, June 25, 1955. Copyright 1955 by the Associated Press. Reprinted with permission of the Associated Press.

Thirst and exposure claimed two companions, Calvert Wilson, 49, prominent southern California Democratic politician, and James R. Thompson, 75, retired Joshua Tree businessman.

Bunker told a reporter that Thompson died Thursday after "going berserk." The body of Wilson, who had struck out alone for help, was found near Cadiz Dry Lake.

The four men started out early Wednesday to size up land which Bunker said "is ripe for development."

All went well until they swung around the Iron Mountains on the way home. "Walking" (wind-shifted) sands bogged down their four-wheel-drive vehicle and they decided to wait until nightfall for cooler digging weather.

Then they found the front differential had broken.

Although they had water bags, they had brought no food.

Wilson, who knew some celestial navigation, set out Wednesday night for aid. He thought he could follow the stars to a highway fifteen miles away. He was found five miles away.

"The rest of us figured we had more chance of being seen on Cadiz Dry Lake, and we did," said Bunker.

When the next day's sun seared and their water ran out, Bunker, Robertson, and Thompson lay down, took off their shirts, and put them over their heads to protect against the rays.

"But Thompson got away from us and started running in circles," said Bunker. "I passed out and didn't wake up until the next (Friday) morning when the cold air brought me to. Then Robertson told me Thompson was dead.

"That was about all he said and I could hardly answer. Our tongues were pretty well frozen to our mouths."

A civilian plane spotted them about 8:30 that morning and an Air Force helicopter whisked them to a hospital.

This is an interesting story. It would be too bad to miss it just because the first sentence contains four words that may be unfamiliar to you. It would be too bad, particularly, because the story gives many clues to the meanings of these words. By reading on, you can find those clues.

There are no clues, however, in the words themselves. To understand them, you have to think about the whole context. Take the word *survivors* first. You may not know exactly what it means. But you know that it was not one of the two dead men who told this story. *Survivors* must refer to one of the people who lived through the experience.

Let's take the word *grim*. You may not know its exact meaning, but you can pretty well figure out that it is not a favorable word. It probably does not mean anything pleasant, happy, or gay. You know this because you know that two men lost their lives.

Suggestion 2

Keep on reading. The meaning of the unfamiliar words may be cleared up in later sentences. You can come back to these words later and figure out their meaning from the rest of the words in the story.

Take the word *ordeal*, for example. You know that it was something that lasted for two days because the sentence reads "two-day ordeal." A later sentence says, "It was the worst thing I've been through in twenty years on the desert." This gives you a clue to what an ordeal is.

Take the word *searing*. A later sentence in the story says that the temperatures were between 120 and 130 degrees. Still later you find a sentence beginning, "When the next day's sun seared and their water ran out . . ." You can figure out that searing has something to do with the sun and with heat.

Exercise 48

Let's see how much meaning you have read into the hard words in the first sentence of the news story.

Write the numerals 1 to 4 on your paper. Copy the letter for the word or phrase that is closest in meaning to each numbered word.

1. grim
   A. sad
   B. frightful
   C. long
   D. thirsty

2. searing
   A. frightening
   B. boiling
   C. burning
   D. shivering
3. ordeal
   A. camping trip
   B. accident
   C. painful experience
   D. celebration
4. survivor
   A. explorer
   B. reporter
   C. businessman
   D. one who lives through an experience

Suggestion 3

Try to pronounce the unfamiliar word. You know many thousands of words by sound that you have not yet learned to read. If you recognize a new word by its sound, you often find that you know its meaning.

Suggestion 4

Analyze the word itself by breaking it into syllables. See whether one of these syllables is a short word that you do know. For example, in the word *impressionable* you recognize the word *press*.

Look for prefixes and suffixes that you may know. The prefix *im-* in *impressionable* could mean "not" or it could mean "in." You would have to try both meanings to see which one fits. But you can always rely on the suffix *-able*. It always means "able" or "able to be." And the suffix *-ion* in this case adds little or no meaning to the word.

By breaking *impressionable* into its syllables—*im-pres-sion-a-ble*—and studying the prefixes and suffixes, we come to the meaning "able to be pressed in." Now try this word out on your family and friends in a sentence like this: "You can't always depend on Lynn's judgment, because she is so impressionable."

You can learn to pronounce new words

The English language has been growing for many hundreds of years, and it is still growing. It did not grow according to any plan. It did not grow according to the rules of any grammar book or dictionary. It grew because people pushed it out here and pulled it in there. When they needed new words, they made them up. When a pronunciation was too hard, people chopped it down. As a consequence, there are few easy rules to follow, but there are some worth knowing.

The vowel sounds

The letters *a, e, i, o, u,* and sometimes *y* are vowels. At the bottom of every page in your dictionary you will see a table of sounds. This table gives examples of the most common vowel sounds and the marks that are used to indicate them, such as these: ¯, ˘, ¨, and ^. Thus you will see *făt, āpe, cär*.

Every vowel has a short sound marked ˘, and a long sound marked ¯: *căt, cāpe; bē, bĕd; bĭt, bīnd; hŏt, hōle; ŭp, ūse.* Say these words over to yourself until you are sure which are the long sounds and which are the short ones.

Two vowels often appear together. Sometimes only one of them is sounded, as in *road, ease, height.* Sometimes the two vowels make an entirely new sound, called a diphthong: *ou* sounds like *ow* in *cow; oi* sounds like *oy* in *boy.*

Be careful! The letters *ou* do not always make the *ow* sound—*dough, rough, fought,* for example. The letters *oi* do not always make the *oy* sound—*going,* for example.

Sometimes when two vowels appear together, both of them are sounded, as in *usual, Indian, going.*

When a word ends in a vowel-consonant combination, the vowel is nearly always short: *economic, hotel, referendum, hat.* The *e* at the end of a word is almost never pronounced: *escape, rotate, plate.* But when a word ends in a vowel-consonant combination plus final *e,* the final *e* gives the preceding vowel a long sound: *site, cope, use, plate, complete.*

The consonants

All the letters except *a, e, i, o,* and *u* are consonants. There are many words in which one or more consonants are silent. The *g* and *h* in *flight* are silent. The *k* and *w* in *know* are also silent.

Sometimes we combine consonants to make new sounds. These are called consonant blends. The most common of these blends are:

bl ch dr fl gl pl sl th wh ng
br cl fr gr ph sh tr
cr pr st
str
shr

The *ch* blend has three sounds: like *sh*, as in *chef;* like *k*, as in *chorus;* and like the *ch* sound in *chest*. The *th* blend has two sounds: one as in *thin*, the other as in *the*.

The letters *c* and *g* have hard sounds, as in *cash* and *gun*. They also have soft sounds, as in *cent* and *genius*. When *c* is followed by *e* or *i*, it is almost always soft. When *g* is followed by *e* or *i* it is usually soft, but not always (for example, *give* and *get*).

Pronunciation

Exercise 49

A short vowel sound is shown by placing this mark (ˇ) over the vowel. A long sound is shown by placing this mark (ˉ) over the vowel.

Write the numerals 1 to 20 on your paper. Copy only the italicized vowel in the words below. Mark it to show whether it has a long or a short sound. Say the words to yourself.

1. g*e*nial
2. dig*i*t
3. ign*i*te
4. ac*i*d
5. budg*e*t
6. ref*u*te
7. red*u*ce
8. b*a*t
9. reb*a*te
10. gl*a*ss
11. gl*a*ze
12. emphas*i*s
13. imm*u*ne
14. comp*o*se
15. regul*a*te
16. sn*i*pping
17. m*i*splace
18. s*u*preme
19. democr*a*t
20. syst*e*m

Pronunciation

Exercise 50

The *ch* sound in *chef* is a soft sound. The *ch* sound in *Christmas* is hard. The *c*

in *call* is hard. The *g* in *general* is soft. The *g* in *go* is hard.

Write the numerals 1 to 12 on your paper. Write *hard* or *soft* to show the sound of the italicized letters in the words below. Say the words to yourself.

1. *c*ongress
2. *c*oroner
3. *c*ollege
4. suffra*g*e
5. so*c*iety
6. vo*c*ation
7. inte*g*er
8. effi*c*ient
9. ma*ch*ine
10. stit*ch*
11. or*ch*estra
12. *ch*lorine

Pronunciation

Exercise 51

Copy the ten words below on your paper. Circle all of the silent letters. Say the words to yourself.

1. involve
2. frighten
3. knowing
4. growing
5. repeat
6. measure
7. broad
8. waist
9. decrease
10. whole

Break a word into syllables

The sounded parts of a word are called syllables. In every syllable there is only one vowel sound. The word *send* has only one vowel sound. Therefore it has only one syllable. The word *usual* has three vowel sounds. Say it to yourself and listen for these sounds. Its syllables would be shown thus: *u-su-al*. You can see that a vowel can be a syllable all by itself.

Three rules usually work in breaking a word into syllables. (1) Never divide a consonant digraph (two consonants with a single sound) or a diphthong (two vowels with a blended sound): *ma-chine; boil-ing*. (2) Prefixes and suffixes are always separate syllables: *ad-here, sing-ing, cup-ful, pre-cise*. (3) When two consonants appear together in the middle of a word, divide between them unless they form a digraph: *sum-mer, star-dom, graph-ic, diph-thong*.

The reason for knowing about syllables is that it helps you to pronounce a new word, part by part.

Syllables

Exercise 52

The following words appear in regular ninth-grade school subjects.

Copy the words on your paper. Divide them into syllables. Place a mark (–) between each syllable.

1. commission
2. indictment
3. majority
4. referendum
5. obsolete
6. bibliography
7. vacuum
8. concave
9. solstice
10. nucleus

Learn how words are put together

Words are used to name things and ideas. They are used to show relations between things and ideas; they are used to show what people and things do.

Because new things are constantly being invented and new ideas developed, our language must be constantly growing. It grows in many interesting ways.

Sometimes we form new words, such as *astronaut* or *radiotelescope*.

More often we put old familiar words into new combinations: *cover girl, double take, hot rod*. When such words have been used together a long time, they are sometimes joined by a hyphen: *hot-foot, light-year, merry-go-round*.

The hyphen stays in some of these words for a long time. But gradually it disappears. Then we have compound words like *battleground, backfield, housewife, hothouse*. Sometimes compound words are made without going through the hyphen stage.

We also make new words by adding certain words to others. They are added (fixed) either at the beginning or the end of words. If at the beginning, they are called prefixes; if at the end, they are called suffixes.

Among the most useful prefixes and suffixes are these:

-less (without; not)
 hopeless.......without hope
 witless........having no sense or
     intelligence

-ful (full of; having the qualities of; having the measure of)
 hopeful......full of hope
 cupful........as much as a cup
     will hold
 masterful....having the qualities
     of a master

out- (located at a point outside; going away; greater, better, more than)
 outrun........run better than
 outstation.....a station far away
 outpour.......a pouring out or
     away from

over- (in a position above; too much; passing beyond)
 oversee.......to supervise from a
     top position
 overflow.......to flow too much
 overrun.......to run beyond

under- (beneath; below; in a lower rank; too little)
 underpaid....paid too little
 undercoat.....a coat beneath
     another, as a coat
     of paint
 undergraduate.a student who has
     not yet earned a
     degree

-most (the most)
 foremost......first in place or time
 innermost.....the farthest inside
     or toward the center

-wise (in the direction or position of; in the manner of)
 sidewise......in a side position
 clockwise......in the same direction followed by
     the hands of a clock

Be careful in using prefixes and suffixes

The English language of today is made up of words and parts of words borrowed from many languages. Among them are many from Latin and Greek. Latin was the language of ancient Rome. It was a rich language and an expressive one. But the Romans built new words for themselves just as we do today in English.

Sometimes they used words like *de* just to make the meaning of other words stronger. For example, they had a word *dicare*, meaning "to dedicate." They added *de* as a prefix and made the word *dedicare*, which also means "to dedicate." Our English word *dedicate* comes from *dedicare*, but the prefix has no meaning today in the English word.

In the same way, the Romans added the prefix *ad*, meaning "to" or "toward," to the word *judicare*, meaning "to judge." Our English words *adjudicate* and *adjudge* come from the Latin word, but the prefix *ad-* has no meaning in the English words.

This is the way with many English words. We must not think that a prefix always adds meaning to a word.

There is another thing to keep in mind: prefix + word base + suffix gives us one literal meaning for a word. Actually, most English words have many different meanings. And some of them go far, far away from the literal meaning.

If you are interested in words, you can have fun with a good dictionary. Look for words whose literal meaning gives no clue to their current meaning. You will come across words like *jeopardy*, which means "danger, chance of being caught." *Jeopardy* is made up of *jocus*, meaning "joke or game," and *partitus*, meaning "divided." The two words mean "a divided game."

Preposterous is another interesting word, one that you ought to have in your vocabulary because it shows very strong disapproval. When you say that something is preposterous, you mean that it is contrary to reason or common sense. It is made up of the Latin words *prae*, meaning "before," and *posterus*, meaning "behind." Maybe you would say that it is contrary to reason to have "the behind before." But just knowing the prefix *pre-* does not give you the meaning of the word as we use it today.

Some prefixes are a great help in getting word meaning

Remember that (1) an English word is much more than the sum of its parts, and (2) most common words in English have more than one meaning. With these two facts in mind, you can make good use of prefixes in approaching unfamiliar words.

To begin with, there are a number of Latin and Greek forms that we use constantly in both old and new words. Here is a list that you should know:

Prefix	Meaning
auto-	self
biblio-	book
bio-	life
geo-	earth
homo-	man
hydro-	water
micro-	small
mono-	one
omni-	all
phono-	sound
photo-	of or produced by light
poly-	many
tele-	at a distance

Using word parts

Exercise 53

Here is a list of words that are used in many junior high school courses.

Write the numerals 1 to 20 on your paper. Write down the prefix or suffix that you recognize. After it, write its meaning. You are responsible only for the prefixes and suffixes presented thus far. The correct answers are shown in the answer key.

1. undersell
2. telescope
3. photosynthesis
4. bibliography
5. biology
6. monocotyledon
7. nameless
8. teletype
9. polygon
10. telegraph
11. polynomial
12. micrometer
13. hydrometer
14. monopoly
15. geography
16. hydroelectric
17. clockwise
18. overestimate
19. microscope
20. automatic

More about prefixes

There are a few other prefixes that are especially useful to know. They all have more than one meaning, so when you meet them in an unfamiliar word, you must try their several meanings. Here is a list of the most useful prefixes in English words.

Prefix Meaning

in- 1. not, as in *incomplete*
     2. into or within, as in *indent*

re- 1. back, as in *repay*
     2. again, as in *restate*

anti- 1. against, as in *antilabor*
ant- 2. opposite, as in *antisocial*

ex- 1. out of, as in *expel, exclude*
     2. beyond, as in *excess*
     3. formerly, as in *ex-President*

dis- 1. away, as in *dispel, disperse*
     2. deprive of, as in *disarm*
     3. opposite of, as in *dishonest*
     4. fail or cease, as in *disappear*

de- 1. down from, as in *descend, decline*
     2. away from, as in *detour*
     3. opposite of, as in *demerit*

pro- 1. before in position, as in *protrude*
     2. before in time, as in *prologue*
     3. in behalf of or in favor of, as in *proponent, prolabor*

pre- 1. before in place, as in *precede*
     2. before in time, as in *precaution*
     3. first in rank, as in *preeminent*

sub- 1. under, below, as in *submarine*
     2. lower in rank, as in *subordinate*
     3. less than, as in *subhuman*

Using prefixes

Exercise 54

In the list of words below, some of the prefixes have only one meaning. You should have no trouble with them. Other prefixes may have two or three meanings. Try to decide which one seems right for the word.

Write the numerals 1 to 20 on your paper. Write the meaning of the prefix in each of these words. They are words that appear in many high school courses. Look back over the preceding pages for help if you wish. The correct answers are shown in the answer key.

1. exhale
2. indistinct
3. decompose
4. preposition
5. address
6. exclamation
7. dependent
8. decode
9. prehistoric
10. subdivision
11. repetition
12. subgroup
13. discomfort
14. profession
15. expel
16. discontinue
17. repel
18. preview
19. extract
20. incorporate

Prefixes

Exercise 55

Write the numerals 1 to 20 on your paper. Write the meaning of each prefix. Most of the prefixes in these words have more than one meaning. Look at the list of prefixes in column 1 if you need to. The correct answers are shown in the answer key.

1. include
2. review
3. exceed
4. reprint
5. substandard
6. adjoin
7. dispossess
8. provision
9. subsoil
10. defrost
11. precedent
12. prophesy
13. subscribe
14. expression
15. degrade
16. protrude
17. inalienable
18. report
19. preface
20. repair

What context is and why it is important

From your study of prefixes, you know that the prefix *con-* means "together with." The context of a word is the other words used together with it—in the same sentence or in the same paragraph, chapter, or book.

There are two things you should know about context. First, context determines which meaning of a word is the right one for a particular sentence. Second, there are often clues in the context to the meaning of an unfamiliar word.

The key fact that you must keep in mind about words is that most of them have more than one meaning. The word *run*, for example, has more than one hundred different meanings. For example:

• a run on the bank
• to run for office
• to run a show
• a run in a stocking
• a run of bad luck
• a run in baseball

Can you think of others?

The interesting thing is that the more common a word is, the more meanings it has. The word *set* has more than fifty meanings, the word *fix* more than twenty. Quite often, even with words that have only four or five meanings, these meanings are entirely different from one another. The word affluent may mean "wealthy." It may also mean "flowing toward." The word *disposition* may mean (1) the way a person acts towards others; (2) management; (3) the giving away of something; or (4) an orderly arrangement.

With so many words having so many meanings, how do we ever choose the right one? This is the point at which context helps us. If you are talking about baseball and use the word *plate*, no one would think of "an object on which food is served." The context of baseball helps you to cast off the meanings of a word that do not relate to what you are talking about.

Context gives clues to meaning

A writer tries to make sure that his readers know what he is talking about. If he uses a word that is out of the ordinary, he can explain it in a number of ways.

1. *Definition.* The most obvious way of explaining a word is to define it. You can spot this explanation by watching for three words: *means*, *is*, and *consists of*. When an author says "This word means _____," he is defining it. But he may not be so direct. He may say, for example, "On a submarine a watch is a four-hour period of duty." Or he may say, "The electoral college consists of all the electors from the fifty states."

2. *Examples.* One of the best ways of explaining a word is to give examples of how it works, what it does, or how it is used. When a writer does this, he may use any of the following words: *such as*, *like*, *especially*, *for example*. See how these words signal an explanation in these sentences:

- On her vacation, Betty will travel on a boat *like* the one piloted by Mark Twain.
- Girls always seem to do better in tests of an aesthetic nature, *such as* matching colors and shapes.

- President Jefferson tried by economic measures *such as* the embargo to halt English raids on our ships.
- A study of homonymns—*meet* and *meat, for example*—helps build a vocabulary.

3. *Modifiers.* An effective way to explain a word is to use phrases and clauses after it.

- The suffragettes, *seeking a new law to permit women to vote*, marched in parades and held demonstrations.
- One clue is given by metabolism tests, *which measure the speed of chemical and physical processes going on in the body.*
- We have a city manager, *who runs all the service departments of the government and takes charge of buying for the city.*

4. *Restatement.* If a writer is not sure that a word will be understood, he may say it over in different words. In doing this he often uses signal words to catch the reader's eye; for example, the word *or* followed by a synonym. Thus:

- The Post Office tries to discourage the abbreviation, *or shortened form*, of state names on envelopes.

Another kind of restatement is known as an appositive.

- The sentence fragment, *a group of words that is less than a sentence*, is a common error in student writing.

Sometimes the writer uses these words as signals: *in other words, that is to say*, or *that is*.

- Inoculation, *that is*, the injection of a serum into the blood, is one way of preventing disease.

Using context clues

Exercise 56

First read each passage carefully. Then answer the questions that follow. The questions will test your ability to get meaning from context. The correct answers are shown in the answer key.

- A helicopter does not have wings like an airplane. It is moved through the air by a large four-bladed propeller, called a rotor. One of the newest helicopters can carry thirty-three combat-equipped men.

The interior, or payload, compartment is thirty feet long.

1. The rotor of a helicopter is
   A. the propeller
   B. the wings
   C. the engine
2. The payload compartment of a helicopter is
   A. the tail assembly
   B. the carburetor
   C. the interior

• Adolescence, or the period between childhood and adulthood, is a time of great physical growth. It is a time also of personal growth, when a young person begins to make decisions. One of these decisions is the choice of a career. Aptitude tests, which tell you what special skills and abilities you have, are valuable aids at this time.

3. Adolescence is
   A. a group of skills
   B. the period between childhood and adulthood
   C. a childhood disease
4. Aptitude tests measure
   A. attitudes toward school
   B. intelligence
   C. special skills and abilities

• The biological sciences, such as physiology and pathology, offer many opportunities for people who do not want to become doctors. The general practitioner, that is, the family doctor who answers all calls, depends a great deal on laboratory workers in the biological sciences.

5. A general practitioner is
   A. a family doctor
   B. a surgeon
   C. a specialist in childhood diseases

Dictionaries are the surest source of word meanings

Up to this point in this lesson you have approached an unfamiliar word in three ways. First, you try to pronounce it because you may know it by sound even though you don't recognize it in print. Second, you look at the base of the word and at the prefix and suffix for clues to meaning. Third, you look for clues in the context.

None of these three ways is sure to give you the meaning of a word. The only sure way is to go to a dictionary. There you will find the various meanings of the word, and your job is to choose the one meaning that fits the particular passage you are reading.

Dictionaries vary greatly in size and in the amount of information they contain. The *Oxford English Dictionary* contains thirteen volumes, each several hundred pages long. Dictionaries do not always agree. There is no final, fixed definition for any word in general use.

The people who make dictionaries gather examples of the use of words. They get these examples from writings and from listening to people speak. Then they group these uses and interpret the meanings that the writers and speakers have given the words. Dictionary makers may not agree on what the writers meant. That is why dictionaries differ. It is a good reason why you should use more than one dictionary.

Dictionaries offer a rich variety of information

Let's look at one of the good new dictionaries, *Webster's New World Dictionary of the American Language*. Notice that it is a dictionary of the American, not the English, language. Our use of words frequently differs from that of the English people.

This dictionary has on its inside covers a key to pronunciation and a table of symbols and abbreviations. The pronunciation key shows you how the different vowel and consonant sounds are marked throughout the book. This dictionary does not use the short vowel mark (˘). The symbols and abbreviations are used in the etymologies. These are the histories of the words—what language they come from and how they have changed in spelling and meaning.

There is a foreword that tells about the scholars who worked on the dictionary. This is followed by a guide to the use of the dictionary that explains how the words are arranged, how syllables are shown, and how to find a variant form of a word. The next section is a twenty-page study of the language. Here is a statement about pronunciation and how it varies from one section of the country to another. Here also is an interesting, concise study of grammar. The section ends with a history of the English language.

Then comes the letter *A* and all the entries on to the last word, *zymurgy*. Do you know what this word means?

This dictionary closes with a supplement that lists colleges and universities, forms of address, weights and measures, and a table of special signs and symbols.

In the main body of the book you will find the names of historical events, brief biographies of famous persons, and names of all important towns, lakes, rivers, countries, and mountains. In this particular dictionary you will find slang terms and common phrases such as *hot rod* and *bull*.

Most good dictionaries have the features described above. They are therefore handy general reference books.

Looking for word meanings in a dictionary

When you look up the meaning of a word, you must take to the dictionary the whole sentence in which the word is used. This is the only way to get out of the dictionary the meaning that will fit in your context.

It will help if you know the part of speech of the word you are studying. Some words have one set of meanings when used as a verb, another set when used as an adjective, and still another set when used as a noun. This, by the way, is another good reason for taking the whole sentence to the dictionary.

Here is what you would find in the *New World Dictionary* for *hurdle*.[3]

hurdle (hŭr′d'l), *n.* [ME. *hurdel, hirdel;* AS. *hydrel* < base **hurd-*, wickerwork, hurdle (cf. HOARDING); IE. base **qert-*, to plait, twist together, seen also in *crate*], 1. a portable frame made of interlaced twigs, etc., used for temporary fences or enclosures. 2. a kind of frame or sled on which prisoners in England were drawn through the streets to execution. 3. a movable, framelike barrier for horses or runners to jump over in a race. 4. an obstacle; difficulty to be overcome. *v.t.* [HURDLED (-d′ld), HURDLING], 1. to enclose or fence off with hurdles. 2. to jump over (a hurdle) in a race. 3. to overcome (an obstacle).

the hurdles, a race in which the contestants must jump over a series of hurdles.

Notice the following specific points of information:

1. First the word appears in **bold** type. The pronunciation is given in parenthesis; the *d′ l* shows that there is a very short vowel sound between the *d* and *l.*

2. The letter *n* after the parenthesis stands for "noun". It means that the meanings to follow are those for the word when it is used as a noun.

3. Within the brackets you find the history of the word. It goes back to Anglo-Saxon (AS), where it meant wickerwork. The letters *cf.* in parentheses mean "compare." You are advised to look up and compare the origin of the word *hoarding.* An older base, *qert,* in Indo-European (IE) has a similar meaning—"to plait, twist together." This base is the origin of our word *crate.*

4. Notice that the first three noun meanings indicate that a hurdle is movable.

5. The fourth noun use shows how we take a concrete word like *hurdle* and extend its uses to other situations. It is not just something to be jumped over; it is any difficulty or obstacle we meet in any situation.

6. The letters *v.t.* stand for "verb transitive," which means that this verb is followed by an object. That is, you hurdle *something.*

7. In the brackets are shown the past tense and the *-ing* form of the verb. Once again the pronunciation is given in parentheses. Then follow three meanings of the word when used as a verb.

---

3 From *Webster's New World Dictionary*. Copyright © 1962 by The World Publishing Company.

Using a dictionary entry

Exercise 57

The questions below are based on the entry for *hurdle*, which is given above. Write the numerals 1 to 4 on your paper. Write the letter for the correct answer to each question. The correct answers are shown in the answer key.

1. In which meaning of the word *hurdle* do you find the influence of the Indo-European base word meaning "to plait"?
   A. noun 1
   B. verb 2
   C. noun 4

2. If you add *-ing* to *hurdle*, you spell the word
   A. *hurdleing*
   B. *hurdling*
   C. *hurdeling*

3. Which meaning fits this sentence? "The explorers hurdled the clearing to keep out wild animals."
   A. noun 2
   B. verb 2
   C. verb 1

4. Which meaning fits this sentence? "Tom had expected algebra to be a difficult hurdle in his freshman year, but he found it fairly easy."
   A. noun 3
   B. verb 2
   C. noun 4

Practice Reading 12

In a book, magazine, or newspaper that you like, practice reading for speed and comprehension. Make a record of this reading in Chart 3 on page 8 of the progress folder.

12
article

How we kept Mother's Day [4]

by Stephen Leacock

Of all the different ideas that have been started lately, I think that the very best is celebrating Mother's Day.

It is especially in a big family like ours that such an idea takes hold. It made us all realize how much Mother had done for us for years, and all the sacrifices that she had made for our sake.

So we decided that we'd make Mother's Day a holiday for all the family, and do everything we could to make Mother happy. Father took a holiday from his office, and my sister Anne and I stayed home from college classes, and Mary and my brother Will stayed home from high school.

We planned to make it a day just like Christmas or any big holiday. So we decided to decorate the house with flowers and with mottoes over the fireplace, and all that kind of thing. We got Mother to make and arrange the decorations, because she always does it at Christmas.

The two girls thought it would be nice to dress in our very best for such a big occasion, and so they both got new hats. Mother trimmed both the hats, and they looked fine. Father bought silk ties for himself and for us boys as a souvenir of the day to remember Mother by. We were going to get Mother a new hat, too. But she seemed to really like her old gray bonnet better than a new one.

Well, after breakfast on Mother's Day, as a surprise for Mother, we arranged to hire a motor car. We would take her for a beautiful drive into the country. Mother is hardly ever able to have a treat like that, because we can only afford to keep one maid, and so Mother is busy in the house nearly all the time. And of course the country is so lovely now that it would be just grand for her to have a lovely morning, driving for miles and miles.

But on the very morning of the day, we changed the plan a little bit, because Father thought that taking Mother fishing would be even better than taking her for a motor drive. Father said that as the car was hired and paid for, we might just as well use it for a drive up into the hills where the streams are. As Father said, if you just go out driving without any object, you have a sense of aimlessness. But if you are going to fish, there is a definite purpose in front of you to heighten the enjoyment.

So we all felt that it would be nicer for Mother to have a definite purpose. And anyway, it turned out that Father had just got a new fishing rod the day before. He said that Mother could use it if she wanted to. In fact, he said it was practically for her, only Mother said she would much rather watch him fish and not try to fish herself.

So we got the trip all arranged. We got Mother to make a lunch. Of course, we were to come back home again to a big dinner in the middle of the day, just like Christmas or New Year's Day. But we wanted a lunch in case we got hungry.

When the car came to the door, it turned out that there wasn't as much room

4 Reprinted by permission of Dodd, Mead & Company and The Bodley Head Ltd. from *Laugh with Leacock*, by Stephen Leacock. Copyright 1930 by Dodd, Mead & Company.

in it as we had supposed. We hadn't reckoned on Father's fishing basket and the rods and the lunch. We saw plainly enough that we couldn't all get in.

Father said not to mind him. He said that he could just as well stay home. He was sure that he could put in the time working in the garden; there was a lot of rough dirty work that he could do, like digging the trench for the garbage. We were not to let the fact of his not having had a real holiday for three years stand in our way. He wanted us to go right ahead and be happy and have a big day, and not to mind him. In fact, he said he'd been a fool to think there'd be any holiday for him.

But of course we all felt that it would never do to let Father stay home, especially as we knew he would make trouble if he did. The two girls, Anne and Mary, would gladly have stayed and helped the maid get dinner, only it seemed such a pity to, having their new hats. But they both said that Mother had only to say the word, and they'd gladly stay home and work. Will and I would have dropped out, but unfortunately we wouldn't have been any use in getting the dinner.

So in the end it was decided that Mother would stay home. She would have a lovely restful day around the house, and get the dinner. It turned out that Mother doesn't care for fishing. Also, it was a little bit cold and fresh out of doors though it was lovely and sunny, and Father was afraid that Mother might take cold if she came.

He said he would never forgive himself if he dragged Mother around the country and let her take a severe cold when she might be having a beautiful rest. He said it was our duty to try and let Mother get all the rest and quiet that she could, after all that she had done for all of us. He said that young people seldom realize how much quiet means to people who are getting old. He could still stand the racket, but he was glad to shelter Mother from it.

So we all drove away with three cheers for Mother. She stood and watched us for as long as she could see us. Father waved his hand back to her every few minutes till he hit his hand against the door of the car. Then he said that he didn't think that Mother could see us any longer.

Well, we had the loveliest day up among the hills that you could possibly imagine. Father caught such big fish that he felt sure that Mother couldn't have landed them anyway, if she had been fishing for them. Will and I fished too, though we didn't get so many as Father. And the two girls met quite a lot of people that they knew as we drove along. There were some young men friends of theirs that they met along the stream and talked to. And so we all had a splendid time.

It was nearly seven o'clock in the evening when we got back, but Mother had guessed that we would be late. She had kept the dinner ready and hot for us. Only first she had to get towels and soap for Father and clean things for him to put on, because he always gets so messed up while fishing. That and helping the girls get ready kept Mother busy for a while.

But at last everything was ready. We sat down to the grandest kind of dinner—roast turkey and all sorts of things like on Christmas Day. Mother had to get up and down a good bit during the meal, fetching things. But at the end Father noticed it and said she simply mustn't do it, that he wanted her to spare herself. He got up and fetched the walnuts from the sideboard himself.

The dinner lasted a long while, and was great fun. When it was over, all of us wanted to help clear the things up and wash the dishes, only Mother said that she would really much rather do it. So we let her, because we wanted just for once to humor her.

It was quite late when it was all over. When we kidded Mother before going to bed, she said it had been the most wonderful day in her life, and I think there were tears in her eyes. So we all felt awfully repaid for all that we had done.

Record your finishing time in the time box. Then take the reading test.

Read each test item and choose the best answer. Print your answers on page 7 of the progress folder.

Getting main ideas

1. The day turned out to be a holiday for everyone except
   - **A.** Father
   - **B.** Anne
   - **C.** the author
   - **D.** Mother
   - **E.** Mary

2. The person whose plans were changed most often was
   - **A.** Mother
   - **B.** Father
   - **C.** the author
   - **D.** Anne
   - **E.** Mary

3. This story was written to make you
   - **A.** cry
   - **B.** feel unhappy
   - **C.** feel angry
   - **D.** feel happy
   - **E.** laugh

Understanding important details

4. To celebrate Mother's Day, the family decided to put over the fireplace some
   - **A.** mottoes
   - **B.** pictures of Mother
   - **C.** flowers
   - **D.** bells
   - **E.** tinsel

5. As a souvenir of the day, Father and the boys got new
   - **A.** shoes
   - **B.** suits
   - **C.** hats
   - **D.** ties
   - **E.** canes

6. As a surprise for Mother the family arranged to hire
   - **A.** a fishing rod
   - **B.** a maid
   - **C.** a motor car
   - **D.** a man to do the rough work
   - **E.** a special cook

7. Father said Mother should stay home because she might
   - **A.** hurt herself
   - **B.** catch cold
   - **C.** not like the lunch
   - **D.** be frightened
   - **E.** not like a drive

8. While Father and the boys fished, the girls

    A. fished too
    B. met some young men friends
    C. had a brief sleep
    D. fell into the stream
    E. sewed

Reading with a keen eye

9. The family returned home from its outing at

    A. seven o'clock
    B. noon
    C. four o'clock
    D. midnight
    E. nine o'clock

10. Father said young people seldom realize how much quiet means to people who

    A. like fishing
    B. live in the country
    C. celebrate Mother's Day
    D. were getting old
    E. like turkey dinners

Choosing the best reason

11. The boys would not let Father stay home because

    A. they did not know the way to the stream
    B. they wanted him to teach them how to fish
    C. they were lonesome
    D. they knew he would make trouble if he stayed
    E. only he knew how to drive the car

12. The family left Mother home for a restful day around the house. Yet they expected to return home to

    A. play cards
    B. eat a big roast turkey dinner
    C. sit quietly by the fire
    D. a party of friends and neighbors
    E. go right to bed

13. Mother stayed home because she

    A. was angry
    B. was expecting company
    C. knew she was expected to
    D. wanted to clean the house
    E. wanted to visit her sister

14. Father said that Mother would enjoy a chance to

    A. fish
    B. go shopping
    C. visit friends
    D. go to the movies
    E. stay home

15. Here are five events mentioned in the story. Which one came first?

A. Mother prepared a roast turkey dinner.
B. The family hired a motor car.
C. The family decided to celebrate Mother's Day.
D. Father and the children went fishing.
E. Father fetched the nuts from the sideboard.

Understanding words

16. "During the meal Mother got up and down a good deal, fetching things." As used here, *fetching* means

A. throwing
B. bringing
C. warming
D. watching
E. cooking

17. "Father wanted Mother to spare herself." As used here, *spare* means

A. be good to
B. teach
C. punish
D. wash
E. sing

18. Five words taken from the story have been divided into syllables. One has been divided incorrectly. Which one?

A. col/lege
B. ar/range
C. suppos/ed
D. hun/gry
E. beau/ti/ful

19. "The family wanted to humor Mother." As used here, *humor* means

A. fool
B. make fun of
C. ignore
D. punish
E. keep happy

20. Sometimes little words can be found in big words. Here are five words taken from the story. Only four of them contain a smaller word. Which one does *not?*

A. everything
B. forgive
C. fireplace
D. fishing
E. trouble

Follow the directions (Steps 8–13) on page 1 of the progress folder.

How you can build a better vocabulary

Notice the title of this lesson. What we are interested in is not just a big vocabulary, but a better vocabulary.

For a better vocabulary you will need more words, to be sure. But more important, you need a more thorough knowledge of the words you already know. A better vocabulary will be not only larger, but more precise. Your goal should be to have the right word ready in any situation.

As you move forward in school, you will need an improved general vocabulary. You will need technical words, too. And you will need words that are used in a special way in chemistry, shop, or mathematics. This lesson will give you some suggestions for improving both kinds of vocabulary.

You will not often need technical words like *valence, mitosis,* or *logarithm* in conversation. Nor will you need them frequently for your general reading. But you do need for your general reading a large stock of commonly used words.

Most useful words are not pretentious. They will not make you sound as though you were trying to show off. They are the kind of words that the world's greatest speakers have used with telling effect.

One of the most eloquent speakers of our times is Winston Churchill, the great British statesman. He seldom uses a long and unusual word when there is a short and simple one to do the job. He said in England's darkest moment during World War II: "I have nothing to offer but blood, toil, tears, and sweat." At another time, when the British air force had beaten the Nazi air force, he remarked simply, "Never in the field of human conflict was so much owed by so many to so few."

These are great phrases—memorable phrases. They are powerful and moving. Note that they are composed of simple words familiar to you, but chosen carefully and with precision.

You must be interested in words

One thing is sure: to improve your vocabulary you need most of all an interest in words.

You can develop this interest by watching and listening carefully. When someone uses a new word, or a word that strikes you as colorful, make a note of it. Think of the other words that might have been used. Think of the words you yourself might have spoken. Try to figure out why the word used was especially effective.

The more you learn about words, the more interested you will become in them. The more attention you give to words, the more you will learn about them.

As your interest grows, you will discover how words and meanings develop. You will find the key to the amusing plays on words that you hear on radio and television programs. You will find why so many people are fascinated by words.

And your vocabulary will grow stronger, richer, and more flexible.

Some words sound so funny that it is a wonder people can use them without laughing. Take the word *banana,* for example. Say it out loud. Doesn't it sound ridiculous? *Coconut* is another word that sounds rather funny.

One scholar gives this list of the funniest-sounding English words:

pink	bananas
people	caboose

He puts them all together in this sentence: "Pink people eat bananas while riding in cabooses." Query: Do you know what a caboose is? What's the difference between a caboose and a calaboose?

To the person who is interested in words, they are an endless source of amusement. He enjoys making plays on words. Have you ever heard this verse?

Hark to the whimper of the sea-gull;
He weeps because he's not an ea-gull.
Suppose you were, you silly sea-gull,
Could you explain it to your she-gull?[1]

Another source of fun with words is in puns. A pun often employs two words that are alike in form or sound but different in meaning. By exchanging them, you get amusing results.

Some people frown on puns. You may have heard it said that anyone who would make a pun would pick a pocket. But punsters are in good company—William Shakespeare, for example. Thomas Hood, another English poet who loved puns, is said to have written this reply to his critics:

If I were ever punished
For every pun I shed
I'd hie me to a puny shed
And there I'd hang my punnish head

Radio and television comedians often use puns to good effect. In a picture made by the famous Marx brothers, the following conversation takes place.

GROUCHO: Let's take up the matter of taxes.

CHICO: Dat'sa where my brother lives.

GROUCHO: Your brother lives where?

CHICO: In Texas.

GROUCHO: I'm talking about taxes—money—dollars.

CHICO: Dat'sa right. Dallas, Texas.

Learning about puns and other kinds of wordplay may not increase your vocabulary greatly. But if you keep your eyes and ears open for amusing uses, your interest in words will increase. As your interest increases, your vocabulary will grow.

---

1 Copyright 1940 by Ogden Nash. From *Verses from 1929 On*, by Ogden Nash, by permission of Little, Brown and Co. and J. M. Dent & Sons, Ltd.

Three interesting words

Do you know what *abracadabra* means? It is pronounced *ab'ra-ca-dab'ra*. It is so strange a word that some dictionaries do not list it. It is an interesting word because it is supposed to have magical powers. You may have heard it in childhood magic games.

Speaking of magic, do you know what *prestidigitation* means? It is accented on three syllables: *pres'ti-dig'i-ta'tion*, with the heaviest accent on the *ta* syllable. It means "the performance of tricks by the skillful use of the hands." A prestidigitator is nothing more than a magician. Words like this are fun because they have a rollicking rhythm in their sound.

Here is certainly one of the longest words in the English language—*antidisestablishmentarianism*. With what you know about prefixes and suffixes, you will have little trouble in breaking this word into its parts.

Start with the familiar word *establish*. You know that to establish something is to get it started. When you have done that, you have an establishment. The suffix *-arian* here means "one who believes in." So anyone who believes in establishing something is an establishmentarian.

The prefix *dis-* here means "the opposite of." So a disestablishmentarian would be someone who believes in breaking up or putting an end to an establishment. The prefix *anti-* here means "against." In short, people who want to break up an establishment have enemies. The suffix *-ism* means here "belief or practice."

Now you can put the whole word together and pronounce it syllable by syllable. Put the accent on the *tar* syllable. And one of the longest words in the language is yours.

Some words have interesting origins

You can remember some words and use them more accurately if you know how they started. The word *rather* originally meant "earlier." The word *than* once was *then*. In the early days of our language people might have said, "I would earlier have a horse then an ox." Today we say, "I would rather have a sports car than a motorcycle."

Our word *pencil* comes from a Latin word meaning "little tail." The word was first used to name a brush with hairs, used by artists.

Precocious comes from a Latin word meaning "to cook or ripen beforehand." So a precocious child is literally one who has ripened ahead of time.

Word origins

Each person in the class should choose at least one word from the following list, and give a report on the origins of the word. Use a large unabridged dictionary if possible. You will find this information set in parentheses or brackets either after the pronunciation or after the meanings. Use the word in a sentence and see how the current meaning of the word compares with its original meaning.

abet	neighbor
acumen	parasite
ambitious	pecuniary
assassin	precipitate
boycott	prevaricate
candidate	recalcitrant
companion	record
curfew	remorse
dexterous	salary
hazard	senate
impediment	stigma
journey	supercilious
monster	tantalize

Idioms repay study

An idiom can be either of two things. It can be a group of words that change their meaning when used together. Or it can be the manner in which the words are used that gives them a special meaning. Literal translation from one language to another would give an entirely different meaning to the words.

We make many English idioms by adding to a verb. Let's take the word *look*, for example. If you "look up" something,

you do not raise your eyes. If someone tells you to "look out," you may already be "out" on the street in the path of a speeding car. If you "look down on" a practice such as cheating, you may not actually be looking at it at all. If you "look over" your notes, you are certainly not going to look above them.

You use idioms so naturally that you sometimes forget what they mean. They will serve you better if you give them a little thought.

Idioms

Exercise 58

Here is a list of idioms built around the verb *go:* (*Went* or *goes* may also be used.)

go about	go hard with
go after	go under
go along with	go off
go around	go on
go down	go out
go by	go through with
go beyond	go with

Write the numerals 1 to 14 on your paper. Write the idiom that fits each sentence. There is one sentence for each idiom listed above.

1. Whom does Jane go _____ now?
2. The amount of paper collected went _____ our wildest hopes.
3. Our married sister goes _____ her maiden name in business.
4. The team went _____ to defeat in its first four games.
5. I don't think I can go _____ this course.
6. My parents do not let me go _____ on school nights.
7. A rumor went _____ that there would be no school on Friday.
8. Our adviser is willing to go _____ our request for more free time.
9. The old trapper was too tired to go _____ any farther.
10. Bill went _____ down the road to look for help.
11. If the store doesn't get more customers soon, it will go _____.

12. Jane went _____ the hard problems with real determination.
13. The boy went _____ the job as though he knew what he was doing.
14. If you don't get these reports in on time, it will go _____ you.

The correct answers are shown in the answer key.

A second exercise on idioms

Nine students will each choose one of the following words and bring to class as long a list of idioms as they can find. There are some dictionaries that will help. The lists should be discussed in class and tested to see that the phrases really are idioms—that one cannot get their meaning by adding the meaning of one word to the meaning of the other.

get	do	give
make	set	come
fix	play	put

What is the difference?

If someone says "What's the difference?" he may be asking for information. Or he may be expressing the opinion that the point someone is making is of little importance.

There are many pairs of words in English that look alike and sound alike but are actually quite different. Anyone interested in accurate reading must learn to keep these words apart.

Suppose you read this statement in the newspaper. "The imminent writer Haroun Tazieff will be in town tomorrow." Does the sentence look right? Does it sound right? If *imminent* is the wrong word, what is the right word?

This is one of two words that look and sound very much alike but that have quite different meanings: *eminent*, meaning "famous and outstanding"; *imminent*, meaning "threatening and likely to happen at once."

You would normally speak of an *eminent* writer. Or you might find that a reporter who wrote an inaccurate story about the writer was in *imminent* danger of losing his job.

Here are a number of word distinctions to keep in mind:

1. affect.........to act upon
   effect..........a result of action
2. council........a group that meets to discuss or to govern
   counsel........advice; an adviser
3. coarse.........vulgar; rough
   course.........school subject; part of a meal; plan of action
4. complement.....something that completes or supplements
   compliment.....an expression of courtesy or admiration
5. formerly.......some time ago
   formally.......in a formal manner
6. official.........one holding an office
   officious.......meddlesome
7. rhyme..........repetition of sound
   rhythm........a regular pattern of light and heavy accents
8. uninterested....not interested
   disinterested....not influenced by
9. precede........to go before or to come before
   proceed........to go on or to continue
10. moral.........a lesson; the point of a story
    morale........the state of one's courage, confidence, and enthusiasm

Recognizing word distinctions

Exercise 59

Write the numerals 1 to 20 on your paper. Write the correct word for each of these sentences.

1. Many people believe that a trip to the moon is (eminent, imminent).
2. The student (counsel, council) will meet on Tuesday.
3. The attractive draperies were made of (course, coarse) material.
4. The chairman paid the speaker a (complement, compliment).
5. We have never been (formerly, formally) introduced.

6. Dr. Watson is an (imminent, eminent) scholar.

7. Why not ask the principal to (counsel, council) us.

8. The whole class seemed to be (disinterested, uninterested) in the story.

9. Next year we will have a (course, coarse) in auto shop.

10. An intransitive verb does not have an objective (complement, compliment).

11. (Formally, Formerly) the store was open until 9 P.M.

12. The coaches are looking for some (uninterested, disinterested) person to act as referee.

13. The usher in a very (official, officious) manner kept telling us to be quiet.

14. Music used for marching is played with a very strong (rhyme, rhythm).

15. After the special announcement, the program was allowed to (proceed, precede).

16. The (moral, morale) of the troops was high before the attack began.

17. The (moral, morale) of the story is to think before you speak.

18. A young person should allow an elderly person to (proceed, precede) him into a room.

19. An (officious, official) paper arrived two days later.

20. The ghost story had a strange (affect, effect) on all of us.

The correct answers are shown in the answer key.

Synonyms can improve your vocabulary

When the meanings of words are very similar, the words are called *synonyms*. If their meanings were exactly alike, they could be substituted for one another in any sentence. But no two words ever have exactly the same meaning in all contexts.

For this reason, one of the similar words is usually better for a particular sentence. The ability to tell which synonym is best is a mark of a good writer or speaker. A knowledge of word differences will make you a better reader, too.

In every good dictionary there are

comparisons of synonyms. You will find it interesting and useful to study these comparisons. They are called synonymies.

Here is an interesting synonymy from the *New World Dictionary*.[2]

SYN.—**appreciate,** in this comparison, implies sufficient critical judgment to see the value or to enjoy (he *appreciates* good music); to **value** is to rate highly because of worth (I *value* your friendship); to **prize** is to value highly or take great satisfaction in (he *prizes* his Picasso collection); to **treasure** is to regard as precious and implies special care to protect from loss; to **esteem** is to hold in high regard and implies warm attachment or respect (an *esteemed* statesman); to **cherish** is to prize or treasure, but connotes greater affection for or attachment to the thing cherished (she *cherished* her friends). See also **understand.**—*ANT.* despise, disdain.

The last part of this synonymy gives two antonyms, words of opposite meaning. In the comparison you find six words that are closely related but different in meaning. You can see that a study of synonymies would lead quickly to a larger, more precise vocabulary.

Using synonyms

Exercise 60

Study the synonymy above. On your paper, write the word that fits each sentence. The correct answers will be the six words in the synonymy.

1. Ann loved her husband deeply and _____ him.

2. Mr. Bodkin was _____ by his fellow townsmen as a public-spirited citizen.

3. "Money is not everything," Mark said. "In fact I _____ the respect of my friends much more."

4. My mother _____ the letters that my father wrote to her when he was in college.

5. Our principal _____ the letter he received from the governor thanking him

---

2 From *Webster's New World Dictionary.* Copyright © 1962 by The World Publishing Co.

for taking part in the statewide study of health education.

6. "Don't worry. Miss Glick can _____ the difference between careful preparation for an assignment and the slick talk of some student who hasn't bothered to do any real research."

The correct answers are shown in the answer key.

Color in language

Someone once pointed out that when it comes to insulting people, our language is colorless. It isn't, however, the fault of our language. The words are there, but we never use them. In the old days, he went on to say, a curse was a masterful and eloquent thing. Today, when annoyed with someone, we call him a fool and let it go at that.

Not too long ago in our history, the mule skinner or bargeman could string out his opinion of someone in a sentence stretching from Buffalo to St. Louis. He was admired and looked up to by his fellows and anyone within earshot. Today our descriptive poetry is delivered by the TV comedian. It might not be colorful, but it's short.

Color in language is like color in a picture, and we react to it in the same way. We make pictures with words, and our pictures can be dull black-and-white or sparkling with color.

Suppose you go to a special sale at a department store. When asked about it, you might say, "It was very crowded." But how much more colorful it is to say, "It was a madhouse. People were pushing and shoving, snatching things from the counters and from each other. They were shouting for the salesman and elbowing each other out of the way." You are painting a picture, and your listener can see it in his mind's eye. Color in language makes you a more interesting speaker.

The mule skinner, the bargeman, and Shakespeare might seem strange bedfellows at first, but in their use of colorful language they had much in common. In Shakespeare's *Henry the Fourth*, Prince Hal describes Falstaff as follows: ". . . that trunk of humors, that bolting-hutch of beastliness, that swoln parcel of dropsies, that huge bombard of sack, that stuffed cloakbag of guts, that roasted Manningtree ox with the pudding in his belly, that reverend vice, that grey iniquity, that father ruffian, that vanity in years . . ."

Although it heightens your appreciation if you understand Shakespeare's references, it isn't really necessary. The tone of insult comes through, and the colors are vivid.

Falstaff, in his defense, describes himself as ". . . sweet Jack Falstaff, kind Jack Falstaff, true Jack Falstaff, valiant Jack Falstaff . . ."

The colors in Falstaff's language are not the same as Prince Hal's; but their quiet repetition makes them effective.

You might say, "Well, but that's Shakespeare!" And you are right. But even though you are not Shakespeare, you can make your language more colorful, more vivid, more descriptive.

Words to describe things and people

An English scholar once developed a simple vocabulary to make our language easier for foreign people to understand and use. This simplified vocabulary is called Basic English.

In Basic English there are only 850 words. There are only 16 verbs, such as *come*, *get*, *make*. There are 200 nouns naming objects that can be pictured and 400 "general" nouns, such as *summer*, *talk*, *taste*, referring to things that cannot be pictured. There are 150 descriptive words, called qualifiers.

Basic English may be all right for travelers from abroad who want to learn the language quickly. They can say nearly everything they might want to say with the 850 words. But a knowledge of Basic English is not enough for anyone whose native language is English.

Do you know anyone who sounds as though he were using a limited vocabulary? Everything he likes is "good" or "great." Everything he dislikes is "corny" or "square."

You need a supply of specific words in talking about things and people. The more varied your supply, the more interesting your conversation will be, and the more accurate and rewarding your reading.

Suppose you find a book or a school course uninteresting. You can say it is "dumb," if you want to, but this word doesn't show what you think. It shows only how you feel. You might use words like these to show what you think: *dull, heavy, lifeless, impractical, tedious.*

On the other hand, suppose you like a book very much. You can say, "It's terrific. It's great. It's the most." But these phrases do not explain why you like the book. You might express your approval in these words: *entertaining, engrossing, gripping, moving.*

If you like a person, perhaps you say, "He's smooth. He's great." But can you say what you like about him? Do you ever use these words of approval?

sympathetic	pleasant
understanding	gay
agreeable	imaginative
friendly	buoyant
thoughtful	considerate
amusing	entertaining
bright	ingratiating
enthusiastic	

If you like a boy's tie and sports jacket or a girl's dress, do you know how to express your approval? Do you use words like these?

stunning	well-cut
attractive	colorful
bright	beautiful
becoming	

You will find it profitable to build up your words of approval and words of disapproval. By studying their shades of meaning, you will become a better reader and a more interesting speaker.

What about slang?

Slang is bright, racy, salty, effective, and communicative. In formal conversation or very informal writing, slang is effective.

But the habitual use of slang is dangerous. Slang expressions like "It really swings" or "That's the most" or "What a blast" are used in all sorts of situations, whether they are adequate or not. The danger is that slang is so easy to use that it keeps a person from seeking the right word, the precise word, the most expressive word. Do not use slang to the point where it stunts your vocabulary growth.

Words that name ideas present difficult problems

You will recall that in Basic English there are 200 nouns naming objects that can be pictured. These words and thousands of others present a minimum of difficulty for the reader. If the writer says "We sat on the radiator to keep warm," most readers will know what he means. Radiators have many shapes, but nearly everyone has seen a radiator that he could sit on.

But if a writer says "The young man showed initiative and a sense of responsibility," the reader may have trouble. What one person thinks of as responsibility or initiative may not be at all another person's idea. And since you cannot draw a picture of responsibility, it is hard to make sure just what it does mean.

Our language is full of words that cannot be pictured. They are called "abstractions." The most important words in our language are abstractions—words like *loyalty, justice, truth, honesty.* These words stand for ideas rather than objects or living things, and they are so important that men and women have died for what they believed them to represent.

Nonetheless, they do present problems in communication. You cannot be sure that your idea of "loyalty" is the same as the idea someone else has. Good writers take care to pin down their meanings for words like these.

The easiest way to do this is to describe a situation in which loyalty, as you understand it, has been demonstrated. You show in this description how people act. You show the effect of loyalty. You show how it operates. This kind of explanation is called an "operational definition." It is an effective way of getting agreement between two people as to the meaning of a word that cannot be pictured.

You may not agree that the situation described represents your idea of loyalty.

But at least you know what the word means to the other person. And you don't have to waste your time arguing about meanings.

Which are the abstract words?

Exercise 61

Copy the words from the list below that cannot be explained by pictures.

1. justice
2. dog
3. democracy
4. courthouse
5. house
6. home
7. school building
8. education
9. holdup
10. crime
11. girl
12. beauty

The correct answers are shown in the answer key.

How to double your vocabulary

In Lesson 12 you learned some of the ways in which English words are made. You found out that prefixes and suffixes are added to a base word to make new meanings. This process of word building should suggest to you a way to increase your vocabulary enormously.

If you will take a simple word such as *house*, or *press*, or *form*, and add prefixes and suffixes, you will come up with hundreds of words having a common base meaning.

Let's take the word *press* for example. Its basic meaning is "to push." From what you know of prefixes, you can see that *impress* means "to press in." You know that the suffix *-ion* merely makes a noun. You can add *impression* to your vocabulary. People often use the word to refer to a memory. "My impression of Jack is that he is very reliable."

You know that the suffix *-ive* means "associated with." Therefore *impressive* means something associated with pressing in. An impressive speech is one that presses in or sinks into the minds of the people who hear it. In Lesson 12 you learned that *impressionable* means "easily impressed."

By adding one prefix and three suffixes

to the base word *press*, you have added four words to your vocabulary. Do you know of an easier way to build your vocabulary quickly?

Forming new words

Here are four base words to use in expanding your vocabulary:

form   sign
stand   serve

Here is a list of prefixes to use in making new words with the four base words:

under-   dis-
com-(co-, con-)   ad-(as-, af-)
with-   in-(im-, ir-)
re-   per-
de-   pre-

Here is a list of suffixes to use:

-ation (-tion)   -ard
-ance   -ing
-ice   -or (-er)

On a separate piece of paper, write the new words that you can build on the four base words. Consult a dictionary to enlarge your list. Read the dictionary entries carefully. Note the various meanings for each of the new words you have built.

How to make a word yours

When you hear a new word or meet a new word in your reading, you will want to fix its meaning in your memory. If you don't, you will have to study it over again every time you meet it.

To master a new word, you need a notebook. Copy the word and underline it. From a dictionary, get the correct way of breaking it into syllables, and make a note of this.

Let's suppose that the word is *benevolent*. You divide it thus: *be-nev'o-lent*, marking the accented syllable.

Examine the word for prefixes and suffixes. By using the dictionary, you discover that *bene-* is a prefix meaning "well." The root of the word is *vol*, meaning "wish." The suffix *-ent* adds little meaning to the word. Write down the prefixes and suffixes with their meanings.

The next step is to copy the phrase in which the word was used. You copy the phrase *benevolent despot*. A despot is a man who has absolute power of government. A benevolent despot acts for the benefit of the people and the state. Leave room for other phrases that you will meet later. When you see the word *benevolent* used again, enter the phrase in which it occurs.

Below these phrases write the meanings given in the dictionary. If the dictionary says "See _____," look up this reference. It may lead you to synonyms and antonyms. You will discover, for example, that the antonym for *benevolent* is *malevolent*. The prefix *mal-* means "bad or evil." By this simple means you have added *malevolent* to your vocabulary.

While you are at it, look over the nearby entries in the dictionary. You will discover other forms of the word. Jot these down in your notebook.

To sum up: (1) Copy the word in your notebook. (2) Indicate syllables and accents. (3) Examine it for prefixes and suffixes and write these down with their meanings. (4) Copy the phrases in which the word appears. (5) Copy the meanings for the word given in your dictionary. (6) Look up synonyms and antonyms and record them. (7) Make a note of related words.

This is a good deal of work on one word. You will not have time to take all these steps for many words every week. But if you keep steadily at it, your vocabulary will be several hundreds of words richer each school term.

But still these words are not yours. They are not yours until you can use them readily. The next step is to use each new word in your speech and writing. Every time you enter a new word in your notebook, think how you can use it. Then try it out on your friends. After you have used it two or more times, you can depend on it for future use.

Finally, review the entries in your notebook once a week. Keep the new words fresh in your memory. Make sure that you do not lose them through disuse.

Practice Reading 13

In a book, magazine, or newspaper that you like, practice reading for speed and comprehension. Make a record of this reading in Chart 3 on page 8 of the progress folder.

After you read Article 13 and complete the test, skim the article and make a list of the words you do not understand. Read carefully the sentence in which each unfamiliar word appears. Then look up the word in the dictionary. You may also wish to add these words to your vocabulary notebook.

13

article

Ships and masters[3]

by Robert Carse

Speed meant everything, the clipper captains understood very clearly, and they drove the ships with persistent, furious abandon. Each day saved at sea counted as thousands of dollars in profit for their owners. The first vessel home from China with the new tea crop received the highest bids at auction and a captain got his share in a bonus or a percentage of the cargo price. But he constantly gambled with the lives of his crew, with his own, and with the survival of the ship.

Due to the rigors of the trade, nearly all of the captains were young. On sailing day they swaggered a little, and it was traditional to dress as a dandy.

The captain climbed the gangplank without a word and only a nod to the mate. He stowed his chronometers in his cabin, where they would be safe and dry beside the chart table. Then he took his logbook and the coastal chart and tide tables from the shelf.

He went up the companionway ladder to the quarterdeck and took his habitual position between the binnacle and the leeward rail, just a few feet from the wheel.

The captain slid forth his massive hunter's watch from his waistcoat pocket. Tide and wind were exactly as he wanted them. He drew a deep breath and let go his awaited shout to the mate: "All right, Mister! A man for the wheel. Single up. Give me a jib now, and the fore-tops'l."

Ladies who carried parasols over their shoulders waved at the ship from the esplanade. Children watched by nursemaids yelled excitedly. Ragamuffins in sketchy cotton drawers claimed attention by diving from the Battery seawall. It was quite a scene, the captain realized, and he would leave it to sail across more than half the world.

Half-smiling, wryly, he remembered the famous question asked all deepwater sailors: Who'd leave a farm and go to sea? But only veteran frontier troops assigned to Indian duty at Western posts and the trappers who worked the beaver ponds in the Rocky Mountain wilds had to meet the sort of demands put on him. His senses were acutely attuned to register and to identify each sound, each motion, and the slightest wind change. They remained alert even during sleep.

He used at sea aboard this ship, day and night, thirty-one sails. There were no lights to illuminate the darkness a hundred feet aloft where the skysails strained and the little moonrakers twitched and dipped with the roll and then the pitch of the ship. All of the rigging was of rope, the blocks and pulleys of wood; sudden, undue stress could tear them before anything might be done to ease the ship.

A snapped topmast in the middle of a typhoon, sails blown tattered from the boltropes one after the other, sprung seams, decks awash all the way from the bow to the quarterdeck were common features of a China run in the 1840s.

The captain would raise his hands to

his salt-rimed mouth then and give a shout for his mate. Men already fearful and tense went into the lee rigging with the mate's yell. They climbed and swung out over the black, black void of the sea where the ship was only a dim white arrow wedged in foam. Beneath them was just the foot-rope, and the canvas they fisted tore fingernails ragged, hit with blows that could break ribs. But they got the canvas in; they furled it, and passed the gaskets, and secured it. They went on like that, down one mast, up the next, down and up until the ship sailed bare-poled in the storm and the captain in his long oilskin coat rested motionless beside the wheel.

There were, though, in spite of the similarities of temperament, two kinds of captains in the clipper ships. One was the bully type, the man who drove his crew harder than he did his ship. The other was the captain who had learned early that the sea was enemy enough and treated his men well, sheltered them, encouraged them. As a consequence, he was given their respect and unquestioning, loyal performance in any emergency.

Robert H. Waterman, who really gloried in the nickname of "Bully," was an outstanding example of the rough-and-tough type, and the reputation of his former chief mate, a man named George Fraser, was equally bad. They took a sheer and what must have been cruel delight in banging drink-stupefied, vomiting sailors around the deck. They equipped themselves with brass knuckles, blackjacks, and revolvers, never went forward without a belaying pin in hand.

Waterman was hated by sailors in every seaport in the world, and in New York his name along the waterfront was an epithet. His most famous ship was one of the very early clippers, *Sea Witch*, and he made marvelous runs in her to China and back. It was said that he could smell the wind, and he was certainly a very close student of Maury's weather charts. But *Sea Witch* had as figurehead a big black Chinese dragon with a gaping mouth and partly coiled tail. Sailors, drunk or sober, knew that figurehead, and they took coastal ships to get out of port. They became fervently if briefly religious in the bethel missions, gave up liquor and their usual

haunts to escape being shanghaied into a Waterman crew.

A posse of vigilantes was needed to save Waterman in 1851 in San Francisco. It was strongly stated that he had killed three of his sailors while at sea, and he was lucky to keep his life. But he went on with his psychopathic cruelty, seemed somehow pleased to turn men against him in final, desperate mutiny.

His type was given a good deal of false glorification at the time, and a number of shipowners bragged openly about the aggressive tactics of their captains and mates. A legend was started by them which is not yet completely disbelieved, and more than one writer has picked it up as fact. Bully-boy captains were supposed to come over the side in all their finery and immediately dump buckets of seawater upon themselves. This was done quite invariably in freezing weather, to make sure the crew knew just how tough they were. Then, with no change of clothing, the bullyboys took their ships out and set every sail.

There was between the extreme Waterman type and the considerate, thoughtful captain a man such as Samuel Samuels. Just as tough physically as Waterman and no less a sailor, he commanded the exceptionally beautiful packet ship *Dreadnought* which often broke New York–Liverpool records. Samuels had run away from home when he was thirteen, gone to sea in all sorts of vessels, and learned his trade the hard way. Homeward-bound to New York in *Dreadnought* during a heavy-weather voyage, some of his sailors mutinied. They were Liverpool packet sailors, violent, savage, and uncaring. Samuels knocked one of them cold with a fist blow, took a pistol and a belaying pin and, alone, went forward to the fo'c'sle for the others.

They listened to him and he made his peace with them. Their knives were tossed onto the deck from the fo'c'sle door. Then the men came out and said they would work and Samuels turned them to without hesitation.

When the ship was alongside the dock in New York he called the ringleaders into his cabin. He said quietly that all he had to do was summon the police, make a statement and show his logbook of the voyage. Mutiny was punished in United States courts by a sentence of five years in prison and a fine of five thousand dollars. But he would not bring in the police; a sentence like that, with the fine to be worked out, meant practically a lifetime in prison. There was also no reason for him to show the logbook entries. The men were free to go ashore, and here was their pay. If they couldn't find another ship, they should come back aboard *Dreadnought* and he'd hire them.

The Liverpool men left the cabin with the silence of the devout departing from church.

Record your finishing time in the time record for Article 13. Then take the reading test. Read each item and choose the best answer. Write your answers on page 7 of the progress folder.

Reading Test 13

Getting main ideas

1. The life of a seaman on the clipper ships was

    A. monotonous and dull
    B. guaranteed to be short
    C. hard and cruel
    D. relaxing and healthy
    E. luxurious

2. The captains of the clipper ships

    A. were dandies and ladies' men
    B. were poor navigators
    C. let the mate and officers run the ship
    D. cared more for safety than speed
    E. drove the men as hard as the ships

3. The author intended this story to be

    A. complete directions for sailors
    B. a complete history of the sea
    C. a description of the China trade
    D. an interesting bit of history
    E. a humorous sketch

Remembering key facts

4. The ships raced to be first one home

    A. with the new tea crop
    B. to beat the British
    C. to win a gold cup
    D. for the best anchorage
    E. because of the storms

5. As soon as the captain boarded the ship

    A. the mate left the bridge
    B. the men came to see him
    C. it sailed from the harbor
    D. he stowed his chronometers away
    E. the mate took charge

6. Captain Waterman's *Sea Witch* used as a figurehead

    A. a statue of a mermaid
    B. a big black Chinese dragon
    C. a snake with coiled tail
    D. a red, fiery dragon
    E. a spouting whale

7. Captain Robert Waterman's nickname was

    A. Blackbeard
    B. Bobby
    C. Buddy
    D. Stony
    E. Bully

8. On sailing day, it was traditional for the captain to

    A. ignore the rest of the crew
    B. dress as a dandy
    C. let the mate handle the ship
    D. line up the men for inspection
    E. salute the owner

Choosing the best reason

9. Captain Samuel Samuels treated his crew well because

    A. he was afraid of the tough sailors
    B. it was easier than beating them
    C. the shipowners told him to
    D. he received good work in return
    E. the men were afraid of him

10. During a typhoon, sails are taken in because

    A. they slow down the ship
    B. it's a good time to practice
    C. it's easier to steer
    D. they might be blown off
    E. they might get soaked

Understanding descriptive phrases

11. When the ship sailed *bare-poled*, it moved

    A. without sails
    B. round the pole
    C. without a rudder
    D. fully rigged
    E. with a damaged hull

12. Captain Samuels learned his trade *the hard way*. This means

    A. he took a course in navigation
    B. he studied a long time
    C. he learned through experience only
    D. he wasn't a good student
    E. his teacher was strict

13. Captains who dressed as *dandies* dressed

    A. in their oilskins and boots
    B. warmly and comfortably
    C. in red and blue
    D. quickly and carelessly
    E. in the latest fashion

14. The article mentions one clipper ship that sailed with

- **A.** thirty-seven sails
- **B.** twenty-one sails
- **C.** thirty-one sails
- **D.** forty-one sails
- **E.** eleven sails

15. Mutiny was punished by a sentence of

- **A.** death
- **B.** 5 years and $5000
- **C.** life imprisonment
- **D.** 3 years and $3000
- **E.** 4 years and $4000

Knowing word meanings
16. To *shanghai* someone into a crew means to

- **A.** kidnap him
- **B.** make him sign a contract
- **C.** find him in China
- **D.** carry him to China
- **E.** enlist him

17. To *furl* canvas means to

- **A.** sew the rips
- **B.** spread it out
- **C.** throw it away
- **D.** hang it up
- **E.** roll it up

18. When the captain's lips became *salt-rimed*, they were

- **A.** covered by a thick mustache
- **B.** covered with rhyme
- **C.** edged with salt
- **D.** cut and bruised
- **E.** shut tightly

19. ". . . and the canvas they fisted tore fingernails ragged." *Fisted* means

- **A.** handled
- **B.** punched
- **C.** scraped
- **D.** sewed
- **E.** stretched

20. The *rigors* of a trade are the

- **A.** requirements of a trade
- **B.** hardships of a trade
- **C.** builders of a trade
- **D.** tricks of a trade
- **E.** experience of a trade

Follow the directions (Steps 8–13) on page 1 of the progress folder.

How you can read better for school assignments

Much of the reading you do at this time in your life is for schoolwork. If you improve your reading skills, you will be able to study more effectively. You can cover your assignments more quickly, more easily, and with greater understanding. This will give you more time to do other things and to read books that are not part of the school assignment.

In a sense, every lesson in this book is related to studying. If you gain greater efficiency in getting main ideas and important details as you read, if you learn to adjust your speed to your purpose, if you think about what you read, if you improve your ability to recall—you will almost certainly improve your ability to study.

"Almost certainly" is as strong a phrase as can be used. It is not a sure thing that you will become a better student if you improve your reading. There are good readers who are poor students. There is more to effective study than reading. But good reading is perhaps the most important single factor in successful studying.

What is a good student?

If you were asked what makes a good reader, you could probably give a satisfactory answer. But what is meant by the phrase *a good student*?

The obvious answer is that anyone who gets high grades is a good student. Anyone who gets high grades may be a hard worker, but he may not be a really good student. The important question is, What did he do to get the high grades? Did he memorize everything in the course? Did he spend so much time on studies that he could do nothing else? Or was he one of those rare persons who already knew most of the material in their assignments?

Let's set down a tentative description of a good student and think about it. Let's say that a good student does the best work he is capable of doing with a reasonable expenditure of energy. A good student is not satisfied with mediocre work. A good student gets his work done when it is due without spending all of his time on it the night before. A good student plans his day or week so that he has time for study and time for recreation. And he follows his schedule regularly.

Study habits are important

You can see that there is a great deal more to effective study than just reading. Efficient studying, the kind that produces the best results in the shortest time, depends upon attitudes, habits, and interests.

Let's consider the important attitudes first. A very important attitude is confidence. The student who begins an assignment by saying, "This is too much for me—I can never understand it," places himself under a severe handicap. If you say you can't do something, you probably won't do it. On the other hand, if you approach an assignment as a job that you can do, you have the right attitude.

Throughout your life you are going to have problems to solve. Difficulties will come up in new combinations all the time. It is likely that you won't have enough time, or enough money, or enough energy, to do everything you want to do.

Life is a constant succession of problems for everyone. The person who thinks of every problem as a complete roadblock will never get anywhere. But the person who thinks of a problem as something to be solved can usually find solutions that will lessen his difficulties. Most of the problems you face are not new or yours alone. Other students have faced them and have often found satisfactory solutions. You must try to do this too.

A second attitude of great importance is interest. You will do your best work in a field or on a topic you like, but it is also possible to do a good job at something you find dull or uninteresting at first. After you develop a background, you will find that many formerly uninteresting subjects become interesting. Then, too, a certain amount of routine work is necessary in every job, however glamorous it may appear. The movie star must memorize his lines, he must rehearse, he must often go through a scene over and over until the director says it is right. Such repetition is often boring; but it is extremely important to the actor's success.

Likewise, in your schoolwork, if you develop an interest in a subject you are more likely to listen attentively in class, to contribute more to the class, and to attack your assignments with confidence. And you can develop an interest. One of the easiest ways to become more interested in anything is to find out more about it through study. Another way is to read widely in books and magazines that contain related material.

A third attitude of importance in studying is the determination to concentrate. It is hard at first to concentrate. There are so many exciting and wonderful things in the modern world that everyone could put in a twenty-four-hour day just amusing himself. But if you are going to be a good student, you must plan to give uninterrupted time to your work. And you must attend to your work and seek to master each job as you meet it. Soon you will acquire the habit of concentrating.

Let us look further at the meaning of concentration. When you concentrate on a job, you put other things out of your mind. You keep your attention on what you are doing. You sit down to your math assignment and you think exclusively about that assignment. When a thought of a quarrel or tomorrow's party or today's basketball game intrudes, you suppress it immediately. You do not interrupt your work to talk on the telephone or to watch television.

It is hard work to concentrate, but it is essential and it is rewarding. If you form the habit of sticking to the job in hand, you will learn to work rapidly and effectively. When your study is done, you will have more time for relaxation. Your recreation will then be earned and enjoyed.

Concentration

Exercise 62

Here is a paragraph to test your powers of concentration. Give yourself three minutes to read it and to answer the questions that follow. Make a check on your paper for every time your mind wanders to some other subject.

Accompanied only by my escort—the 1st U.S. Cavalry, about two hundred strong—I reached Jettersville some little time before the 5th Corps. Having nothing else at hand, I at once deployed this handful of men to cover the crossroads till the arrival of the corps. Just as the troopers were deploying, a man on a mule rode into my pickets. He was arrested, and being searched there was found in his boots this telegram in duplicate, signed by Lee's commissary general: "The army is at Amelia Court House, short of provisions. Send 300,000 rations quickly to Burkeville Junction." I surmised that the telegraph lines north of Burkeville had been broken, which would account for this order being sent by messenger. There was thus revealed not only the important fact that Lee was concentrating at Amelia Court House, but also a trustworthy basis for estimating his troops. My troops, too, were hard up for rations, so I concluded to secure, if possible, these provisions intended for Lee.[1]

Write on your paper the letter for the phrase that correctly completes each of the following statements.

1. The writer of this paragraph was
   A. General Grant
   B. General Lee's commissary general
   C. General Phil Sheridan

[1] From *The Personal Memoirs of General P. H. Sheridan.*

2. In the boots of the messenger was found
  A. a telegram
  B. a letter
  C. an order signed by General Lee
3. The papers found in the messenger's boots showed
  A. the location of General Lee's supplies
  B. the location of General Lee's army
  C. the location of General Sheridan's army

How many checks did you mark down? How many times did your attention wander? Compare your number with those of your classmates.

Concentration

Exercise 63

How well can you concentrate when there are distracting noises around you? Here is a test that will show what you can do. While you are reading the paragraph below and answering the questions that follow, two of your classmates will stand at the rear of the room reading aloud. They will read from any textbook in the classroom.

Your teacher or another student will give you a signal to start. When three minutes have passed, he will give you a signal to stop. As you read, make a check every time your mind wanders from your reading.

Thomas Jefferson, as President of the United States, purchased the Louisiana Territory from France in 1803. The purchase doubled the size of the United States. President Jefferson sent two men, Lewis and Clark, to explore the new territory. The expedition was formed at St. Louis in 1804. In special boats, the men set out up the Missouri River to the Northwest. It took them a year to reach Montana. The river being impassable, they left their boats and traveled overland. Guided by Indians, they found their way over the Rocky Mountains to the headwaters of the Columbia River. There they built new boats and sailed downstream to the Pacific Ocean. Their experience made the return trip easier. In less than a year they were back at St. Louis. The 8000-mile trip took two years and four months.

Write on your paper the letter for the phrase that correctly completes each of the following statements.

1. The Louisiana Territory was purchased from France by
  A. President Johnson
  B. Lewis and Clark
  C. President Jefferson
2. After crossing the Rocky Mountains, the expedition reached the Pacific by sailing down the
  A. Mississippi River
  B. Missouri River
  C. Columbia River
3. The 8000-mile round trip to the Pacific took
  A. two years and four months
  B. two years and ten months
  C. one year and four months

How many times did your attention wander? Was the number greater than for the first test on concentration? Compare your results with those of your classmates.

You can learn to concentrate better. It will require effort and practice. It will have to be all your own effort, but you will have a chance to practice every time you sit down to study. Make an effort to give your full attention to your assignment. Try to do this on every lesson. In a month you will show great improvement. Fortunately, once you have started improving you will gain rapidly. Concentration will become a habit.

Good study conditions are important

You probably discovered in the second exercise on concentration that disturbing noises make it harder to keep your mind on what you are doing. The ideal way to study is in a quiet room where you are shut off from distractions.

If you can arrange this at home, you are fortunate. Most students have to do their homework while the rest of the family carries on its regular activities. In some homes where two or more children have homework to do, the family agrees on an evening study hour. During this period television and radio are off. Telephone callers are asked to call later. There is no music practice. When the study hour is over, the normal pattern of family life begins again. But even if your family does not follow such a procedure, you can usually find a relatively quiet place for regular study.

You have time to study, too, during school hours. If you plan your work, you can get a great deal done during study hours. If you try and are really interested in your work, you can learn to concentrate with people around you.

Planning is essential

In every school there are a few students who seem to get a great deal more accomplished than the rest of the class. They play in the band or orchestra, practice on their instruments, take part in sports, work on committees, and still get good grades. Other students never have time to do a good job of anything. They are always in a frantic rush.

The difference may be in planning. Within limits, the more you have to do, the more you can do—if you plan.

Have you ever kept a record of how you use your time during the week? How many of the 168 hours in each week do you devote to study? to recreation? to movies? to TV? to chores? to outside jobs?

In your notebook make a chart like the one below. Keep a record for one week. Bring your record to class and compare it it with the records of other students.

The person who gets things done, the efficient person, looks ahead and plans his activities. He makes a general plan for each week and a specific plan for each day.

A plan for the week ahead might look like the one on page 219.

Make out your own plan for next week. If an unexpected event comes up, change the plan so that you can work at the things you must do. But don't change your schedule unless it is necessary.

Each night during this week, make a plan for the next day. Try to arrange a regular time—the same time if you can—for study. Take advantage of your study hours in school. If the plan works, try it again the following week. Gradually, as you get used to planning, you will find that you are accomplishing everything you need to, with time left for the extra things you would like to do.

Hours devoted to

	Sleep	Meals	Home chores	Outside jobs	Going to and from school	Class	Extracurricular activities	Home study	TV or radio	Movies	Unaccounted for	Total
MONDAY												
TUESDAY												
WEDNESDAY												
THURSDAY												
FRIDAY												
SATURDAY												
SUNDAY												
TOTAL												

	MORNING	AFTERNOON	EVENING
MONDAY	finish book report in study hall	band practice go to library	television 7–8 study 8–10
TUESDAY	copy science notes in study hall	dentist appointment	work on stamp collection 7–8 study 8–10
WEDNESDAY	copy theme in study hall	help Jim on paper route	work on stamp collection 7–8 study 8–10
THURSDAY	band practice in study hall period	help Jim on paper route	television 7–8 study 8:30–10
FRIDAY	band practice in study hall period	television 4–5	basketball game
SATURDAY	shopping for mother	movies	Jim's party
SUNDAY	church	clean out garage	finish preparing for science exams homework in English

Make sure you know what your assignments are

Now let's be more specific. Let's consider what to do about a particular assignment. The first thing to do is to be sure you know what the assignment is. Before each class ends, your teacher tells you what you are to prepare for the next day. Listen carefully. If you are not sure what is expected, raise your hand and ask for specific directions.

Are you supposed just to read through a certain number of pages in a textbook? Are you to take notes on your reading? Are you to write something? If so, must it be written in ink? Exactly which practice exercises are you to do? Make sure you know the exact assignment. Copy it into your notebook so that you can refer to it later.

A general plan for preparing an assignment

Suppose that you have been assigned a passage in your American history textbook. (For this example, we have chosen *The American Adventure*, by Bertrand Wainger.) You are to read pages 284–92 in Chapter 15, "West to the Pacific." If you

do not have this book, get another history and read a chapter in the same way.

You turn to page 284. What is the best thing to do? Do you start right in reading? Here are some suggestions:

1. Look over the whole chapter. Most of it is divided into short sections. Each section covers part of a general topic. You can see how each part fits into the whole.

In Chapter 15 you will find five numbered sections with the following titles:[2]

- *The frontier reaches Arkansas and Iowa*
- *The United States acquires the great Southwest*
- *American pioneers settle Oregon*
- *The gold rush brings settlers to California*
- *Immigrants take part in American expansion*

From these five headings you can see that you are going to start west from Iowa and Arkansas. You are going to take up in order the Southwest, Oregon, and California. In the last section you are going to read about immigrants and the part they played in the nation's westward march to the Pacific. Similar headings appear in

---

2 From *The American Adventure*, by Bertrand M. Wainger. Copyright 1955. McGraw-Hill Book Company, Inc. Used by permission.

other history books too. Look at them carefully in whatever book you use.

2. Look at the illustrations in the chapter. The illustrations in textbooks are carefully planned to help you visualize what the printed matter is about. There are both pictures and maps in this chapter. By looking them over and reading the captions and legends, you can find out a great deal about the content of the chapter.

The first picture is a drawing of covered wagons, with mountains in the background. This is one means that Americans used to go westward to the Pacific. There is a picture of a great Indian educator who taught his people to read. Clearly there will be something about Indians in this chapter. There is also a picture of a river ferry about to carry a covered wagon across the river. Another picture shows the first travelers arriving in Oregon. It is interesting because it shows how people dressed in those times.

The maps in this chapter show you the routes that people followed as they moved west across the country. One map is of the Republic of Texas; another shows four huge sections of the United States, with the dates when they were acquired. These maps give you a good idea of the general content of the chapter. They tell you some of the things that you are going to study.

3. Read the first and the last paragraph of the chapter. You can read these paragraphs fast the first time, because you will come back to them again.

There is an interesting introduction to Chapter 15. It contains a key word that will give you the theme of the whole chapter. Here is that introduction:

Once a man who had spent many years studying the history of our nation was asked if he could give one word that would describe the period between the election of John Quincy Adams (1824) and the election of Abraham Lincoln (1860). He thought, and then said, "Of course no single word can really describe all the events that happened in the United States during those thirty-six years, but if I must use just one word, that word will be *expansion.*" As you read the following chapter, you will easily see why he chose that word. The period from John Quincy Adams to Lincoln was the period of the Texas Revo-

lution, the Oregon Trail, the California gold rush. It was a time when the restless, hopeful pioneers pushed west across the plains, long labeled the Great American Desert, to seek their fortune on the Pacific coast. Some of them sang to the tune of "Oh, Susanna":

California,
You're the land for me;
There's plenty of gold, so I been told
In Cali-for-ny-ee.

Europeans, too, traveled west: across the Atlantic to seek their fortune in the United States. Some of them stopped in eastern states, where they worked in factories or helped build canals and railroads. Some of them continued their journey until they found land in the West where they could settle. Many immigrants worked hard and lived happily. They were building our nation, whether they settled new lands or helped develop the older sections. They helped make the years from John Quincy Adams to Lincoln a period of expansion.

In any history you may find a key word, phrase, or sentence in the introduction to a chapter. Look for them.

On pages 304 and 305 you will find a summary. This is a brief statement of the main points in the chapter. It would be well to read it at the beginning of your study of the chapter as well as at the end. Here is the summary:

Summary

Now you can see why *expansion* is a good word to use in describing what happened to our nation between 1824 and 1860. People were moving west to make homes on new farms and to build new cities. Southerners filled in the empty spaces in Georgia, Alabama, and Mississippi and settled Arkansas. Northerners filled in the north and central parts of Illinois and Indiana and expanded into Michigan, Wisconsin, and Iowa. With improved transportation, the hardships on these frontiers did not last so long as on earlier frontiers.

From 1821 to 1830 about twenty thousand Americans settled in Texas, then a part of Mexico. Unhappy under Mexican rule, they won their independence in 1836 and established the "Lone-Star Republic." Ten years later Texas was admitted into the Union as a state. A war with Mexico followed. The United States won and annexed a huge territory reaching from Texas to California.

Other pioneers, eager for another chance to make a better living, crossed the Great American Desert and the Rocky Mountains to Oregon. On the 2300-mile journey they went through every kind of hardship. In spite of the difficulties they had to face to get there, by 1846 there were enough American settlers in Oregon to make it necessary to agree with Great Britain on a boundary. The forty-ninth parallel was made the boundary.

Just about the time that California became part of the United States, gold was discovered there. In 1849 thousands of eager gold seekers made their way to California by land and water. Only a small number struck it rich. As gold mining declined, Californians turned to farming, lumbering, and manufacturing.

Immigrants from Europe came to the United States in large numbers between 1840 and 1860 to take part in the rapid expansion of the nation. The largest groups were the Irish and the Germans. Many of them settled in cities and did the hard manual labor needed in a growing country. They learned American ways and made important contributions to American life. Many immigrants—or their children—won success in business, politics, and the professions.

By 1860 the United States had extended its boundaries from the Atlantic to the Pacific. Its people, including those born here and those newly arrived from other lands, had settled a vast area.

The summaries of chapters in other books will help you too.

4. Now look over your assignment. Before you begin reading, look at the paragraph headings printed in heavy black type. They point out the most important ideas in your assignment.

Your main job in reading a textbook assignment is to find the most important ideas and to understand them. You do this by attaching to those ideas the facts that explain them. Incidentally, this is the best known device for remembering the facts themselves. And it is the basis for outlining.

The headings in heavy type for the topics on pages 284–92 in *The American Adventure* are as follows:

- *The Indians are moved west of the Mississippi*
- *Settlers east and west of the Mississippi*
- *Frontier conditions disappear rapidly*
- *American settlers in Texas*
- *Texas wins independence*
- *Annexation of Texas brings war with Mexico*
- *The United States annexes the Southwest and California*

Here, clearly set forth by the author, are the seven big ideas that you should get from reading your assignment. As you read, you will look for facts that help explain these ideas. In other histories the main ideas are often set forth with equal clarity. Look for them.

5. Make up questions before you start reading. When you read to answer questions, you read more carefully and remember better what you read.

Here again, the headings in the chapter are a good guide. You can turn these headings into questions. Here are some of the questions you might set for yourself before reading the assignment:

- Why were the Indians moved west of the Mississippi?
- Just where were they moved?
- Who moved them?
- How did the settlers get west of the Mississippi?
- How many settlers were there?
- How did Americans get into Texas?
- Why did Texas want independence?
- From whom did Texas want to be independent?
- What does *annexation* mean?
- What are "frontier conditions"?
- How and why did the United States annex the Southwest?

With questions such as these in front of you, your reading will be more purposeful, more to the point. If you can answer these questions when you have finished, you need have no fear of any test.

Writing questions

The third section of Chapter 15 is called "American Pioneers Settle Oregon." Here are the main headings in this section:

- *Trappers and missionaries open a trail to Oregon*
- *Settlers follow the long trail to Oregon*
- *Dangers and hardships of the trail*
- *Oregon at last!*
- *The Oregon boundary*
- *The Mormons settle at Great Salt Lake*

On your paper, make a list of ten questions that you might ask about "American Pioneers Settle Oregon." Several of your questions should probably begin with "Why and "Who."

Take notes as you go along

For every course you study, you should take good notes. These notes should cover—

1. Important ideas and details from your text.

2. Ideas and details from your outside reading.

3. Ideas, methods of solving problems, outlines, and other related information and material.

Two things are necessary if your notes are to be useful to you:

First, your notes must be readable. You can use any shorthand system you like, provided that you can understand it later. Take enough time to write clearly and legibly. It is not necessary to write complete sentences, but it is necessary to include enough information so that your notes will mean something to you later.

Second, give your notes clear and accurate headings. Such headings will help you recall the main ideas and will be of great help to you in reviewing.

Review as you go along

A few minutes spent in review each week will save you hours of frantic cramming before tests and examinations. Before you start a new chapter or a new topic, go over your notes and the pages of your text covering the topic you have just completed. Go back over yesterday's work. Or go back to the beginning of the chapter and skim through it. This procedure will help you fit the parts into the whole. It will help you keep your direction. It will aid you in seeing the relation of one part of a subject to another. And it will often help you to get the most out of later chapters.

If you were studying Chapter 15 of *The American Adventure*, for example, this kind of review would call to your attention an earlier chapter. You would recall that in Chapter 11, "Americans Move West," you read about the westward movement from 1816 to 1825. It would be interesting to turn back to that chapter and make comparisons. You might ask questions like these, for example:

- Did the early settlers move west for the same reasons as the later settlers?
- Were the early settlers the same kind of people as the later settlers?
- Did the early settlers use the same kinds of transportation as the later settlers?
- Did the later settlers follow the same routes as the early settlers?

In finding the answers, you would learn a great deal about American history that is not definitely stated in the textbook.

Look for the relation between facts and ideas

Consider the difference between reasoning and memorizing. You do not learn facts by reasoning; you memorize facts. What you do learn by reasoning is how facts are related. To be a good reader, it is necessary to recognize this kind of relation.

American settlers began moving into Texas in the 1820s. What relation does this fact have to the war with Mexico? Mexico won its independence in 1825. What relation does this fact have to American settlement? Most of the settlers were slave owners. The new Mexican nation decreed that it would not permit slavery in its territory. What relation do these facts have to one another?

In reading history, science, and most other subjects, you should keep asking the question why. (Why did things happen as they did? What causes led to what results?) In this way you will discover the most important relationships.

In reading science and geography, space relationships are important. Where is Ceylon? How would you get there? In what direction would you travel? How long would it take you?

In reading a narrative, the time relationship is usually very important. What happened first? In what order did these other things happen? If you can keep time order straight, you can find out more easily why things happened.

Overlearn the most important facts and ideas

What does this word *overlearn* mean? Suppose you are memorizing a list of chemical elements for your science course. You write down the list. You read it aloud. You name the items without looking at the list. The next day you can write the list perfectly on your test.

But now what happens? If you do no more work with the list, it will gradually drop out of your memory. Two weeks later you may not remember more than two-thirds of it. By examination time you will have forgotten so much that you will have to learn it all over again. This is clearly a waste of time and energy.

There is a way to avoid this waste. When you think you have a poem or a list of important details memorized, don't stop there. Learn the material better than you need to for tomorrow's test. *Overlearn* what you are memorizing. Say your poem or list over to yourself half a dozen more times than you think necessary. You will be surprised how much better it stays with you if you repeat it again and again.

An exercise in overlearning

Here is an eight-line poem by Emily Dickinson. You should be able to memorize it by reading it silently and aloud seven or eight times. Take ten or fifteen minutes to do it. Then have one of your friends read it aloud. By this time you will be able to repeat the lines without error. Thus you see the value of concentration. But you may like this poem very much and want to recite it at some later time. If you do, you will probably need to overlearn the lines still further. After a week, repeat the poem several times; after a few more weeks, repeat it again. With spaced practice such as this, you will finally be able to recall the poem accurately whenever you wish.

I'M NOBODY[3]

by Emily Dickinson

I'm nobody. Who are you?
    Are you nobody too?
Then there's a pair of us—don't tell!
    They'd banish us, you know.
How dreary to be somebody!
    How public like a frog
To tell your name the livelong day
    To an admiring bog!

There are many other poems you will enjoy. Some of them you will want to learn. Find some poems you like and memorize them. You are almost sure to like some of Carl Sandburg's poems, or those by Stephen Vincent Benét or Robert Frost. And you will enjoy the poetry of Jesse Stuart, particularly the colorful descriptions of rural life in *Kentucky Is My Land*. Look at some of the limericks by Ogden Nash—you may want to memorize some of them.

Get acquainted with your textbooks

Many modern textbooks are carefully planned, handsomely illustrated, and beautifully printed. They are designed to make

---

3 From *The Poems of Emily Dickinson*, published by Little, Brown and Co.

study as interesting and as easy as possible. It will pay you to become well acquainted with your textbooks, so that you can use the many aids they provide.

There are certain parts of a book that you should know even though they are of little help in reading. Every book opens with a title page. On this page appear the title of the book and the name of the author. Sometimes the name of the publishing company is given, along with the cities in which the company has offices.

In some books a whole page may be given to the copyright notice. This is called the copyright page. A copyright is the right granted by act of Congress to a publisher or author to sole use of the printed material for twenty-eight years. At the end of that time the copyright may be renewed for another twenty-eight years. No other publisher or author may print copyright material unless he has the permission of the copyright holder.

If you look through the articles in this book, you will see (in most instances) footnotes at the bottom of the first page of each selection. These footnotes say that the publisher of *How to Improve Your Reading* has obtained permission to reprint from the copyright holder.

Right after the copyright page, a table of contents usually appears. Publishing practice varies, but this table usually gives a great deal of information. It lists the chapters and shows the page on which each chapter begins. In an anthology or a reader, every selection is listed.

Either as part of the table of contents or right after it, a textbook usually gives a list of maps and charts so that you can refer to them easily. Special reference materials placed at the end of the book are also listed in the table of contents.

There is often a page of acknowledgments, in which author and publisher acknowledge their debt to the persons who have assisted them with the book and express their appreciation.

How a textbook helps you in reading

A most useful feature of your textbook is the index, which appears at the end. Here you will find the names of people, events, important topics, and general subjects mentioned in the book. Page numbers are given. A good index also puts together related items appearing in widely separated parts of the book.

The following entry appears in the index of *The American Adventure*.

Clothing: in colonies, 72–73, 76, 81–*86*, 90; of hunters, *118*; of explorers, *216*; changes in, 247, *248*; shown in toys, 330; of cowboys, 410.

Anyone who wants to write a report on changes in American clothing would find information on fifteen pages of this book. The figures given in italics (such as *118*) refer to pages on which there is an illustration. In some books illustrated pages are indicated by figures in heavy black type.

When you are looking for information, turn first to the pages where a topic is treated at some length. The longest discussion of clothing appears on pages 81–86 of *The American Adventure*. The dash between the two numbers shows that the discussion continues from page 81 to page 86.

Occasionally you will come across the notation "see also" followed by the names of related topics. It is worthwhile to look up these references, because you may find there just the information you want. In some indexes there will be topics followed only by a reference. In the index of *The American Adventure*, for example, occurs this entry:

Confederacy (*see* South; War Between the States).

Under both of these topics there are several references to the Confederacy.

When do you use an index? You use the index of your textbook in reviewing. You use it to help you locate the answer to a specific question. In what year was the Erie Canal opened? What was the Gadsden Purchase? You could spend five minutes thumbing through the pages of your book for the answer. You can find it in less than a minute by using a good index.

If you cannot find the topic you are looking for in the index, do not give up. Think of related general headings under which it might appear. The Erie Canal, for example, is listed under "Transportation" and "Canals" in *The American Adventure*.

The study questions at the end of sections and chapters are useful guides. They cover important facts and ideas. Some questions call for specific facts. Others require you to examine several separate facts and to see how they are related.

Most good textbooks give the pronunciation of unfamiliar words or names. On page 215 of *The American Adventure*, for example, you would meet the Indian woman who guided Lewis and Clark into the West. Her name was Sacajawea. The pronunciation appears in parenthesis right after the name: (*săk-a-ga-we'-a*). In other books, pronunciations are given in footnotes. At the back of many science texts or technical books you will find a glossary. A glossary is a list of difficult words, with their definitions and pronunciations.

Getting acquainted with a text book

Exercise 64

The questions below are based on this book, *How to Improve Your Reading*. Write the answers on your paper.

1. What is the number of the page on which the first lesson begins?
2. To find information on taking notes, would you use the index or the table of contents?
3. On what page would you find information about the author of this book?
4. On what page will you find information about antonyms?
5. Who is the author of *Ships and Masters*?
6. On what page does the bibliography begin?
7. On what page do you find the poem *The Ballad of Reading Gaol*?
8. Who is the copyright holder of the selection in Article 2?
9. On what pages do you find instructions on how to use this book?
10. To which lesson would you turn for help in improving your reading rate?

Reading to make a report

Your textbooks are only one source of information for your school studies. Mag-

azines, newspapers, biographies, and reference books are valuable sources also. Here are a few suggestions to help you use sources of information effectively:

Suggestion 1

Skim the source materials to see whether they have the information you want. Before you settle down to read an article or a book carefully, look it over quickly. It may not contain anything that you can use. Look first to see whether it is a factual work or just a general statement of the writer's opinions. If it is too general in nature, it will probably not help you. Look second to see whether it really relates to your topic. It may deal with a phase of the topic that you are not interested in.

To skim an article, follow these steps:
- Read the title and any subtitles or introductions that may tell about the content.
- Read the first and the last paragraph.
- Read the first sentence of six or seven other paragraphs. This much reading will usually take no more than three or four minutes. It will give you a good idea whether the article suits your needs.

Suggestion 2

Go carefully through the table of contents and the index of a reference book. If you are writing a report on forest fires, you will look up entries for "fires" and "forests." But you will also look for entries on related topics, for example, "conservation," "natural resources," "timber resources," "forest protection," "U.S. Forest Service."

Single-volume reference works always have a full index. Encyclopedias sometimes have an index in each volume. They often have an index volume that covers the entire series of books; in an index of this kind you would find references to several different volumes.

In the *Britannica Junior* index volume, for example, under the heading "Fire, prevention and fighting of," you will find ". . . forest 4–438b, 6–163a . . ." The first reference is to Volume 4, page 438, second column. The second is to Volume 6, page 163, first column.

Under the heading "Forestry" you will find ". . . fire, 6–76a, 12–55a." The first figures direct you to Volume 6, page 76, first column; the second to Volume 12, page 55, first column.

Suggestion 3

In taking notes on your reading, be sure to write down the exact name of the book, author, article, and page number. If you copy the exact words of the writer, put quotation marks around them. This will help you later when you write your report. In writing, you may restate the writer's ideas in your own words. But if you copy the writer's exact words, you should always use quotation marks. If your notes are carefully written, you can tell which words are your own and which are quoted.

As you go farther in school, you will use more and more reference materials for reports. You will be asked to compare one author's ideas with another's. You may have to read through a dozen articles to get the information you need.

To do this kind of reading successfully, you will have to learn to adapt your reading rate to your purpose. Your first purpose is to look over an article to see whether it is what you want. To do this, you should read very rapidly. When you have found a good article, your purpose changes. You now want to read it carefully to get ideas and details. To do this, you will read more slowly and think carefully about what you are reading. You will find related references, too. You must decide how each one should be read.

Practice Reading 14

In a book, magazine, or newspaper that you like, practice reading for speed and comprehension. Make a record of this reading in Chart 3 on page 8 of the progress folder.

In this selection, make a special effort to increase your reading rate and your comprehension and vocabulary score.

Record your starting time in the time record on page 7 of the progress folder. Then read the selection. Read as fast as you can, but make sure you understand what you are reading.

14
article

Houdini — the handcuff king[4]

by Beryl Williams and Samuel Epstein

The *Holyoke Daily Democrat* for December 2, 1895, published the following story:

No Use for Handcuffs

Harry Houdini, appearing at the Empire this week, walked into the police station yesterday afternoon to see if the police had any handcuffs which they couldn't manage. Mr. Houdini is an expert in unlocking these instruments. He can manage them as well when they are around his wrists as when fastened to someone else.

Said he to Officer Chamberlain, "I thought I would drop in and show you a trick with the handcuffs. Put any sort of cuffs around my wrists, lock them and take away the key. Let me go into a side room for a second and I will return with the cuffs unfastened."

"A rather doubtful statement," thought Officer Chamberlain, but he thought he would give the fellow a chance. So he pulled out his own cuffs and fastened them around Mr. Houdini's wrists. He put the key in his pocket. Then the fellow walked into the next room and shut the door. In less than a minute he returned carrying the handcuffs in his hand. He did the same thing again several times with equal success.

It makes no difference with Mr. Houdini what kind of handcuffs are used. He opens them all with as much ease as if they were strings wound around his wrists.

Harry Houdini, the magician, was delighted with this story. People read it and then bought tickets at the local theater to see him. After that he always visited police stations to make the same offer. But at that time his show was playing only in the smallest towns. Even with good newspaper stories, he could not make the big-time theaters in the cities.

The years 1896, 1897, and 1898 were discouraging. The magic shows put on by Houdini and his wife, Bessie, brought in very little money.

Then one day Houdini suddenly said, "We're going to Europe, Bess." Bess stared.

"We'll get bookings when we get there," he quickly added. "All the big agencies here grab imported talent. Well, we will be imported. They'll want to hire us, all right. You wait and see."

Houdini arrived in England with his scrapbook under his arm, a list of agents in his pocket, and high hope in his heart. But for some reason, the moment Houdini began to quote notices describing his handcuff escapes as "marvelous," the agents quickly dismissed the Houdinis.

They marched into an office in London one morning, when their money was almost gone. Harry rushed into his spiel despite the feeble protests of the young man behind the desk.

---

4 Condensed and adapted from *The Great Houdini: Magician Extraordinary*, by Beryl Williams and Samuel Epstein, published by Julian Messner, Inc. Copyright 1950 by Beryl Williams and Samuel Epstein. Reprinted by permission of Julian Messner, Inc.

"I say," the young man said, "you must really be rather good. That's my name, too, you know," he continued. "Harry, I mean. Harry Day, it is."

After that things happened with a rush.

"Look here," Harry Day said, "I'm going to call Slater, the manager of the Alhambra, and ask him to give you a tryout!"

But Slater was not as impressed as Harry Day had been. He had seen thousands of vaudeville acts in his time. It took a good deal to interest him. And when Houdini tried to show his skill with the cuffs by showing Slater the clippings that referred to Houdini as "a marvel," the manager closed his eyes wearily.

"We've had enough marvels here," he said. "I wouldn't be interested in another Handcuff King unless he could open the cuffs at Scotland Yard."

Harry Houdini smiled, "Can you go with me to the Yard now?" he asked.

"Yes," Slater said slowly. "Yes, I could do that."

The superintendent of Scotland Yard, Mr. Melville, told Mr. Slater, "Our handcuffs aren't made for variety acts. They hold!"

"Maybe," Houdini said. "But I still want to try them."

Melville shrugged. He opened a drawer and took out a pair of glittering new bracelets.

"May I see them?" Houdini asked politely.

Melville silently handed them over. Houdini studied them for a moment and then handed them back.

"Still want to try them?" Melville's tone made it clear that he expected "no" for an answer.

"Sure."

"All right." Melville rose quickly to his feet. "Put your arms around that post." When Houdini did so, Melville snapped the cuffs around his wrists, and locked them down hard. Melville and Slater moved toward the door. Melville looked back at the cocky young American locked to the post. "We'll come back for you in a couple of hours," he said.

"Wait!" Houdini spoke before they had taken half a dozen steps. "I'll go with you." And as he stepped away from the pillar the cuffs fell to the floor with a clatter.

Melville's jaw fell.

Slater smiled for the first time since the Houdinis had walked into his office.

"Come back to the theater with me," he said. "We'll sign a contract right now."

The press releases were sent out, the handbills printed. "THE GREAT HOUDINI," they announced, "THE HANDCUFF KING."

Houdini finally learned why he had been turned down by so many English agents. Two "marvels" had recently appeared on London stages—one at the Alhambra itself—and had been exposed as fakes.

Houdini was as near to nervous as he had ever been in his life as he paced the wings of the Alhambra stage on that opening night. Finally his act was announced.

"Ladies and gentlemen," he said, "tonight I want to—"

"Stop!" came a loud shout from the audience. "I am the great Cirnoc!" A huge man leaped to the stage. "I am the original Handcuff King. This man is a fake!"

Houdini's surprise left him voiceless. Houdini was not even an American, Cirnoc insisted, and had never been in America.

The audience waited, excited but not surprised. They seemed to be waiting for another "marvel" to be exposed.

But suddenly another man from the audience stood up. His calm voice cut through Cirnoc's shouts.

"That is not true," he said. "I know that the young man is an American. I am also from America. Several years ago I saw him doing his handcuff act there."

The audience burst into applause. The exposer himself was this time being exposed.

Houdini stepped forward. "Get the Bean Giant," he whispered to Bessie. When she returned with the terrible thing, Houdini held it so that the audience might see. Then he said to Cirnoc, "I'll give you five hundred dollars if you can get out of these cuffs."

Cirnoc glared at the irons and then at Houdini.

"Let me see you get out of them," he said.

The audience was spellbound now. The irons were larger than ordinary handcuffs. No one had ever freed himself from the Bean Giant until Houdini had learned its secret.

"Lock me in," Houdini offered. He gave the cuffs to Cirnoc and held out his own hands.

Cirnoc did a careful job. It took him some time to be sure that the lock had snapped tightly shut. Houdini took less time to disappear into his cabinet and step out again, the cuffs hanging freely in his hand.

Again Houdini challenged Cirnoc to free himself from the Bean Giant. There was nothing else for the original Handcuff King to do but accept. The audience would not have allowed him to do otherwise.

Houdini snapped the cuffs on and, with a dramatic gesture, offered Cirnoc the key. The audience chuckled. Even if Cirnoc freed himself as quickly as Houdini had done—which was likely, since he held the key—the young American would still have shown himself the cleverer of the two. Cirnoc disappeared into the cabinet.

Long moments passed. The chuckles from the audience grew louder. Finally the audience roared with laughter.

When Cirnoc stepped out of the cabinet at last, his hands were still clamped by the Bean Giant. His face was red with fury. He was barely able to ask Houdini to release him. The audience burst into loud applause and shouts of congratulations.

Houdini bowed stiffly. But even his formal manner could not put them off. They had just crowned a new Handcuff King.

Record your finishing time in the time box. Then take the reading test.

Read each test item and choose the best answer. Print your answers on page 7 of the progress folder.

Reading Test 14

Getting main ideas

1. Houdini was pleased with the newspaper story because it
   A. was a long story
   B. made people come to see his show
   C. said he was clumsy
   D. showed how hard he had to work to escape
   E. showed that the police were stupid

2. Houdini's trick of escaping from handcuffs
   A. was performed by other men
   B. was simple enough for a child to learn
   C. was understood by the police
   D. is explained by the writer
   E. was extremely rare

3. Houdini went to England
   A. because it was cheaper to live there
   B. to make a reputation that would impress American theater managers
   C. because it was easier to get into theaters there
   D. because he could make more money there
   E. to learn new escape tricks

4. The English theaters would not hire Houdini because they

    A. thought his fee was too high for an unknown performer
    B. did not believe his newspaper clippings
    C. had been fooled recently by men who were fakes
    D. did not like his act
    E. had other good escape acts

Seeing the time order

5. Which of these things happened first?

    A. Houdini escaped from Scotland Yard handcuffs.
    B. Houdini escaped from the Bean Giant.
    C. Houdini decided to go to Europe.
    D. Houdini had trouble getting into big-time theaters in America.
    E. Harry Day took Houdini to Slater's office

6. Which of these things happened last?

    A. Cirnoc was released from the Bean Giant.
    B. The London audience crowned Houdini Handcuff King.
    C. Cirnoc asked Houdini to let him out of the Bean Giant.
    D. An American in the audience identified Houdini.
    E. Slater signed a contract with Houdini.

Remembering key facts

7. Harry Day was

    A. a magician
    B. a theater manager
    C. an agent who got jobs for actors
    D. a newspaper writer
    E. the superintendent of Scotland Yard

8. When Houdini went to Europe, he

    A. had plenty of money
    B. was famous in the United States
    C. went alone
    D. was well known in England
    E. had very little money

9. The superintendent of Scotland Yard

    A. refused to let Houdini try to open his handcuffs
    B. was not surprised when Houdini got out of the handcuffs
    C. thought Houdini would not try to escape the handcuffs
    D. took Houdini to see a theater manager
    E. locked Houdini in a cell

10. Slater, the theater manager, agreed to hire Houdini because

A. Houdini escaped from the Scotland Yard handcuffs
B. he was impressed by Houdini's newspaper clippings
C. he had heard of Houdini's success in America
D. there had been no handcuff escape acts recently
E. Harry Day recommended him

11. Cirnoc said that Houdini was

A. an American
B. an old friend
C. the original Handcuff King
D. a fake
E. a great magician

12. When Houdini began his act at the Alhambra, he was

A. self-confident
B. nervous
C. sure he would fail
D. angry at the audience
E. sick

Reading between the lines

13. The Bean Giant was probably

A. a set of chains with padlocks
B. a large beanstalk
C. a huge sack filled with beans
D. an extra-large set of handcuffs
E. a straitjacket

14. Harry Day probably decided to help Houdini because he

A. liked Houdini's looks
B. was afraid of Houdini
C. was impressed by what Houdini had to say
D. was impressed by Houdini's newspaper clippings
E. felt sorry for Houdini

15. Cirnoc was released from the Bean Giant

A. by Houdini
B. when he manipulated the cuffs gently
C. by Harry Day
D. when he unlocked the cuffs with a key
E. when he smashed the cuffs against the wall

Knowing word meanings

16. "At the end Houdini bowed in a formal manner." This means that he

A. was sneering at the audience
B. laughed and waved his hands
C. bowed awkwardly
D. was quiet and dignified
E. acted very excitedly

17. The prefix *un-* may mean to reverse an action, as in *untie*. It may mean "not," as in *unusual*. In which one of these words does *un-* mean "not"?

A. unable
B. unlock
C. unfasten
D. unroll
E. unstring

18. The prefix *dis-* may mean (1) "opposite," as in *dishonest;* (2) "to take away," as in *dispossess;* (3) "away" or "apart from," as in *dismiss*. In which one of these words does the prefix *dis-* mean "to take away"?

A. disagreeable
B. discourage
C. displeased
D. disappear
E. disband

19. "Houdini could not make the big-time theaters in the cities." The words *make the big-time theaters* mean

A. force the big theaters to give him a job
B. succeed in getting his act into the most popular theaters
C. appear in theaters where audiences were small
D. build theaters
E. get the right to put on a long show

20. "All the agencies here grab imported talent." This means that the American agents who place acts in theaters

A. preferred American acts to foreign acts
B. did not like foreign acts
C. preferred acts that came from Europe
D. liked actors brought in from little towns
E. wanted to send American actors to Europe

Follow the directions (Steps 8–13) on page 1 of the progress folder.

How you can continue to improve your reading

For several weeks you have been working with this book as a guide. Your teacher and your classmates have helped you. What happens next? What happens when you do not have this book at hand?

During these past few weeks you have certainly learned more about reading than you knew before. You have kept a record of your progress in understanding what you read, in developing your vocabulary, and in improving your reading rate. What does the record show? Are you pleased with the gains you have made? Do you feel that you might have done better?

If you have made a substantial gain, you should feel encouraged to keep on trying to improve. Even if your gains have not been very great, you have taken steps toward making them greater.

That is really the point of this lesson. You are finishing this book, but you have just begun to improve your reading. You can continue to make progress on your own. The gains you make from here on will be up to you. In this lesson you will find suggestions as to what you can do to make yourself a better reader.

Do you want to improve your reading?

If you want to improve, you can do so, and you will find this last lesson helpful. But you must be honest with yourself about reading improvement. If you are satisfied to go along with your present reading level, it would be a waste of time for you to carry out the suggestions in this lesson. It would be a waste of time because if you don't really want to improve, you won't improve.

In Lesson 2 you made a list of reasons for reading better. Here is the list that was suggested by this author:

Better reading will help you—

- To become a more interesting person.
- To do better schoolwork and do it more easily.
- To get ready for more training and education in high school and after.
- To get and hold a more interesting and better-paying job.
- To prepare for military service.
- To become a better-informed citizen.
- To lead a fuller and happier life.

How do these reasons strike you now? It might be interesting for your class to talk them over again. Have you had any experience since you read Lesson 2 that supports these ideas?

Let's face a few facts

How did you like the selections in the reading exercises? Most students find them very interesting. They would like to read the books from which the selections were taken. Or they would like to read more stories by the same writers. Would you?

There is something you should know about these selections. All but three or four of them were adapted—that is, the original story or article was shortened or simplified for this book. There is a valid reason for this. Reading experts are agreed that materials used for practice exercises should be reasonably easy for the students who use them.

But suppose now that you go to the magazines and books from which these selections were taken. Will you be able to read what you find there?

If your progress record shows that you have made good gains during the past few weeks, you will have no trouble. Immediately following this lesson is a list of books that you will enjoy reading.

You can see the point. You can't go on reading shortened, simplified selections all the rest of your life. To begin with, there are not many available. To enjoy the really exciting books and magazines that are published every year, you will have to continue to improve your reading ability. If you do this, you will find more and more publications that you can read with ease and pleasure. You will get more and more satisfaction out of reading the daily newspaper. You will find many, many books to enjoy. You will find books to satisfy every mood and to gratify your interests. These books will be of various kinds: short stories, biographies, books on travel, plays, poetry, and so forth.

Let's face a few job facts

There is no place in American life for "the idle rich" or for the idle poor either. The American tradition is that every able-bodied person works at something until he reaches retirement age. The number of married women who hold jobs has steadily increased over the past fifty years. No matter who you are, you are likely to find yourself in a job sooner or later.

It is true that some people take a job—any job—just to be doing something. It doesn't matter much to them how well they do their work or how well they are paid. But the great majority of people want to do their job so that they will win promotions and better pay.

Employment studies show clearly that the ability to read is an important factor in job success. The number of jobs in which reading ability is not important is growing smaller every year. You can improve your chances of job success by sharpening your reading skills.

Perhaps you are thinking that you will get a civil service job or enter a trade such as plumbing. You may suppose that on such jobs reading skill is not important. Nothing could be further from the truth.

To get a civil service job, you have to pass an examination with a high score. To become a plumber, you must have a license. To get a license, you must pass an examination. To pass the examinations, you

have to be able to read reasonably well. And if you have read widely, your chances of making a high score are very good.

Exercise 65

Here are three questions of the kind you would meet on a civil service examination. How well can you do them?

For each question several answers are given. Only one is correct. Write the letter that stands before the correct answer.

1. (from a test for firemen). Hose lines should not be charged with water until brought to the point from which they will operate. Of the following, the chief justification for this rule is that
   A. in many cases water will spread a fire rather than extinguish it
   B. pump operators should usually be told the precise location of the fire in the building
   C. fire hose usually varies in length and diameter
   D. running water weighs less than standing water
   E. a charged hose line weighs more than an uncharged hose line

2. (from a test for a plumber's helper). In a building water system which operates at a pressure of 40 pounds per square inch, it is desired to convert this pressure to read in feet of water. This is done by
   A. multiplying 40 by 0.43
   B. multiplying 40 by 2.30
   C. dividing 40 by 2.30
   D. multiplying 40 by 1.13

3. (from a test for a police patrolman). A statute of limitations
   A. limits the time within which a criminal prosecution or civil action must be commenced
   B. prohibits a second prosecution for a crime for which a person has once been tried
   C. regulates the descent and distribution of the property of a person dying intestate
   D. limits the sentence that may be imposed upon conviction for a particular crime

There is another point to consider. The number of jobs for unskilled workers is fast decreasing. The number of professional, clerical, and sales jobs is increasing. Jobs are hard to get unless you have the skills that an employer needs. One of those skills is the ability to read fast and accurately.

Your improvement is up to you

You will remember that in Lesson 3 you learned why reading is an active process. You learned two things in particular. First, just saying the words on a page is not reading. Second, the reader has to try to find out the writer's meaning.

As you go on to higher grades in school, your textbooks will become more difficult. You will meet more and more unfamiliar words and abstract ideas. You will have to work harder to discover what they mean—much harder than you had to work with the reading selections in this book.

Just to keep up with your regular work, you will have to improve your reading ability. How much you really do improve it will depend on how much thought you give to it.

People learn how to do something by doing it properly. You learn to swim by swimming. You learn to read and to read better by using certain reading methods. You can learn to read better by thinking about what you are doing—and by trying to do it better.

In general, the more you read, the better you will read. But don't depend on wide reading alone to make you a more efficient reader. The rest of this lesson will suggest positive steps you can take.

Step 1. Check up on your eyesight and hearing

If you have trouble seeing print on a page, or if your eyes tire easily, you should have your eyes examined. You might need glasses. Persons with visual difficulties usually do not read much.

You are the one who knows how well your eyes seem to do their job. But you do not know whether you need glasses. Only a doctor can tell you. Have your eyes checked regularly.

If you need glasses, get them and wear them. Some boys have the foolish notion that wearing glasses is a sign of weakness. These boys ought to read something about the professional baseball and football players who wear glasses while they are playing.

Some girls object to wearing glasses because they think glasses spoil their appearance. Glasses may not be romantic, but neither is there anything romantic about headaches and poor school grades. Some girls actually appear to be more attractive with glasses, particularly when the glasses are carefully chosen. If you need glasses when you read, wear them. Don't try to be someone you are not. Contact lenses have been perfected so that most people can wear them. They may seem expensive, but they do not have frames to be replaced and the lenses are unbreakable. The prescription does not have to be changed frequently.

You may wonder what hearing has to do with reading. If you are hard of hearing, you may have difficulty hearing the sounds of words. If you do not know how a word sounds, you may have difficulty getting its meaning.

If you have trouble hearing what is said in class, see your doctor. He will be able to advise you.

Step 2. Adopt a positive attitude toward reading

Reading is not a punishment: it is an opportunity. If you are assigned reading to do outside of class, it is not because your teachers are trying to punish you. The most amazing information, the most thrilling discoveries, the most exciting adventures are recorded in print. They are yours for the asking.

Have you ever heard someone say, "I read myself to sleep at night"? Of course, some good readers do read just before they go to sleep, but what they read is usually light fiction or a mystery story. Most reading should not be regarded as a sleeping pill. From what you know about reading—it is an active process—you know that good reading will keep you awake. Don't let yourself get into the habit of giving only half your attention to reading. If you do develop this habit, it will be harder for you to read actively when you need to. If you can't stay awake and participate in what you are reading, put the book aside.

Nothing else you have learned in this book is more important than this: good reading requires concentration.

There is no easy road to learning how to concentrate. It is a skill you can develop only by hard practice. But the effort is worthwhile, because by concentrating you can greatly reduce the amount of time your studying requires.

Your reading skills are like a set of mechanic's tools. If you have ever watched a good mechanic work, you know what good care he takes of his tools. The cutting edges are kept sharp; the surfaces are free of rust. Your reading skills are among the best tools you have. Take good care of them.

Step 3. Provide the best reading conditions you can get

When you read, you should have enough light to see the print without straining. If there is not enough light, your eye muscles have to work harder. Too much light is just as bad as too little. Have you ever tried to read a book in the bright sunlight? If you have, you know that the glare of the light on the page tires your eyes. If you tire your eyes needlessly, you cannot give enough of your energy and attention to what you are reading. Day or night, try to get indirect light on your reading, and seat yourself so that your shadow does not fall across the page.

Step 4. Make your own practice exercises

More and more high schools are giving their students courses in reading. If your high school is one of these, you are fortunate. If it is not, there are many things you can do to keep your reading skills in shape.

It takes practice to keep any skill in top form. At the height of her career, Babe Didrickson Zaharias, the great athlete, used to practice regularly. She would stand on the practice tee working at her golf shots until her hands were bleeding. Reading skills—if they are to be developed—need constant practice. You can have fun if you try to build your own exercises.

Practice reading several word groups together. Pick up a book or magazine and try the first sentences in the chapters or articles. Your object in this practice is not to see how fast you can read. Your object is to see how much you can take in at once —how far you can read without having to stop and retrace what you have read.

You will be trying to increase your span of attention. You will be reading in thought units, for that is what word groups are. You will avoid stopping in the middle of a word group, because such a stop will break the writer's thought and your own.

The first step in this practice is to get a feeling for word groups. You do not have to be an expert in grammar to do this, although a knowledge of grammar will help you. Suppose, for example, that you saw this beginning sentence: "Perhaps because he lives in a fantastic world where pigs can talk and rocks can walk, Walt Disney has come to believe that nothing is impossible."

In the early stages of practice you might begin by dividing the sentence into word groups like this: Perhaps—because he lives—in a fantastic world—where—pigs can talk—and rocks can walk—Walt Disney—has—come to believe—that nothing— is impossible.

At a later stage in your development you would combine word groups something like this: Perhaps because he lives in a fantastic world—where pigs can talk and rocks can walk—Walt Disney has come to believe—that nothing is impossible.

The ability to group words in this way will give you greater pleasure, more understanding, and a faster pace. The good thing about this kind of practice is that you need no special equipment. You can use any book or magazine.

Practice to get the writer's main ideas. In Lesson 5 you learned that getting main ideas will help you organize and remember what you have read. You do not really understand a piece of writing unless you get the writer's main points.

You can practice this skill every day. Make a habit of stopping after every paragraph or two and asking yourself, "What was this about?"

Practice reading to remember details. You can do this every day with your newspaper. Try it with a half-page advertisement. Give yourself thirty seconds to look over the ad. Then write down as many details—prices, styles, articles—as you can remember.

Perhaps you can talk one of your friends or someone in your family into a memory-of-details contest.

But keep this in mind: practicing with newspaper ads will do you no good unless you use the same skill with regular reading material. Try it with a paragraph from your science or social studies book. If you work at this skill steadily, you will get into the habit of noticing details.

Step 5. Think about your reading

On the whole, if a book, story, or magazine article is worth reading at all, it is worth thinking about. But was it really worth reading? Making a judgment like this is in itself thinking. Your judgment may not agree with that of many other readers, but you are entitled to your opinion—provided you can back it up.

If you dislike something you have read, there must be a reason for your dislike. If you can state your reason, your friends and teachers will respect your judgment.

What kinds of faults might you find with something you have read? You might say that—

- The characters in the story did not act like real people.
- The writer gave only his own opinion without backing it up with facts.
- The writer did not make his points clear.
- The sentences are too long and involved to follow.

If you liked what you read, perhaps you liked it for the opposite of these reasons.

There are many good ways to think about your reading. Here are two that you can put to use at once:

1. Ask yourself questions about what you have read. Why did the writer make this statement or that? What were the reasons for things turning out as they did? Did the author prove his points? How did the author feel about what he was writing?

What was his purpose—to amuse the reader, to persuade him, or to give him information?

2. Relate what you read to your own experience. Does the article explain something that has happened to you? Do you remember something that you have read before on the same subject? Can you think of a friend who would enjoy reading the same story or article?

Step 6. Become a versatile reader

A person who is versatile can turn easily from one thing to another. A versatile reader is one who can read many different kinds of materials—comics, science, history, newspaper stories, thoughtful articles about human affairs, and good novels.

Do you know how much time you spend now on just one kind of reading? Many people give this question no thought at all. They go on from month to month reading the same kind of thing. For the next month, keep a record of everything you read. It will surprise you. Perhaps you will then start a permanent record of your reading just to make sure that your reading diet is varied.

A versatile reader also knows how to vary the rate at which he reads to suit the kind of material he is reading.

Step 7. Read to answer questions

You will always read better if you know why you are reading—if you know what you are looking for. It may be that you have picked up a story just for entertainment. Your purpose in this kind of reading is very clear.

But for other reading, your purpose may not be clear at all as you begin the first sentence. Suppose that you are turning over the pages of a magazine. A dramatic picture catches your eye. Or an interesting title arouses your curiosity—"Diamonds in the Junk Pile," or "The Man Who Won the War," for example.

Stop a moment before you start reading. Begin with the title. What does it promise you as a reader? What kind of junk piles are diamonds found in? How did they get there? What kind of diamonds?

If you begin your reading with questions, you will get more pleasure and profit out of it.

In your school studies, reading to answer questions will fix what you read more firmly in your mind. Some of your textbooks raise the questions for you.

Pick a partner from your family or friends and start a contest. Read a paragraph in advance. Pick out some detail. Build a question around it. Give your partner a time limit and make him find the answer with only one reading.

Try this yourself. Here is a question, which is answered in the paragraph below it. Give yourself one minute to find the answer.

Exercise 66

Question: How did the Indians save some of the early pioneer settlements?

The first settlers in the American colonies had to deal with many Indian tribes. Some were simply small bands of hunters who seized every chance to pillage and steal. Other tribes were organized into settled communities of fishermen, hunters, and farmers. Such tribes offered peace and friendship to the white man. Many settlements would have starved if it had not been for food brought to them by friendly Indians. Roger Williams in Rhode Island and William Penn, who founded Pennsylvania, made treaties with the Indians. They paid for their land and kept the white man from cheating the Indians. These territories were relatively free from Indian uprisings for a long time. Dishonest traders and broken treaties soon caused the Indians to mistrust all white men.

The answer is shown in the answer key.

Step 8. Keep up your interest in words

You cannot build an instant vocabulary. Experiments show that memorizing lists of words and meanings is perhaps not the best way to build a vocabulary. A more effective way is to learn words as you meet them in your reading.

You cannot be expected to make a study of every new word you meet. But if you meet the same new word several times in a short period, you will do well to master it.

Try to figure out the meaning from the words with which it is used. Look it over for prefixes and suffixes that may give clues to meaning. Look for a base word within the new word that is familiar to you. Go to the dictionary to check the meaning you think the word has. Note carefully the different meanings that are listed.

Write the word down. Say it aloud. Then use it in conversation with your friends. Before long the word will be yours.

At the start of your work with this book you measured your reading ability by answering questions on a checklist. Since then you have spent several weeks studying how to improve your reading. What progress have you made? It is time to go over that checklist again.

Write your answers to these questions:

1. Do you read as well as you would like to?
2. Do you need to read better to do better schoolwork?
3. Do you read books often?
4. Do you use the public library?
5. Are you in the habit of reading newspapers and magazines regularly?
6. Do you remember well what you read?
7. Do you think about what you are reading?
8. Do you get the main ideas from stories when you read them rapidly?
9. Do you get the important details when you are reading in fields such as science?
10. Do you understand and follow directions quickly and accurately?
11. Do you understand pictures, maps, and graphs?
12. Can you read aloud with accuracy, clearness, and ease?
13. Can you figure out the meanings of new words when you meet them in your reading?
14. Do you know how to use a variety of books when you are studying?
15. Do you know the best sources of information?

16. Do you appreciate good writing?
17. Do you enjoy reading so much that you sometimes read just for fun?
18. Do you ever read to understand and improve yourself?
19. Do you read to become a good citizen?
20. Have you honestly tried to improve your reading?

Now ask your teacher to return the answers you gave to these questions when you started this course. Which answers are different? To which questions do you still answer "no"? These are the aspects of reading for you to work on in the future.

Remember this: improvement depends on reading. Develop the habit of reading. There will be many rewards for this. In the words of Bennett Cerf:

"Reading is like eating peanuts: once you begin, you tend to go on and on. Every book stands by itself, like a one-family house, but books are like houses in a city. Although they are separate, together they all add up to something; they are connected with each other and with other cities. . . . Books influence each other; they link the past and the present and the future and have their own generations, like families. Whenever you start reading you connect yourself with one of the families of ideas, and, in the long run, you not only find out about the world and the people in it; you find out about yourself, too."[1]

1 "The Pleasure of Reading," in *The Wonderful World of Books* (edited by Alfred Stefferud), p. 25. A Mentor Book published by The New American Library, 1953. Reprinted with permission of the publisher and the author.

Practice Reading 15

In a book, magazine, or newspaper that you like, practice reading for speed and comprehension. Make a record of the reading in Chart 3 on page 8 of the progress folder.

The next selection—"How Long Is Life?"—is a fascinating article. When you have finished it, you should go on to read the last three selections. You will find them exciting, interesting, and informative.

15
article

How long is life?[2]

by Paull M. Giddings

A Dane born in the seventeenth century, a man named Christen Jacobsen Drakenberg, married when he was 111. Though his wife was little more than half his age, he outlived her by almost three decades. He finally died in 1772—at the age of 145.

Drakenberg is only one of many men whose lives have lasted well over a century. Yet at the other extreme of human lifespan are countless children who are born, live a few minutes or hours, and die.

Human differences, accidents, and illness will probably always make it impossible to predict accurately how long a single individual will live. Yet today we know more about lifespan than ever before. We can make highly accurate predictions about the lifespans of classes of people within a large group. These predictions are summed up in mortality tables.

A mortality table could theoretically be designed to show what effect any human characteristic has on length of life. In practice, though, most mortality tables are based on the single factor that has the greatest effect: age.

One representative mortality table lists all ages from 0—the first year of life—to 99. Assuming 1000 persons of each age, the table shows how many can be expected to die within one year of reaching that birthday, as well as the number of years the typical member of each age group can be expected to live.

Consider 1000 persons aged 35, for example. This table shows that 2.51 members of the group can be expected to die before another year is out. But the typical 35-year-old will live another 36.69 years. Put another way, half the group of 35-year-olds will die within the next 36.69 years; the other half will live longer.

The figures in this example are from a new mortality table based on the records of many life insurance companies. Called the Commissioners 1958 Standard Ordinary Table, it was approved in 1962 for use in life insurance computations in all states.

This table is based on records of life insurance policyholders, who are selected to screen out the most serious health and other hazards to normal lifespan. As a group, then, policyholders are undoubtedly longer-lived than the general public. But figures in this table can nevertheless be applied to the general public, because a special safety factor is built into all mortality tables used for life insurance computations. The safety factor, required by law, assures that insurance companies will always be able to meet their obligations, even if the death rate should climb unexpectedly.

Construction of the new mortality table was a triumph of the computer age. The compilers of the table fed hundreds of thousands of figures into modern electronic data-processing equipment. Within three months the basic table took shape. The same job would have taken two years to complete using the now outmoded method of punching figures into desk calculators.

The new table shows clearly that

---

2 Courtesy of Paull M. Giddings, Institute of Life Insurance.

people are living longer, on the average, than they used to. The basic mortality table used previously, the Commissioners 1941 Standard Ordinary, showed that a newborn baby's life expectancy was about 62 years. The new table shows an expectancy at birth of about 68 years. In fact, the increase in human lifespan during the two decades before the preparation of the new table was greater than in the previous half century.

But while average lifespan is lengthening, not all ages are benefiting equally. The new mortality table, compared with the one it replaces, shows that by far the greatest increase in life expectancy is in the youngest part of the population. The death rate among infants in the first year of life, for instance, dropped by about two-thirds in less than twenty years. But there has been no great increase in the number of people now living to extreme old age. Instead, the new table indicates that many more babies and children can now be expected to live out the biblical standard of a lifetime: threescore years and ten.

Many people expected life insurance rates to drop with the adoption of a new mortality table. The fact is, though, that the new table has no direct effect at all on premium rates. The basic table is used in such technical calculations as determining policy cash values and the amount of assets companies are legally required to hold in reserve to back policy guarantees.

How are life insurance rates set, then? In contrast to the way the new mortality table was developed—by the cooperative effort of many insurance companies—premium rates are set competitively by the nearly fifteen hundred companies. They base premiums on experience with their own policyholders, and adjust the rates frequently to reflect changes.

The method of adjusting rates depends on the type of company. Mutual companies, owned by their policyholders, charge enough to cover the highest foreseeable death rate among policyholders. Part of the premium is returned as a dividend after the company has analyzed its experience. Stock companies, owned by investors, sometimes pay dividends too. More often, though, they set lower "net" premiums aligned with their most recent experience.

Mortality figures are not limited to the "standard risk" — the typical life insurance policyholder. Figures are also compiled for special groups of people, such as those with selected physical defects or diseases. Life insurance companies use these figures to judge the extra risks of insuring people with a wide range of health impairments. Some five million persons who now own life insurance would have been uninsurable for medical reasons a generation ago. Most of them pay a higher premium for their insurance, the amount of the additional premium depending on the extra risk.

Special mortality figures are also compiled on many occupations. Some jobs carry so much risk that applicants for new insurance must be charged an additional premium as long as they hold these jobs. Until a few years ago, many occupations were totally uninsurable. Now only one—civilian test pilot of jet aircraft—is generally uninsurable. And some insurers report they have offered extra-rate coverage even to a few members of this last "uninsurable" group. A key factor in the extension of life insurance coverage to people in risky jobs has been the increasing refinement of occupational mortality figures.

Life insurance companies have so increased their knowledge of mortality among high-risk groups that today only a tiny minority of insurance applications are turned down. About three out of every hundred applicants are now refused insurance for reasons of health, occupation, habits, or family medical history. Two generations ago the rejection rate was between three and four times as high.

While life insurance is the best-known application of mortality tables, it is far from the only one. The planner in both government and industry must have accurate mortality projections. How much housing for the elderly will be needed in 1980? Mortality tables can help give the answer. Physicians and public health officials use mortality figures in their planning and in allocating research funds. Any industry whose product is used chiefly by a single age group, as bubble gum or wheelchairs are, will want to know the size of the potential market in years to come.

Compilers of mortality tables are confirmed trend-watchers. They have seen average life expectancy grow steadily longer owing to medical and social advances in this country. The death rate among young adults is now so low that more than half of all deaths are due to accident. And the death rate among infants and young children, already slashed, continues to drift lower.

The next major improvement in life expectancy will almost certainly come with the control or conquest of the diseases of old age. The leading causes of death at ages over 60, apart from accident, are circulatory and coronary diseases and cancer.

A medical breakthrough in any of these areas could bring a considerable increase in the length of life.

On the other hand, it is possible that if each of these major causes of death were controlled, the death rate might not be significantly decreased. In the past, whenever one disease of old age has been controlled, another has replaced it as a cause of death.

What we do know certainly is this: anyone alive today has a greater chance of living out a full life than ever before in human history.

Record your finishing time record for selection 15. Then take the reading test. Read each test item and choose the best answer. Print your answers on page 7 of the progress folder.

Reading Test 15

Getting main ideas

1. This article deals mainly with
   A. the insurance rates you pay
   B. measuring life expectancy
   C. the life expectancy of infants
   D. the insurability of test pilots
   E. modern computer systems

2. Most mortality tables are based on one factor:
   A. type of job
   B. birthplace
   C. accident
   D. age
   E. the birthrate

3. The new mortality table is used to determine a company's
   A. charges for insurance
   B. investment policy
   C. ability to expand
   D. required cash reserve
   E. net cash value

4. The greatest increase in life expectancy is for
   A. older persons
   B. infants
   C. test pilots
   D. the physically handicapped
   E. young adults

Remembering details

5. Christen Drakenberg died at the age of 145, in the year

A. 1672
B. 1782
C. 1872
D. 1882
E. 1772

6. Comparing the 1941 table with the 1958 table, we find that a baby's life expectancy has changed from

A. 72 to 78 years
B. 52 to 68 years
C. 62 to 68 years
D. 62 to 78 years
E. 72 to 68 years

7. The biblical standard of a lifetime is

A. threescore years and ten
B. fourscore years and seven
C. threescore years and seven
D. fourscore years and ten
E. threescore years and eleven

8. Christen Drakenberg lived in

A. Corsica
B. Finland
C. Germany
D. Sweden
E. Denmark

9. Insurance companies that are owned by their policyholders are called

A. mutual companies
B. asset companies
C. investment companies
D. stock companies
E. rate companies

10. That part of the premium payment which is returned by the company is called a

A. derelict
B. dividend
C. deduction
D. divisor
E. declaration

Choosing the best reason

11. Insurance policyholders are longer-lived than the general public because

A. they are more careful
B. they live healthier lives
C. the company watches them
D. they are carefully screened by the company
E. their rates are lower

12. People with health impairments pay higher premiums for their insurance because

A. the company loses money on them
B. of the extra paperwork required
C. of the extra risk to the company
D. they require special attention
E. they sometimes have difficulty finding employment

13. It is impossible to predict how long a single individual will live because of

A. variations in temperature
B. differences in education
C. various human differences, accidents, and illness
D. mathematical errors in the tables
E. his occupation

Reading with a keen eye

14. The job of assembling the new mortality tables took only

A. three months
B. four months
C. three weeks
D. one year
E. five weeks

15. The number of persons owning life insurance today who could not have been insured a generation ago is

A. 3 million
B. 5 thousand
C. 6 million
D. 4 million
E. 5 million

Understanding words

16. The figuring of mortality rates from a table is called a

A. consultation
B. conformation
C. combination
D. computation
E. differentiation

17. A person living for only three decades would die at the age of

A. 45
B. 60
C. 30
D. 9
E. 27

18. An element that affects the result is called a

A. factor
B. factory
C. fallacy
D. figure
E. fantasy

19. One who gathers information is called a

    A. conciliator
    B. computer
    C. companion
    D. confider
    E. compiler

20. As used in this article, the word *potential* means

    A. carrying ability
    B. future possibility
    C. high-ranking person
    D. camping out of doors
    E. an extra dividend

Follow the directions (Steps 8–13) on page 1 of the progress folder.

Record your starting time in the time record on page 7 of the progress folder. Then read the selection. Read as fast as you can, but make sure you understand what you are reading.

16
article

Mama finds a way [1]

by Kathryn Forbes

For as long as I could remember, the small cottage on Castro Street had been home. The familiar background was there: Mama, Papa, my only brother Nels. There was my sister Christine, closest to me in age, yet ever secret and withdrawn—and the littlest sister, Dagmar.

Mama had tried everything she knew of to stop Dagmar's earache. She'd warmed sweet oil and garlic, and used the medicine Mr. Schultz had sent from the drugstore, but nothing had helped.

When Dr. Johnson came, he told Mama that Dagmar must be taken to the hospital.

"At once," he said. "We will have to operate."

Mama's eyes grew dark with fright.

"Can wait?" she asked. "Until my husband comes home from work?"

"No time," the doctor said. "You must decide this morning. An immediate operation is her best chance."

Operation! Mama took a deep breath. "We go," she said, and took down the Little Bank and emptied its contents onto the kitchen table. Then she looked up at the doctor. "Is enough?" she asked hopefully.

The doctor looked uncomfortable. "I was thinking of the County Hospital," he explained.

"No," Mama said. "No. We pay."

"Well, then, take her to the Clinic Hospital."

"Clinic?"

"Yes. There you pay what you can afford," Dr. Johnson explained. "Your child will have the same care as the other patients."

Mama looked worried. "I—I do not understand so well."

"Just leave it to me, then. Dagmar will be well taken care of, I promise you. I myself will do the operation."

"Is so good of you," Mama said gratefully, and sent Nels for a blanket to wrap around Dagmar. And because Papa was at work, Nels and I went to the hospital with Mama.

When we got there, two nurses put Dagmar on a high table and started to wheel her down the hall. Mama tried to go along too.

"She is my little girl," Mama explained.

"Hospital rules," the nurse said firmly. "You must wait here."

Mama let go of Dagmar's hand then, and walked with slow steps to the desk. They gave her papers to sign, but she didn't even try to read them. Her eyes kept looking down the hall.

Nels and I had never been in a hospital before. With great interest we watched ladies in blue-and-white uniforms and important-looking men with little black bags hurry in and out of doors; watched the cleaning women as they took mops and buckets and long-handled brooms out of the closet by the elevator.

"Dr. Johnson is fine doctor," Mama said suddenly. "Surely Dagmar will be all right."

1 From *Mama's Bank Account*. Copyright, 1943, by Kathryn Forbes. Reprinted by permission of Harcourt, Brace & World, Inc.

I started to cry then, and Mama patted my shoulder and told stories of the old country. But Mama didn't tell the stories as usual; she kept forgetting parts of them.

When Dr. Johnson came hurrying down the hall, Mama stood up quickly.

"Dagmar came through it fine," he told us. "She is sleeping now, from the anesthetic."

Mama smiled tremulously and shook hands twice with the doctor.

"I go to her now," she said happily.

Dr. Johnson coughed. "Sorry, against clinic rules. See her tomorrow."

"But she is so little," Mama said. "When she wakes, she will be frightened."

"The nurses will take excellent care of her. Don't worry. You see, for the first twenty-four hours, clinic patients are not allowed visitors. The wards must be kept quiet."

Mama didn't seem to understand. "I will not make a sound," she said.

Dr. Johnson lifted his hat politely, and hurried out of the hospital.

Mama looked worried. "Come," she said to Nels and to me. "We go find Dagmar."

The nurse at the desk had quite a time explaining rules to Mama.

"Your child is getting the best of care, madam," the lady kept repeating.

"Is fine hospital," Mama agreed. "I see her now?"

"No visitors for the first twenty-four hours, madam.

"Against—the—rules!" The nurse spoke loudly and slowly and with great finality.

Mama stood looking down the hall for such a long time that I had to touch her arm to remind her that Nels and I were still there.

She held my hand tightly as we walked to the streetcar and never said a word all the way home.

Christine had kept lunch hot for us, but Mama just drank two cups of coffee. She did not take off her hat.

"We must think of some way," she worried.

"They'll let you see Dagmar to-morrow," Nels reminded her.

"But unless I see her today," Mama asked, "how will I know that all is well with her? What can I tell Papa when he comes home from work?"

She shook her head. "No. Today I see Dagmar."

She stood up suddenly and took paper and string out of the kitchen drawer. Carefully, she wrapped Dagmar's little doll in one neat package and our big picture book in another. We watched uneasily.

"It will be like this," Mama explained. "I will go past the hospital desk very quickly. If anyone asks where I go, I will just say, 'Delivering packages to Dagmar.'"

When Mama came back—still carrying the packages—we knew she'd been unsuccessful. We knew, too, that she was upset, because she answered us in Norwegian.

"Almost," she said wearily, "almost did I get down the hall."

Then she tied the big apron around her waist, filled the bucket with hot soapy water, and started to scrub the kitchen floor.

"You scrubbed yesterday," Christine reminded her.

"And the floor isn't a speck dirty," I said.

"It's almost time to get dinner," Nels protested.

"Comes a time," Mama answered strangely, "when you must get down on your knees."

And the whiteness of her face made me want to cry again.

Mama had scrubbed all but the part near the back door when she stood up suddenly and handed the scrub brush to Christine.

"You finish the floor. Katrin, you come with me." And she sent me for my coat.

"Come where, Mama?"

"To the hospital." Her face was serene. "I have thought of way to see Dagmar sure."

We walked in so quietly that the nurse at the desk didn't even look up. Mama motioned for me to sit in the big chair by the door. While I watched—Mama took off her hat and coat and gave them to me to hold. Only then did I notice that she'd kept her apron on. She tiptoed over to the big closet by the elevator and took out a damp mop. She pushed the mop past the desk, and as the nurse looked up, Mama nodded brightly.

"Very dirty floors," Mama said.

"Yes, I'm glad they've finally decided to clean them," the nurse answered. She looked at Mama curiously. "Aren't you working late?"

Mama just pushed more vigorously, each swipe of the mop taking her farther and farther down the hall. I watched until she was out of sight and the nurse had turned back to writing in the big book. Then I saw that I had held Mama's hat so tightly, one side was all out of shape.

After a long time, Mama came back. Her eyes were shining.

While the nurse stared with amazement, Mama placed the mop neatly back in the closet, put on her hat and coat, and took my hand. As we turned to go out the door, Mama bowed politely to the nurse and said, "Thank you."

Outside, Mama told me: "Dagmar is fine. No fever; I felt her forehead."

"You saw her, Mama?"

"Of course. She wakened while I was with her. I told her about clinic rules; she will not expect us until tomorrow."

"You won't try to see her again," I asked, "before then?"

"Why," Mama said, "that would be against the rules. Besides, I have seen for myself that all goes well with her. Papa will not worry now."

I swallowed hard.

"Is a fine hospital," Mama said happily. Then she clicked her tongue disapprovingly. "But such floors! A mop is never good. Floors should be scrubbed with a brush."

Record your finishing time in the time box. Then take the reading test.

Read each test item and choose the best answer. Print your answers in the answer record on page 7 of the progress folder.

Reading Test 16

Getting main ideas

1. Which of the following sentences best explains the story?

    A. Doctors never make mistakes.
    B. Hospital rules are unfair.
    C. Hospital floors should always be clean.
    D. An operation is not dangerous.
    E. Mother love will find a way.

---

2. The author wrote this story to

    A. puzzle you
    B. amuse you
    C. frighten you
    D. surprise you
    E. inform you

---

3. This story is a

    A. true story
    B. fairy story
    C. ghost story
    D. nature story
    E. mystery story

Remembering key facts

4. Dagmar was sick with

    A. a cold
    B. a headache
    C. an earache
    D. a broken arm
    E. a toothache

5. Mama tried to see Dagmar the first time by

    A. sneaking in the back door
    B. making believe she was a nurse
    C. delivering packages to her
    D. making believe she was a doctor
    E. taking Dagmar a mop and pail

6. Mama could not get in to see Dagmar because

    A. there was a nurse in the hall
    B. Mama didn't know where she was
    C. the hospital door was locked
    D. the door was locked
    E. Dagmar was too sick

Choosing the best reason

7. Mama wanted to see Dagmar because

    A. Dagmar might have been frightened
    B. Dagmar might have been very sick
    C. she had told Dagmar that she would
    D. she thought the doctor was not good
    E. she had told Papa that she would

8. Dagmar went to the Clinic Hospital because

    A. it was free
    B. it was so costly
    C. Mama wanted to pay something
    D. it was nearby
    E. the doctor wanted her to

9. Mama scrubbed the kitchen floor again because

    A. the floor was dirty
    B. it was time for dinner
    C. she wanted the children to be busy
    D. she liked housework
    E. she wanted time to think

10. Mama got in to see Dagmar by making believe she was

    A. Dagmar's sister
    B. a nurse
    C. a doctor
    D. a cleaning woman
    E. Dagmar's aunt

Reading between the lines

11. Mama forgot parts of the stories she told in the hospital because

    A. the stories were too long
    B. she was worried
    C. she was making up stories
    D. she had told too many stories
    E. she did not know the stories well

12. When Mama emptied the Little Bank, there was

A. not enough money
B. too much money
C. only one dollar
D. enough money
E. no money

Understanding descriptive expressions

13. When Mama's eyes grew dark with fright, she was

A. happy
B. amused
C. lonely
D. scared
E. tired

14. The ladies in blue-and-white uniforms were

A. lady doctors
B. cleaning women
C. visitors
D. patients
E. nurses

15. Mama said that sometimes you have to get down on your knees. She meant that

A. the floor should be scrubbed by hand
B. everyone should learn how to scrub floors
C. the floor mop was no good
D. sometimes people have to pray
E. sometimes people need exercise

16. Mama told stories about the old country. She meant

A. the United States
B. Africa
C. Canada
D. Mexico
E. Norway

17. When Mama was upset, she was

A. on her knees
B. upside down
C. worried
D. puzzled
E. happy

18. When Mama tiptoed to the door, she

A. crawled
B. walked quietly
C. skipped
D. ran
E. hopped

19. When Mama started to wash the floor, Christine said

A. "You flubbed yesterday."
B. "You scrubbed yesterday."
C. "You dubbed yesterday."
D. "You shrubbed yesterday."
E. "You slubbed yesterday."

20. Katrin crushed one side of Mama's hat all out of

A. drape
B. state
C. tape
D. shape
E. mate

Follow the directions (Steps 8–13) on page 1 of the progress folder.

17
article

Motivations of the space program [1]

by Dr. A. R. Hibbs

In telling you the reasons why man will go into space, let me tell you first some of the reasons which you might hear. Many of these have nothing to do with the matter. But still, these false reasons are often the subject of great debate. In many cases they are discussed at great length either to justify or to condemn some aspect of the space program. For example, one often hears that the purpose of manned space flights is to conduct scientific experiments which cannot be made by automatic instruments. Naturally, this arouses the interest of those who feel that instruments can do the job better. They point out that a large spacecraft would be needed. They add that much of the cabin would be used only to house the pilot. Given this extra space, they say, they could design instruments which would outperform any human being.

That's one side of the argument. On the other side is the fact that although such designs may be a future possibility, we are still a long way from that.

A typical project for such an instrument would be to land on the surface of Venus. It would then eject a small craft to explore the planet. This craft would wander over the surface collecting and analyzing samples of rock or anything else that it might find. It would then return to the landing vehicle and radio the results of its analysis back to Earth.

It is possible to design instrument systems that could do a job like that. We could carefully carry one to the Mojave Desert in the back of a truck and place it gently on the surface of the ground. It would then, without human help, make an analysis of the surface of the earth and report back its findings. And yet, our remote planetary craft must be taken on its journey, not in the back of a truck, but on the front end of a rocket. It will not be set down by gentle hands on the surface of Venus. Instead, it will arrive at Venus after coasting for several months through space to scream down through an atmosphere about which little is known. Its speed will be more than double that of an intercontinental ballistic missile (ICBM) warhead. If it completes a safe descent it may find itself on the side of a cliff, on the bottom of a ravine, or even in the middle of an ocean.

We have gone very far and made much progress in the field of automation. The problem of operating a remote mineral analyzer should be fairly simple. However, even the complex automatic instruments that we have today require the presence of a human being. Someone must at least watch for the telltale red light that will tell him to go in and fix the equipment. This might not be so easy to do if the human being is on Earth and the red light on Venus.

In spite of our progress, we are still a long, long way from the day when we will have a rocket able to carry a human being to Venus. It is very possible that by then we will have also solved the problems in the design of reliable automatic instruments.

[1] From "Motivations of the Space Program," by Dr. A. R. Hibbs, CEC Recordings, 1961.

Another reason is often brought up to prove the need for manned space flight. This is the ability of a man to make judgments and act on them. There might be many surprises for us in space! After all, automatic instruments can only do what they're told to do, or what the designer thinks they might have to do. To cope with the wholly unexpected, human judgment is required.

There are many who disagree with this. They point out that human beings are quite prone to make mistakes. In space a human being must gain his information through the use of instruments. His eyes and ears will be of little use to him. The information with which he must deal will be of a type outside his normal earthly experience. Thus, it is quite likely that he will misinterpret an event which is quite ordinary and expected in outer space. To him it might seem very odd or unusual. In this situation he may decide that it would be best to override the automatic controls. He would probably cause a disaster more times than he would avert one. In fact, there are some who say that there is only one real way to ensure the safety of a human passenger in space. That way is to keep him asleep until he returns safely to the ground. In this way he would have no power to interfere with the more reliable operation of his automatic equipment.

Another argument for manned space travel is the idea that a human being will be called upon to play the role of a pilot. He would guide his craft in maneuvers which could not be made by automatic equipment. As you might imagine, this philosophy has the greatest number of opponents. They point out that the role of the pilot is even disappearing from modern aircraft. For the modern jet fighter entering on a combat mission, it is the pilot who guides the plane during its takeoff from the field. As soon as the plane is in the air, the pilot turns over control of the aircraft to the automatic equipment. The robot pilot flies the plane toward its target and points its rocket weapons in the right direction. It then fires the rockets and performs the pullout maneuver. After guiding the craft back to the airport, it turns the controls back to the pilot. He makes the landing. However, landing and takeoff also could be done with automatic equipment. Rocket weapons certainly do not need an airplane to carry them into position. After all, they are perfectly capable of taking off under their own power. So we find that the Air Force is bringing to a close the role of the piloted combat plane.

In space, these problems would be much more complex. There would be less time to react to each maneuver or event. Each decision must be carefully made on the basis of instrument readings by complicated computing machinery. A pilot would really have very little to do.

There are many other arguments both for and against manned space flight. The ones I have described here are the most common. In reading my description of these arguments, you may have found yourself agreeing with one side or the other. In spite of which side you choose, I am sure that you can see in all of them the seeds of an almost endless argument. Now there is a curious fact that I would like to bring up. None of these discussions have anything to do with the real reasons which drive man to travel into space. They are little more than camouflage.

Man will be driven to explore the planets by the same urge which drove him across the unknown Atlantic. This same force drove the American colonists to explore the West. It is the same urge that took Marco Polo from Europe across Asia on the way to China. In more modern times the lure of the unknown has taken Admiral Byrd and Sir Edmund Hillary across the desolate wastes of Antarctica to the South Pole. Man will someday be able to reach the stars. This same urge will drive him on to other galaxies.

It is possible that negative opinions of a great part of the population could postpone manned space travel for a few years. Life began on Earth a billion years ago, and will be carried to the stars in a few million more. A few years one way or another at this stage of history is not important. So I am not trying to sell an idea, but merely to inform you of a fact. Regardless of whether you accept this fact, your descendants will reach the stars.

Record your finishing time in the time box. Then take the reading test. Read each test item and choose the best answer. Print your answers on page 7 of the progress folder.

Reading Test 17

Getting main ideas

1. The exploration of space will go on because of
   - A. man's urge to explore the unknown
   - B. man's fear of instruments
   - C. the population growth on the earth
   - D. the money it will cost
   - E. man's fear of starvation

2. The best method of controlling a spacecraft is
   - A. to use a pilot
   - B. through solar energy
   - C. from the Mojave Desert
   - D. yet to be decided
   - E. by automatic instruments

3. The article presented some opinions for and against
   - A. the Army and Air Force
   - B. the exploration of space
   - C. a landing on Venus
   - D. the development of spacecraft
   - E. two kinds of spacecraft control

Choosing the best reason

4. Manned spacecraft would waste
   - A. too much time
   - B. valuable cabin space
   - C. too much rocket fuel
   - D. time and money
   - E. instrument systems

5. After landing on Venus a craft could
   - A. easily take off again
   - B. attack anything it meets
   - C. collect samples of rock
   - D. radio for help
   - E. take pictures of the sun

6. To cope with the wholly unexpected,
   - A. better instruments are needed
   - B. larger instruments are needed
   - C. human judgment is required
   - D. more training is needed
   - E. faster rockets are needed

7. A space passenger might be safe if
   - A. he didn't try to steer
   - B. he landed in the ocean
   - C. the cabin were larger
   - D. more instruments were used
   - E. he were kept asleep

Remembering key facts

8. Admiral Byrd and Sir Edmund Hillary crossed the

    A. wastes of Asia
    B. Himalayan Mountains
    C. wastes of Antarctica
    D. Mojave Desert
    E. North Pole

9. Modern jet fighters are controlled and flown by

    A. pilots and FM radio
    B. pilots and automatic instruments
    C. engineers on the ground
    D. intercontinental stations
    E. solar energy

10. Life began on the earth

    A. a million years ago
    B. a billion years ago
    C. a century ago
    D. when two planets crashed
    E. a decade ago

11. The journey to Venus would take

    A. several weeks
    B. several months
    C. a few days
    D. more than two years
    E. two months

12. On arrival at Venus the speed of the spacecraft will be

    A. the same as that of an ICBM
    B. slowed down considerably
    C. double that of an ICBM
    D. double that of a jet fighter
    E. controlled from the earth

13. The complex automatic instruments we have today

    A. require the presence of a human being
    B. are all carried on trucks
    C. will survive a crash landing
    D. can repair themselves
    E. are very simple

Drawing conclusions

14. In the argument of piloted spacecraft versus instruments

    A. time is of the utmost importance
    B. foolish statements are always made
    C. there's only one right answer
    D. both sides may be right
    E. neither side is right

15. When it comes to exploring the unknown

    A. man has almost come to the end
    B. man will stop at the stars
    C. man will never be satisfied
    D. animals are more curious than man
    E. man has become discouraged

Knowing word meanings

16. "In spite of our progress . . ." *Spite*, as used here, means
    A. grudge
    B. annoyance
    C. except for
    D. speed
    E. regardless

17. ". . . the complex automatic instruments that we have today . . ." *Complex*, as used here, means
    A. complicated
    B. obsession
    C. complete
    D. exaggerated
    E. simple

18. ". . . prone to make mistakes." *Prone*, as used here, means
    A. able
    B. lying down
    C. dried raisin
    D. likely
    E. careful

19. ICBM stands for
    A. Inevitable Ballistic Missile
    B. Incompetent Ballistic Missile
    C. Intercontinental Balanced Missile
    D. Interplanetary Ballistic Missile
    E. Intercontinental Ballistic Missile

20. *Robot pilot* means
    A. senior pilot
    B. training instruments
    C. assistant pilot
    D. automatic instruments
    E. training pilot

Follow the directions (Steps 8–13) on page 1 of the progress folder.

18
article

Great-grandma[1]

by Ray Bradbury

She was a woman with a broom or a dustpan or a washrag or a mixing spoon in her hand. You saw her cutting piecrust in the morning, humming to it, or you saw her setting out the baked pies at noon or taking them in, cool, at dusk. She strolled but twice through any garden, trowel in hand, and the flowers raised their quivering fires upon the warm air in her wake. She slept quietly, as relaxed as a white glove to which, at dawn, a brisk hand will return. Waking, she touched people like pictures, to set their frames straight.

But now . . .?

"Grandma," said everyone. "Great-grandma."

Now it was as if a huge sum in arithmetic were finally drawing to an end. She had stuffed turkeys, chickens, squabs, gentlemen, and boys. She had washed ceilings, walls, invalids, and children. She had laid linoleum, repaired bicycles, wound clocks, stoked furnaces, swabbed iodine on ten thousand grievous wounds. Her hands had flown all around, about and down, gentling this, holding that, throwing baseballs, swinging bright croquet mallets, seeding black earth, or fixing covers over dumplings, ragouts, and children wildly strewn by slumber. She had pulled down shades, pinched out candles, turned switches, and—grown old. Looking back on thirty billions of things started, carried, finished and done, it all summed up; the last decimal was placed, the final zero swung slowly into line. Now, chalk in hand, she stood back from life a silent hour before reaching for the eraser.

With no further ado, she traveled the house in an ever-circling inventory, reached the stairs at last, and, making no special announcement, she took herself up three flights to her room where, silently, she laid herself out like a fossil imprint under the snowing cool sheets of her bed and began to die.

Again the voices:

"Grandma! Great-grandma!"

The rumor of what she was doing dropped down the stair well, hit, and spread ripples through the rooms, out doors and windows and along the street of elms to the edge of the green ravine.

"Here now, here!"

The family surrounded her bed.

"Just let me lie," she whispered.

"Great-grandma, now listen—what you're doing is no better than breaking a lease. This house will fall down without you. You must give us at least a year's notice!"

Great-grandma opened one eye. Ninety years gazed calmly out at her physicians like a dust-ghost from a high cupola window in a fast-emptying house. "Tom . . .?"

The boy was sent, alone, to her whispering bed.

"Tom," she said, faintly, "in the Southern Seas there's a day in each man's life when he knows it's time to shake hands with all his friends and say good-by and sail away, and he does, and it's natural—it's just his time. That's how it is today. I'm so like you sometimes, sitting through Saturday matinees until nine at night when we send your dad to bring you home. Tom, when the time comes that the same cowboys are shooting the same Indians on the same mountaintop, then it's best to fold back the seat and head for the door, with no regrets and no walking backward up the aisle. So, I'm leaving while I'm still happy and still entertained."

Douglas was summoned next to her side.

"Grandma, who'll shingle the roof next spring?"

Every April for as far back as there were calendars, you thought you heard woodpeckers tapping the housetop. But no, it was Great-grandma somehow transported, singing, pounding nails, replacing shingles, high in the sky!

"Douglas," she whispered, "don't ever let anyone do the shingles unless it's fun for them. Look around come April, and say, 'Who'd like to fix the roof?' And whichever face lights up is the face you want. Because up there on that roof you can see the whole town and the country and the edge of the earth and the river shining, and birds on the trees down under you. Any one of those should be enough to make a person climb a weather vane some spring sunrise. It's a powerful hour, if you give it half a chance. . . ."

Her voice sank to a soft flutter.

Douglas was crying.

She roused herself again. "Now, why are you doing that?"

"Because," he said, "you won't be here tomorrow."

He looked at her face as she said, "Tomorrow morning I'll get up at seven and wash behind my ears; I'll run to church with Charlie Woodman; I'll picnic at Electric Park; I'll swim, run barefoot, fall out of trees, chew spearmint gum . . . Douglas, Douglas, for shame! You cut your fingernails, don't you?"

"Yes'm."

"And you don't yell when your body makes itself over every seven years or so, old cells dead and new ones added to your fingers and your heart. You don't mind that, do you?"

"No'm."

"Well, consider then, boy. Any man saves fingernail clippings is a fool. You ever see a snake bother to keep his peeled skin? That's about all you got here today in this bed is fingernails and snakeskin. One good breath would send me up in flakes. Important thing is not the me that's lying here, but the me that's downstairs cooking supper, or out in the garage under the car, or in the library reading. I'll be around a long time. A thousand years from now a whole township of my offspring will be biting sour apples in the gumwood shade. That's my answer to anyone asks big questions! Quick now, send in the rest!"

At last the entire family stood, like people seeing someone off at the rail station, waiting in the room.

"Well," said Great-grandma, "there I am. I'm not humble, so it's nice seeing you standing around my bed. Now next week there's late gardening and closet-cleaning and clothes-buying for the children to do. And since that part of me which is called, for convenience, Great-grandma, won't be here to step it along, those other parts of me called Uncle Bert and Leo and Tom and Douglas, and all the other names, will have to take over, each to his own."

"Yes, Grandma."

"I don't want any Halloween parties here tomorrow. Don't want anyone saying anything sweet about me; I said it all in my time and my pride. I've tasted every victual and danced every dance; now there's one last tart I haven't bit on, one tune I haven't whistled. But I'm not afraid. I'm truly curious. Death won't get a crumb by my mouth I won't keep and savor. So don't you worry over me. Now, all of you go, and let me find my sleep. . . ."

Somewhere a door closed quietly.

"That's better." Alone, she snuggled luxuriously down through the warm snowbank of linen and wool, sheet and cover, and the colors of the patchwork quilt were bright as the circus banners of old time. Lying there, she felt as small and secret as on those mornings eighty-some-odd years ago when, wakening, she comforted her tender bones in bed.

A long time back, she thought, I dreamed a dream, and was enjoying it so much when someone wakened me, and that was the day when I was born. And now? Now, let me see . . . She cast her mind back. Where was I? she thought. Ninety years . . . how to take up the thread and the pattern of that lost dream again? She put out a small hand. *There* . . . Yes, that was it. She smiled. Deeper in the warm snow hill she turned her head upon her pillow. That was better. Now, yes, now she saw it shaping in her mind quietly, and with a serenity like a sea moving along an endless and self-refreshing shore. Now she let the old dream touch and lift her from the snow and drift her above the scarce-remembered bed.

Downstairs, she thought, they are polishing the silver, and rummaging the cellar, and dusting in the halls. She could hear them living all through the house.

"It's all right," whispered Great-grandma, as the dream floated her. "Like everything else in this life, it's fitting."

And the sea moved her back down the shore.

Record your finishing time in the time box. Then take the reading test. Read each test item and choose the best answer. Print your answers on page 7 of the progress folder.

Reading Test 18

Getting main ideas

1. The main point of the story is that Great-grandma is a happy, contented woman who

   A. keeps busy all the time
   B. loves shingling roofs
   C. is very old
   D. is a very good cook
   E. is not afraid to die

2. Great-grandma tries to tell the family that

   A. we all must die
   B. it's time to do late gardening
   C. she's left many children behind
   D. her death is not a tragedy
   E. she'll picnic in Electric Park

Choosing the best reason

3. Great-grandma reminds Tom about his Saturday matinees so that

   A. he won't stay too long next time
   B. he'll think about her
   C. he'll understand it's time for her to go
   D. he'll remember the fun he had
   E. he'll remember to come home

4. Shingling roofs should be done only by

   A. someone who can climb the roof
   B. an experienced shingler
   C. Tom
   D. Douglas
   E. someone who thinks it's fun

5. Great-grandma went quietly to her room because

   A. she didn't want any fuss made over her
   B. she was too tired to talk
   C. she had checked everything in the house
   D. she was feeling very sick
   E. everybody was busy

6. ". . . that part of me which is called,
   for convenience, Great-grandma, won't
   be here." She means that

   A. they should forget her
   B. names don't mean anything
   C. she'll change her name
   D. they shouldn't call her again
   E. Uncle Bert will be boss

7. ". . . those other parts of me called
   Uncle Bert, and Leo and Tom and
   Douglas . . ." She means that

   A. she will live through her children
   B. her children are separated
   C. they must help one another
   D. she has many children
   E. the family is very large

Remembering key facts

8. Great-grandma would shingle the roof
   every

   A. May
   B. July
   C. June
   D. September
   E. April

9. Snakes, after peeling off their skin,

   A. leave it behind
   B. bury it in sand
   C. become very sunburned
   D. change their color
   E. dry up and die

10. Great-grandma called the mourning
    period after death

    A. a vacation party
    B. a Halloween party
    C. a celebration party
    D. a good time to work
    E. an anniversary

11. When Tom went to Saturday mat-
    inees, he would stay until

    A. he got hungry
    B. the show ended
    C. his father came for him
    D. the cowboys beat the Indians
    E. his grandma came for him

12. Great-grandma's age is given in the
    story. It is

    A. ninety years
    B. eighty years
    C. one hundred years
    D. seventy-nine years
    E. ninety-five years

Recognizing the right word

13. When Great-grandma was finally
    alone, she

    A. shuffled up the stairs
    B. scuffled her way upstairs
    C. struggled down into bed
    D. snuggled down in the bed
    E. struggled up to bed

14. To extinguish candles, Grandma used to

    A. call someone
    B. puff on them
    C. punch them
    D. pinch them
    E. drop them

Knowing word meanings

15. A trowel is a

    A. long journey
    B. gopher hole
    C. drying cloth
    D. long hook
    E. small shovel

---

16. The word *victual* means

    A. food
    B. victor
    C. punctual
    D. victim
    E. event

---

17. The word *inventory* means

    A. new invention
    B. list of property
    C. canning process
    D. thorough investigation
    E. fairy tale

---

18. ". . . the flowers raised . . . upon the warm air in her wake . . ." This means

    A. she took a long journey
    B. she made the flowers bloom
    C. she roused them from sleep
    D. there was a gathering of mourners
    E. she transplanted flowers

---

19. The word *serenity* means

    A. flood
    B. awe
    C. calmness
    D. superiority
    E. boredom

---

20. "And whichever face lights up is the face you want." *Lights up* means

    A. seems very familiar
    B. can be recognized
    C. is scrubbed and clean
    D. becomes bright and cheerful
    E. reflects the light

Follow the directions (Steps 8–13) on page 1 of the progress folder.

bibliography

Here is a list of books that you may want to read:

Adventure, travel, and sports

ANDREWS, MARY EVANS. *Hostage to Alexander*. Longmans, Green, 1961.

BIRD, ANTHONY. *Veteran Cars*. Viking, 1962.

CAMERER, DAVE. *Winning Football Plays*. A. S. Barnes, 1954.

CLEMENS, SAMUEL L. (Mark Twain.) *The Adventures of Huckleberry Finn*.

COOKE, DAVID COXE. *Flights That Made History*. G. P. Putnam's Sons, 1961.

CRISP, FRANK. *Devil Diver*. Coward-McCann, 1954.

DECKER, DUANE WALTER. *Rebel in Right Field*. William Morrow, 1961.

DODSON, KENNETH. *Away All Boats*. Little, Brown, 1954.

FRANCHERE, RUTH. *Jack London: The Pursuit of a Dream*. Thomas Y. Crowell, 1962.

GENDRON, VAL. *Powder and Hides*. Longmans, Green, 1954.

GODDEN, RUMER. *Hans Christian Andersen*. Knopf, 1955.

HERSEY, JOHN. *A Bell for Adano*. Knopf, 1944.

HERZOG, MAURICE. *Annapurna*. Dutton, 1953.

HEYERDAHL, THOR. *Kon-Tiki: Across the Pacific by Raft*. Rand McNally, 1950.

HOFFMAN, GAIL. *The Land and the People of Israel*. Lippincott, 1960.

HUNT, JOHN (Sir). *The Conquest of Everest*. Dutton, 1954.

MELVILLE, HERMAN. *Moby Dick*.

MURRAY, MARY F. *Skygirl*. Little, Brown, 1951.

NORTON, ALICE M. *At Swords' Points*. Harcourt, Brace, 1954.

O'BRIEN, JACK. *Silver Chief to the Rescue*. John C. Winston, 1937.

PINTO, ORESTE. *Spy Catcher*. Harper & Bros., 1952.

POLO, MARCO. *The Travels of Marco Polo*.

POOLE, LYNN. *Science the Super Sleuth*. McGraw-Hill, 1954.

PRICE, WILLARD. *Underwater Adventure*. John Day, 1954.

ROBERTSON, KEITH. *Three Stuffed Owls*. Viking, 1954.

SKIDMORE, HUBERT. *Hill Doctor*. Doubleday, 1959.

STEVENSON, ROBERT LOUIS. *Kidnapped*.

———. *Treasure Island*.

TAZIEFF, HAROUN. *Caves of Adventure*. Harper & Bros., 1953.

ULLMAN, JAMES RAMSEY. *Banner in the Sky*. Lippincott, 1954.

WERSTEIN, IRVING. *The Battle of Midway*. Thomas Y. Crowell, 1961.

Science fiction

CAPON, PAUL. *The World at Bay*. John C. Winston, 1955.

CONKLIN, GROFF. *Possible Worlds of Science Fiction*. Vanguard, 1951.

——— (ed.). *Invaders of Earth*. Vanguard, 1952.

DEL REY, LESTER. *Steps to the Stars*. John C. Winston, 1955.

FRENCH, PAUL. *Lucky Starr and the Oceans of Venus*. Doubleday, 1954.

HEINLEIN, ROBERT A. *Star Beast*. Charles Scribner's Sons, 1954.

NORTON, ANDRÉ. *Catseye*. Harcourt, Brace & World, 1961.

WOLLHEIM, DONALD A. *The Secret of Saturn's Rings*. John C. Winston, 1954.

Animals

BAGNOLD, ENID. *National Velvet*. Rev. ed. William Morrow, 1949.

BRELAND OSMOND PHILIP. *Animal Facts and Fallacies*. Harper & Bros., 1948.

BRONSON, WILFRID SWANCOURT. *Coyotes*. Harcourt, Brace, 1946.

CHAPIN, HENRY. *The Remarkable Dolphin and What Makes Him So*. William R. Scott, 1962.

CLARK, DENIS. *Boomer*. Viking, 1955.

CLEMENS, SAMUEL L. (Mark Twain). "A Dog's Tale." (*Great Short Stories from the World's Literature*, ed. C. NEIDER, pp. 478–87.) Holt, Rinehart & Winston, 1950.

COLLINS, HENRY HILL. *The Bird Watcher's Guide.* Golden Press, 1961.

DITMARS, RAYMOND L. *Strange Animals I Have Known.* Harcourt, Brace, 1931.

FENNER, PHYLLIS (comp.). *Dogs, Dogs, Dogs: Stories of Challengers and Champions, Heroes and Hunters, Warriors and Workers.* Franklin Watts, 1951.

_____. *Horses, Horses, Horses: Palominos and Pintos, Polo Ponies and Plow Horses, Morgans and Mustangs.* Franklin Watts, 1949.

HEGNER, ROBERT WILLIAM and JANE (Zabriskie). *Parade of the Animal Kingdom.* Macmillan, 1935.

JAMES, WILL. *Smoky.* Charles Scribner's Sons, 1926.

KNIGHT, ERIC MOWBRAY. *Lassie Come Home.* John C. Winston, 1940.

O'HARA, MARY. *My Friend Flicka.* Lippincott, 1944.

OLLIVANT, ALFRED. *Bob, Son of Battle.* Grosset & Dunlap, 1904.

RAWLINGS, MARJORIE. *The Yearling.* Charles Scribner's Sons, 1961.

SANDERSON, IVAN T. (ed.). *Animal Tales: An Anthology of Animal Literature of All Countries.* Knopf, 1946.

STREET, JAMES. *Goodbye, My Lady.* Lippincott, 1954.

Science and mathematics

AHNSTROM, D. N. *Complete Book of Helicopters.* World Publishing Co., 1954.

BAKER, ROBERT H. *When the Stars Come Out.* Rev. ed. Viking, 1960.

BROWN, BILL. *Rain Forest.* Coward-McCann, 1962.

CARSON, RACHEL L. *The Sea Around Us.* Rev. ed. Oxford University Press, 1961.

COOMBS, CHARLES IRA. *Skyrocketing into the Unknown.* William Morrow, 1954.

COOPER, ELIZABETH K. *Silkworms and Science: The Story of Silk.* Harcourt, Brace & World, 1961.

CURIE, EVE. *Madame Curie.* Doubleday, 1949.

EDEL, MAY. *The Story of People.* Little, Brown, 1953.

FARB, PETER. *The Story of Dams.* Harvey House, 1961.

FREEMAN, IRA MAXIMILIAN. *All About Sound and Ultrasonics.* Random House, 1961.

GARDNER, MARTIN. *Mathematical Puzzles.* Thomas Y. Crowell, 1961.

GOLDMAN, IRVING and HANNAH. *First Men: The Story of Human Beginnings.* Abelard-Schuman, 1955.

HEUER, KENNETH. *Men of Other Planets.* Viking, 1951.

HYDE, MARGARET O. *Driving Today and Tomorrow.* McGraw-Hill, 1954.

JAFFE, BERNARD. *Crucibles.* Rev. ed. Fawcett Publications, 1960.

KENDALL, JAMES. *Great Discoveries by Young Chemists.* Thomas Y. Crowell, 1954.

KNIGHT, DAVID C. *Robert Koch: Father of Bacteriology.* Franklin Watts, 1961.

LEY, WILLY. *Engineers' Dreams: Diagrams and Maps.* Viking, 1954.

MEEUSE, B. J. D. *The Story of Pollination.* Ronald Press, 1961.

MEYER, JEROME. *Fun with Mathematics.* Fawcett Publications, 1961.

MORGAN, ALFRED P. *Boys' First Book of Radio and Electronics.* Charles Scribner's Sons, 1954.

NEWCOMB, ELLSWORTH, and KENNEY, HUGH. *Miracle Metals.* G. P. Putnam's Sons, 1962.

OSBORN, FAIRFIELD. *Our Plundered Planet.* Little, Brown, 1948.

PEI, MARIO. *All About Language.* Lippincott, 1954.

SCHNEIDER, LEO. *Space in Your Future.* Harcourt, Brace & World, 1961.

SOLOMON, LOUIS. *Telstar: Communication Break-Through by Satellite.* McGraw-Hill, 1962.

Home, family, and community life

DALY, MAUREEN. *Seventeenth Summer.* Dodd, Mead, 1948.

DAY, CLARENCE. *Life with Father.* Knopf, 1935.

FERBER, EDNA. *So Big.* Doubleday, 1924.

FORBES, KATHRYN. *Mama's Bank Account.* Harcourt, Brace, 1949.

GILBRETH, FRANK B., and CAREY, ERNESTINE G. *Belles on Their Toes.* Thomas Y. Crowell, 1950.

_____. *Cheaper by the Dozen.* Grosset & Dunlap, 1948.

CORSLINE, DOUGLAS WARNER. *Farm Boy.* Viking, 1950.

263

LANDON, MARGARET DOROTHEA. *Anna and the King of Siam*. John Day, 1944.

PATON, ALAN. *Cry, the Beloved Country*. Charles Scribner's Sons, 1948.

SAHGAL, NAYANTARA. *Prison and Chocolate Cake*. Knopf, 1954.

TARKINGTON, BOOTH. *Seventeen: A Tale of Youth and Summertime and the Baxter Family, Especially William*. Harper & Bros., 1932.

THURBER, JAMES. *The Thurber Album: A New Collection of Pieces About People*. Simon & Schuster, 1952.

Humor

BENCHLEY, NATHANIEL (ed.). *The Benchley Roundup*. Harper & Bros., 1954.

CERF, BENNETT A. *Good for a Laugh*. Garden City Books, 1952.

————. *Shake Well Before Using*. Simon & Schuster, 1948.

————. *Try and Stop Me*. Simon & Schuster, 1944.

DUNNINGER, JOSEPH. *100 Houdini Tricks*. Arco, 1954.

HERZBERG, MAX J., and MONES, LEON (eds.). *Humor of America*. Appleton-Century-Crofts, 1945.

MARQUIS, DON. *Lives and Times of Archy and Mehitabel*. Doubleday, 1950.

NASH, OGDEN. *I'm a Stranger Here Myself*. Little, Brown, 1941.

PAPASHVILY, GEORGE and HELEN. *Anything Can Happen*. Harper & Bros., 1945.

SHULMAN, MAX. *The Many Loves of Dobie Gillis*. Doubleday, 1953.

THURBER, JAMES. *Thurber's Dogs*. Simon & Schuster, 1955.

You and other people

BAILARD, VIRGINIA, and STRANG, RUTH MAY. *Ways to Improve Your Personality*. McGraw-Hill, 1951.

BETZ, BETTY. *Your Manners Are Showing: The Handbook of the Teen-Age Know-How*, with verses by ANNE CLARK. Grosset & Dunlap, 1946.

BROOKMAN, DENISE CASO. *The Young in Love*. Macrae Smith Co., 1962.

CORNELL, BETTY. *Betty Cornell's Teen-Age Popularity Guide*. Prentice-Hall, 1953.

COSGROVE, MARJORIE C., and JOSEY, MARY I. *About You*. Science Research Associates, 1952.

DAHL, BORGHILD MARGARETHE. *Finding My Way*. Dutton, 1962.

DALY, SHEILA JOHN. *Personality Plus*. Rev. ed. Dodd, Mead, 1952.

KELIHER, ALICE VIRGINIA. *Life and Growth*. Appleton-Century-Crofts, 1941.

LUDDEN, ALLEN. *Plain Talk for Men Under 21!* Dodd, Mead, 1954.

RAVIELLI, ANTHONY. *Wonders of the Human Body*. Viking, 1954.

RUCHLIS, HYMAN. *Clear Thinking*. Harper & Bros., 1962.

SHACTER, HELEN. *Understanding Ourselves*. Rev. ed. McKnight & McKnight, 1959.

STRAIN, FRANCIS BRUCE. *Teen Days: A Book for Boys and Girls*. Appleton-Century-Crofts, 1946.

How-to-do-it

BAER, MARION E. *Sound: An Experiment Book*. Holiday House, 1952.

BROWN, VINSON. *How to Make a Home Nature Museum*. Little, Brown, 1955.

FRANKEL, GODFREY. *Short Cut to Photography*. Sterling Publishing Co., 1955.

LEEMING, JOSEPH. *Real Book of Science Experiments*. Garden City Books, 1955.

MARSHALL, LUCILLE ROBERTSON. *Photography for Teen-Agers*. Prentice-Hall, 1957.

ZARCHY, HARRY. *Ceramics*. Knopf, 1954.

The world

ALDERMAN, CLIFFORD LINDSEY. *Samuel Adams: Son of Liberty*. Holt, Rinehart & Winston, 1961.

ALLEN, FREDRICK LEWIS. *The Big Change*. Harper & Bros., 1952.

ATTWOOD, WILLIAM. *Still the Most Exciting Country*. Knopf, 1955.

BAITY, ELIZABETH C. *Americans Before Columbus*. Viking, 1951.

COLVER, ANNE. *Theodosia: Daughter of Aaron Burr*. Holt, Rinehart & Winston, 1962.

COOLIDGE, OLIVIA E. *Men of Athens*. Houghton Mifflin, 1962.

DUGGAN, ALFRED. *Growing Up in 13th Century England*. Pantheon Books, 1962.

FINDLAY, BRUCE ALLYN, and BLAIR, ESTHER. *Your Rugged Constitution*. Science Research Associates, 1952.

FISHER, AILEEN LUCIA. *My Cousin Abe*. Thomas Nelson & Sons, 1962.

FISHER, DOROTHY CANFIELD. *A Fair World for All.* McGraw-Hill, 1952.

FLETCHER, DAVID. *The King's Goblet.* Pantheon Books, 1962.

FORBES, ESTHER. *Johnny Tremain.* Houghton Mifflin, 1943.

FRITZ, JEAN. *San Francisco.* Rand McNally, 1962.

GALT, TOM. *How the United Nations Works.* Rev. ed. Thomas Y. Crowell, 1956.

GIDAL, SONIA and TIM. *My Village in Italy.* Pantheon Books, 1962.

JOHNSON, ANNABEL and EDGAR. *Wilderness Bride.* Harper & Row, 1962.

KELLY, REGINA ZIMMERMAN. *Chicago: Big-Shouldered City.* Reilly & Lee, 1962.

LEY, WILLY, and the editors of *Life. The Poles.* Time, Inc., 1962.

LISITZKY, GENEVIEVE HELEN. *Thomas Jefferson.* Viking, 1933.

McNEER, MAY YONGE. *America's Mark Twain.* Houghton Mifflin, 1962.

PYLE, ERNEST TAYLOR. *Brave Men.* Grosset & Dunlap, 1944.

REYNOLDS, QUENTIN. *The FBI.* Random House, 1954.

ROOSEVELT, ELEANOR, and FERRIS, HELEN. *Partners: The United Nations and Youth.* Doubleday, 1950.

SANDBURG, CARL. *Abe Lincoln Grows Up.* Harcourt, Brace, 1931.

STONE, IRVING. *Immortal Wife.* Doubleday, 1948.

WATSON, SALLY. *Witch of the Glens.* Viking, 1962.

WILDER, LAURA INGALLS. *On the Way Home: The Diary of a Trip from South Dakota to Mansfield, Missouri, in 1894.* Harper & Row, 1962.

WITTY, PAUL, and KOHLER, JULILLY. *You and the Constitution.* Childrens Press, 1948.

Careers and Jobs

BIEGELEISEN, JOHN ISRAEL. *Careers in Commercial Art.* Rev. ed. Dutton, 1952.

DE KRUIF, PAUL. *Microbe Hunters.* Harcourt, Brace, 1932.

HILL, LORNA. *Veronica at Sadler's Wells.* Holt, 1954.

HUMPHREY, J. ANTHONY. *Choosing Your Career.* Rev. ed. Science Research Associates, 1949.

JONES, CHARLES REED (ed.). *Your Career in Motion Pictures, Radio and Television.* Sheridan House, 1949.

LARIAR, LAWRENCE. *Careers in Cartooning.* Dodd, Mead, 1950.

PATTON, FRANCES GRAY. *Good Morning, Miss Dove.* Dodd, Mead, 1954.

POLLACK, PHILIP. *Careers and Opportunities in Science: A Survey of All Fields.* Dutton, 1954.

Art, Music, and the Dance

EATON, JEANETTE. *Trumpeter's Tale.* William Morrow, 1955.

GLUBOK, SHIRLEY. *The Art of Ancient Egypt.* Atheneum, 1962.

HAGGAR, REGINALD G. *Sculpture Through the Ages.* Roy Publishers, 1962.

KAINZ, LUISE C., and RILEY, O. L. *Exploring Art.* Harcourt, Brace, 1947.

KOBBE, GUSTAV. *Kobbe's Complete Opera Book.* Edited and revised by the EARL OF HAREWOOD. G. P. Putnam's Sons, 1954.

MUNCH, CHARLES. *I Am a Conductor.* Oxford University Press, 1955.

SAMACHSON, DOROTHY and JOSEPH. *The Fabulous World of Opera.* Rand McNally, 1962.

SHAKESPEARE, WILLIAM. "Yale Shakespeare." Ed. by Department of English, Yale University. Yale University Press.

answer key

Lesson 1

How well do you read?

Exercise 1

1. B		3. C		5. A		7. A		9. D
2. B		4. B		6. B		8. C		10. E

Exercise 2

1. T		3. F		5. F		7. T		9. F
2. T		4. T		6. F		8. F		10. T

Exercise 3

1. A		3. C		5. C
2. E		4. A		6. B

Article 1

Elephants—Giants on the Land

1. A	5. A	9. C	13. B	17. A
2. B	6. D	10. A	14. D	18. D
3. B	7. D	11. E	15. E	19. C
4. E	8. C	12. E	16. B	20. C

Lesson 2

Why you should learn to read better

Exercise 4

1. monkey	5. fish
2. fish	6. pig
3. pig	7. mule
4. mule	8. fish

Article 2

A Secret for Two

1. C	5. C	9. D	13. D	17. D
2. A	6. A	10. A	14. E	18. E
3. B	7. C	11. E	15. A	19. B
4. B	8. E	12. B	16. C	20. D

Lesson 3

What is reading?

Exercise 5

1. The school band—was practicing—in the hall.
2. An elderly lady—helped the truck driver—to his feet.

3. A weather-beaten face appeared—in the dim light—of the entrance.
4. The science teacher—had been talking about —the solar system.

Exercise 6

2

Exercise 7

1. C		4. F		7. G		10. L
2. H		5. D		8. J		11. B
3. I		6. E		9. K		12. A

Exercise 8

B; C

Exercise 9

1. F		2. T		3. T		4. F

Article 3

A, B and C—The Human Element in Mathematics

1. B	5. C	9. D	13. A	17. C
2. D	6. B	10. B	14. E	18. D
3. A	7. E	11. A	15. D	19. A
4. E	8. C	12. E	16. B	20. C

Lesson 4

How you can remember what you read

Exercise 10

1. Never play at "doctoring." If a case is at all serious, get a doctor.
2. When treating a "hurry case," jump to the job. A second saved may mean a life saved.
3. Stop severe bleeding with pressure and bandages.
4. Give artificial respiration when breathing has stopped—and keep it up.
5. If a poison has been swallowed, dilute it.
6. Always treat the patient for shock. Have him lie down. Keep him warm, comfortable, and quiet.

Exercise 11

Comprehension Test

1. B		2. D		3. A		4. C

Vocabulary Test

1. **D**	5. **D**	9. **S**	13. **D**	17. **D**
2. **S**	6. **S**	10. **D**	14. **D**	18. **S**
3. **S**	7. **S**	11. **S**	15. **S**	19. **D**
4. **S**	8. **S**	12. **D**	16. **S**	20. **D**

Article 4

Jungle Zoo Without a Cage

1. **D**	5. **A**	9. **B**	13. **E**	17. **E**
2. **D**	6. **D**	10. **A**	14. **C**	18. **B**
3. **C**	7. **C**	11. **E**	15. **B**	19. **C**
4. **E**	8. **D**	12. **A**	16. **A**	20. **B**

Lesson 5

How you can get main ideas

Exercise 12

1. All day long the storm had battered the northern Michigan mainland.
2. They realized the *Bradley* was in mortal danger.
3. Now we know that the substance we call coral is composed of the skeletons of innumerable tiny marine animals.
4. Good habits are as hard to break as bad habits.

Exercise 13

1. Opportunities in the world of work today are unlimited.
2. But the world of work is in the future, and you have some decisions for tomorrow morning.
3. "Know thyself."
4. The Delphian advice is good today, and it will go on being good advice.
5. When we have the answers to these questions, we will find that a good many other questions have been answered also.
6. "Who you are" is a composite of all your characteristics.

Exercise 14

1. **C**   2. **B**   3. **B**   4. **A**   5. **B**

Article 5

The Lonesome Bear

1. **A**	5. **E**	9. **B**	13. **E**	17. **D**
2. **A**	6. **C**	10. **C**	14. **B**	18. **A**
3. **B**	7. **D**	11. **A**	15. **C**	19. **E**
4. **D**	8. **E**	12. **B**	16. **C**	20. **D**

Lesson 6

How to read for details

Exercise 15

1. house	7. lilacs
2. window	8. robin
3. sun	9. brother
4. roses	10. laburnum
5. violets	11. swing
6. lily cups	12. fir trees

Exercise 16

1. He commanded the sloop *Hero*.
2. He sailed nine thousand miles to the Antarctic.
3. He discovered unknown islands abounding with seals.
4. He designed some of the first clipper ships.
5. He made record-breaking runs to China.

Exercise 17

1. **F**   2. **T**   3. **F**

Exercise 18

1. **C**   2. **B**   3. **A**   4. **C**   5. **C**

Exercise 19

1. when	10. who
2. who	11. what
3. what	12. where
4. where	13. who
5. where	14. what
6. who	15. how
7. why	16. who
8. where	17. what
9. when	18. why

Exercise 20

1. **C**   2. **B, A, D, C**   3. **E**

Exercise 21

Part 1

1. no   2. no   3. no   4. yes   5. no

Part 2

1. **A**	3. **D**	5. **C**	7. **B**
2. **E**	4. **E**	6. **C**	8. **D**

Article 6

Terror in the Woods

1. **B**	5. **A**	9. **E**	13. **E**	17. **B**
2. **E**	6. **C**	10. **C**	14. **B**	18. **D**
3. **E**	7. **C**	11. **A**	15. **D**	19. **A**
4. **C**	8. **A**	12. **D**	16. **D**	20. **B**

Lesson 7

How to read to follow directions

Exercise 22

1. **F**   2. **T**   3. **T**   4. **T**   5. **T**

Exercise 23

1. A. cork or sponge   2. C, E, D, B, A
   B. candle   3. oxygen
   C. glass   4. oxygen

Exercise 24

1. **B**   2. **C**   3. **A**   4. **A**   5. **C**

Exercise 25

Test on the whole article

1. **C**   2. **C**   3. **C**

Part 1
1. **C**   2. **B**   3. **B**   4. **C**

Part 2
1. **T**   2. **F**   3. **T**   4. **T**

Part 3
1. **A**   2. **C**   3. **C**

Part 4
1. **A**   2. **A**   3. **A**

Part 5
1. **A**   2. **B**   3. **B**   4. **C**

Part 6
1. **A**   2. **C**   3. **C**   4. **A**   5. **C**

Part 7
1. **A**   2. **A**   3. **B**   4. **A**

Article 7

Whales—The World's Largest Animals

1. **B**	5. **E**	9. **A**	13. **A**	17. **B**
2. **C**	6. **D**	10. **D**	14. **E**	18. **E**
3. **B**	7. **C**	11. **C**	15. **D**	19. **A**
4. **C**	8. **A**	12. **E**	16. **B**	20. **E**

Lesson 8

How to think about what you read

Exercise 26

Part 1
1. yes   2. yes   3. no   4. no

Part 2
1. It gets its food by filtering it out of the water that is constantly flowing through.
2. It has no nerves.
3. It has no way of knowing that the diver is near. It is tightly attached to the rock or sea bottom.

Exercise 27

The clerk gave $8.57 change.
It was the correct amount.
The statements that give the necessary information are 5, 6, and 8.

Exercise 28

1. **B**   2. **C**   3. **A**   4. **C**

Exercise 29

3

Exercise 30

1. **F**	4. **F**	7. **O**	10. **F**	13. **O**	16. **F**
2. **O**	5. **F**	8. **F**	11. **O**	14. **F**	17. **F**
3. **O**	6. **F**	9. **F**	12. **F**	15. **O**	

Exercise 31

Part 1
1. **C**   2. **C**   3. **B**

Part 2
1. **C**   2. **D**

Exercise 32

Part 1
1. a newspaper
2. a collar that fits
3. a six-foot leash
4. a twenty-foot rope

Part 2
1. no   3. sit   5. stay
2. heel   4. down   6. come

Part 3
1. **T**	3. **T**	5. **T**	7. **F**	9. **F**
2. **F**	4. **F**	6. **T**	8. **T**	10. **T**

Exercise 33

1. **A**	3. **C**	5. **B**	7. **A**	9. **A**
2. **A**	4. **A**	6. **A**	8. **B**	

Article 8

Elastic Metal

1. **C**	5. **E**	9. **B**	13. **B**	17. **E**
2. **B**	6. **A**	10. **D**	14. **B**	18. **D**
3. **A**	7. **C**	11. **C**	15. **E**	19. **C**
4. **D**	8. **A**	12. **D**	16. **E**	20. **A**

Lesson 9

How to read at the right speed

Exercise 34

Part 1
1. **C**   2. **B**   3. **C**

Part 2
1. **B**   2. **C**   3. **A**   4. **C**   5. **A**

Part 3

1. B	2. C	3. A

Part 4

1. A	2. C	3. B

Part 5

1. B	2. B	3. B

Exercise 35

1. B	3. A	5. C	7. C
2. B	4. A	6. A	8. B

Exercise 36

1. A	5. C	9. A	13. A	17. A
2. C	6. C	10. B	14. C	18. A
3. B	7. A	11. A	15. B	19. C
4. B	8. C	12. B	16. B	20. A-6;

B-2; C-4; D-1; E-5; F-3

Article 9

Midshipman Aboard the "Half Moon"

1. D	5. D	9. B	13. D	17. E
2. E	6. C	10. E	14. B	18. B
3. C	7. B	11. A	15. E	19. A
4. A	8. D	12. A	16. C	20. A

Lesson 10

How to read illustrations

Exercise 37

1. B	3. C	5. B
2. B	4. C	6. B

Exercise 38

1. C	2. A	3. B	4. B

Exercise 39

Part 1
C
Part 2
B
Part 3

1. C	2. B	3. A

Exercise 40

1. A	2. A	3. C	4. D

Exercise 41

1. C	2. B	3. B

Exercise 42

1. C	3. C	5. C
2. B	4. A	6. A

Exercise 43

1. A	3. A	5. B	7. C
2. C	4. A	6. C	

Exercise 44

1. B	3. A	5. C	7. B	9. C
2. C	4. A	6. C	8. A	10. D

Article 10

Clipper Ship Boy

1. C	5. C	9. B	13. E	17. A
2. B	6. C	10. E	14. C	18. D
3. D	7. D	11. E	15. B	19. C
4. E	8. B	12. A	16. D	20. A

Lesson 11

How to read aloud

Exercise 45

1. C	2. B	3. A	4. C

Article 11

For the Benefit of All

1. C	5. B	9. A	13. E	17. C
2. D	6. E	10. C	14. B	18. E
3. D	7. B	11. A	15. D	19. E
4. A	8. A	12. D	16. C	20. B

Lesson 12

How you can read unfamiliar words

Exercise 46

1. B	3. B	5. B
2. A	4. C	6. A

Exercise 47

1. B	2. A	3. A	4. B	5. B

Exercise 48

1. B	2. C	3. C	4. D

Exercise 49

1. ē	5. ĕ	9. ā	13. ū	17. ā
2. ĭ	6. ū	10. ă	14. ō	18. ē
3. ī	7. ū	11. ā	15. ā	19. ă
4. ĭ	8. ă	12. ĭ	16. ĭ	20. ĕ

Exercise 50

1. hard	5. soft	9. soft
2. hard	6. hard	10. soft
3. soft	7. soft	11. hard
4. soft	8. soft	12. hard

Exercise 51

1. e	3. k, w	5. a	7. a	9. a, e
2. gh	4. w	6. a, e	8. i	10. w, e

Exercise 52

1. com-mis-sion
2. in-dict-ment
3. ma-jor-i-ty
4. ref-er-en-dum
5. ob-so-lete
6. bib-li-og-ra-phy
7. vac-u-um
8. con-cave
9. sol-stice
10. nu-cle-us

Exercise 53

1. under
2. tele
3. photo
4. biblio
5. bio
6. mono
7. less
8. tele
9. poly
10. tele
11. poly
12. micro
13. hydro
14. mono
15. geo
16. hydro
17. wise
18. over
19. micro
20. auto

Exercise 54

1. out of
2. not
3. opposite
4. before in place
5. toward
6. out of
7. down from
8. out of
9. before in time
10. less than
11. again
12. under
13. opposite
14. before in place
15. out of
16. cease
17. away
18. before in time
19. out of
20. into

Exercise 55

1. into
2. again
3. beyond
4. again
5. less than
6. nearness to
7. deprive of
8. before in time
9. under
10. opposite
11. before in time
12. before in time
13. under
14. out
15. down
16. before in position
17. not
18. back
19. before in place
20. again

Exercise 56

1. A   2. C   3. B   4. C   5. A

Exercise 57

1. A   2. B   3. C   4. C

Article 12

How We Kept Mother's Day

1. D	5. D	9. A	13. C	17. A
2. A	6. C	10. D	14. E	18. C
3. E	7. B	11. D	15. C	19. E
4. A	8. B	12. B	16. B	20. E

Lesson 13

How you can build a better vocabulary

Exercise 58

1. with
2. beyond
3. by
4. down
5. through with
6. out
7. around
8. along with
9. on
10. off
11. under
12. after
13. about
14. hard with

Exercise 59

1. imminent
2. council
3. coarse
4. compliment
5. formally
6. eminent
7. counsel
8. uninterested
9. course
10. complement
11. formerly
12. disinterested
13. officious
14. rhythm
15. proceed
16. morale
17. moral
18. precede
19. official
20. effect

Exercise 60

1. cherished
2. esteemed
3. value
4. treasured
5. prizes
6. appreciate

Exercise 61

justice	education
democracy	crime
home	beauty

Article 13

Ships and Masters

1. C	5. D	9. D	13. E	17. E
2. E	6. B	10. D	14. C	18. C
3. D	7. E	11. A	15. B	19. A
4. A	8. B	12. C	16. A	20. B

Lesson 14

How you can read better for school assignments

Exercise 62

1. C   2. A   3. B

Exercise 63

1. C   2. C   3. A

Exercise 64

1. page 1
2. Index
3. title page
4. page 205
5. Robert Carse
6. page 262
7. page 168
8. Littauer and Wilkinson
9. page 10
10. lesson 9

Article 14

Houdini—The Handcuff King

1. B	5. D	9. C	13. D	17. A
2. E	6. B	10. A	14. C	18. B
3. B	7. C	11. D	15. A	19. B
4. C	8. E	12. B	16. D	20. C

Lesson 15

How you can improve your reading

Exercise 65

1. E   2. B   3. A

Exercise 66

Many settlements would have starved if it had not been for the food brought to them by friendly Indians.

Article 15

How Long Is Life?

1. B	5. E	9. A	13. C	17. C
2. D	6. C	10. B	14. A	18. A
3. D	7. A	11. D	15. E	19. E
4. B	8. E	12. C	16. D	20. B

Article 16

Mama Finds a Way

1. E	5. C	9. E	13. D	17. C
2. B	6. A	10. D	14. E	18. B
3. A	7. A	11. B	15. D	19. B
4. C	8. C	12. A	16. E	20. D

Article 17

Motivations of the Space Program

1. A	5. C	9. B	13. A	17. A
2. D	6. C	10. B	14. D	18. D
3. E	7. E	11. B	15. C	19. E
4. B	8. C	12. C	16. E	20. D

Article 18

Great-grandma

1. E	5. A	9. A	13. D	17. B
2. D	6. B	10. B	14. D	18. B
3. C	7. A	11. C	15. E	19. C
4. E	8. E	12. A	16. A	20. D

index

A, B and C—The Human Element in Mathematics, 38 f.

A A Is for Aardvark, 162–67

Abstract words, 207 f.

Airways and map of standard time zones of the United States, 147

Alexander the Great, 86, 88

American Adventure, The, 219–23, 224

American Porcupine, The, 73

Animal Kingdom, The, 6

Annual mean income, 144

Answer key, 266–71

Antonyms, 205

Aqualung, 90

Are There Sea Serpents? 106 ff.

Aristotle, 88

Assignments, preparing, 219–23

Athletes, 122 f.

Attitude, 235

Ballad of Reading Gaol, The, 168 f.

Bar graphs, reading of, 142–45

Barkham, John, 51

Barnum, P. T., 100

Basic English, 206 f.

Bathyscaphe, 90, 91

Bathysphere, 90

Be Prepared! 72

Beebe, William, 90

Bees, 56

Bends, the, 89

Better reading, reasons for, 19, 20, 21, 22

Bibliography, 262–65

Big Rock Candy Mountain, The, 162

Bradbury, Ray, 257

Bruun, Anton, 106, 107

Buckley, F. R., 2

Bumblebee, 136 ff.

Burke, Johnny, 19

Caisson disease, 89

Campsite, How to Choose a Good, 83

Cape of Good Hope, 106

Captions, 135

Carroll, Lewis, 161

Carse, Robert, 210

Cartoons, reading, 140 f.

Celli, Jack, 103

Cerf, Bennett, 159, 239

Checklist of reading needs, 9

Chicago Daily News, 183, 184

Chili, recipe for, 81

Chodorov, Jerome, and Fields, Joseph, 171

Churchill, Sir Winston, 201

Circle graphs, reading, 142

Clipper Ship Boy, 150-52

Cochran, Rice E., 124

Colons, 71

Comic strips, 184

Commas, 71

Compound words, 189

Comprehension tests, 5, 7, 37, 49

Concentration, 216 f.

Conquest of the Depths, 84–91

Consonants, 187 f.

Contents, table of, 10

Context, 191, 192 f.

Copyright page, 10

Cousteau, Captain Jacques-Yves, 89, 90

Danny Deever, 118 f.

Dashes, 70

da Vinci, Leonardo, 88

de Corlieu, Louis, 88

Details
   as reasons for beliefs, 68
   clues to finding, 69
   descriptive, 67
   explanatory, 67
   importance of, 68
   in finding facts, 71–74
   kinds of, 67
   reading for, 67–74

Diagrams, reading, 135 f.

Dickinson, Emily, 223

Dictionaries, 193 ff., 209

Directions, following, 80–91

Discovering Your Real Interests, 58

Diving bell, 86, 88; *see also* Bathyscaphe; Bathysphere

Diving helmet; *see* Helmet, diver

Diving suits, 90

Dormice, 156

Doucette, Earl, 75

Elastic Metal, 109–11

Elephants—Giants on the Land, 12–14

Elman, Mischa, 57

Embargo Act of 1807, The, 119 f.

Emrich, Duncan, 159

Enunciation, 158 f.

Epstein, Samuel, and Williams, Beryl, 227

Estimated lifetime income, 145

Exercises
   and memory, 46, 48
   in bringing experience into reading, 99, 100, 101
   in checking reading rate, 116

in choosing the right reading speed for concentration, 216 f.
in evaluating opinion, 101, 102, 106
in finding the main idea of a passage, 58
in getting main ideas, 30, 57 f., 59 f.
in getting meaning of quantity words, 70
in identifying opinion, 102
in new language, 31
in noting details, 68 f., 71 f., 72 f., 73 f.
in organizing information, 103 f.
in overlearning, 223
in reading rates, 121 f., 124 ff.
in reading to follow directions, 81 f., 82 f., 83–91
in seeing word groups, 30
to find facts, 98 f.

Experiment, 81 f.
Exposure suit, 90
Eye movements, 36
Eyesight, 235

Facts and ideas, relating, 222 f.
Fields, Joseph, and Chodorov, Jerome, 171
Fighting Words, 156
First Aid, 46–48
Fisher, Robert Moore, 37
Fleuss, Henry, 89
Flying saucers, 102 f.; *see also* UFOs
For the Benefit of All, 178–80
Forbes, Kathryn, 246
Franklin, Benjamin, 88
French, 31
Friedman, Ralph, 162

Gagnan, Émile, 89
General directions for using this book, 10
Giddings, Paull M., 240
Glossary, 225
Goethe, 35
Goggles, 87
Gold-Mounted Guns, 2–5
Good Deed Daily, A, 124 ff.
Goodyear, Charles, 109
Graphs, reading, 141–48
Great-grandma, 257–59

Halley, Sir Edmund, 88, 89
Harding, Lowry W., 129
Hay, John, 156
Hearing, 235
Heifetz, Jascha, 57
Helmet, diver, 85, 87, 89
Henry, Patrick, 156
Herblock, 141, 142
Hibbs, A. R., 252
Hitches Dreams to Balloons, 8
Hobos' Heaven of Song, 162
Hofmann, Josef, 57
Hood, Thomas, 68
Horses and mules and tractors, 146
Hotchner, A. E., 106

Houdini—The Handcuff King, 227–29
Houot, Lieutenant Commander Georges, 86, 91
How About the Weather? 37
How Americans spent their income in 1959, 143
How Long Is Life? 240–42
How to Choose a Good Campsite, 83
How to File Your Income Tax Return, 117 f.
How We Kept Mother's Day, 196 f.
Hyphen, 189
I Hear America Singing, 170
I Remember, I Remember, 68
Idioms, 203 f.
Illustrations, how to read, 135–49
I'm Nobody, 223
Italics, 70

Jabberwocky, 161
Jefferson, Thomas, 217
Jim Bludso, 156
*Job Opportunities for Women as Food Service
Managers,* 120 f.
Jungle Zoo Without a Cage, 51–53
Junior Miss, 170–77

Kemp, F. W., 107
Key, Francis Scott, 48
Keyhoe, Major, 103
Kinney, Harrison, 61
Kipling, Rudyard, 118
Klingert, Otto, 89
Knight's Night Out, A, 22

LaFrance, Ernest, 122
Langley, Major W. H., 107
Language, new, 31 f.,
Leacock, Stephen, 38 f., 196
Legends of pictures, 135
Le Prieur, Commandant Yves, 89
Line graphs, reading, 146, 148
Loch Ness monster, 107
Lonesome Bear, The, 61–63

Main idea, 56–60
of a paragraph, 56
of a passage, 58
of stories and articles, 58, 59
Mama Finds a Way, 246–48
Maps, reading, 147–48 f.
Masks, 87
McMorris, William B., 162
Memory, improving, 43–50
meaningful, 44
rote, 44
Midshipman Aboard the "Half Moon," 129–31
Montgomery, Elizabeth Rider, 109
Motivations of the Space Program, 252 f.
Mud Pies and the Weather, 37

Nemo, Captain, 89
Neoprene suit, 90

Newspapers, reading, 183–86
Notes as help in studying, 222

Opinion, evaluating and identifying, 102
Or Better Still, Bring the Body, 184
Oral reading, 35, 36, 156–77
  and silent reading, compared, 35
Order to the Careless Driver, An, 156
Organizing information, 103
Overlearning, 223
Oxygen "rebreathing" unit, 89

Paragraphs, getting meaning from, 30 f.
Pearson, Captain H. L., 107
Photograph, how to read, 139 f.
Piccard, Auguste, 90
Pictures; *see* Illustrations
Plays: *Junior Miss*, 170–77
Poems
  Ballad of Reading Gaol, The, 168 f.
  Danny Deever, 118 f.
  I Hear America Singing, 170
  I Remember, I Remember, 68
  I'm Nobody, 223
  Jim Bludso, 156
Practice exercises, 236
Prefixes
  in analyzing unfamiliar words, 187, 189 ff., 208
  in making new words, 189 f.
Project Blue Book, 102
Pronunciation, 159
  of unfamiliar words, 187 f.
Punctuation marks, 70
Puns, 202

Quarles, Air Secretary Donald A. 102, 103
Quotation marks, 71

Reading Accelerator, 10
Reading needs, checklist of, 9
Reading rate
  adapted to purpose, 114–28
  how to test, 115
  improving, 121 f., 128
Recipe for chili, 81
Remembering, helps in, 43–50
Review, as aid in remembering, 46, 222
Reynolds, Quentin, 24
Rote memory, 44
Ruppelt, Colonel, 103

School assignments, 215–26
Science picture story, reading a, 136 f.
Scuba diver, 85
Sea serpents, 106 ff.
Secret for Two, A, 24–26
Self-contained underwater breathing apparatus, 85, 89
Semicolons, 71
Shakespeare, William, 206
Shapiro, Morton, 138, 139

Ships and Masters, 210–12
Shrew, The, 6
Siebe, Augustus, 89
Skimming, 115, 225
Skin diver, 85
Slang, 207
Smeaton, John, 89
Smith, Louis, 150
Snorkels, 87 f.
Sponge, 97 f.
Sports College, 122, 123
Star-Spangled Banner, 48 f.
Steppingstones into Space, 135 f.
Study, planning for, 218 f.
Study Calls Flying Saucers a Myth, 102
Study conditions, 217 f.
Study habits, 215 f.
Suffixes
  in analyzing unfamiliar words, 187, 189 f., 208
  in making new words, 189 f.
Survivor Tells Two-Day Desert Ordeal, 185 f.
Swinging on a Star, 19 f.
Syllables, in analyzing unfamiliar words, 187, 188 f.
Synonyms, to improve vocabulary, 205 f.

Tall Tale, A, 156
Tannehill, Ivan Ray, 178
Terror in the Woods, 75–77
Textbooks, 223 ff.
Thorndike, Edward L., 35
Thorndike-Barnhart Comprehensive Desk Dictionary, 32
Through the Looking-Glass, 161
Time record, directions for, 11
Title page, 10
Tom Sawyer, 33 f.
Tongue twisters, 159
Training for a Dog's Life, 103 ff.
Trieste, 90
Twenty Thousand Leagues Under the Sea, 89

UFOs, 99 f., 102 f.
Understanding Life's Chemical Code, 59 f.
Underwater archaeology, 83
Unfamiliar words, 183–95
Unidentified flying objects, 99 f., 102 f.
United States Air Force, 102, 103
United States Air Force Academy, 116 f.
United States Marines, 103

Van Heusen, Jimmy, 19
Verne, Jules, 89
Vocabulary, building a, 201–9 tests, 9, 49, 60, 100, 183, 184, 186
Vowel sounds, 187, 188

Wainger, Bertrand M., 219
Walsh, Lieutenant Don, 90

Weather, Mid Pies and the, 37

Webster's New World Dictionary of the American Language, 193, 194

Whales—The World's Largest Animals, 92–94

Whitman, Walt, 169, 170

Why Don't Athletes Do Better?, 122 f.

Wilde, Oscar, 168

Wilderness Ways, 136 ff.

Williams, Beryl, and Epstein, Samuel, 227

Wilm, Pierre, 86, 91

Word Groups, 29 ff.

Words
    abstract, 208 f.
    descriptive, 206
    developing an interest in, 201 f.
    distinction of, 204 f.
    new, 208
    origins of, 202 f.
    unfamiliar, 183–95

Time-to-rate table for the reading selections

(each Article contains about 1,350 words.)

Reading time	Reading rate	Reading time	Reading rate	Reading time	Reading rate
1:00-1:14	1209	7:00-7:14	190	13:00-13:14	103
1:15-1:29	988	7:15-7:29	183	13:15-13:29	101
1:30-1:44	835	7:30-7:44	177	13:30-13:44	99
1:45-1:59	723	7:45-7:59	172	13:45-13:59	97
2:00-2:14	638	8:00-8:14	166	14:00-14:14	96
2:15-2:29	570	8:15-8:29	161	14:15-14:29	94
2:30-2:44	516	8:30-8:44	157	14:30-14:44	92
2:45-2:59	471	8:45-8:59	152	14:45-14:59	91
3:00-3:14	433	9:00-9:14	148	15:00-15:14	89
3:15-3:29	401	9:15-9:29	144	15:15-15:29	88
3:30-3:44	373	9:30-9:44	140	15:30-15:44	86
3:45-3:59	349	9:45-9:59	137	15:45-15:59	85
4:00-4:14	328	10:00-10:14	133	16:00-16:14	84
4:15-4:29	309	10:15-10:29	130	16:15-16:29	82
4:30-4:44	292	10:30-10:44	127	16:30-16:44	81
4:45-4:59	277	10:45-10:59	124	16:45-16:59	80
5:00-5:14	264	11:00-11:14	121	17:00-17:14	79
5:15-5:29	252	11:15-11:29	119	17:15-17:29	78
5:30-5:44	240	11:30-11:44	116	17:30-17:44	77
5:45-5:59	230	11:45-11:59	114	17:45-17:59	76
6:00-6:14	221	12:00-12:14	111	18:00-18:14	75
5:15-6:29	212	12:15-12:29	109	18:15-18:29	74
6:30-6:44	204	12:30-12:44	107	18:30-18:44	73
6:45-6:59	197	12:45-12:59	105	18:45-18:59	72

Use the Time-To-Rate Table on this page to change your reading time for an article into your reading rate for that article. This table shows reading time in minutes and seconds. It also shows reading rate in number of words per minute.

In the column headed, "Reading Time," find the time range which includes your reading time. At the right of this range, find the corresponding number in the column headed "Reading Rate." This number is your reading rate for the article.

Suppose that your reading time for Article 1 is 7:18 (7 minutes 18 seconds) as given on page 4 of the Progress Folder. This time, 7:18, is in the range, 7:15-7:29. For this time range, the reading rate is 183 words per minute. That is, if your reading time is 7:18, your reading rate is 183 words per minute. Write this rate in the Progress Folder (page 4 or 7).